but at any rate we shall
have some bea[...] [...]ny.
~~by all as~~ also [...] [...]lled
brewery or distillery.   This
latter will recall happy
memories at any rate.

I was very pleased
to hear ~~some~~ account of Dan
Murphy. He never answered
a letter which I wrote him abo[ut]
November last so we have got
out of touch.   They can all
be having a good laugh at u[s]
now but I dont think they
are somehow.   Even if

MICHAEL
COLLINS
THE MAN
AND THE REVOLUTION

At an event described by the photographer W.D. Hogan as a 'Free State demonstration', Collins delivers a speech to an attentive crowd at the Grand Parade in Cork in March 1922. (*National Library of Ireland*)

MICHAEL
COLLINS
THE MAN
AND THE REVOLUTION

ANNE DOLAN AND WILLIAM MURPHY

The Collins Press

First published in 2018 by
The Collins Press
West Link Park
Doughcloyne
Wilton
Cork
T12 N5EF
Ireland

A CIP record for this book is available from the British Library.

Hardback ISBN: 978-1-84889-210-1

Design and typesetting by Anú Design
Typeset in Minion
Printed in Poland by Białostockie Zakłady Graficzne SA

Contents

Acknowledgements

A book so richly illustrated owes an enormous debt of gratitude to a host of libraries and archives and their wonderful archivists, curators and librarians. We would like to thank the following institutions for their courtesy in both granting permission to reproduce the documents and images and supporting the publication through the supply of images: the British Cartoon Archive, the British Library, British Pathé, the Churchill Archives Centre, the Hugh Lane Gallery, the Imperial War Museum, the Library of Congress, the Life Picture Collection, Getty Images, the London Transport Museum, Mercier Press, the Military Archives of Ireland, the Museum of London, the National Archives of Ireland, the National Archives UK, the National Library of Ireland, the National Museum of Ireland, N&S Syndication, the Parliamentary Archives, the Post Office Museum London, the Royal Irish Academy, Solo Syndication, the Board of Trinity College Dublin, Trinity Mirror Publishing Ltd and UCD Archives. Thanks to Margarita Cappock of the Hugh Lane Gallery, Lisa Dolan of the Military Archives, Sandra Heise and Brenda Malone of the National Museum, John McDonough of the National Archives of Ireland, and Kate Manning of UCD Archives, who answered our many queries with great good will. We would particularly like to thank Mary Broderick, a treasure of the National Library in her own right.

We imposed upon a number of people to read full drafts of, or chapters of, the manuscript and it is certainly a better book because of their reflections and insights. Any mistakes, of course, are our own. Sincere thanks to Marie Coleman, Mark Duncan, James McConnel, John Mullen, Conor Murphy, Eunan O'Halpin, and Ciarán Wallace. Thanks to Susan Hegarty and the MA in History, DCU, class of 2018 for their map-making skills. We would like to thank our colleagues and students at the School of History and Geography, Dublin City University and the Department of History, Trinity College Dublin. Thanks also to all at The Collins Press, designers Karen Carty of Anú and Sarah Farrelly of Artmark, and indexer Doreen Magowan.

And thanks to all who indulged the Collins anecdotes when no doubt their patience was wearing thin: Ciaran Brady, Rosemary, Danny and Matthew Burnell, Frances Clarke, Pauline and Podge Dolan, Leeann Lane, Pat McGarty, R.S. McStiggins, Con, Marie, John, Ellen, Joe and Peter Murphy.

As ever, special thanks to Joseph Clarke and Catherine Cox – Mick won't be coming home with us again.

A young Collins, photographed here in his Volunteer uniform, possibly in 1917, was already acutely aware of the power of his image. *(National Museum of Ireland)*

Timeline

16 October 1890	Michael Collins is born at Woodfield, Clonakilty, Cork
March 1897	His father, Michael, dies
October 1903	Moves to Clonakilty to attend school
February 1906	Takes civil service exams
Summer 1906	Moves to London to work for the Post Office Savings Bank
March 1907	His mother, Mary Anne, dies
c. 1908	Joins Sinn Féin
July 1909	Becomes Secretary of the Geraldines GAA Club
November 1909	Joins the IRB
April 1910	Leaves the Post Office for a stockbroking firm, Horne & Co
December 1913	Irish Volunteers founded in London and Collins joins
1914	Becomes member of the Executive (treasurer) of South of England IRB
January 1916	Military Services Act passed and Collins moves to Dublin
24 April 1916	Joins the Easter Rising, based at the GPO
May 1916	Deported and interned at Stafford and then Frongoch Camp
December 1916	Released from Frongoch Camp
3 February 1917	North Roscommon by-election: Collins works for Count Plunkett
14 February 1917	Appointed Paid Secretary of the INA & VDF

19 April 1917	Key player at Count Plunkett's Mansion House Conference
June 1917	Becomes a member of the Supreme Council of the IRB
16—18 June 1917	1916 convicts return from prison
25 September 1917	Thomas Ashe dies on hunger strike: Collins becomes Secretary of the Supreme Council of the IRB
25—26 October 1917	Sinn Féin Árd Fheis, Collins elected to the Executive
27 October 1917	Becomes Director of Organisation of the Irish Volunteers
March 1918	Becomes Adjutant General of the Irish Volunteers
2 April 1918	Arrested at Dublin, relating to a speech at Legga, County Longford
18 April 1918	Military Service (No. 2) Act becomes law: Mansion House Conference
20 April 1918	Instructed while in Sligo Jail to accept release on bail
May 1918	Becomes a member of Sinn Féin Standing Committee (SFSC)
6 July 1918	Ceases to be Secretary of INA & VDF
19 September 1918	SFSC confirms Collins as candidate for South Cork
December 1918	Returned, for South Cork, unopposed at the general election
21 January 1919	Dáil Éireann meets for the first time.
22 January 1919	Becomes Minister of Home Affairs, Dáil cabinet
3 February 1919	Participates in rescue of Éamon de Valera from Lincoln prison
1 April 1919	De Valera elected President of Dáil Éireann

2 April 1919	Collins appointed Secretary for Finance, Dáil cabinet
May/June 1919	Harry Boland and de Valera depart for USA
***c.* May 1919**	Collins replaces Boland as President of the IRB
mid-1919	Appointed Director of Intelligence of the Irish Volunteers
30 July 1919	Shootings of DMP officers by 'The Squad' begin
September 1919	Dáil loan launched
9 August 1920	Restoration of Order in Ireland Act
September 1920	Dáil loan closed
21 November 1920	Bloody Sunday
1 December 1920	Appointed 2nd Deputy, in effect Acting, President of Dáil Éireann
10 December 1920	Martial law imposed in four Munster counties
23 December 1920	Government of Ireland Act becomes law; de Valera returns to Dublin
4 January 1921	Martial law extended to four further counties
13 May 1921	Elected to southern parliament unopposed, for Cork
24 May 1921	Elected to northern parliament, for South Armagh
11 July 1921	The Truce comes into force
26 August 1921	Re-appointed Secretary of State for Finance
14 September 1921	Appointed a plenipotentiary to Anglo-Irish Conference
6 December 1921	Signs Anglo-Irish Agreement (The Treaty)
19 December 1921	Addresses Dáil Éireann, defending the Treaty
***c.* 1 January 1922**	Collins and Kitty Kiernan become engaged

7 January 1921	Dáil Éireann approves the Treaty
9 January 1921	The opponents of the Treaty withdraw from Dáil Éireann
10 January 1922	Appointed Minister for Finance (Dáil cabinet)
14 January 1922	Becomes Chairman of the Provisional Government of the Irish Free State
21 January 1922	First Craig–Collins Pact signed
March 1922	Makes a series of speeches defending the Treaty
30 March 1922	Second Craig–Collins Pact signed
20 May 1922	Signs pre-election pact with de Valera
14 June 1922	Makes speech in Cork which is seen as breaking the pact
16 June 1922	Irish Free State Constitution published, general election held, and Collins re-elected TD
22 June 1922	Sir Henry Wilson killed in London
28 June 1922	Civil War begins
5 July 1922	Republican forces in Dublin surrender
12 July 1922	Collins appointed Commander-in-Chief of the army at head of a three-man War Council
10 August 1922	Cork city falls to pro-Treaty forces
12 August 1922	Arthur Griffith dies
22 August 1922	Collins killed at Béal na mBláth, Cork

Arriving at Earlsfort Terrace, at some point during the Treaty debates in December 1921 or early January 1922, Collins bounds from the car, as his first biographer, Hayden Talbot, described him, 'the embodiment of speed'. *(National Library of Ireland)*

Introduction

'Anything that can be said about me, say it'[1]

So, how do we begin? We might start with the first infant cries, by picking over the early scraps, looking for signs that somewhere there was greatness here to come. We might wait to meet him at the docks, watch him off the mailboat, start only when he comes back from London, start everything with 1916. Of course, we could kill him first, but Neil Jordan's *Michael Collins* has already carried off that trick.[2] We could traipse through all the Collinses that his many biographers have conjured up and argue that, despite all that the other books have done, we need yet another one. But there might not be much point in that. Whether we look back to the early and jealous keepers of the legend, back to Hayden Talbot's Collins of 1923, 'another George Washington – another Thomas Jefferson', to a Collins who was 'the finest character', 'the greatest natural leader of men I have ever known', or whether it is to Piaras Béaslaí's Collins of 1926, the 'child, the embodiment', indeed, the maker of a 'new Ireland' itself, we all just craft a Collins after our own lights.[3] Peter Hart's 'real' *Mick* was, in its own ways and intentions, a Collins for 2005, just as Frank O'Connor's *Big Fellow*, Margery Forester's *Lost Leader*, Tim Pat Coogan's *Michael Collins*, each of them, and all the others, made a Collins to the measure of their own times.[4] We might acknowledge that the path is both well worn and trodden well, but this is not the reason why we write. We harbour no notion that we will solve the Collins puzzle, unpick the riddle, finally fathom the fascination with this man. We write, instead, because there are simply more questions to be asked.

At the beginning of his biography of Napoleon, Alan Forrest set out the pitfalls of his task. Biography went against his historian's better instincts; it too easily shaped 'a period, a country, a culture' in the likeness of a single man, too readily gave 'weight to a mythology', and took too much for granted that one man alone 'dictated the history of his age'. 'In the beginning was Napoleon', in a sentence, summed up all that Forrest wanted to avoid.[5] While Collins may not have inspired even his most ardent detractors or admirers to scale such biblical heights, Forrest's warnings are worth heeding. The willingness, if not almost insistence, to see Collins as the sum of what amounted to an Irish revolution, and in turn to reduce him to a simple caricature of his many parts, leaves our sense of both man and revolution much reduced. So, like Forrest, we might start this book with a clear sense of what it is not. Collins will not emerge as some colossus to bestride his age. Here he is instead a creature of it; he is one of many who might have risen to play his part.

Equally, this book makes no pretence to save him. It is not going to wrest him free of the myths amassed around him, nor pare back the 'man of legend' for the sake of something seemingly more honest underneath.[6] Although it has been a powerful impulse for his biographers, whether Frank O'Connor in 1937 desperate to protect him from the pieties of the plaster saint, or Hart hoping to rescue him from 'the story' of his life, Collins valued the legend too much for us to cast it so eagerly aside.[7] In May 1921 he pondered how the latest failure by British forces to capture him might be perceived: 'it was the most providential escape yet. It will probably have the effect of making them think that I am even more mysterious than they believe me to be, and that is saying a good deal.'[8] Collins knew precisely the power of this persona, and capitalised when he could on what people wanted or seemed willing to believe. 'Anything that can be said about me, say it' was how he responded to Minister for Defence, Cathal Brugha's

Dear Rory.

12 APR 1920

Would you met me at
No 21 Dawson St — top of the house
over Milners Safes. You will
see the name Miss McGrane
on door on second floor Ring
bell 3 times
    I have some further news.
    Time 9 O'Clock.
                Mick

accusations during the Treaty debates that he had played up to the newspapers to exaggerate his role.[9] Someone who opted in such circumstances for such a reply cannot be neatly separated from the stories, wheat from chaff. The 'real Michael Collins' was only ever in the eye of the beholder, and Collins, even from his earliest days in London, was quick to make a virtue out of that.

No different from any of the other Collinses, we make him here piecemeal from what he has left us, ragtag from the glimpses others give us of a man who was at once and by turns effusive and cajoling, ambitious, idealistic, brutal, bullying and cantankerous. In eight thematic chapters, we focus on aspects of his life that will hopefully complicate our understanding of him, and which also allow us to bring new approaches from the wider study of the revolution to bear. *Michael Collins: the Man and the Revolution* is not a narrative, not a chronological summation of his life: there have been books enough not to need another rehearsal here of that. Instead the opening timeline provides chronological ballast to this life, anchoring him, when anchoring is needed, as the book considers the forces that formed him, the organisations that shaped him, the parts he played, the roles he relished, and the things he believed in. It is there to lean on as we ask questions of his politics, his wars, the figure he became, the fixation with his death, and the persistence of his afterlife. It is there to allow us to ask questions of them all.

Of course, there were other questions we might have asked, other parts of his life we might have explored: there is Collins holding various purse strings, Collins as Minister for Finance; there are his friendships, his enmities, and while some are here, there are certainly more to explore.[10] For readers seeking more on his rivalry with Éamon de Valera, this book will disappoint. It is, by now, an old and rather hackneyed story, exaggerated beyond proportion, and too easily reductive of both men, never mind the wider times they lived through.[11] Equally, the gossipier side of his private life is largely absent here; it has been drawn out vividly elsewhere from mildly torrid might-have-beens to the fury of some women scorned.[12] There is much in this book that might have borne more detail, aspects that deserved and already have warranted books in their own right: his wars, the machinations of spying and intelligence, his role as peacemaker, the nature of the Treaty and its negotiation, the pressures to avoid and then to fight a civil war, and each reader might add to what is only the beginning of this list.[13] With all of this in mind, this book is written to provoke questions rather than to answer them, to encourage more curiosity, particularly about all of the aspects

23 Queensboro' Terrace
Hyde Park. W.

July 24th/4

Dear Mr Collins

I am having a few people here on August 8th. For the afternoon + evening. I want you to come, there will be no restrictions. or anything. so you'll be quite free to get some of those "holy books off" your club —

Yours Sincerely
E— Copley.

PS I have a very nice little girl for you, but the only fault I am afraid. she will be too slim — her name is Miss Cox. Don't forget —

A note from July 1914 suggests some of what might amount to Collins's early romantic life. It also encapsulates just how much most of it will always remain beyond our ken. *(UCD Archives)*

Pictured here at the Gresham Hotel on the night after the Treaty was accepted in the Dáil by 64 votes to 57, this photograph seems to sum up a weary but welcome victory. The empty bottle in the background suggests at least some celebration at the result.
(National Library of Ireland)

of his life and the much broader contexts of the revolution we could not manage to incorporate into one short book. It is written most to prompt the questions we did not even think to ask.

In search of the young man who would become a revolutionary, the first chapter explores Collins's formation and background, asking not just what makes a revolutionary but what makes a revolutionary generation as well. A number of authors have asked varieties of Peter Hart's question: 'what kind of people became guerrillas?' This allows us to assess the extent to which Collins shared the characteristics of those he would later come to surpass.[14] Collins would become exceptional, but it is worthwhile considering the ways in which he was typical, little different from all the rest. The chapter looks at the Cork he came from and the London he went to; it looks at the opportunities and the excitements he found there, and the versions of himself he tried and tested in those early years.

From the moment he entered Irish separatist circles in London Collins began to amass a series of organisations, cliques and alliances. For Collins, the Gaelic Athletic Association, the Gaelic League, the Irish Volunteers, the Irish Republican Brotherhood (IRB), Sinn Féin and the fraternity to emerge from Frongoch internment camp all played their parts, but Chapter 2 will focus on Collins's role in a vital prisoners' support organisation, the Irish National Aid and Volunteer Dependents' Fund as a case study of something of what he was to become. As paid secretary and general office manager of this organisation during the crucial period of his career from February 1917 to the following July, we can watch Collins's working methods emerge. It is perhaps his assiduous striving within such organisations, his exploitation of the positions he acquired that distinguishes Collins from most of his colleagues, his friends and his enemies. This chapter will explore Collins the joiner, Collins the cultivator of circuits of influence, the engineer of functioning and potentially revolutionary structures. It reveals Collins the worker hungry for responsibility, but also Collins the self-promoter eager to make a name for himself, keen above all for a chance to get on.

Like many of the revolutionary generation, Michael Collins liked to claim the part of the plain soldier above any other role. Although the photographs of him in uniform during the last weeks of his life may sway our sense of him, although he possessed all the positions and monikers of the fighting man, Collins saw very little of the actual fight. He was an organiser and strategist based in a series of Dublin offices through the more intense periods of 1920 and 1921, with arguably

A chara

Dublin 12·10·18

Enclosed a 3 copies of An t-Óglác. We have printed an equivalent no of take offs of Ruthless Warfare. There is however no necessity to send this in separate form to you. If the contributor thinks anything has been left out I [will] attack just tell him — "considerations of space."

Have got your other letters. Thanks for that appertaining to Kerry especially. I had already written to both the men confirming the intentions of meeting & generally on the lines you suggest. I am glad I had the right people but I did not know them. The few Kerry men that have been up since P's arrest don't know as much as myself about Tralee.

I'm fed up to-day. It's the first time for 8 years I've felt it necessary to stay in bed, & which in addition to the physical disability makes me smart under a feeling of vicarious shame. Of course I'll be alright tomorrow but I'm very very impatient

Letter enclosed from the diplomatic Sec.

Slán leat — The best to you all.

M.

MS 5,848/12

Writing to Austin Stack, who was then in prison in Belfast, in October 1918, Collins was already his own hardest taskmaster. *(National Library of Ireland)*

far less control of the war than his lofty titles and later reputation as 'another David with his sling' would suggest.[15] In Chapter 3 we reflect upon Collins as 'the man who won the war'.[16] We will look at the types of violence he has become intimately associated with, his reputation as shadowy spymaster, and just how important the Collins he was alleged and believed to be actually was when it comes to understanding Collins's wars.

Collins may have thought of himself as a soldier, but how effective and committed a politician was he? He participated in the creation of the new Sinn Féin as it emerged between the spring and autumn of 1917. He sought to influence the positions, policies and personnel of the party; he served on the executive, built alliances, made enemies and played, through both his failures and successes, a fundamental part. It was as Minister for Finance in Dáil Éireann's cabinet he became one of the most influential, and admittedly fractious, politicians and administrators in that team. So should we remember Collins as a master of the mundane rather than the more romantic figure who seems too readily to occupy our thoughts? If 'politician' was a label he eschewed, then Chapter 4 will see how 'committee room schemer', 'statesman', 'negotiator', 'state builder' sit, looking at his methods, achievements and failings during his last year as the separatist movement first divided and then fought.

For all the many accounts of Collins's life, it is striking how very few of his biographers have thought it worth their while teasing out his ideals or beliefs. Indeed, his beliefs often seem to be taken as given, dispensed with in a couple of paragraphs, that he straightforwardly adhered to those grand, vague terms, 'independence', 'nationalism', 'freedom', like all the rest. For those who conscript him readily as a purveyor of their own views, for all the coulds and mights and should-have-beens, for all the certainties of how he would have made it different, better, quicker, Chapter 5 comes as a necessary counterweight. Here we begin the task of considering him at his own words rather than just surrendering him to those eager to put their words in his mouth. What was the nature of Collins's nationalism? Did he have a social or economic vision? What had he to say of democracy, religion, partition? Did he have an 'Ireland that we dreamed of' of his own?[17]

Drawing on a point made by Nancy Brandt of Collins's near contemporary, the Mexican revolutionary, Pancho Villa, who too became a very modern legend, Collins was born just five years after linotype transformed the pace of

Photographed in London during the Treaty negotiations in late 1921 at a desk surrounded by paper, does this best represent a typical Collins day?
(National Library of Ireland)

news, and two years after the invention of the Kodak camera. He was three years old when Edison produced moving pictures and five when Marconi invented the telegraph.[18] And each contributed to his fame. Given all that most people knew was the Collins that they had stitched together out of rumours and gossip and what the newspapers said, we have to take account of at least some of the Collinses produced. By the time he travelled to London for the negotiations in October 1921 his name was sufficiently famous, or notorious, that he was the one the press and the public wanted to see. Mobbed, feted, even propositioned, he had become a type of celebrity, the sum of what amounted to the Irish revolution in many British eyes, at least as they read it fresh each morning with their tea and toast. Chapter 6 will grapple with the celebrity Collins had inexorably become.

In Chapter 7 we will let him die, but only after examining some of the sensation and speculation caused by his death. While his death certainly questions any conception of him as the great fighter – he died in a type of ambush a hardened War of Independence veteran should have had the sense to avoid – that fight at Béal na mBláth quickly became something more mysterious and profound. While some resorted to conspiracy theories to explain it, and others chose to believe that Collins foresaw his own death with some sort of mysterious second sight, this chapter will try to get some measure of why the nature of his death just would not do. Such an extraordinary life, it seems, demanded a much more remarkable and imposing end.

In light of how we have started here it would make no sense to leave him in 1922. Collins had and has an afterlife unrivalled by any of his Irish revolutionary peers, and we will trace it through its early vivid manifestations, on through some awkward fallow years, and wait for Hollywood to come and cast him in even brighter lights. Chapter 8 will consider where many of the Collinses have hailed from, why some have stayed with us and persisted, why others quickly served their purpose and were gone. For all sorts of reasons Michael Collins has come to embody the Irish revolution. That chapter, this book, goes some way to wonder why.

One of the earliest photographs of Collins in the uniform of Commander-in-Chief of the new National Army, this image has shaped perceptions of him for decades. The inclusion of the smiling Alphonsus Culleton, a runaway-turned-sometime-mascot, no doubt humanised Collins while suggesting a status of national father-hero. *(National Library of Ireland)*

COUNTY OF *Longford*

County Inspector's Office,

Longford 6th *March* 1918

Submitted for information :—
Michael Collins is visiting this locality
very much of late & working up the
Volunteer movement. I am afraid his
influence if unchecked will have a
bad effect —

The D.I. [illegible]   *Reginald Heard*
                                                C.I.

By March 1918 it was already obvious to some in the Royal Irish Constabulary that an 'unchecked' Collins might have 'a bad effect'. *(The National Archives, London)*

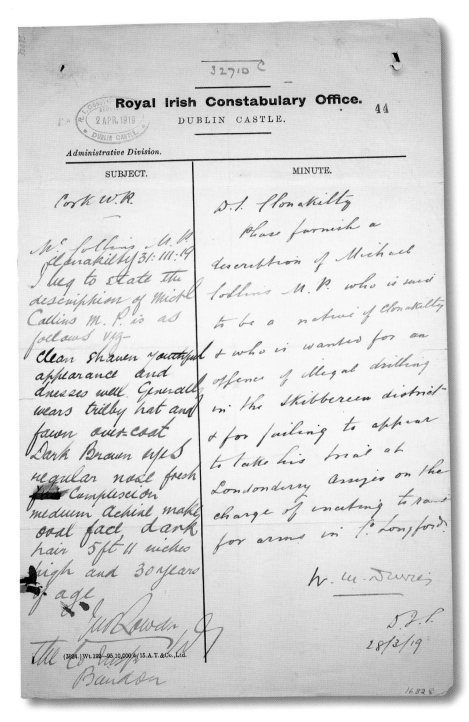

Royal Irish Constabulary Office.   44

DUBLIN CASTLE.

Administrative Division.

SUBJECT.	MINUTE.

Cork W.R.

M⁺ Collins . M.P.
Clonakilty 31: III: 19
I beg to state the
description of Mich⁺
Collins M.P. is as
follows viz—
Clean shaven youthful
appearance and
dresses well. Generally
wears trilby hat and
fawn over-coat
Dark Brown eyes
regular nose fresh
Complexion
medium actual make
oval face dark
hair 5 ft 11 inches
high and 30 years
of age

D.I. Clonakilty
Please furnish a
description of Michael
Collins M.P. who is said
to be a native of Clonakilty
+ who is wanted for an
offence of illegal drilling
in the Skibbereen district
+ for failing to appear
to take his trial at
Londonderry Assizes on the
charge of inciting to raid
for arms in P. Longford

W. M. Davies

D.I.
28/3/19

(3824.) Wt. 192—95. 10,000. 4/15. A.T. & Co., Ltd.

A growing cause for concern: Dublin Castle sought a description of Collins in March 1919. *(The National Archives, London)*

1

'We chose to consider ourselves outposts of our nation':

Making Michael Collins

In any biographical study the origins chapter is treacherous. This is especially true if the subject is a 'great man'. The longer that chapter becomes the more sceptical the reader should grow. Usually, without the benefit, or perhaps the encumbrance, of too many mundane, contemporary sources authors are fated to chase down and present the select reminiscences of the subject, the nostalgia of family, the sanitised versions of friends, the myths of acolytes, the inevitabilities of hindsight, the spite of enemies, the exaggerations that accrete to stories told and retold, and all of that before they reach for Freud.

It is not surprising then that the opening pages of Piaras Béaslaí's life of Michael Collins became a hunt for the exceptional origins of the exceptional subject. It is, however, a striking example of the tendency. Following the conventions of heroic biography, Béaslaí tells us that Collins's greatness was founded in breeding and foreshadowed in childhood. He was descended from chieftains and bards, was the son of a 'remarkable' father who was an Irish-Ireland ideal in being both of the soil and highly cultured, and, of course, the soon-to-be great man was an 'exceptionally handsome and good-tempered baby.'[1] In general, later biographers have been less brazen, though they have continued to rely on Béaslaí to a remarkable degree.

Given this, it is perhaps useful to think about the ways in which Collins might have been typical, rather than a youth apart. Over recent decades, historians of the Irish revolution have continued to write biographical studies of key revolutionary figures but they have also begun to ask, often in quite systematic ways, what made an Irish revolutionary in the years 1912 to 1923? What were the social origins and occupations, the familial circumstances, the cultural and intellectual influences, the generational markers, and the motivations most often shared amongst the revolutionary activists of the period?[2] In his novel *The Magic Mountain*, the German writer Thomas Mann put it thus: 'A man lives not only his personal life, as an individual, but also, consciously or unconsciously, the life of his epoch and his contemporaries.'[3] And so, in search of the man who would become a revolutionary, it seems important to ask to what extent Collins was a young man of his age. Collins would become extraordinary, but how ordinary was he?

Born on 16 October 1890, Collins's revolutionary years would be his twenties. In this, it seems, he was typical of IRA officers of the period. National and local studies indicate that between 1917 and 1921 over 60 per cent, sometimes and in some places more than 70 per cent, of the Irish Volunteer or IRA officers were in their twenties. Ordinary members were likely to be even more youthful, but the leaders, like Collins, tended to be 'neither young enough to be despised as mere adolescents, nor old enough to have lost their physical vigour or bachelorhood' as David Fitzpatrick put it when discussing County Clare.[4] Many of those most closely associated with Collins in the leadership of the IRA were of a similar age:

Richard Mulcahy was born in 1886, Eoin O'Duffy in 1890, Gearóid O'Sullivan in 1891, and Diarmuid O'Hegarty in 1892.

Like O'Sullivan and O'Hegarty, Collins was born in west Cork. Some 30 years ago, when Tom Garvin attempted to describe what he called, 'the Sinn Féin elite', he pointed out that rural Munster was their heartland and that of all regions west Cork was 'the most conspicuous area of origin' for members of that elite.[5] Cork would also, of course, prove the most violent county during the revolutionary period, although Collins was a member of a Cork set who would make their reputations through activity elsewhere. These Cork men – in London and in Dublin – reinforced each other's enthusiasm on the way up and brought each other along as they climbed the revolutionary hierarchy.

The rural IRA was built on farmers' sons and the urban IRA on clerks, shop assistants and civil servants, who were very often the sons of farmers, usually comfortable farmers. Again, in this regard, Collins seems standard model rather than bespoke Irish revolutionary, though his background was somewhat more comfortable than the average. At the time of his birth, Collins's parents (Michael and Mary Anne), along with his bachelor uncle, Patrick, were the tenant farmers of a quite substantial holding of 136 acres in the townland of Woodfield, near Clonakilty. Michael was their eighth child. In 1901 of the 40,043 holdings in County Cork only 4,174 (10.4 per cent) were a hundred acres or more. By then, Michael was the youngest of six – three daughters and three sons – still at home, in a household headed by his 45-year-old widowed mother. Their farm had more outbuildings (nine) than any of the other twenty holdings in the townland, and their house had more rooms (eight).

John, Michael's eldest brother, who became known as Seán, would inherit the tenancy after Mary Anne's death in 1907 and he would buy half the holding in 1911. This seems a little late for a comparatively prosperous and ambitious family to avail of the Land Acts, but during the preceding two decades much of the family's resources were evidently devoted to ensuring that Seán's seven siblings were educated and set up in life.[6] This enabled them to pursue careers as civil servants, teachers or in the religious in Ireland, Britain and America. For Michael it would be London. Not yet sixteen, he arrived in Shepherd's Bush in the high summer of 1906. It must have been exciting. He had left Clonakilty for the comparative safety of a job in the Post Office in West Kensington, and a flat with his sister Johanna (Hannie), but he also left Clonakilty for London, perhaps

In April 1921, at the height of the War of Independence, the British Army came to the Collins family home at Woodfield and, using petrol and hay, set it ablaze. Sometime after, Collins and his brother Seán posed in the ruins for the *Irish Independent*. *(National Library of Ireland)*

More than twenty years earlier, a rather sullen eight-year-old Collins was photographed at the family home with his mother (right) and grandmother (rear).

the most dynamic city in the world: a city with a population of 4.5 million and all the attractions of modern urban life. Collins would be 25 before he returned to Ireland for good, nine and a half years later.

It was during that time, in London, that he became a man. 'He grew rapidly during the first few years,' Hannie remembered.[7] It is tempting to imagine his rhythms synchronise with those of the city, with the plunge and surge of the crowds in and out of the Central Line, which opened in 1900 and ran from Shepherd's Bush to Bank; or the Great Northern, Piccadilly and Brompton Railway (the Piccadilly Line), which opened six months after his arrival and coursed conveniently through South Kensington, pulsing the populace around the metropolis;[8] or, on Saturday night with his young-buck friends and 2,300 others, pushing and shoving in the crowds at the shining Shepherd's Bush Empire, just opened in 1903, one of the last in a new generation of mass-market music halls established across Britain's cities from 1885;[9] or watching the twenty palaces, 120 exhibition buildings and a stadium for 110,000 spectators climb into the Shepherd's Bush sky at the White City complex, all built for the Franco-British Exhibition and Olympics of 1908, before, surely, joining the eight million visitors to those events;[10] or participating in the new craze for sitting in the dark, sometimes with a girl, to watch the flash of light on screen in one of the thousand or more film venues available to Londoners in the years 1906 to 1914 – more and more of these were purpose-built cinemas that 'appeared overnight' (383 by 1914);[11] or queuing with the curious and self-improving thousands when the

Clonakilty was Collins's childhood metropolis. In autumn 1903, he moved the few miles there to attend school and live with his sister Margaret and her husband, P.J. O'Driscoll. Clonakilty was connected to the world. There was the railway and P.J. owned the local newspaper, but it was quiet. *(National Library of Ireland)*

CLONAKILTY. Co.CORK. 3248. W.L.

Shepherd's Bush was different. This photograph was taken on a May afternoon in 1903. Just three years later, Collins would join the bustle. *(London Transport Museum Collection)*

new Victoria and Albert Museum building opened in Kensington in the summer of 1909;[12] or, just maybe, hiding amongst the throngs for a surreptitious look at the Festival of Empire at the Crystal Palace in 1911;[13] or, more mundanely, each working day, writing and writing at the Post Office Savings Bank to meet the demands of his supervisors and the eight million customers beyond.[14]

And there were the public houses and the dance halls. In an affectionate recollection of Collins in London, P.S. O'Hegarty, a leading figure in the Irish nationalist scene in the city during those years, wrote that he 'fell into spasmodic association with a hard-drinking, hard-living crowd from his own place, and their influence on him was not good'. Collins was, O'Hegarty noted, 'in the "blast and bloody" stage of adolescent evolution'. He was regarded as 'a wild youth' and 'spoiled by his wildness',[15] but this is the same O'Hegarty who wrote in 1909 in *Inis Fáil*, the journal of the London Gaelic League, which he edited, that dancing 'is not really an art, it's a survival of primitive barbarism ... I don't dance myself, and have never tried to.'[16] Albeit with more humour than average, O'Hegarty was numbered among those revolutionaries who embraced asceticism, even puritanism, as an ethic. Collins was not. This made Collins friends, but it would also win him disapproval.

Collins brought more than the energy of youth to London. He arrived with, as Tim Pat Coogan put it, 'ideological baggage'.[17] The influence of family, and in particular parents, upon the revolutionaries of this era has prompted contrasting observations. Fearghal McGarry wrote of Collins's generation that 'no one was born a revolutionary, but many were born into revolutionary families' while noting that many of the revolutionaries were also born into families in which the parents had always been or had become 'committed to parliamentary methods', prompting 'intergenerational conflict'.[18] Roy Foster has argued that for many of the radicalised men and women of that era the process of becoming a revolutionary involved a conscious rejection of their parents' generation, whom they came to see as colluding and compromised. Further, Foster seems to imply, a particular subset may have been motivated by a drive for fulfilment rooted in loss: Terence MacSwiney, P.S. O'Hegarty and his brother Seán, Liam de Róiste, Éamon de Valera, Erskine Childers and Patrick Pearse, he notes, all 'came from families with a dead or absent father'.[19]

Collins offers an interesting if not very conclusive case study in this regard. His father died when he was six, so if Foster's psychological speculation reflects

CENTRAL LONDON (TUBE) RAILWAY.

TAKING THE TICKET AT BANK STATION.

DISPOSING OF THE TICKET.

SAFE & COMMODIOUS LIFTS.

TAKE THE TWOPENNY TUBE

No Worry about accidents

AND AVOID ALL ANXIETY

SHEPHERD'S BUSH. — HOLLAND PARK. — NOTTING HILL GATE. — QUEEN'S RD. — LANCASTER GATE. — MARBLE ARCH. — BOND ST. — OXFORD CIRCUS. — TOTTENHAM COURT RD. — BRITISH MUSEUM. — CHANCERY LANE. — POST OFFICE. — THE BANK.

CENTRAL LONDON RAILWAY.

ENTERING THE TRAIN.

LEAVING THE STATION AT SHEPHERD'S BUSH.

This 1905 poster promotes the convenience of the Central Line, showing all the stops from Shepherd's Bush to Bank. *(London Transport Museum Collection)*

Collins worked here at the Post Office Savings Bank Headquarters, Blythe House, on Blythe Road, West Kensington. It was built between 1899 and 1903 and when it opened it accommodated about 4,000 staff. *(The Postal Museum)*

a reality then Collins should be added to his list. Hart has suggested that a series of replacement father figures would 'guide the way' as Collins became more and more committed to nationalism.[20] His family's politics was nationalist, but the texture of that nationalism at the time of Collins's childhood, and how he experienced it, is less clear. Coogan tells us that, 'according to family tradition', a cousin who had been a friend of Wolfe Tone taught Collins's father and that, in turn, Michael senior had been in the Fenians, though he did not rebel in 1867. As such, Coogan continues, in his childhood Collins 'had a not insignificant link with the founder of Irish Republicanism.'[21] The contorted double negative would suggest that not even Coogan had much confidence in that assertion. Hart's portrait of Collins's father evokes a man who, during his later years at least, 'disliked radical politics', leaned toward the conservative end of the Home Rule spectrum and subscribed to the *Weekly Freeman's Journal*.[22] And Coogan does acknowledge that 'at home Collins received a gentler, more complex, but nevertheless complementary vision of history and politics' than that offered by local firebrand republicans whom the young boy knew.[23]

On balance, Collins's family and community seem to have exposed him to a mix of nationalist influences and ideas that were characteristic of the period: a mix that produced many nationalists but fewer active separatists. McGarry's reading of the oral history statements given by revolutionary activists to the Bureau of Military History during the 1940s and 1950s has led him to note that 'many separatists regarded their education as a radicalising experience.'[24] Writing from Frongoch to a friend in 1916, Collins emphasised that finding his path to revolutionary nationalism had involved long searching on his part and guidance from 'other men', and identified his first tutors as Denis Lyons and James Santry. Santry was a local blacksmith. Lyons was the local teacher and he, wrote Collins, 'had this pride of Irishness that has always meant most to me.'[25]

While at the individual level future rebels, like Collins, came under the influence of occasional inspiring local teachers, the role of education in creating revolutionaries was, at its most important, more structural than that. As David Fitzpatrick has put it, education

> equipped artisans, clerks and shopkeepers' children to attend debates, join youth clubs and form coteries in which revolution could be imagined if not realised in practice. It was such people, remote

from the world of universities and artistic elites, whose unexpected transformation through the act of rebellion so startled Yeats.[26]

While still in Cork, Collins's education opened up to him the vibrant print culture that, from the middle of the nineteenth century, engendered and sustained a public conversation saturated in the idea of, and aspiration to, a distinct Irish nationhood. This was a crucial formative experience. We shall explore Collins's conceptualisation of nationality in Chapter 5 but as far as his youthful reading goes, Béaslaí offered up a standard menu: Thomas Davis, the Sullivan brothers (*Speeches from the Dock*), Charles J. Kickham (*Knocknagow*) and the contemporary journalism of D.P. Moran and Arthur Griffith. If this seems rather too like a list of the material that Collins should have read when avoiding 'trashy fiction', then it is also entirely plausible, and subsequent biographers have repeated it.[27] When Hannie Collins wrote to Béaslaí in September 1923, she made a point of letting him know that Collins 'got through a good course of the English classics before he was 16' and that he continued to read the best literary fiction. For Hannie, still living among the English, it was vital to emphasise both her brother's intellectual capacity and his sober respectability through his reading habits. The term hooligan was coined in London in 1898 in the context of a moral scare about a 'new' youth gang problem. The popular press blamed this alleged development, at least in part, on the nurturing of boys on a diet of cheap penny-dreadful novels. Evidently, Hannie wanted it known that Michael was not some murderous corner-boy.[28] While on remand in prison in Sligo in April 1918, Collins returned to old editions of the *Irish Review*. 'Many and many an hour of occupation have these copies given me in the days gone by', he wrote. This quality literary journal, which appeared between 1911 and 1914, was edited in succession from 1912 by Padraic Colum and Joseph Plunkett, with Thomas MacDonagh as associate editor, and it was the Colum and Plunkett numbers that Collins owned.[29] Later in 1918, he wrote to Austin Stack, who was then in prison, offering to send books from his personal library, providing a listing that was dominated by nationalist memoir, history, literature, poetry, and ballads.[30] Joe Good has provided further confirmation of these impressions of Collins's cultural grounding and interests. Admittedly, Good, who knew Collins in London, may have been exaggerating when he recalled that Collins had memorised and could recite as many as 350 Irish – many of them nationalist – songs, poems and ballads.[31]

[S. 293.]

To be filled up by the Candidate himself, and returned within a week, in the accompanying envelope.

6 FEB 1906

Situation *Temporary Boy Clerk*

Write here your **Number.** G49888
(See Examination Order.)

NOTE.—Should any of the particulars furnished, in answer to the undermentioned Queries, be found to be false within the knowledge of the Candidate, he will, if appointed, be liable to be dismissed; and if otherwise entitled to Superannuation Allowance, he will forfeit all claim thereto. The wilful omission of any Situation or the suppression of any material fact will be similarly punished.

Christian name and surname (*in full*) ... *Michael James Collins*

Date .... *2nd* day of *February* 190*6*

Address (*in full*) .... *90 P. O Driscoll, Sloghen Nol Male National School Clonakilty Co Cork*

Day and year of birth*.................. *Friday Oct 16th 1890*
Age last birthday... *15 years*

Place of birth (*give Parish, Post Town, and County*) .... *Rosscarbery parish. Clonakilty post town Co Cork*

* *Note.*—Date of Birth. Before answering this question Candidates should take pains (by consulting public registers if necessary) to ascertain the exact date of their birth, as any erroneous statement may be held to affect their eligibility in respect of character.

Father's name .... *Michael Collins (Deceased)*
    „   address .... *Woodfield. Clonakilty Co Cork*
    „   profession or trade .... *Carpenter.*
(*If deceased, give the last address, profession, &c.*)

Names and addresses in full of two *referees as to character. These should be responsible persons of mature age,* not employers or relations, *but well acquainted with you in private life.*

I. Name ...... *J.C. O'Sullivan Esq,*
   Address ... *Sovereign St, Clonakilty*
   Occupation *Merchant.*

II. Name...... *J. O'Brien Esq. J.P.*
    Address... *Western Rd Clonakilty*
    Occupation *Merchant*

Schools.
(*Mention the school or schools at which you were educated, stating the kind of schools, whether public or private, Collegiate, National, British, &c.*
Mention the length of your stay in each, and the names of the Masters of the schools attended. If you have been a Pupil Teacher you should state the date on which you were apprenticed.)

First School.
Name and Address of the School - } *Lisavaird National School Clonakilty Co Cork*
Name of the Master *Mr. D. Lyons.*
Date of entry and leaving - - - } From *June 4th 1895* , to *Oct 1st 1903*

Second School.
Name and Address of the School - } *Nol Male National School Clonakilty Co Cork*
Name of the Master *Mr J. Crowley.*
Date of entry and leaving - - - } From *Oct 1st 1903* , to *Present time 18*

Third School.
Name and Address of the School - }
Name of the Master
Date of entry and leaving - - - } From   18   , to   18

Age on finally leaving school.................. *at school still*

Are you free from pecuniary embarrassments ? .... *Yes.*

Have you been on any former occasion examined by the Civil Service Commissioners ? .... *No.*
(*If so, state when, and for what situation.*)

W B & L (891·)—23303—5000-7-4
31213 —5000-3-5

[TURN OVER.

According to Collins's application form to join the Post Office as a boy clerk, dated 2 February 1906, he attended Lisavaird National School between 1895 and 1903, where he was taught by Denis Lyons, whom he would later describe as an important influence. He then received a further two and a half years of schooling in Clonakilty, where he lived with his sister Margaret and her husband, P.J. O'Driscoll. In 1906 both of his referees lived in that town: Jeremiah C. O'Sullivan, for example, was a prosperous merchant. *(The National Archives, London)*

2 Nevertheless it must be conceded that the training in clerical and routine work acquired in the Savings Bank was exceedingly useful to him in his later career. He was naturally a neat and quick worker, and his books and papers were so arranged that he could put his hand on anything required in a moment. This was characteristic of him from a very early age, for he kept his books and personal belongings in his own small bedroom at home, which was a model of neatness to some of his elder brothers and sisters whose habits were far otherwise. There were no loose ends about Michael, physically or mentally, and he was very impatient of loose statements and vague information, holding that no one had any business speaking on a subject which he had not studied.

He was an omnivorous reader; like the other members of his family, he had got through a good course of the English classics before he was 16: Scott, Dickens and

In September 1923 Johanna (Hannie) Collins wrote to Piaras Béaslaí providing him with what she called 'a short account of Michael's life in London'. Michael had lived with her throughout his time there. Hannie emphasised how 'changed and cold and lonely the world without him is for his friends, and above all for me, who had the privilege of making a home for him during his young and impressionable years'. This sisterly intimacy and admiration makes her account valuable but should also render the reader cautious. *(National Library of Ireland)*

and Thackeray — Swift, Addison, Burke,
Sheridan, Dryden, Pope — and
Shakespeare and Milton as well as
Moore, Byron, Shelley and Keats.
Later he read Hardy and Meredith,
Wells, Arnold Bennett and Conrad,
also Swinburne and Oscar Wilde,
as well as contemporary writers like
W.B. Yeats, Padraig Colum and James
Stephens. No one appreciated Bernard
Shaw more than he, and he felt his
influence, as all among the younger
generation who think at all have come
under that same salutary influence.
How we discussed literature together
and how often have we sat up long
after midnight discussing the ~~to~~
merits and demerits of the English and
Irish and French writers who happened
to be our idols at the time. He was
thoroughly modern and liked realism
and the plays of the younger dramatists
who wrote for the Abbey Theatre. How
many a little brown-covered book of those plays

THE HOME AND COLONIAL TEA STORES
(FOR PRICES, SEE MIDDLE OF BOOK.)

Divination	Act of foretelling future events
Doge	The chief magistrate in Republican Venice
Doggerel	Wretched verse.
Doric	Earliest & plainest form of Greek architecture
Dormitory	Place to sleep in
Dryad	Wood-nymph.
Ductile	Tractable - flexible
Dulcet	Sweet harmonious
Durance	Imprisonment, custody,

E -

Ebullition	Sudden burst.
Eclat	Burst of applause - Renown - Splendour.
Ecumenical	General - universal - applied to Church Councils.
Effete	Worn out Exhausted.
Effigy	The image or likeness of a person Portrait - figure -
Effluvium	Nauseous odour -
Effrontery	Audacious impudence - Shameless Boldness

Effulgent	Sending out a flood of light - Gleaming - Splendid.
Egregious	Remarkable - Enormous.
Egress.	Exit departure
Eisteddfod	Meeting of the Welsh bards & minstrels
Eleemosynary	Given in Charity
Elision	Suppression of a vowel or syllable
Embouchure	A mouth or aperture as of a river cannon
Embrasor	One who attempts to influence illegally a jury
Emetic	A medicine that provokes vomiting
Emollient.	A substance that softens or allays irritation. Softening making supple
Empiric	A quack a charlatan
Encomium	Eulogy - praise
Ennui	Dulness of spirit Listlessness weariness
Entomology	Zoology pertaining to insects
Ephemeral	For one day only - for a short time
Epic	Poetic narrative of a one event
Epilepsy	called falling sickness - also makes patient lose all sense

Collins's urge to self-improvement and his humour are illustrated by a notebook from his time in London during which he created his own dictionary, noting down words and their definitions in a diligent and ordered manner.
(UCD Archives)

This nationalist reading did not inoculate Collins against a desire 'to live in the biggest city in the world' or to seek there a career that would 'satisfy' his 'ideas of opportunity'.[32] Nor did it prevent him from writing a composition for his successful civil service entrance examination in which he lauded the study of history because through it one could learn how 'an island such as Great Britain came to be the greatest power on the face of the earth', before listing a series of English and British military victories through the ages.[33] The composition was, of course, a means to an end, but the end remained respectable employment and advancement via an arm of the British state. For the Collins of 1906 this was perfectly compatible with being a proud Irish nationalist. Perhaps it had to be. For the youngest son of a Cork farmer, with an education that was real but modest, opportunities were not manifold. Nonetheless, to begin with at least, Collins regarded London as an opportunity, not an exile. Once more, Collins is part of a trend. From about 1870 the children of middle-class and lower-middle-class Irish Catholics increasingly crammed for, and effectively pursued, posts in a metropolitan civil service that had become more meritocratic, at least at the entry levels.[34]

For Collins, this would prove a frustrating and disillusioning experience. He spent four years as a boy clerk, a low-status and tedious job. Some of his then colleagues remembered that Collins found it 'particularly irksome'.[35] When, in the summer of 1910, following another examination, he was offered a somewhat better civil service job, Assistant Clerk, he turned it down. By then his keenness to improve himself had led him take up a position as a clerk at a stockbroking firm, Horne & Co., and he decided to stay there. He would move to another such firm, The Guaranty Trust Company, in September 1914. There are different versions of his role at the latter firm, but it is clear that in eight years Collins's advancement in London had not met his ambitions or his estimations of his own abilities. As such, Collins seems to constitute an instance of the Irish middle and lower-middle classes of this period, described by John Hutchinson in *The Dynamics of Cultural Nationalism*, who, finding their upward mobility hobbled, if not blocked, turned to nationalism.[36]

Ernest Gellner, one of the great theorists of modern nationalism, believed that such frustration among an educated and ambitious yet excluded ethnic group was more likely to turn toward nationalism in the context of modern, multi-ethnic cities, where an emphasis on difference was fostered.[37] This rings true in the case of Collins and that of the London-Irish separatists amongst whom he was radicalised during these years. In 1922 Collins told the Dáil that 'I know very well that the people of England had very little regard for the people of Ireland, and that when you lived among them you had to be defending yourself constantly from insults … Every man that has lived amongst them knows that they are always making jokes about Paddy and the pig, and that sort of thing.'[38] Collins seems to have been more likely than the average to call out and confront such slights immediately,[39] but he also adopted the typical response of seeking out and sticking with one's own: 'I had Irish friends in London before I arrived, and in the intervening years I had made many more friends among Irishmen resident in London. For the most part we lived lives apart. We chose to consider ourselves outposts of our nation. We were a distinct community – a tiny eddy, if you like, in the great metropolis.'[40] In 1922, at a moment when his opponents charged that he had allowed the atmosphere in London to contaminate and dilute his commitment to Irish freedom, it is likely that Collins exaggerated in retrospect the extent to which he and his Irish friends were isolated and isolated themselves a decade earlier. Nonetheless, there is no doubting the seriousness and intensity of his engagement with his Irish cultural and political identity during those years in London.

When Collins arrived in London the most visible and active organisational manifestations of that distinct community were associational forms of cultural nationalism. The Irish-born population of London then numbered around 50,000 men and women, and in 1906 the Gaelic League had about 3,000 members. This membership was largely drawn from the 'Irish-born Catholic lower intelligentsia comprising minor civil servants, teachers and postal officials.' It is not surprising then that Collins should join, although like many other members, perhaps the majority, he was primarily attracted to the League for the social events where he met other Irish people.[41] His attendance patterns suggest he was less enthusiastic about language classes; however, he was tenacious. He attended classes more regularly from 1910, though general membership figures for the League had fallen dramatically since his joining.[42]

Maybe he took to heart one of the regular chidings of dilettantes penned by P.S. O'Hegarty in *Inis Fáil*. O'Hegarty was severe in many matters, but especially in his role as GAA correspondent for that paper. When he reported on the first-ever victory in a hurling match of the Geraldines Gaelic Athletic Club, on 15 March 1908, at Finchley against Rapparees – a game in which Collins played at half back for the Geraldines – O'Hegarty complained that the 'hurling was poor, and dangerous into the bargain, and accidents were averted rather by good luck than by skill.' Neither did he give the Geraldines much credit for their win, explaining that the 'result was practically due to the fact that four Rapparees missed the train from Forestgate . . . and they were, therefore, four men short throughout.'[43] On this matter, O'Hegarty's judgement seems to have been sound. When the hurling team he captained, Rooneys, played the Geraldines in the semi-final some weeks later, the Geraldines lost 7 goals and 17 points to 2 points.[44] It was this rather ramshackle club, based in west London, which added seventeen-year-old Collins to its committee in January 1908 and would elect him vice-captain of the hurling team in July of that year, in the immediate aftermath of the defeat to Rooneys. He quickly became a regular attendee at, and vociferous contributor to, committee meetings. By July 1909 he was the club secretary.

Such committee positions are avoided more often than coveted and, in the case of the Geraldines, could not be mistaken for glamorous. Collins's minutes record that their meeting of 12 January 1910 took place 'near some trees Wormwood Scrubs',[45] while he spent a lot of time hectoring the membership for their fees. Though Collins proved to have the stomach for the humdrum necessities of club life, Hart was surely wrong when he argued that the fact that Collins served as secretary for seven years, but never as president or vice-president, suggests that he was regarded as 'a valuable foot soldier . . . still not officer material.'[46] As well as being the most onerous and tedious position in a GAA club, the post of secretary was the most influential and facilitated high levels of networking. If one was intent on making a mark, as Collins appears to have been from the beginning, then it was ideal.

It also provided young Collins with the opportunity to try out some personalities. The minutes suggest that he was, by turn, hot-headed and emollient, demanding and resigned, dogmatic and ironic. His accounts of the first and second half-yearly general meetings to which he was secretary, in January and July 1910, show that he had also developed a tendency toward wry self-dramatisation. He wrote, 'the secretary's report which was extremely pessimistic – not to say cynical – was adopted with practically no comment' and, he recorded, 'the secretary read his report. It was not flattering to the members & advocated disbanding as the club had been unable to field a team for more than 6 months. This suggestion was of course repudiated & the report, after the exhibition of marked enthusiasm by a few members, was adopted'.[47]

This broadside poster from 1913 by the artist Cesca Trench promoted the Gaelic League's Seachtain na Gaeilge. Collins joined the League in London. There he met and socialised with people from home and second-generation London-Irish, including Art O'Brien, president of the London League from 1914 and an important ally in the years ahead. *(National Library of Ireland)*

connrad na zaedilze

⚜ lonndain. ⚜

an szrúduzad bliadantamail

1912.

Dearbuizeann an teirbear ro zur éiniz le

Miċeál ó Coileán

1 zcéim a ....4..... 'ran rzrúduzad, azur zo

bruair re 84.5% de na máincannaib

..................................uaċtarán.

..................................Rúnaire.

brúin 7 nuallám, Spáid napad, baile áta cliat.

Collins also learned some Irish at Gaelic League classes. This certificate dates from 1912. *(UCD Archives)*

Geraldine G. A. Club.

Report for half year ending December 1909

An eventful half year has followed a somewhat riotous general meeting. Great hopes instead of having been fulfilled have been rudely shattered. An unhappy accident to an old and very prominent member tended to increase the gloom always attendant on persistent ill fortune. Your committee granted a little assistance to the stricken member, and you will be gratified to learn that Mr Kingston is now on the high road to recovery. Another episode of which I shall speak later helped to make confusion worse confounded.

Our internal troubles were saddening but our efforts in football and hurling were perfectly heartbreaking. I speak first of football. In no single contest have our colours been crowned with success. In hurling we haven't even the consolation of a creditable performance. But to speak first of football. At our July meeting we had high hopes of winning the nss cup — alas such hopes were vain. The Hibernians proved their superiority on July the 15th but after a well contested game. We have played one match for the 1909 championship — and been beaten in that. Our men quite obviously showed their want of training, and as this has not since been remedied — as far as one can judge by the practices — it looks as if we would make a very poor fight indeed for the championship. But our hurling record is infinitely worse. During the half year we were drawn to play 5 matches. but disgraceful to say in only one case did we field a full team — Agst the Mils on July 5th

This report was Collins's first to a half-yearly general meeting of the Geraldines club, London. He drafted it in December 1909 and presented it on 8 January 1910. Collins was clearly amused by his own performance at the meeting, but the critical tone is one that would become familiar to those who corresponded with him.
(National Library of Ireland)

Collins was a vigorous competitor on the hurling field and at GAA athletics meetings. This photograph of a hurling match in London dates from *c.* 1902, and gives a strong sense of the London GAA world that he joined. *(Museum of London)*

An active commitment to cultural nationalism did not necessarily lead to, or go hand in hand with, sympathy for militant separatism, but a tight clique of separatists operated within London's GAA in these years and the internal politics of the GAA reveal early tangible evidence that Collins's nationalism had acquired a harder edge. The first decade of the twentieth century witnessed a heated debate within the GAA between an influential element – prominent among them leading IRB men – who successfully campaigned to reinstitute an automatic suspension from the association for any member who played 'foreign games' and others who resisted this. The rule that grew from the campaign would become known as 'the ban'. From 1903, the opponents of this development, recognising that some form of 'the ban' was inevitable in the short term, tended to coalesce around the position that each county board should have discretion as to whether to enforce the rule within their jurisdiction. After success at the annual congress of 1903, proponents of 'the county opt out' position were defeated at the 1904 congress. From then, an automatic ban would remain in place until 1971, but the debate remained a live one for a number of years after 1905, appearing on the agenda at a series of annual congresses.[48]

In London during those years one's attitude to 'the ban' was a barometer of one's politics. At club and county board level the contest was particularly fierce as hardliners such as O'Hegarty, Sam Maguire, Liam MacCarthy and Patrick Belton (all IRB men) struggled to hold the line. In 1911, much to their disgust, they found themselves in a minority. When the County Board put a motion to the Annual Congress of the association of that year, proposing the rule should not apply in London, MacCarthy, who was supposed to be the county delegate, refused to attend. Instead, he wrote a letter urging Congress to reject the motion and in doing so show to his back-sliding colleagues in London, 'whose environments had made them shoneens', that 'there is no room in the GAA for them.' Congress took MacCarthy's advice.[49]

Collins was unequivocal and loud in his support for the hard-line position. In January 1909 he was the proposer of a motion at the Geraldines' half-yearly general meeting condemning the County Board for 'asking back into the GAA' athletes who had served five months only of a fifteen-month suspension for breaching 'the ban'.[50] He had by then, it is generally suggested, been attending and contributing at Sinn Féin meetings while his entry into the Irish Republican Brotherhood is usually dated to November 1909. He was becoming part of that minority among Irish nationalists for whom the expression of cultural identity or voting for the Irish Party or taking pride in a rebel history was not enough. Depending on whose account one believes, he was sworn in to 'the Brotherhood' by Belton or Maguire. Either way, the GAA connection appears to have been crucial.[51] Years later, Brian Cusack claimed that O'Hegarty had kept Collins 'on the mat waiting for quite a long time before he was taken in as he – Collins – had been drinking too much.'[52] It is possible that O'Hegarty took this stance, though Cusack had opposed the Treaty and was a founder member of Fianna Fáil, and is not necessarily a sympathetic source.

The IRB that Collins entered was showing the first signs of awakening from a dormant phase, yet in 1909 a young man joining the brotherhood in Ireland might reasonably have imagined that he was expressing an attachment to a particular ideal rather than committing himself to imminent revolutionary action. In London, however, he was joining a secret society in the context of a heightened awareness of 'terror'. For example, in January two anarchists had killed a policeman and a boy, and injured as many as twenty others, in an incident known as 'the Tottenham outrage', while in July, in South Kensington, Madan Lal Dhingra, an Indian nationalist, had assassinated Sir William Curzon Wyllie, the political aide-de-camp to the Secretary of State for India. Dhingra was hanged in August.[53] Later, from 1912, radical suffragettes would escalate their concerted campaign – centred on London – of window-breaking, acid attacks, arson and even bombings.[54] When Collins returned to Ireland, he did so with some feel for the sensation that such events could generate. Furthermore, Collins was attracted to those who favoured action and risk in pursuit of their ends. In an essay from these years on the theme 'Nothing Ventured Nothing Have', written for night classes he was attending, he argued, 'In the history of the world's most famous men we find that all of them were ready to venture even their existence on the attainment of their ends. Washington played for a large stake, and it was only by venturing everything that he was master of that he won it. The same was true of Garibaldi in Italy, and in England Richard III unfeeling [sic] sacrificed his nephews because they were in his way to the throne.'[55] The puckish pleasure he took in teasing his English instructor through the examples he selected is as evident as his admiration for ambition. Hannie claimed that her brother read Joseph Conrad around this time, if he did then he did not heed Conrad's warnings about the dangers of revolutionary commitment and terror in *The Secret Agent* (1907) and *Under Western Eyes* (1911).[56]

Once in, Collins became part of the change that was occurring within the IRB as a new generation brought renewed energy.[57] The speed at which he climbed the hierarchy of the London IRB was, however, disputed later by Béaslaí and O'Hegarty. Béaslaí claimed, on the basis of an interview with Sam Maguire it appears, that Collins was appointed a 'section master', head of a basic unit, as early as 1910: Maguire went so far as to say that Collins was 'very good at it'.[58] According to O'Hegarty, this promotion did not occur until 1913. By 1914 he was, it is certain, on the executive for the south of England: they appointed him treasurer.[59] He had by then joined the Irish Volunteers upon its establishment in London. This new paramilitary group, founded in Dublin in November 1913, constituted an Irish nationalist response to the establishment of the Ulster Volunteers, which had been formed by unionists to oppose Home Rule for Ireland. Hart emphasised his lack of significant rank in that organisation but, in their recollections, contemporaries such as Joe Good and Jeremiah O'Leary stressed his prominence and influence: according to Good, 'this man, Michael Collins, meant to be in command.'[60]

The coming of war in Europe must have affected Collins's daily life. During those early weeks London was transformed. Anxious crowds gathered, at Buckingham Palace for instance, on 4 August, the day Britain entered the conflict, but more significant were the practical signs of mobilisation – the soldiers, reservists and military vehicles always in the streets – and the early alarm as people rushed to 'withdraw money' or 'amass food stores in their houses'. Working as he did for a stockbroking firm, Collins's life changed even before the official declaration of war because the London Stock Exchange closed on 31 July in response to panic on the financial markets. It did not reopen until January 1915. As August turned into September, Collins would have watched increasing numbers of his co-workers sign up and disappear in response to the now ubiquitous recruitment leaflets, posters and meetings.[61] Over time, the London Collins had moved to was transformed. Union flags appeared everywhere, wartime restrictions closed the pubs at 10pm, most of the galleries and museums shut, the once-bright evening lights went out or were dimmed in anticipation of Zeppelin air raids that eventually came in May 1915. As one contemporary observer of the city wrote: 'As I go about I can see the wide spaciousness of London and its vast variety of characteristics slowly but surely contracting to a War Camp.'[62]

Separatists living in Ireland, such as Desmond FitzGerald, recalled that even there the war atmosphere and increased levels of jingo heighted their sense of being outsiders.[63] This feeling must have been even more stark for Collins and the small cohort of radical nationalists living in London. Despite or because of this they persisted. Sam Maguire credited Collins with keeping many of the London members with the radical minority when the Volunteers split over John Redmond's support for the war effort. Maguire stated that 'from that time forward he [Collins] was a leading light in Volunteer circles in London.'[64] In October 1915, the *Irish Volunteer* paper reported breezily on the activity of the London company, despite the 'difficulties of Irish Volunteering in London under war conditions'.[65]

Through all of this, Collins was, it seems, that apparent contradiction, an extrovert conspirator. Restless, confident, ambitious, committed, sometimes gauche, he made his presence felt. Cracking various local networks and organisations, he demonstrated both a willingness to take on responsibility and a capacity to do the work. By late 1915 if one moved in nationalist or republican circles in London it would have been almost impossible to miss Michael Collins, yet he was hardly remarkable. He was just another young enthusiast, finding some fulfilment and purpose in the apparently marginal world of separatist associational life. Not only that, as a resident of London he was on the periphery of the Irish separatist world. Very few separatists in Ireland would have been aware of him in 1915, but that was about to change.

How do you know? Define what you mean by "good luck"

good luck knocks at least once at each man's door but ~~the tide~~ it must be ~~taken at the flood and~~ received in a lively and vigorous manner. In the history of the world's famous men we find that all of them were ready to venture even their existence on the attainment of their ends. Washington played for a large stake, and it was only by ~~venturing~~ risking everything he was master of, that he won it. The same was true of Garibaldi in Italy, and in England Richard III unfeelingly sacrificed his nephews because they ~~were in~~ hindered him in his way to the throne.

Mixed metaphors, a "tide" does not knock at the door.

Avoid clashing of words with a similar sound, as venture & venturing

Is this an example of the desirability of venturing all?

We must not however be too rash. It has been truthfully said that 'vaulting Ambition o'erleaps itself' and history is rich in instances of this truth. Wolsey aimed at being pope, but he failed, and on his dying bed said:

Cromwell, I charge thee fling away ambition,
By that sin fell the angels: how can man, then,
The image of his Maker, hope to win by't?

Napoleon aspired to being emperor of Europe; but

Waterloo made him a prisoner and an exile, and so forever barred him from being anything greater than an inhabitant of a cell in St Helena.

He was not kept in a cell.

    Fire, when kept under restraint, is a useful servant, but when it gets the upper hand it is a merciless tyrant. The same holds good of ambition. If we take it to mean an unquenchable desire to advance by honest methods towards perfection, it is one of the best qualities a man can be endowed with.

    Avoid a confusion of metaphors and vague statements. Develop your ideas.

195

While working as a boy clerk he attended evening classes at King's College. Several of the essays – with what appear to be the tutor's amendments – survive. 'Nothing Ventured Nothing Have', probably dating from early 1908, considered the value of ambition. He wrote that 'To wait passively for good fortune to smile on us, is like waiting for the stream to run dry.' The tutor did not think much of the simile but the phrase expresses something of Collins's personality. *(UCD Archives)*

P173/46(1)

O.K. If you don't take a chance you will never. (text overwritten)

Chicago.

Dear Michael

I received your letter and Fannies a couple of days ago, was pleased to hear before that you both were well.

Now Michael regarding your coming to Chicago I have no doubt but you will be able to land some thing here even if it comes slow you will be sure to have a place to sleep and eat besides business is getting good all through the country now, and the prospects are pointing to a prosperous future of course

During 1915 Collins appears to have contemplated moving to Chicago where his brother Patrick was a policeman. In this letter Patrick is encouraging if not pushy. It is not clear whether this was ever a serious proposition. We do know, however, that Collins was frustrated by his career by then while the war probably increased the temptation to get out of London. *(UCD Archives)*

2

P123/46(2)

you will have to use your
own discretion and not do
anything you may regret.
I was speaking to Michael
Neary last week about you
he told me that he would
do anything he could for you
and he hooks pretty close
to some bankers I would
take a chance myself to
front a prominent banker,
the only thing to do is to
hew to the line, you know
the big noises of the banks
are very plain so keep your
Ear to the ground and watch
our smoke,
I had a letter from
Uncle Tom I'm going on a
visit to his place for a
couple of weeks. Emma will

Collins's London was transformed by the war. Many of those around him responded to the call in posters such as this one from 1915. *(Library of Congress, Prints & Photographs Division)*

The IRISH VOLUNTEERS

(South London District Committee).

A

NEW CENTRE

FOR VOLUNTEER WORK

WILL BE OPENED

On Sunday, August 2nd,

AT

The North Surrey Poultry Farm

MITCHAM LANE, TOOTING, S.W.

(Five minutes' walk from Tooting Junction Station; and from the corner of Southcroft Road and Mitcham Lane).

Drill Every Sunday, 5 to 6 p.m.

All Irishmen in Tooting, Merton, Mitcham, Streatham, Balham, Wimbledon, and surrounding districts should enrol immediately at this centre. Or apply to Hon. Secretary, 11, Tremadoc Rd., Clapham, S.W.

GENERAL ORDER.—South London Companies will fall in at 4 p.m. each Sunday, commencing August 2nd, at the Clock Tower, Clapham Common, and march *via* Tooting Broadway to above centre.   BY ORDER.

Volunteers meet every Saturday from 5 to 8, at St. George's Hall, Westminster Bridge Road.

GOD SAVE IRELAND.

Instead, Collins chose the Irish Volunteers. This poster is an example of the Irish Volunteer activity in London. *(Bureau of Military History, Military Archives of Ireland)*

2

'Please come in to see me':

The Collins Method

On 14 February 1917 Michael Collins – veteran of the 1916 Rising and ex-internee – received a very separatist valentine from Fred Allan, then secretary to the Irish National Aid & Volunteer Dependents' Fund (INA & VDF). It was a job offer, and not any old job offer. On the previous evening, Allan informed Collins, the executive of the INA & VDF had met and decided to appoint him to the 'position of Paid Secretary and General Office Manager to the Executive',[1] based at 10 Exchequer Street, Dublin. Less than two months earlier, just before Christmas, Collins had been freed from Frongoch camp in Wales as part of the general release of those Easter Rising internees who remained in custody. After a short break in Cork over the new year, Collins had moved to Dublin and begun to seek a role that would allow him to contribute to, perhaps take a prominent place in, the reconstruction of the Irish separatist movement. Now he had found that role.

The INA & VDF had as its purpose the support of the dependents of those rebels killed during the Rising, but also the support of internees, convicts and their families.[2] To this end, resting on the work of pre-Rising republicans and highly motivated neophyte sympathisers, it had built an infrastructure in Ireland for the collection and delivery of aid. Not only did it have active branches all over the country, but it had formed close links with the Irish National Relief Fund (INRF) and the Irish Relief Fund (IRF), which were founded in London and New York respectively, around the same time and for the same purposes. In February 1917, the Irish Volunteers was still shattered and the new Sinn Féin had yet to emerge. Consequently, whomever the INA & VDF appointed 'Paid Manager and General Office Manager', if alive to the opportunity, would become the key employee in the most important extant organisation linking the rebels (including those released and those still in prison) to each other and to their newly enlarged audience. Though rarely recognised as such, the INA & VDF network was arguably the foundation upon which post-Rising separatism sat. It was Collins, who would occupy the post until 6 July 1918,[3] who recognised the potential. During those seventeen months, he would use his new position and draw on his own existing circuits of influence to assume an influential role in rebuilding the IRB and Irish Volunteers, and in constructing the post-Rising Sinn Féin. This chapter tells that story because it is interesting in itself but, more importantly, because it tells us a lot about how Michael Collins worked and networked. In doing so, it will move backwards and forwards in time, explaining how his experience during 1916 put him in a position to get the job and what he did with it during 1917.

Much of the work was mundane. For the most part he wrote letters, day after day, week after week. He answered requests for promotional materials, responded to calls for collection books, explained whether fund-raising events required permits and how to apply for a tax exemption on the proceeds, reassured local committees and individual donors that their efforts were appreciated and would be publicly acknowledged, fielded appeals from former prisoners for weekly allowances or one-off grants or jobs, asked trusted local organisers to provide information on the circumstances of applicants, organised appointments for and interviews with various INA & VDF subcommittees, solicited visits for and forwarded comforts to remaining prisoners, and arranged to meet the recently released. He delivered good news and bad, and he was no less conscientious or effective because he did it with an ulterior motive.

In all these various ways the INA & VDF looked like, and was, an organisation designed to support prisoners and their families, yet it had also become a mechanism for remaking and then growing separatism. It was the first channel into which the new enthusiasm for separatism could legitimately, and comparatively safely, be directed, as people subscribed, collected and served on local committees. Through it too the prisoners became aware that they were not abandoned, that they could yet become more than defeated rebels, that there might be a post-Rising movement. Practically speaking, those ex-rebels who were provided with some means of living were in a better position to think about rebelling again.[4] This process was under way before Collins was released, but it continued to gather momentum during 1917 and he was at the centre of it. That he got the job was not an accident: he had lobbied his IRB contacts and, in turn, they had swayed their contacts on the INA & VDF committee. Once in the position, his personal network and profile expanded rapidly. The work could be tedious and wearying but Collins had an appetite and aptitude for it, and he had his eye on the prize.

Of course, before Collins worked for the INA & VDF he had been an object of its attentions. The body had its origins in the weeks after the Rising. Then, rapidly, two groups had emerged in Ireland with the purpose of supporting the dependents of dead volunteers and prisoners. The first, the Irish Volunteer Dependents' Fund, grew out of radical separatism and was closely associated with the IRB. The female relatives of rebels dominated the face it presented to the world, most prominently Kathleen Clarke, wife of Tom Clarke. The Irish National Aid Association (INAA), on the other hand, drew from a broader base within nationalism and emphasised its philanthropic rather than political character. 'No doom of law condemns to deprivation and penalty the relatives of imprisoned men, or the families of the sentenced', its appeal insisted, defying contradiction from those who doubted that their motivations were charitable. 'We make our appeal to all human hearts', it continued, 'whose noble compassion can reach over every obstacle to redress wrongs and alleviate suffering'.[5]

By August 1916, despite their differences in emphasis and origin, it was obvious (even if both committees resented and resisted the conclusion) that one organisation was likely to be more effective and efficient than two. This realisation was crystalised when the American fund-raising body, the IRF, made

Michl. Collins released.
Sinn Fein (interned) prisoner
circular 27:12:16

S.
4438
D.M.P.

218
76008

78

County of Cork M R

Clanakilty 31:12:16

I beg to report that
on 26th inst. Michael
Collins a native of
Woodfield Miltown
Sub Dist. returned to
his brothers home in
this District. He was
not arrested in this
District or at the instance
of the Dist police in
any way. This young man
was employed in the Post
office — in Dublin I understand
latterly — and was
apprehended for some
connection recent rebellion
or Sinn Feinism there.
He boasts to his friends
that he was in the rebellion
fighting in Church
street Dublin for four
days
the County Insp
Bandon

C.C. D.M.P.
Transmitted for information &
favour of report as to his
history in Dublin.
He is apparently not the Mr. Collins
clerk of Dublin — who is now at
Sunday's Well cork. (see S/4378 81/17)

J E Rodhus

C. M Reg
9.1.17

Supt. G div
W R J
10.1.17

On 6 January 1917, the RIC at Bandon reported the arrival of Michael Collins at Woodfield on 26 December.
Interestingly, the Collins family are described as '"brainy" people' and 'disloyal', though it is clear that the local
police know little about Michael. *(The National Archives, London)*

He is a young man of
fair complexion clean
shaven strong jaws
and features may
be 28 years of age.
He belongs to a family
"brainy" people who
are disloyal and
of advanced Sinn
Fein sympathies
they are of the farming
class

Geo Lordan
DI

Bandon 6. 1. 17
Submitted.

J. Tweedy
CI.

The Insp. General

" unemployment at the present date; that the list
" be kept up to date by weekly notification from
" the Distribution Comtee, and that the Registry
" Clerk be directed to send to the secretary
" of the Distribution Comtee a weekly list of names
" on that list who have not registered during the
" week."

A further report was submitted from the
auditor as to the applicants for position of paid
secretary and office manager. It was decided
that the successful candidate be required to complete
a fidelity guarantee bond to the extent of £500 in
an approved office; the premium to be paid by the
executive.

The selected candidates were then interviewed
individually; and a ballot having been subsequently
taken, Mr Michael Collins received a majority
of the votes of those present, and was declared
duly appointed to the position.

A letter was read from Mrs Wyse Power
regarding the question raised at the previous
meeting and after some discussion it was decided
That the matter be postponed to the next
ordinary weekly meeting; and that Mrs Power be
written to, to ask her to endeavour to obtain
a satisfactory answer from Mr Schawlers, and
also some definite statement from the Foley family.

The balance of the agenda was adjourned to the
special meeting to be held on the following Sunday.

Patrick T. Keohane

20/2/17

As the minutes of the INA & VDF executive committee of 13 February 1917 show, Collins was one of several candidates interviewed for the job of paid secretary, and was selected on the votes of a majority. *(National Library of Ireland)*

Comhluct Conganta na nzaodal
agus
Spleadac Oglac na hÉipeann

Longpopt: 10 Spáid an Ciste, Át Cliat.

Irish National Aid
AND
Volunteer Dependents' Fund

Offices: 10 EXCHEQUER ST., DUBLIN.

24th May, 1917.

The Governor,
H. M. Prison,
L E W E S.

Dear Sir,

      I enclose two volumes of the "Irish Homestead" and will
ask you to be so good as to hand them to Mr. Con O'Donovan.
Under separate cover I am sending you a volume of the "Farmer's
Gazette" from April 1st 1916 to March 24th 1917. I would also ask
you to be kind enough to inform Mr. O'Donovan that I have not been
able to get copies of the later publications beyond the date
mentioned. I enclose a stamped addressed envelope so that you can
let me know if the above mentioned articles have reached you.

      Yours truly,

Michael Collins

Secretary.

Books received with thanks. Prisoner informed

R.A. Marriott
29.5.17 Governor

In this rather typical piece of correspondence, dating from May 1917, Collins sent copies of the *Irish Homestead*
and the *Farmer's Gazette* to the governor of Lewes prison for Con O'Donovan. O'Donovan, who had attended
the same school in Clonakilty as Collins, had fought in, and been convicted in the aftermath of, the Rising. A
month after he sent this letter, Collins would travel with O'Donovan to Clonakilty to celebrate the latter's release.
(National Library of Ireland)

a merger a condition of handing over the considerable monies it had raised. Despite being the smaller organisation, the IVDF drove a hard bargain. At their insistence, several figures associated either with the Irish Party (for instance, former Lord Mayor of Dublin Lorcan Sherlock) or John Redmond's National Volunteers (Maurice Moore, for example) who had served on the INAA committee were excluded from the new body. In late August, one of the first initiatives of the new INA & VDF was to establish a subcommittee charged with the task of considering, and then pursuing, measures to improve the conditions of the internees held at Frongoch camp in north Wales.[6] A propaganda campaign focused on their treatment was one of the consequences. This campaign was not only intended for the internees' benefit but it involved their active participation. When the internees, who received newspapers and followed proceedings in parliament, became aware that their complaints would be given a public airing, they complained more often and more vigorously. Collins was one of these internee complainants, playing a role in the authoring of a pamphlet entitled *Official Report of the Ill-Treatment of the Irish Prisoners of War Interned at Frongoch Camp*. It was published in Cork by the INA & VDF in late 1916 and purported to tell 'The Truth About Frongoch' to 'The People of Ireland'.[7]

In the immediate aftermath of the Rising, Collins, like 3,500 or so others, was arrested. Initially, he was held at Richmond Barracks, Dublin, before being among those transferred, in early May, to Stafford in England to a jail that had become a military detention centre. From there, in mid-June, he was transferred again. This time to Frongoch, which had been emptied of German prisoners of war to make way for the Irish. He made his presence felt on the camp sports field, quickly, and in the field of camp politics, gradually, taking a leading part in the formation of an IRB clique.[8] Forceful well past the point of pushy in both arenas, Collins attracted admiration and antipathy.[9] In the confines of a small, closed community he was certainly unavoidable, and he was still there in early September, at which point the population had been cut, through releases, to around 540 men from a peak of 1,775 in mid-July. From September, a militant core of this reduced cohort (including Collins) became more aggressive in its attitude toward the camp authorities, engaging in a number of disputes.[10] One of the key causes of conflict was an attempt by the camp authorities, at the request of the War Office, to identify and remove a number of those internees who were liable for conscription under the Military Service Act of January 1916. That Act had declared that any unmarried male British subject between the ages of 18 and 41, who was 'ordinarily resident in Great Britain' on 15 August 1915, was liable for military service.[11] As such, quite a few of those at Frongoch were vulnerable, including Collins.

The vulnerable group consisted of rebels who had been born in Britain to Irish parents and men who, like Collins, had migrated to Britain and had been working and living there on 15 August 1915. Consequent to the passing of the Act, a body of 'refugees' from conscription had moved to Dublin during the early weeks of 1916. These single young men, with radical nationalist tendencies, found sanctuary with the Plunkett family at Larkfield, Kimmage, and then joined the Plunkett brothers (Joseph, George and Jack) at the GPO on Easter Monday.[12] Collins too, both aware of the threat of conscription and alert to the possibility of action in Ireland, had left London for Dublin. He did not live at Larkfield but he did, for a time, have a job with the Plunkett family, secured, it seems, on the recommendation of an IRB and GAA contact, Patrick Belton.[13] Very soon Geraldine Plunkett, who was as rebellious as her brothers, had formed the impression that he was 'shrewd, serious and downright, very quick and clear.'[14] When the Rising came, Collins would be Joseph Plunkett's aide-de-camp at the GPO. This gave Collins a certain status, as Plunkett, who was recovering from an operation, was a signatory to the rebel proclamation and was Director of Military Operations for the Irish Volunteers.[15]

Having fled conscription once, these men now faced its imminent imposition, and at Frongoch, on the face of it, there was nowhere to hide. But there was. To conscript the liable men the authorities had to identify them amongst the camp population, a task that proved very difficult in the case of Michael Murphy when, in early November, the military made him and Fintan Murphy their next targets. The Murphys refused to present themselves and when the camp authorities called a roll more than half of their fellow internees refused to answer in a show of solidarity. The camp officials detected Fintan quite quickly, but Michael Murphy remained elusive. A stand-off lasting weeks ensued with those internees refusing to give their names separated from the others and punished by the withdrawal of various privileges.

That Collins was at the forefront of this conflict is perhaps not a surprise: he was by then the camp secretary and he had more to lose than most if solidarity on this issue was not maintained. He encouraged both the 'refugees' and other internees to stand firm. He dismissed as 'cowards' those who, resenting the hardships involved, considered abandoning the fight.[16] He publicised the conflict by sending out a series of letters, most significantly to Art O'Brien, the head of the INRF, based in London, whom Collins knew from his days in the Gaelic League there. The letters, which were intended to arm the INRF and INA & VDF in their campaign of support for the internees, addressed the issue of conscription itself, but also made a series of allegations about the treatment of the protesting internees.[17] Even some of his fellow internees regarded the content to be exaggerated.[18] By 9 December the camp commandant, Colonel F.A. Heygate Lambert, numbered Collins among fifteen ringleaders he wished to remove from the camp altogether. Amongst the others were several who would remain close allies of Collins in the months and years to come, including Seán Hales, Gearóid O'Sullivan, Eamon Price and the prisoners' then commandant, Michael Staines.[19] They were not removed but instead, two weeks later, all the internees were released.

In February 1917, the INA & VDF brought Staines and Collins together again: Collins in the office and Staines in the field. This facilitated the use of the INA & VDF in building a renewed revolutionary infrastructure and momentum. Staines remembered that he was employed to 'tour the country investigating claims for assistance for dependants of Volunteers' though he had a parallel task, to assist in the 're-organization of Volunteer Companies throughout the country.'[20] Collins's letters to him show that Staines spent much of the spring in Galway.[21] In May, they decided he would go to Lewes in Sussex to give support to what was evidently a well-planned prison revolt: most of those who had been convicted, rather than interned, in the aftermath of the Easter Rising were still in custody and held together there. The prison rebellion and the persistent protests that proceeded from it were a propaganda success. When the government released the convicts in mid-June, presenting their action as a gesture of good will in the context of the Irish Convention, Collins could counter that 'it was the men themselves who were responsible' and that the government was 'in a most humiliated position'.[22] Although he was in the employ of the Gaelic League rather than the INA & VDF, and organising in Cork and Kerry, Richard Mulcahy, the future Chief of Staff of the Irish Volunteers, was also in regular contact with Collins during these months. As in the case of Staines, Mulcahy was busy with the parallel project of reorganising the Volunteers and the IRB. From Exchequer Street, Collins sent him copies of the *Irish Volunteer* and advice on people to meet when in the Clonakilty district.[23]

TELEPHONE No. 21081. (3 LINES)   TELEGRAMS: "CERTIFY, DUBLIN".

CRAIG, GARDNER & Co.
CHARTERED ACCOUNTANTS.

D. TELFORD
G. H. TULLOCH
E. BUCKLEY
G. BROCK
J. RUSSELL
E. J. SHOTT
J. WALKER   McA

Belfast Office:
DONEGALL HOUSE, 7, HOWARD STREET.

TRINITY CHAMBERS,
39-41, DAME STREET,
DUBLIN. C.I.

21st July 1936

Frank O'Connor Esq.,
Abbey Theatre,
Marlborough Street,
Dublin.

Dear Mr. O'Connor,

I have looked up our past records and all that I can
find in regard to Michael Collins is that he came into our office
in a temporary capacity on the 23rd February 1916, and that he
left some time in the month of April.   The date is not mentioned,
but he appears to have only received about one week's salary for
that month.

My own impression is that he was sent to the country
(I think Co Wexford) on a liquidation matter and that we never
saw or heard of him after Easter week.

Am I right in thinking that a Life of Collins was
published early in the year 1927 in which he is stated to have
been employed here at the time of the Rising?

It is just possible that Mr. Scott, our Cashier, might
be able to give you some more information.   I might refer you

In July 1936 J.H. Tulloch of Craig, Gardner & Co., accountants, confirmed to Frank O'Connor, who was then researching *The Big Fellow*, that Collins had worked for the firm for two months in early 1916. Collins did not, it seems, make a lasting impression. *(National Archives of Ireland)*

This photograph shows post-Rising internees interacting with visitors. Such visits were crucial to the morale of the internees such as Collins. *(National Museum of Ireland)*

Initially, Collins was deported to Stafford prison, north of Birmingham, where this photograph was taken. Collins is identified by the 'X' over his head. *(Military Archives of Ireland)*

Irish Prisoner of War
Stafford
June 24th '16

Dear Mollie

Very many thanks indeed for that parcel. The fruit especially was beautiful. Indeed I don't know in the world what I shall ever be able to do for all my friends who are being so kind.

Think we shall be off to the old camp sometime during this coming week. By all accounts it will hardly be a change for the better, but at any rate we shall have some beautiful scenery. by all as also a dismantled brewery or distillery. This latter will recall happy memories at any rate.

It was very pleased to hear some account of Dan Murphy. He never answered a letter which I wrote him about November last so we have got out of touch. They can all be having a good laugh at us now but I don't think they are somehow. Even if the camp is a more unpleasant

On 24 June 1916 Michael Collins wrote from Stafford to Mary 'Mollie' Woods of Dublin. His letter conveys the conditions. The regime had been relaxed in late May, following a difficult few weeks during which the internees had experienced the full rigours of prison. Frongoch had begun to fill with Irish internees on 9 June and Collins was anticipating a move. He had evidently received some word of the conditions there. *(National Museum of Ireland)*

place than this it is something
to look forward to meeting many
of my old friends again.

We've been doing
greatly here for the last few
days. Someone brought in
a melodion & a flute so we
have music go bar. It will
be better still when we get to
the camp. I'm afraid though
that we shall be only allowed
to write one letter each week
so it will take me some time
to reach all my friends.
Ofcourse we may receive
all the letters that are sent us.
We had Mr Ginnell

here not long since. He said
a few words to us and we
gave him a great ovation.

Well goodbye — if
you don't hear from me you'll
know its because we're on the
one letter a week. I hope
Stella & Bessie are having
a fine time in the old
country. I fear it will be some
time before any of us see it
again.

With many thanks
& best wishes
Yours sincerely
M Collins

We've been doing
here for the last few
Someone brought in
lodion & a flute so we
music go bar. It will
ter still when we get to
amp. I'm afraid though
we shall be only allowed
te one letter each week

Well goodbye —
you don't hear from me
know its because we're o
one letter a week. I hop
Stella & Bessie are hav
a fine time in the old
country. I fear it will be
time before any of us see

This watercolour, one of a series by a Carlow internee Cathal Mac Dubhghaill, represents the south camp at Frongoch. It was a converted distillery and you can see the former industrial buildings in the rural setting in north Wales. *(National Museum of Ireland)*

THE
MILITARY SERVICE ACT, 1916

Applies to Unmarried Men who, on August 15th, 1915, were 18 years of age or over and who will not be 41 years of age on March 2nd, 1916.

ALL MEN, NOT EXCEPTED OR EXEMPTED, between these ages who on November 2nd, 1915, were unmarried or widowers without any child dependent on them will on

THURSDAY, MARCH 2nd, 1916,

Be deemed to be Enlisted for the Period of the War.

THEY WILL BE PLACED IN THE RESERVE UNTIL CALLED UP IN THEIR CLASS.

MEN EXCEPTED :

> SOLDIERS, including Territorials who have volunteered for Foreign Service ;
> MEN serving in the NAVY or ROYAL MARINES ;
> MEN DISCHARGED FROM ARMY OR NAVY, disabled or ill, or TIME-EXPIRED MEN ;
> MEN REJECTED for the Army since August 14th, 1915 ;
> CLERGYMEN, PRIESTS and MINISTERS OF RELIGION ;
> VISITORS from the DOMINIONS.

Men who may be exempted by Local Tribunals :

> Men more useful to the Nation in their present employments ;
> Men in whose case Military Service would cause serious hardship owing to exceptional financial or business obligations or domestic position ;
> Men who are ill or infirm ;
> Men who conscientiously object to combatant service. If the Tribunal thinks fit, men may, on this ground, be (a) exempted from combatant service only (not non-combatant service), or (b) exempted on condition that they are engaged in work of National importance.

Up to March 2nd, a man can apply to his Local Tribunal for a certificate of exemption. There is a Right of Appeal. He will not be called up until his case has been dealt with finally.

Certificates of exemption may be absolute, conditional or temporary. Such certificates can be renewed, varied or withdrawn.

Men retain their Civil Rights until called up and are amenable to Civil Courts only.

DO NOT WAIT UNTIL MARCH 2nd.
ENLIST VOLUNTARILY NOW

For fuller particulars of the Act, please apply for Leaflet No. 64 to the nearest Post Office, Police Station, or Recruiting Office.

Published by the Parliamentary Recruiting Committee, London. Poster No. 153.   The Abbey Press, Westminster, S.W.

This poster explains conscription as provided for under the Military Service Act, 1916. *(Imperial War Museum)*

Collins was aware that a degree of circumspection was necessary in the correspondence that left his office. As he wrote to Seán O'Donovan, 'you will understand that this is an official letter, therefore I will omit several things I would like to say.'[24] The evidence of his use of the position is, however, everywhere. For instance, it was surely no accident that among the few correspondents he invited to come to the office to discuss their issues were Oscar Traynor ('if possible I would like you to come in and see me about the matter'), Harry Boland ('If you would prefer to come in and see me I could take particulars direct from you.'), Joe Good ('Please come in to see me about the matter in the morning if you can') and Piaras Béaslaí ('please come in to see me as soon as you return').[25]

Much of the extracurricular business was then conducted, it seems, in a series of pubs – The Stag's Head on Dame Lane, Neary's on Chatham Street, Davy Byrne's on Duke Street – and in the bar or dining room of the Wicklow Hotel on Wicklow Street. All of these were within three or four minutes' walk of the office. Though a non-drinker, Eamon Dore remembered knocking around some of these south-side haunts at that time with Collins, Staines, and others.[26] The bar of Vaughan's Hotel at 29–30 Rutland Square (now Parnell Square) in the north inner city became the most favoured and famous of nocturnal hang-outs for Collins and his cronies. In the summer of 1917 his favoured drinking companions there, according to Béaslaí, were Boland, Diarmuid O'Hegarty, Diarmuid Lynch, Fionán Lynch and Béaslaí himself. Most of them were associated with the Bartholomew Teeling circle of the IRB.[27] Vaughan's was close to the 18 North Frederick Street rooms that hosted the Keating Branch of the Gaelic League, which shared a core membership with the Teeling circle. Nearby too were Gaelic League premises at 25 and 46 Rutland Square, where key meetings of the Irish Volunteer executive were held. Conveniently, Collins lived a few minutes' walk to the north, at 44 Mountjoy Street, in the Munster Private Hotel. It was owned by Myra McCarthy, Fionán Lynch's aunt.[28] And, of course, Croke Park was just ten minutes away. The stadium was another important venue where Collins networked, while living so close facilitated Collins in inviting those who were in Dublin for a match to call on him at his rooms.[29]

All the while Collins was busily trying to influence the shape of any political vehicle that might emerge to carry the colours of separatism in the aftermath of the Rising. He had arrived in north Roscommon just in time to help on polling day, 3 February 1917, and witness Count George Noble Plunkett, the father of

STRIKE

OF

IRISH PRISONERS

IN

LEWES JAIL

PUBLIC MEETING

AT

BERESFORD PLACE

ON

SUNDAY, JUNE 10

AT 7.30, P.M.

This poster, advertising a meeting in support of the 'strike' by prisoners at Lewes, illustrates how separatists both supported those convicted after 1916 and used them to organise around and generate enthusiasm. *(The Board of Trinity College Dublin)*

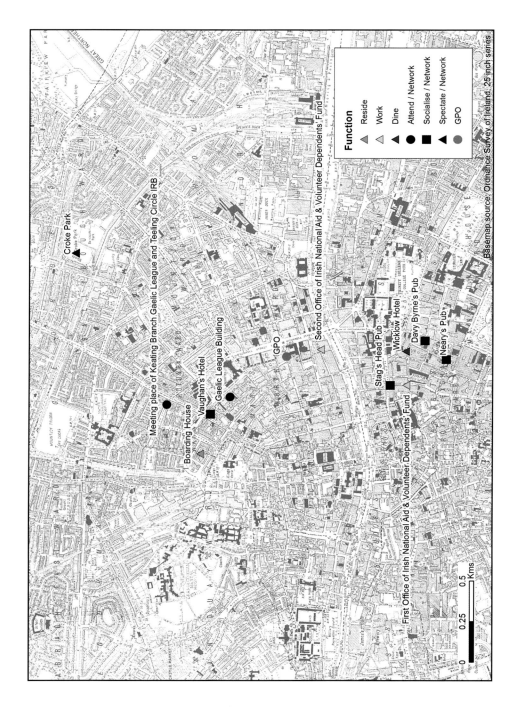

This map shows Michael Collins's world during 1917. It was in some ways large and growing, yet it is striking how confined, tight and enmeshed it was, geographically, socially and politically. *(Susan Hegarty, with Bertie Faulkner, Joseph Rodgers and Gerard Shannon)*

Collins was a regular attendee at matches at Croke Park during these years. This photograph, in which he is pictured in the crowd with Seán MacEoin, dates from September 1921. For a period in late 1918 and early 1919, he attended a series of special meetings of the Central Council to press for a ban on civil servants and to ensure that outstanding monies raised in fund-raising tournaments staged for the INA & VDF would be transferred to a new prisoner support group, the Irish Republican Prisoners' Dependents Fund. *(National Library of Ireland)*

Joseph Plunkett, win the first by-election of 1917. The candidate himself had arrived as late in the day as 1 February, accompanied by his daughter, Geraldine. Plunkett was the separatist candidate and his victory was a first, enormous, electoral shot in the arm for radical opponents of the Irish Party, but Plunkett did not have a party and his platform was vague. In such circumstances, particularly given that Collins had been at Joseph's side in the GPO and knew Geraldine well from Larkfield, he joined Plunkett's retinue with ease.[30]

With various dissident, though competing, factions jockeying around him – including the Irish Nation League (a group founded in the summer of 1916 to oppose partition), pre-Rising Griffith-ite Sinn Féin, and the IRB – Plunkett took the notion that he was not a symbol but a national leader around whom all should come together. To this end, he called a convention for the Mansion House, Dublin, on Thursday, 19 April. If this was the beginning of a new movement, then Collins wanted to ensure that he and other republicans were in the vanguard, exercising as much control as possible, and so he secured 30 per cent of the tickets.[31] It was no accident that he organised an INA & VDF delegate conference for Dublin for Wednesday, 18 April. During the fortnight beforehand he devoted a good deal of his time at Exchequer Street to sending letters that canvassed attendance at Wednesday's proceedings, with Thursday's in mind.[32] Plunkett attempted to use the convention to launch the 'Liberty League', a new body that republicans like Collins hoped would constitute a separatist alternative to Sinn Féin, ultimately displacing it. In the weeks that followed, however, Sinn Féin acquired considerable popular momentum, forcing the barely established Liberty League to merge into Sinn Féin in early June. For Collins, who was on the executive, the task was to ensure that the post-merger Sinn Féin was as republican as possible.[33] Working toward this sometimes took him out of the office and beyond his inner-city beat at weekends. For instance, on 19 August he spent the day in Leitrim, first in Gowel where he spoke to the Roger Casement Sinn Féin club and then in Carrick-on-Shannon where he addressed the inaugural meeting of the Seán Mac Diarmada Sinn Féin club.[34]

By then, Collins's use of the INA & VDF, combined with the evident progress that separatism was making, had begun to attract unwanted attentions for his employers. The tipping point came with the nomination of Joe McGuinness, one of the convicts at Lewes, to contest a by-election for the parliamentary seat of South Longford. His nomination was announced in the days before the Mansion House convention[35] and soon the constituency experienced an invasion of separatist activists from various parts of the country, including Collins (on one of his weekend jaunts) and Staines.[36] Indeed, it was Staines who had been dispatched to ensure that Frank McGuinness, a brother to Joe who was based in Longford and was of known moderate views, would nominate his brother.[37] As the contest neared its conclusion the unsympathetic local newspaper, the *Longford Leader*, suggested that monies misappropriated from the INA & VDF were paying for the well-resourced McGuinness campaign.[38] These allegations, which attracted the interest of the police, were not true – Griffith had issued a very successful appeal for campaign funds through the pages of his paper *Nationality* – and on 23 June, under threat of legal action, the *Longford Leader* issued a withdrawal.[39] This did not stop the rumours and Dr Denis Kelly, the Bishop of Ross and the foremost supporter of the Irish Party among the hierarchy, proved more difficult to menace when Collins wrote to him that summer, 'respectfully' asking that he withdraw a statement he had issued. When refusing the INA & VDF permission to carry out church-gate collections in his diocese, Kelly publicly warned that 'in the minds of some of the promoters of these collections there is concealed under the cloak of Christian Charity the purpose of reckless and ruinous revolutionary propaganda.'[40]

Reckless or not, Collins continued to conceal other work under the cloak of the INA & VDF. On 30 August he wrote to Michael de Lacy, who had been released from prison six weeks earlier having been convicted by court martial for his participation in the Rising at Enniscorthy, County Wexford. Collins assured de Lacy of his help in pursuing a position as a commercial teacher at the Limerick Technical School, promising 'anything I can do for you I shall be only too glad to do'. As proof, he informed de Lacy that he had written to the Limerick Branch and 'to a few friends' (almost certainly code for members of the republican brotherhood), while also mentioning Stephen O'Mara, the wealthy bacon manufacturer and former mayor of Limerick.[41] Collins knew O'Mara because he was a member of the executive of the INA & VDF and had been a prominent representative of the Irish Nation League at the April Mansion House convention. His sons James and Stephen would soon work closely with Collins on financing Sinn Féin and Dáil Éireann. Collins did indeed write to Alphonsus Kivlehan, secretary of Limerick's branch of the INA & VDF, and to Madge Daly of the influential IRB family and sister to Kathleen Clarke, asking them to exert their influence.[42]

De Lacy got the job; once again, however, this was not simply a matter of the INA & VDF looking after the interests of an unemployed ex-prisoner. Collins had been a member of the executive of the Irish Volunteers since May, and they wanted de Lacy to take charge of the Mid-Limerick Brigade. That brigade's area incorporated the city where the Irish Volunteers were by then divided into two mutually antagonistic battalions. The origins of the split resided in recriminations that followed the failure of the city's Volunteers to participate in the Rising, while it appears to have been sustained by class divisions within the brigade. The executive had set de Lacy the difficult task of knocking heads together to produce an effective unit. In the event it proved beyond his capabilities.[43] Within a year Collins had become frustrated at de Lacy's lack of efficiency, and eventually replaced him in the summer of 1919.[44] Collins tended not to be forgiving of failure. When, in October 1920, W.T. Cosgrave mentioned employing de Lacy in Dáil Éireann's Department of Local Government, Collins replied, 'I don't know whether I would feel quite justified in recommending him for the position. He has always appeared to me to be excellent in theory, but rather weak in practical details.'[45]

De Lacy's was not an isolated case of jobbery with a purpose. In October 1917, for example, Collins wrote to Anthony Mackey, of the GAA, the IRB and owner of a fishery at Castleconnel in Limerick. Collins had heard on the grapevine that Mackey had a 'vacancy' and proposed that 'if you would kindly give me particulars I think we may be able to fix you up.' Although Collins sent this request on behalf of the INA & VDF it seems certain that the 'we' he referred to was the IRB.[46] Collins had joined the Supreme Council that summer and by the autumn he was secretary to that too.[47]

Perhaps the most ostentatious way in which the INA & VDF channelled resources to political effect was to pay for the funerals of former prisoners. This was easily justified as a legitimate philanthropic act, yet the political effect could be enormous, and everyone knew it. Funerals had long fulfilled a key function for nationalists in general, and republicans in particular. A timely death could facilitate a considerable show of strength, allowing republicans to occupy the public space, demonstrate their capacity to organise, and make evident the extent to which they had captured public sympathy.[48] In July 1917 the INA & VDF paid for the funeral of William Partridge, who had been released from prison in April due to ill health. In the days afterward, Collins wrote to Madge Daly explaining that Partridge 'had a splendid funeral at Ballaghadereen. But I think his remains should have been brought to Dublin for a public funeral here, as I am of opinion that more good would come of it in that way.'[49] Two months later, when Thomas Ashe (President of the IRB) died following forcible feeding while on hunger strike in Mountjoy prison, Collins insisted on having his way. He persuaded Ashe's family not to take the body home to Kerry for burial but instead to allow the staging of a massive political funeral in Dublin. The INA & VDF paid for it and the Wolfe Tone Memorial Association, an IRB front, organised it. It was Richard Mulcahy and Michael Collins's show.[50] Presumably, Collins was, metaphorically, wearing his IRB cap at Glasnevin cemetery when he delivered a short graveside oration during which he informed the still-gathering crowd that the volley that had just been fired was 'the only speech which it is proper to make above the grave of a dead Fenian.'[51] Certainly, this was the occasion during which he was least careful to protect the fiction that Chinese walls existed between his job at the INA & VDF and his other (multiplying) roles. The funeral was a triumph and funerals became his and Mulcahy's territory. When Pierce McCan died in prison in March 1919, Sinn Féin's standing committee immediately appointed them and Harry Boland 'to make all arrangements'.[52]

On 27 November 1917 the committee of the INA & VDF decided that they would place a notice in *Nationality* informing the public that the fund would soon close. The committee had a considerable sum in hand with which to meet the future needs of the dependents of those who had died during the rebellion.[53] On the other hand, there were growing cohorts of prisoners in Ireland's jails who demanded support and offered new opportunities for the mobilisation of public opinion. In September – around the time of the hunger strike at Mountjoy – a new body had been established, calling itself the Irish Republican Prisoners' Dependents Fund (IRPDF). This was an openly political body, based at Sinn Féin's headquarters on Harcourt Street: in an appeal issued in early December it lauded the actions of prisoners who were at that moment driving 'home the lesson that Ireland's battle can be fought even in prison.'[54] Staines was one of the honorary secretaries and Collins was on the committee. Other officers, including Kathleen Clarke and Margaret Pearse, had been on the committee of the INA & VDF and remained among the trustees as it wound up its business.[55] Anxious that established structures would not go to waste, Collins encouraged local committees of the INA & VDF to shift their energies from the old body to the new. For instance, on 6 December he advised Elizabeth Corr, a key figure on the Belfast committee of the INA & VDF, as follows: 'It would I am sure, be a good idea if you kept your Committee together for the purposes of collecting subscriptions for the new Fund. I am asking Miceal Staines to write you and send you a number of Appeals.'[56]

As the role of the INA & VDF contracted in late 1917, it and Collins moved offices to 32 Bachelors Walk. Collins appears to have become less focused on INA & VDF's work around then. In a statement attached to a pension claim submitted in 1945, Kitty O'Doherty wrote that from autumn 1917, she 'did all his [Collins's] secretarial work in the office of Donal O'Connor, Westmoreland Street while Collins drew his salary for this work for more than a year.'[57] O'Doherty exaggerated, but perhaps only a little. What is certain is that on 1 July 1918 the committee of the INA & VDF decided that Collins's contract should be terminated five days later.[58] It was not that Collins had lost interest in prisoners. His correspondence, particularly with Art O'Brien, and his interventions at meetings of Sinn Féin's Standing Committee indicate that in the following months and years he remained exercised by the issues faced by prisoners and their families.[59] Nor was it simply that he had decided to address and exploit the prisoner issue through the IRPDF instead of the INA & VDF. Rather, as we shall see, by mid-1918 Collins's portfolio of political and military roles had expanded greatly, in part because of the reputation he had made at the INA & VDF. By March, for example, he was both Adjutant General and Director of Organisation on the general staff of the Irish Volunteers.[60]

Each day during his tenure with the INA & VDF, a convenient route to and from work, whether on foot or bicycle, took Collins along the shell of Sackville Street (now O'Connell Street) and by the GPO. From time to time the destruction must have given him pause for thought, but he mentions it only once in all those letters from Exchequer Street and Bachelors Walk. On the morning of 18 June 1917 Collins, Staines and Fred Allan were at Kingstown to greet the returning 1916 convicts and accompany them to Westland Row station.[61] Frank Thornton, one of the freed men and a future close associate of Collins, remembered that the enthusiastic crowds there 'nearly tore us asunder that day.'[62] Two days later, Collins wrote to Alec McCabe, sending news to Sligo of the wonderful scenes and letting him know that 'Republican flags still fly from the ruins of our Easter Week Headquarters.'[63] Janus-faced, Collins knew empathy, sentiment and a sense of responsibility. He looked back, counting loss and cost. It was easier to do so, however, if he also looked insistently forward, hectic with the demands of striving, reassured by the egoism of feeling essential, and presenting his actions in the livery of a shared dream. From early 1917 to the middle of 1918, he did this from a base in the INA & VDF while demonstrating a significant capacity to build connections between and across various groups and organisations. As he did so, he moved from being one of many within the burgeoning movement that was Irish separatism to forging a place among the key movers. Just how important he had and would become is explored through the overlapping arenas of violence and politics, the subjects of the two chapters that follow.

After the Rising, the citizens of Dublin resumed their business on Sackville Street but the ruins of the GPO loom in the background. By 1917 it had become a site not only of memory but of commemoration. At noon on Easter Sunday, 10 April, young republicans had hoisted a flag over the building, and a large crowd gathered. *(National Museum of Ireland)*

This poster explained to the voters of North Roscommon why they should vote for Count Plunkett at the by-election of February 1917. *(National Library of Ireland)*

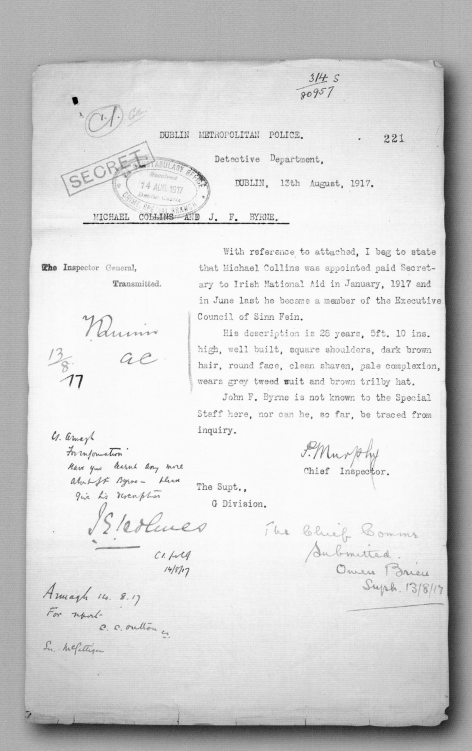

314 S
80957

DUBLIN METROPOLITAN POLICE. · 221

Detective Department,

DUBLIN, 13th August, 1917.

MICHAEL COLLINS AND J. F. BYRNE.

The Inspector General,

Transmitted.

With reference to attached, I beg to state
that Michael Collins was appointed paid Secretary to Irish National Aid in January, 1917 and
in June last he became a member of the Executive
Council of Sinn Fein.

His description is 28 years, 5ft. 10 ins.
high, well built, square shoulders, dark brown
hair, round face, clean shaven, pale complexion,
wears grey tweed suit and brown trilby hat.

John F. Byrne is not known to the Special
Staff here, nor can he, so far, be traced from
inquiry.

P. Murphy
Chief Inspector.

The Supt.,
G Division.

[handwritten annotations]
13/8/17

A. Armagh
For information.
Have you learnt any more
about JF Byrne - than
give his description.

J S Collins
C.I. felg
14/8/17

Armagh 14. 8. 17
For report.
C. C. Oulton
Sn. McGettigan

The Chief Comms
Submitted.
Owen Brien
Suph. 13/8/17

By the summer of 1917 Collins's public positions, working for the INA & VDF and Sinn Féin, ensured he was on the radar of the Dublin Metropolitan Police. *(The National Archives, London)*

By September 1917 Collins was sufficiently prominent to make it onto the poster – albeit just ahead of the 'etc'– for this meeting to establish a Sinn Féin club. *(National Library of Ireland)*

Cırce Muɲᵹaıle na nᵹeımleaċ ı bpoblaċt Éıɼeann.
(Irish Republican Prisoners' Dependents Fund.)

A FURTHER APPEAL.

Started as a temporary expedient for what looked likely to be only temporary imprisonment, this Committee has never been able to build up a reserve fund—indeed, they have seldom had in hands more than enough to meet the expenses of a few weeks ahead. Their work has been heavily handicapped by the Censor from the beginning, and before the Committee was long in existence many of its members were swept into jail. Since its formation in September, 1917, £2,690 has been received, of which £2,670 has been paid out, and over 400 cases have been dealt with. The Committee feel keenly that, owing to the scarcity of funds, they have been unable to deal with many deserving cases. With the exception of stationery, printing and postage accounts, every penny has been spent in the relief of the dependents of the men in prison.

Every day new victims are seized, and to-day it is absolutely necessary to throw the responsibility of this national work on the people of Ireland—every one of whom must feel in honour bound to help in the largest possible way. These men are the brave unpaid army who are fighting our battle in prison cells, and it ought to be our proud right to relieve them from all anxiety concerning the welfare of their families.

Irishmen have many claims on their generosity in these critical days, but the Committee feel this is not a question of generosity—it is a clear duty; and the needs are so urgent that they make no apology for claiming a first call on every Irish citizen who believes the cause for which these prisoners are suffering is just and right.

President:
EAMONN DE VALERA.

Vice-President:
G. N. COUNT PLUNKETT.

Hon. Secs.:

Miss A. O'RAHILLY.

Miss O'BRENNAN.

Hon. Treasurers:
Mrs. PEARSE.
Mrs. WYSE POWER.
M. J. STAINES.
GEORGE NESBITT.

Committee:

Mrs. CLARKE.
Madame O'RAHILLY.
Mrs. GAVAN DUFFY.

JOHN MURPHY.
J. SHOULDICE.
MICHAEL COLLINS.

GEORGE PLUNKETT.

This appeal by the IRPDF is unequivocally political, reflecting Sinn Féin's direct control over that organisation. This is reflected in the membership of the committee, including Collins. *(National Library of Ireland)*

The rifles respond to Collins's oration at the grave of Thomas Ashe, September 1917. *(National Library of Ireland)*

3

'Are you Michael Collins the murderer':

Collins at War[1]

One night during the Truce, it may well have been the late summer of 1921, some Black and Tans took their lady friends for a drive. Too exuberant, too eager to impress the women, maybe just too drunk, they crashed somewhere near Clondalkin, hitting another car. Michael Collins walked unhurt from the wreckage of that other vehicle and set off to find a telephone. When he came to the house of the Oblate Fathers in Inchicore he knocked at the door. 'My name is Michael Collins,' he told the priest who opened it. 'Are you Michael Collins the murderer? Come in, in God's name', was the priest's whispered reply.[2]

This may be just a story, one of many about Michael Collins that lost nothing in the retelling of umpteen years, but whether it is true or not, it sums up the challenge of fathoming Michael Collins's war. For a start, so much of it is about stories greater or lesser than this; about rumours of what he was supposed to be, exaggerations of what he was said to have done. And for a life said to have been lived as 'a significant series of winks', the stories may well mean and have meant more than any truth.[3] But 'Are you Michael Collins the murderer?' takes us to the heart of his kind of war, or at least to the assumptions that were made about it. It challenges us to consider the nature of the violence he was associated with, and was held responsible for. And the priest presents us, not least because of his calling, with the moral ambiguity of it all. That Collins was so quickly invited in, and more to 'come in, in God's name', suggests 'murderer' had come to be more than it usually bluntly meant. It tells us something of what was borne or even condoned by then; maybe more of what heroism now amounted to. But above all the priest's words confirm what had already happened to Michael Collins by 1921: all Michael Collins had come to mean was war.

When Arthur Griffith described Collins in the Treaty debates as 'the man who won the war', the historian Frank Pakenham claimed this 'encomium … drew the loudest cheers of all those vociferous days'.[4] But Griffith's words drew more than just appreciative roars. Out into the open came the disgust and the disquiet at such a claim; out came all the things long-bitten tongues had dearly longed to say, out came the questions about what exactly amounted to Michael Collins's war. Because theirs was a well-known enmity, we might associate Cathal Brugha most with this kind of attack, but Brugha was not its only source. Séamus Robinson may have started it, just as he had arguably started the self-same war at Soloheadbeg.[5] Robinson had had his fill of the braying acclamation of what he called the 'pet hero' in their midst, and he wanted a few home truths made known.[6] He told the Dáil that Collins had skulked home from London to avoid conscription in 1916, and while he admitted leaving Glasgow for the very same reason himself, Collins was the one who went back to commit an 'act of high treason and betrayal' in London in 1921.

'The man who won the war' had riled Robinson and he was not going to stand for rot like that:

suppose you know that such a man was not really such a great man; and that his reputation and great deeds of daring were in existence only on

paper and in the imagination of people who read stories about him …
The Press has called him the Commander-in-Chief of the IRA … and
the 'elusive Mike' and we have all read the story of the White Horse …
I'm forced to think that the reported Michael Collins could not possibly
be the same Michael Collins who was so weak as to compromise the
Republic.

For Robinson, this 'reported Michael Collins did not ever exist'; this Collins was
a sham. And if the 'Dáil, the country, aye, and the world' were still in doubt, he
set out to shame Collins once and for all: 'what positions exactly did Michael
Collins hold in the army? Did he ever take part in any armed conflict in which
he fought by shooting; the number of such battles or fights; in fact, is there any
authoritative record of his having ever fired a shot for Ireland at an enemy of
Ireland?'[7]

It was clear from Robinson's questions what passed by his lights for a good
war. Robinson had been in the ambushes, had had the near-misses that were
by then passing for the stuff of Collins's fight. Robinson was part of that group
that believed you started a war by shooting policemen long before Collins had a
Squad. If Robinson was what passed for a warrior in the War of Independence
then he was clearly saying Collins was never one of 'us'. The Treaty debates were
certainly venomous by the time Robinson rose to speak on 6 January; that might
explain it, or maybe it was just jealousy that Collins was getting the type of
plaudits that Robinson felt belonged to the real fighting men, to the likes of Dan
Breen, Tom Barry and himself. But whatever explains the vigour of this attack or
the certainty of Griffith's defence, Collins's war record mattered, and if we give
in to the temptation to arbitrate between these two extremes we may well miss a
quite fundamental point: when it comes to Collins's war, Griffith and Robinson
both managed to get it right.

It has been clear for quite some time that Collins 'was no warrior in the way
he is usually understood – as a man of the gun and the uniform, uncomfortable
with politics'. Indeed, for Peter Hart this very 'idea is laughable', so much so
that he hammers home the point with what might be heresy still: '[d]e Valera
was more of a soldier – he at least had held a combat command and had led
men in battle'.[8] But it has also been clear for some time that the Irish revolution
was not just, if ever, about that kind of war where men were conventionally led

While Robinson was determined to expose Collins as the arch-pen-pusher, when the debates turned to civil war the anti-Treatyites capitalised on the image of Collins as the tyrannical military figure. Seen here in an image by Countess Markievicz, Collins was portrayed as the swearing, uniformed, gun-toting bully. *(National Library of Ireland)*

and combat followed an orthodox command. At the same time the desire to 'demilitarise' Collins, to show him as more than just the spymaster, more than just the hidden hand at the centre of a clandestine war, has prompted all sorts of interesting investigations of the many other sides of his life and work.[9] We have been variously introduced to Collins the administrator, the accountant, the Minister for Finance; Collins the manager, the negotiator, the networker, the manoeuvrer, the propagandist, the string-puller, and the politician most of all.[10] And we will meet this man in Chapter 4.

But if Robinson wanted to expose him for the pen-pusher or bean counter he no doubt was, it was never going to be as cut and dried as that. He had his others titles too: he was aide-de-camp to Joseph Plunkett during the Easter Rising, became Treasurer of the IRB and took on Patrick Pearse's old job as Director of Organisation of the Irish Volunteers by the end of 1917. He was Adjutant General of the Volunteers by the following March, President of the Supreme Council of the IRB, and Director of Intelligence by mid-1919, though no title, military or otherwise, ever seemed to contain him in his own preserves.[11] It is not as straightforward as tipping a balance back, in remaking him as an administrator who probably never fired a shot or an accountant who did more for Irish freedom with the debit side of the Dáil loan and the credit side of the Volunteer Dependents' Fund, because bean counting and pen-pushing were probably his most obvious weapons of war. Without the money to keep it going, war just stopped. He was 'arms supplier in chief', largely because he was Minister for Finance.[12] His letters and memoranda gave it all the authority of paper, the legitimacy of letterheads, turning what might have been dismissed as 'a squabble to a war'.[13] Ernie O'Malley described him seated at a table once in 1918, how through their conversation the writing never stopped. All the time 'the pile of envelopes increased' as he worried away at an empire with the scrape of his nib.[14] Because he is an untidy sum of so many parts he is what Griffith and Robinson said he was: by turn the man who never fired a shot, by turn the man who did his best to win his war.

For all that, though, the most common construction of Collins has been Griffith's one. Although by 1924 Dan Breen had already recounted the revolution as a sequence of scrapes and escapades to make 'a Wild West show … grow pale', Collins emerged more Richard Hannay to Breen's Tom Mix.[15] From Béaslaí's 1926 biography to Neil Jordan's 1996 film, the man of action has always played the bigger part, not least because we have consistently wanted him to.[16] In the 1930s Seán O'Faoláin knew that writing 'sensationalist pieces on Collins' for the Sunday newspapers was always good for a few bob, a handy £4 a week, when times were tight.[17] And being known as Yitzhak Shamir's *nom de guerre* no doubt kept up the price.[18] 'I killed for Michael Collins' was still the stuff of newspaper headlines well into the 1960s, and our ardour for the whiff of gunpowder has yet to dim.[19]

Why? Well, it suits us. We want him to be 'Ireland's fighting hero', to be the man who 'broke' the 'British Secret Service system in Ireland', to be the one who 'saved the movement for independence', because it is all a better, more inspiring, more straightforward story than the truth.[20] Collins the 'hero of a hundred escapes', Collins the master spy, running rings around his slow-witted Dublin Castle opponents as he read their secret files under their noses, Collins in his uniform leading an army in a tragic civil war, he sets the pulse racing and the books selling in a way all the other Collinses could not.[21] Never mind that it leaves us a Collins who is sorely 'incomplete' or a fighting story that is far more simplistic and reductive than the one Collins probably knew.[22] It may well reflect the obsession of the historiography and its readers with the violence of the Irish revolution, the reduction of something with complex political, economic and social contexts to the sum of just its violent parts. It is an approach that only measures war, as Robinson did, by the sound of a rifle or a revolver shot. Although P.S. O'Hegarty was constant in his criticism of the part Béaslaí's 1926 biography played in reducing all there was of war to Collins and all there was of Collins to war, the 'fighting hero' remains the Collins that is most familiar still.

Unpicking Collins's war from all the myths that have wrapped themselves around it then, and since, is not as simple as separating out what he really did from what others wanted to believe he might have done. The stories were too integral to too much of what Collins understood of war for it to be as straightforward as that. We have known for some time the extent to which Richard Mulcahy, the Chief of Staff of the IRA, was the moving force behind many of the measures Collins has been associated with; even the British admitted that 'during the troubles he had many of the adventures since attributed to Mr Collins'.[23] Apocryphal stories of Collins in battle on a white charger, such as the one Robinson referred to, were directly at odds with what amounted to his war.[24] Indeed, 'one of the keys to Collins's astonishing success during the War of Independence had been precisely

PARTICULARS OF A ACCOUNT (London)

DATE.

PARTICULARS OF GOODS.

DATE	PARTICULARS OF GOODS.	£.	s.	d.
1920 Feb.10th	1-38 colt. with hammer.	4.	10.	0.
" "	1 ditto. hammerless.	4.	0.	0.
" "	1 9 m/m. German. Automatic.	4.	0.	0.
" "	1 Gallery Pistol.	2.	0.	0.
" "	1-45 ordinary.	3.	0.	0.
" "	1 Single action. 476.	2.	0.	0.
" "	1 ditto 44.	1.	10.	0.
" "	1 9/ m/m. German Automatic.	4.	0.	0.
" "	1 Bulldog. 32.	3.	5.	0.
" 15th	1 Small Auto.			
" "	4-45 S & W.	12.	0.	0.
" "	1-38 Auto.	5.	0.	0.
" "	1 Rifle.	2.	0.	0.
" 21st.	2-38 German Autos.	9.	0.	0.
" "	1-32 Auto.	4.	0.	0.
" "	1 Ditto.	3.	10.	0
" "	350 rounds 38 Auto.	3	8.	0.
" 27th	I Machine Gun.	5.	0.	0.
March 4th	1-45 Ordinary.	1.	15.	0.
" "	1 Rifle	3.	0.	0.
" 15th	1-45 Auto. & Am.	6.	0.	0.
" "	Expenses		7.	8.
" 17th	1 Rifle (1917)	6.	0.	0.
" "	1 Trunk, straps, taxi etc.	4.	14.	0.
" "	1 Automatic & 70 rounds.	5.	0.	0.
" "	Expenses to Liverpool½	1.	0.	0.
April 6th	1-45 Auto.	6.	10.	0.
" 9th	German Auto. & 200 rounds.	5.	10.	0.
" 11th	1-38 Hammerless ordinary.	2.	15.	0.
" "	2-45 Colts.	7.	0.	0.
" "	1-9 m/m Automatic	4.	0.	0.
" "	240 rounds Assorted Am.	1.	0.	0.
" 12th	1-45 ordinary	3.	10.	0.
" "	Expenses.	6.	10.	0.
" 20th	20 rifles.	40.	0.	0.
" 22nd.	30 "	60.	0.	0.
March 18th	1-45 ordinary	3.	10.	0.
		240	4	8

This sample from early 1920 of an account recording the precise pounds, shillings and pence spent acquiring arms and ammunition in London reveals the type of detail Collins gathered. From rounds of ammunition to a machine gun for £5, such accounts not only reveal Collins's bookkeeper's mind, but also something of how widely available guns were in post-war Britain. *(National Archives of Ireland)*

The ubiquity of the image of Collins in uniform portrays something of the fascination with him as the 'fighting hero'. Collins wore this uniform only during the last summer of his life but that does not seem to undermine the readiness to portray him as a military man. Seen here at Arthur Griffith's funeral with Richard Mulcahy, Collins was acutely aware, at this vulnerable moment, of the significance of his appearance in uniform. *(National Library of Ireland)*

his ability to stay out of trouble … he had appreciated that he was far more useful as an orchestrator of violence than as a gun-slinging foot soldier'; something that the nature of his death was to highlight.[25]

Even in terms of his intelligence war we have long recognised the part the Tobins and the Thorntons, the Clancys and the McKees have played, that Collins may well have wound the mechanism but the cogs did most of the work.[26] Indeed, they often protected him from threats he could not recognise. John Jameson, really John Byrnes, was one, Patrick Molloy another, while Henry Quinlisk was yet 'another close shave'.[27] All found to be spies of various sorts, each man managed to meet, what Hart calls, 'the ever-trusting Collins', who 'on his own had been fantastically reluctant to act decisively against' these men.[28] The limits of Collins's powers as a spymaster can even be seen in terms of the killing of fourteen men, suspected intelligence agents and courts-martial officers, on Bloody Sunday morning.[29] Frank Thornton later claimed 'the British Secret Service was wiped out on the 21st November 1920', that it was one of Collins's most decisive victories even though more were meant to be killed that morning, even though IRA intelligence spent the rest of 1920 and enough of 1921 tracking down other British intelligence threats, knowing it was not so.[30] While that morning's work may have brought temporary relief for the IRA in Dublin, it came at quite a cost. The fourteen people killed, the more than 60 injured in retaliation that afternoon at a match in Croke Park, was the first price, although the loss of Dick McKee and Peadar Clancy of the Dublin Brigade, both killed later that day in Dublin Castle with Conor Clune, was counted by senior IRA intelligence figures in Dublin far more.[31] But more was to come: that morning 'prompted a backlash that sent the IRA reeling'. The introduction of detention without trial saw hundreds of IRA men rounded up; martial law was declared in Munster; and British intelligence learned that morning about many of the mistakes it should no longer make.[32] Even if Thornton was right, it was all a rather costly boast.

But while Bloody Sunday was called 'a spectacular coup by Michael Collins' and it has been intimately associated with his reputation as intelligence supremo since, even Collins himself admitted it was never so.[33] When Kate McCormack queried why her son, a cousin of Michael Davitt, had been shot in the Gresham Hotel that morning, when she asked Richard Mulcahy in March 1922 to exonerate him of the charge of being a British spy, Collins was prodded to reveal the limits

This photograph, taken from a scrapbook full of similar images, shows something of how information was gathered as part of the intelligence war. Drawing on newspaper notices of all sorts of events, even births, marriages and deaths, and assembling photographs such as these from a wide variety of sources, was a laborious effort beyond any one man. *(National Library of Ireland)*

of his own powers.[34] When Mulcahy asked Collins how he should reply to this woman Collins wrote:

> you will remember that I stated on a former occasion that we had no evidence that he was a Secret Service Agent. You will also remember that several of the 21st November cases were just regular officers. Some of the names were put on by the Dublin Brigade. So far as I remember McCormack's name was one of these. In my opinion it would be as well to tell Mrs McCormack that there was no particular charge against her son, but just that he was an enemy soldier.[35]

There was little comfort for Kate McCormack in this response, especially since she had been living on the charity of her daughter-in-law's family since her son's death, but it certainly recalibrates Collins's role. Bloody Sunday was a Dublin Brigade operation, and it would be simply naïve to go on looking for the hidden hand of Collins when he admitted himself that it was only ever discreetly there. In fact Seán Ó Murthuile, one-time secretary of the supreme council of the IRB, believed that, while Dublin Castle keenly pursued Collins, 'Liam Tobin … was regarded as the most effective Intelligence Officer the Castle people were up against', that without him Collins had only a shadow of an intelligence war.[36] But however much this type of evidence might suggest the nature and the limits of Collins's actions, all of it probably misses a wider point: what people were prepared to believe of him had become a weapon essential to his war. Playing up to the persona was just another way to fight.

In October 1919 the Chief Secretary's Office asked the Commissioner of the Dublin Metropolitan Police (DMP) for a list of those known to be most responsible for the 'murders of police, military and civilians … within the past twelve months'. Michael Collins was returned first on a list of 35 names. He was described as 'Adjutant General of the Irish Volunteers', 'Minister of Finance to Dail Eireann', and most particularly as 'a most violent man'. 'He is said to be the person most responsible for the many outrages committed in this country by Volunteers'.[37] From there the image grew, and he became an easy means to sum up and sensationalise what seemed to be this Irish war. Collins's file was the one Frank Thornton said his friends in Dublin Castle could never smuggle out, because 'it was always with the Auxies or in some other department, moving round'.[38] Rumours circulated among the British forces that he was capable of all sorts of things. He was known as 'a man who was a very good shot with either hand, and who sometimes dressed as a monk'.[39] The more macabre believed he kept 'the personal trinkets of murdered officers' in his home.[40] It was even suggested that he 'had gone about as a woman', albeit 'a giant woman' but a woman just the same, that 'he passed into officers' clubs disguised as an officer, worming secrets out of people' who had secrets to tell.[41] The journalist, C.H. Bretherton, wrote that 'I have seen Dublin clubmen shut the door, and look under the table before whispering the awful name of Michael Collins into each other's ears'; when a critic as stern as Bretherton was convinced, rumour was infinitely more powerful than fact.[42]

In his memoir William Darling recalled meeting Collins by accident just before the Truce. When Collins admitted who he was, Darling confessed he rather rudely said, 'are you the Michael Collins whom the British police have made famous?' When Collins asked him to explain what he meant, Darling, who was then working in Dublin Castle in General Tudor's office, replied: 'A police force has a duty to apprehend criminals … If they fail to apprehend criminals one defence is to say that the criminal … is the most astute, remarkable, astonishing criminal in history', to which Collins apparently laughed aloud.[43] No doubt he was amused by the persona created to save British blushes, but there was more strategic advantage to be taken from it than that. Having a 'mysterious Mike' in your camp raised the spirits of those he encouraged to fight – 'all the boys look to you' – and many on his own side told him and themselves so.[44] 'You are a good second to the Scarlet Pimpernel,' one man told him; for another, it was simpler than that: 'We have the swine now, by Heaven, if you are left'.[45] Even de Valera confided to him, 'Your life is one of the most valuable the country has, if not the most valuable': Collins had become a talisman of their fight.[46]

In turn, he played up to the role, to impress, perhaps, just how important he had become. In June 1921 he told Éamon de Valera how a captured IRA messenger had not been ill-treated by his captors for fear 'that M.C. would murder them all'. In the same letter he confided, 'between ourselves that the escape on Thursday was nothing to four or five escapes I have had since'.[47] 'My journey … certainly did a great deal of good locally' was how he described a trip to Cork in the early days of the Truce; it seems he believed the sight of this 'M.C.' was by then adequate to inspire.[48] That was certainly the logic of putting him in uniform in July 1922, of

No EL.22.   1st June. 1921

<u>PRESIDENT</u>

     I have acknowledged yours No.42, but I did
not formally acknowledge Nos. 39, 40 and 41 - These
did reach me safely.

     <u>CAPTURED MESSENGER</u> No.39. They did not
illtreat him - Thought if they did that M.C would
murder them all. When the first rush at him failed
he told them a wonderful story - it is really
awfully funny, but I am glad he had the resourcefulness,
which was the means of saving him from an awkward
position.

     <u>DEPARTED FRIEND</u> No.40 I saw him yesterday -
we concluded everything. This will have been clear to
you from an earlier memo.

     I may tell you between ourselves that the escape
on Thursday was nothing to four or five escapes I have
had since. They ran me very close for quite a good
while on Sunday evening. The Engineering friend is a
nuisance - he won't do what he is told and take care of
himself.

     <u>MESSENGER No.41</u> I note your recommendation.
I suppose the proper thing to do accordingly is to put
him on the £3 basis, same as my lad was getting. This
will as you recommend take effect from the date he was
taken over. The necessary details are being attended
to.

Writing to de Valera on 1 June 1921 of his fearsome reputation as 'MC' and of his numerous escapes, Collins's tongue may have been planted firmly in his cheek, but he lost no opportunity to remind de Valera of how important he had become. *(National Archives of Ireland)* his occupying the position of Commander-in-Chief of what would be the new National Army; he was a figure to cohere around, to inspire loyalty in a ragtag army facing into civil war.[49] The speed with which newspapers and newsreels distributed his image round the country and the world suggested he was making the most of the personal following he could still muster, and the spirit of 'what's good enough for Mick is good enough for me' was quickly capitalised upon.[50]

It clearly amused him to play the hero. He turned up to the makings of a soirée at the home of surgeon and writer Oliver St John Gogarty, making no attempt to disguise the 'large revolver strapped to his thigh', knowing that the assembled company of George Russell, a visiting American senator and some giddy society gals would have been heartily disappointed if he had arrived with a briefcase full of files.[51] But Collins the hero could go too far: believing he was even a shadow of what the gossip said he was may have been one of his more considerable flaws. Quite detailed reports got back to the Prime Minister, David Lloyd George, about Collins's visit to see Irish prisoners in Wormwood Scrubs in October 1921. Prison guards said he was drunk, passing cigarettes to the prisoners, and 'boasting about all the loyal people he has shot': they threatened to resign if he was permitted in again.[52] Talk of this episode around the fringes of the Treaty negotiations shows just how much damage this one incident had done: 'he fancied he had met and defeated the whole might of the Empire. But, if necessity came, he would find out his mistake. A country which had raised six million men for a great war was not to be so easily defied.'[53] After just more than a week of negotiations, he had already crudely overplayed his hand.

In March 1922, R.M. Smyllie, editor of *The Irish Times*, asked Desmond FitzGerald, pro-Treaty Director of Publicity, for details about Michael Collins: where and when he was born, where he worked, 'and lastly, what is the most important of all, could you let me into at least <u>one</u> of his legendary escapades? One hears of so many, but they generally sound apocryphal'.[54] While it is striking that Smyllie and *The Irish Times* had fallen for the Collins myth, FitzGerald's reply was perhaps more striking still. He outlined a by then oft-repeated run-in Collins had had with some Auxiliaries in the Gresham Hotel on Christmas Eve 1920, but FitzGerald counselled caution otherwise: 'without consulting him [Collins] it is rather shaky ground to talk about his escapes' at all.[55] By then Collins was head of the Provisional Government, the most public face of the new regime, key to the organisation of a new and hopefully orthodox army, and

H.M. Prison Wormwood Scrubs.   20th October, 1921.

Memorandum.

MICHAEL   COLLINS.

The above named arrived at the Prison with two companions at 4.45 p.m. last night.   He had evidently been drinking heavily and reeked of whisky.   When asked who he wished to see, he replied that he would see Kerr of Liverpool first and find out what other friends of his were here.   He said his two companions would also be present at the visit.   I replied that I had only instructions to admit him, Michael Collins.   He then assumed a bullying demeanour saying "Mr. Lloyd George won't thank you for being discourteous to me".   I asked him who had told him his companions could visit prisoners and he replied Mr. Jones, Secretary to the Cabinet.   By this time he had become truculent and announced his intention of seeing all the prisoners.   I informed Mr. Wall ^(Secretary to the Prison Commission) by telephone and he authorized me to permit his two companions to visit prisoners with him.   Acting under Mr. Wall's instructions I had arranged for the visits to take place in the Visiting Committee Room.   He saw three men, viz: 5,278, N. Kerr; 4371, R. Stack; and 4457, L. Breen.   He kept Kerr for 1½ hours, Stack for 45 minutes and Breen for 40 minutes.   He attempted to pass tobacco to Kerr but was prevented, after some difficulty, from doing so by Warder Smeed.   The Chief Warder persuaded him to go about 8.20 p.m.   The Irish prisoners since their meeting

in June have been behaving well and doing good work, but I am afraid the visits of such a notorious individual boasting about all the loyal people he has shot and in liquor will be certain to cause unrest among my prisoners. I trust no more visits will be permitted.

(Signed) J. J. K. GREENWAY.

Governor,

20/10/1921.

Since writing the above Kerr has been reported for persisting in talking, insolence, and refusing to change his place when ordered to do so, 4 other Sinn Feiners have in consequence refused to go to the shed.

Collins's visit to Wormwood Scrubs, lasting nearly four hours, caused a considerable stir. The Governor's report resurrected some of the misgivings on the British side about sitting down to negotiate with Collins at all.
(Parliamentary Archives, London)

trying to convince as many of his old comrades as possible to accept what would become the new state; playing up to the old elusive Pimpernel, the symbol of staunch resistance to Britain, sat perhaps uneasily by then.

By March 1922 it was also very obvious what he was, and, for some, this Collins before them was a poor shadow of what many hoped he might have been. Celia Shaw, who was a convinced pro-Treatyite, wrote in her diary just a month before:

> I fervently hope they would soon get into military togs. It's surprising how different the actual ideal always is – when I saw an obviously slum youth in uniform I almost get a shock, I had never pictured his type in the IRA. I always thought of the tall dark, black haired & flashing eye IRA of my imagination. Michael Collins' grammar is another sore point with me.[56]

During the Treaty debates she criticised: 'Mick is talking too much'.[57] While she may have been especially hard to please, she summed up the disappointing shift from fantasy to fact; no one imagined their Rudolf Valentino mixing up his prepositions and his pronouns, not knowing when to shut his mouth. C.H. Bretherton later wrote that 'Collins should have kept up the role of Unknown Assassin, the man who might emerge from the boot cupboard or up through the floor, pistol you, and depart through the front door after exchanging the password with the house-parlourmaid', that when he came into the open he could 'never be mysterious or terrible' again, almost implying that to be 'mysterious or terrible' was his achievement, his point.[58] The charisma of the creation had overpowered the man.

But where do we begin to find the man in his war? However much he claimed to prefer the company of 'a good soldier … to a dozen like de Valera', Collins never really fitted the soldier mould.[59] While in later years Sam Maguire remembered Collins as 'a leading light in Volunteer circles in London', for others he was always part of the 'awkward squad', never lacking in enthusiasm, but never quite marching to time just as he should.[60] The common thread in his contemporaries' recollections of him in London can be summed up by the brief comment of Pat Brennan, who met him first in 1908: 'he worked very hard in the IRB'.[61] It seems he had from the beginning more of a passion for conspiracy than patience for drill. He had what must have been a frustrating Rising; as aide-de-camp to Joseph Plunkett he was remembered as 'silent to the point of surliness',

Although positioned at the edge of this painting, Collins seems to dominate Leo Whelan's portrayal of the General Headquarters staff. Whelan completed the painting over several months in late 1922 and early 1923, and presents an interesting array of drab men in suits reminiscent of a company AGM rather than an underground military leadership. *(National Museum of Ireland)*

OＧLAIＧ nA h-ÉIＲeAnn.

(IRISH VOLUNTEERS.)

An All-Ireland Convention of the Irish Volunteers has been held recently, and a new Executive elected. The principal duty of this Executive will be to carry on the re-organisation of the Irish Volunteers throughout the country, and put them in a position to complete by force of arms the work begun by the men of Easter Week.

In order that we may not be hampered in our next effort by any misunderstanding such as occurred on the last occasion, as a result of conflicting orders, Volunteers are notified that the only orders they are to obey are those of their own Executive. [See note.]

They are at liberty, and are encouraged, to join any other movement that aims at making Ireland a separate and independent nation.

They are reminded, however, of what occurred when Parnell induced the Fenians to fall into line with him—a fusion that resulted in the almost complete abandonment of physical force as a policy. They are warned, therefore, against devoting too much time or energy to any movement other than their own, but to help them solely for the reason that they may enable them to spread the principles of their own organisation, which is the one to which they owe and must give first allegiance.

Each Volunteer is expected to do his own part under the present difficult circumstances towards making himself an efficient soldier in the National Army, and each county is expected to see to the training and arming of its own men. It must also see that well-defined lines of communication are kept with the surrounding counties. The Executive, of course, are in the last degree responsible for all this work, and they call with confidence on all officers and men to co-operate with them in carrying it out as speedily as possible. They guarantee, in return, that they will not issue an order to take the field until they consider that the force is in a position to wage war on the enemy with reasonable hopes of success. Volunteers as a whole may consequently rest assured that they will not be called upon to take part in any forlorn hope.

Let each one get to his work at once, and when the Executive are satisfied that the right moment has come—that is, when we are strongest and the enemy weakest—they will give the order to strike—*and then let it be done relentlessly.*

By Order,

EXECUTIVE IRISH VOLUNTEERS.

Dated 22nd May, 1917.

NOTE.—All orders of the Executive will be signed " For and on behalf of the Executive." This does not apply to matters of detail pertaining to organisation, training and communication, which will, of course, be signed by the respective directors.

'hovering about somewhat restlessly' as some semblance of readiness was put on Plunkett to fight.[62] Although an injured hand was given as the reason why he was 'prevented from using a gun' that week, he seems to have meandered round the GPO putting in his time.[63] He was with James Connolly on the Monday, and later bullied Desmond FitzGerald, who was trying to hold the line on food rations, into feeding some worn and weary men.[64] By Thursday he was reduced to guarding a ladder to the roof, and in this 'post of little honour or danger', he left the impression of an 'Achilles sulking in his tent'.[65] By Friday he was mucking in to fight the encroaching flames in the post office, and, as if to add insult to injury, this ruined the breeches of the uniform of which he had been so proud.[66] He was just one of 'the many uniformed spare parts' in the GPO that week, but he had dirtied that uniform, done his bit for Ireland, and had become a veteran of at least a type of war.[67]

Collins's comments that the Rising had too much of 'the air of a Greek tragedy about it', that it 'was bungled terribly, costing many a good life', the idea that 'unlike Pearse [Collins] had no Messianic notions, no idea of a sacrifice to bring back a soul into Ireland', have shaped much of our sense of where the violence he went on to espouse came from.[68] Guerrilla warfare has been understood almost as Collins's direct reaction to the military disaster of Easter 1916. But Collins's views of violence are not as straightforward as that. Written on the backs of Geraldine GAA club reports from 1909 are, without coherent beginning or end, snatches of his thoughts about all sorts of things. He writes of the 1882 Phoenix Park murders: 'I do not defend the murder simply as such. I merely applaud it on the ground of expediency.'[69] However, his views on Finland and Russia are maybe more revealing of his attitude to violence than that: 'The Finns are almost less homogenous than the Irish. Altogether there are 2,000,000 of them & they won against the might of Russia. Cannot we go and do likewise? ... The murderers of Bobrikoff & Johnson had their Irish counterpart in those of Burke & Cavendish. The results were not so gratifying in Ireland as they were in Finland. But that was mainly because of ...', and it trails off there.[70] Nikolai Bobrikoff, who had been appointed Governor General of Finland as part of the Russification policy, was assassinated by a lone gunman in June 1904; Johnson or Ionson, the Procurator of the Senate, was killed in his home in February the following year, shot in front of his son for his pro-Russian sympathies.[71] If we add in the 'Tottenham outrage', the assassination of Sir William Curzon Wyllie, which, as we saw in

Chapter 1, took place in the very same year Collins penned the club reports if not these thoughts, he may well have been working out an early draft of what revolutionary violence might mean.

There was clearly more to the development of his ideas on violence than Ireland, than Easter 1916. In that meeting with William Darling, he mentioned his love of Walt Whitman's *Leaves of Grass*, perhaps for its 'resist much, obey little', but Darling was more struck by a favourite of Collins's that he had never heard of: *My Reminiscences of East Africa* by the German general, Paul Emil von Lettow-Vorbeck. Von Lettow-Vorbeck's account of a four-year guerrilla campaign against Allied troops, remarkable for just surviving, for tying up ten times the number of his own men, was well known, if not to Darling then certainly to his superiors, as an account of one of the most serious threats to imperial interests in Africa during the First World War.[72] Collins may just have been keen to impress that he was widely read, but his chosen book was making a point, albeit lost on his listener, that he was well versed in the type of guerrilla warfare his enemy's enemy had used to considerable effect. Of course, in Lettow-Vorbeck Collins may also have been grasping for models and precedents to dignify what his opponents would not publicly concede was war, or trying to impress that he was as dangerous to their interests as Lettow-Vorbeck had once been. But he was crafting, however haphazardly, a defence, a rationale. Given that his fight for freedom was so often at odds with what passed for the little that was honourable and ethical in war, he needed all the Finnish assassins and German generals he could get.

If we look to some of Collins's vindications for the types of violence he was most associated with, we see something of what he thought the point of that violence was, where he drew the lines he would not cross, maybe something of who he conceived his enemies to be. What he seemed to be asked most about, and defended most virulently in return, was the execution, the assassination of 'spies and informers', particularly in Dublin. In all sorts of ways he found himself answering, again and again, versions of F.P. Crozier's rather blunt question: 'but what about the murders?'[73] He held a firm line both in public and in private for the need for force: he told Crozier, the one-time commanding officer of the Auxiliary Division of the RIC, rather simply, 'when you're up against a bully you've got to kick him in the guts!'[74]

Austria & Germany. The diplomatists of all these countries are seeking a Russian alliance, and so Finland can scarce expect much sympathy from them. However there is reason to believe that the Active Resistance party is still alive & working. It may yet be possible for Russia to meddle in Finnish affairs.

I have headed my remarks — Finland & Ireland: You will perhaps be impatient to see what either has to do with Ireland. Let me paint the moral. As a rule I hate morals and hate moralists still more, but in the present case I think it is excusable even desirable. The murders of Bobrikoff & Johnson had their Irish counterpart in the murders of Burke & Cavendish. The results were not gratifying in Ireland as — they were in Finland. But that was mainly
because of

These notes express some of Collins's early thoughts on violence, and show something of his engagement with a political world that encompassed far more than the machinations inside one London GAA club. *(UCD Archives)*

The sense that some sort of moral code had been breached, by the kind of violence it was assumed he directly encouraged, prompted some of his more vivid constructions of what he meant by this type of war. Although Todd Andrews recalled that as a young IRA man he revelled in the fact that the British press 'sucked Roget's *Thesaurus* dry to find words to denounce us. We were gunmen, terrorists, extremists, murderers, assassins, butchers, thugs', murderer was the word that seemed to rankle, the only moniker Collins was said to resent.[75] In his biography of Collins, Rex Taylor transcribed the contents of a note Collins may have composed in London during the Treaty negotiations in case he was cornered about the killings on Bloody Sunday morning, a crib, if one was needed, when the awkward questions came:

> My one intention was the destruction of the undesirables who continued to make miserable the lives of ordinary decent citizens. I have proof enough to assure myself of the atrocities which this gang of spies and informers have committed. Perjury and torture are words too easily known to them. If I had a second motive it was no more than a feeling such as I would have for a dangerous reptile. By their destruction the very air is made sweeter. That should be the future's judgment on this particular event. For myself, my conscience is clear. There is no crime in detecting and destroying, in war-time, the spy and the informer. They have destroyed without trial. I have paid them back in their own coin.[76]

It was a quite remarkable defence for one who felt right was so clearly on his side. 'We shall be call'd purgers, not murderers', Brutus said, and Collins may have read his *Julius Caesar* well.[77]

When asked by Crozier 'why did you murder poor old Mrs Lindsay?' Collins struggled in reply: "'I was sorry about that", he replied, pausing, as he cast his eyes on the ground as if ashamed, "but she wasn't murdered in cold blood. She was executed. Let me explain".[78] He said she had informed against men in Cork, she had been tried, that it was the fault of General Strickland, the commanding officer of the 6th Division in Ireland, for executing five IRA men, that she would not have been killed if Strickland had let them live.[79] But even with those reasons he still admitted:

'there is this about it, they should have referred it to me for decision, but did not do so ... that's why I said I was sorry about it, as I don't think I'd have shot her on account of her age.' We paused while I lit a pipe. Puffing through the smoke, I met the eyes of Collins once more ... 'You think I was a brute?' he said ... 'I'd do anything to free my beloved land'.[80]

That may be, but he clearly found this kind of 'anything', the murder of a 60-year-old widow hard to make right.[81] Her kidnap in the wake of the failed Dripsey ambush, the burning of her home, the murder of her chauffeur, that she was held for over a month before her death, that her eventual execution in March 1921 did not become public knowledge, much to Collins's embarrassment, until July, while the Truce was still a delicate flower, may well have provoked these efforts to exonerate and explain.[82] Missing, Mrs Lindsay had become 'a *cause célèbre*, her fate a subject for newspaper headlines, questions in the House of Commons, and even Virginia Woolf's diary', but dead, she also clearly caused Collins considerable disquiet; she was something, as he admitted to Crozier, 'I was sorry about'.[83] Lionel Curtis, who had acted as a secretary to the British Treaty negotiators and as adviser on Ireland to the Colonial Office, remembered that Collins had proved truculent and difficult over the question of compensation after the Treaty. For Collins, paying compensation conceded some kind of culpability when he wanted his British adversaries to seem the only ones to blame. However, Collins had admitted liability without question or objection to one particular case, a case of rape, because it 'was the kind of crime which genuinely shocked him'.[84] It was Curtis's way of saying that Collins still knew right from wrong.

Paddy O'Daly recalled Collins vigorously reprimanding him when a rumour circulated shortly after the Squad was formed that O'Daly was going to shoot a DMP man because he had once harmed O'Daly's daughter in a raid. When O'Daly claimed 'it was only talk ... Michael Collins then gave me a lecture on revenge and told me that the man who had revenge in his heart was not fit to be a Volunteer'.[85] It was quite at odds with Joseph Sweeney's recollection of Collins delighting that 'we got the bastard' when Percival Lea Wilson, the officer who was said to have mistreated Tom Clarke after the Rising, was killed in June 1920.[86] But for all sorts of reasons it was convenient to conceive of Collins's motives to happily mirror one's own ends. The men who killed for

INTEL.

I/O.23.   25. 7. 1921.

TO:
O/C,
West Clare Brigade.

1.   When I was speaking to you about Miss Burke,
I had forgotten that I had sent you a note (no.I/O 22)
telling you to release her. Please act on this note.
We shall leave the other part of it.

2.   It is very unluckythat she should be got at
this time. But you might question her in the way I
told you to. What I would really like to do would be
to release her through the Cork fellows, but this
would mean revealing a number of our men. Tell her
finally that she may thank God she is not a man.

        In view of above, you will consequently not
expect messenger to report as arranged.

In private correspondence Collins held a similar line, albeit with a somewhat different tone. His instructions to release Miss Bridie Burke, a typist in the military barracks in Cork, who had been taken prisoner by the West Clare Brigade while home on leave during the Truce, reveals a much blunter side to his chivalry. Burke worked for Captain Kelly, described in Béaslaí's notes as 'one of [the] torturers of Tom Hales … "one of their vilest ruffians"'. *(Military Archives of Ireland)* him were well served by the type of Collins they often constructed in the recollections of their later lives. For Joe Leonard, Collins had the authority of the Dáil to kill 'all condemned enemy spies or others at his discretion'. For O'Daly, it was simpler still: 'we did not ask any questions … any execution sanctioned by Michael Collins was perfectly justified'.[87] There is a dull refrain in many of the later statements of those who killed for Collins that all spies were spies, that no mistakes were made, and citing Collins's imprimatur was often central to that. Without Collins's careful orchestration, without his 'authority', his 'discretion', the reputations of the men who carried out these deeds crumbled into dust.[88] They espoused Collins's line of defence long after his death, because maybe, just maybe, his reasons turned the hole-and-corner awfulness of what they had done into a legitimate type of war. Collins salved the conscience of his cause.

Although he espoused what he called 'scientifically applied physical force', there was still a blunt ruthlessness to his war often at odds with his own portrayal of it.[89] Given, as Richard Mulcahy said, the IRA had 'not been able to drive the enemy from anything but from a fairly good-sized police barracks', Collins had neither the resources nor the capacity to conceive of this fight in any other way.[90] But there was, regardless of the scale, and perhaps because of that scarcity of resources, a callousness in what was unleashed and what was asked of those who fought. Men who believed in a fair fight were not wanted when the Squad was formed, an admission in itself that the Squad's fight was far from fair.[91] While a conscience was all very well, from the point of view of carrying out an assassination, it was likely to ruin maybe the one chance that weeks and months of planning had brought to pass. The thought behind the choice of generally young unmarried men, with consciences pliable for the task, was a tactical part of this war, but it was callous and it was ruthless nonetheless. Collins was portrayed in Neil Jordan's film hating himself for being the man who put a gun in 'young Vinny Byrne's hand', but the Squad, even better known as Collins's Squad, his 'twelve apostles', was the work and the conception of the Dublin Brigade, of Dick McKee and Mick McDonnell, not Collins, however Christ-like, alone.[92] Even in this Collins was one of a crowd, but it is rarely remembered so.

It is Collins that many of the Squad members' later reminiscences dwell on; it is Collins they remember encouraging them, telling them how to fight. Vinny

Byrne, who joined the Squad at eighteen, maybe nineteen, later recalled what Collins meant to him in those days:

> the 'big fella', Mick Collins, visited us at least twice a week. Notwithstanding the enormous amount of work he undertook, he found the time to visit his squad. The moral effect of his visits was wonderful. He would come in and say: 'Well, lads, how are ye getting on?', and pass a joke or two with us. He was loved and honoured by each and every one of us.[93]

'Skinner' O'Reilly remembered, 'I met Mick Collins on one or two occasions. I thought he was a little god. He was very very nice he hit me on the back.' O'Reilly also recalled, 'I did in Hoppy Byrnes … I think Collins & Tobin were on the court martial … I was to fire & then give him one in the head.'[94] Jokes and cigarettes, laughs and the odd drink, a few pats on the back, and then 'give him one in the head'. It was Collins's kind of leadership, Collins's kind of war.

And in many respects he certainly affected to like this war. His keenness for new weapons was clear. He was eager to get his hands on a type of 'trench mortar', and 'expressed a wish to have a weapon of that nature to drop some shells on Dublin Castle'.[95] He wrote keenly to Seán Nunan in America that 'I understand there is a Repeating Gun in USA which takes shot gun sized cartridges. Will you look this up please and forward us one if at all possible'.[96] His fondness for the Thompson sub-machine guns brought in from America is well known; indeed, the IRA were the first to buy this new weapon, and he was said to have 'enthusiastically tested' the 'new toy' when the guns arrived.[97] He seemed to think a gun was an appropriate keepsake; he made a present of an automatic to Dáil Director of Publicity, Erskine Childers, and a revolver to the Sinn Féin propagandist, Darrell Figgis. Both may have been intended as a means of protection, but both weapons brought only tragic consequences: Childers's gun cost him his life when, by then a prominent anti-Treatyite, he was tried and executed for possession of it in 1922, while Figgis's wife used the revolver in 1924 to take her own life.[98] When it came to arming the new National Army, Winston Churchill had to temper Collins's instincts, and talk him out of a request for '25,000 Mills bombs and 5,000 rifle grenades'. 'If they fall into bad hands they become a most terrible means of aggression on the civil population … you never

Photographed here with Tom Cullen (right) and Liam Tobin (left), two of his key intelligence officers, at the Gresham Hotel on the night the Treaty was ratified, Collins worked hard to maintain morale and loyalty to him amongst the intelligence cohort in Dublin. *(Mercier Press, Cork)*

know whom a bomb will kill; very likely a woman, probably a widow'.[99] It was Churchill's way of telling him there were weapons for a proper army and there were weapons for a hit-and-run kind of war.

The problem was Collins had loosed a genie from a bottle and, once loosed, it was hard to get back in. When the Cork IRA was told to curb its plans for retaliation after the Lord Mayor of Cork, Tomás Mac Curtain, was killed in March 1920, Tom Hales and Dick Barrett of Cork No. 3 Brigade, mentioned while in Dublin just how annoyed the Cork No. 1 Brigade was. But Collins saw the two men back to the train with a striking piece of advice: 'When you see Sean Hegarty, tell him from me that in future, it is always best to shoot first and to ask permission afterwards.'[100] Connie Neenan felt that 'subsequent events [in Cork] proved how effective this advice and policy turned out to be'.[101] Cork recorded more deaths than any other county during the War of Independence, accounting for just over 23 per cent of the conflict's 2,159 fatalities between 1920 and 1921, with what might be loosely called Collins's Dublin a quite distant second with just over 14 per cent. As the violence continued in the county through the Truce, many in Cork might have begged to differ with Neenan's view.[102] But what Neenan perhaps unwittingly made clear was just how little control Collins had over the nature and the extent of the violence in Cork, and, indeed, in many other parts beyond Dublin: 'shoot first' and 'ask permission afterwards' does not imply the powers he is too often credited with.

Whatever the limits or the extents of his orchestration or control, what cannot be overlooked, even if we persist in seeing the War of Independence as simply Collins's war, is how contained and relatively sedate that war was. By contemporary European standards, it was a relatively small war; while 1920 may well have been 'the bloodiest year in Ireland since the 1798 rebellion', Ireland was never the Balkans, never Poland, and Ireland's war was fought as much by means of propaganda as on any other front.[103] Violence was not about winning in any traditional sense for Collins; it was about making things difficult, provoking something more outrageous in return, trying simply to hold on until the force of 'world sympathy', as he put it, forced the British to stop.[104] He noted, 'They had been oppressing us with murderous violence. At the same time they preached elsewhere the new world doctrine of "government by the consent of the governed"...': there is every reason to think he tried to mete out the violence to push home this point.[105]

It was as if he was trying to win by victimhood. In May 1920, he wrote to

This caricature of a young anti-Treatyite gunman by 'Shemus' (Ernest Forbes), which appeared in *The Freeman's Journal* on 27 July 1922, summed up a view later expressed by P.S. O'Hegarty in *The Victory of Sinn Féin* of 1924. The War of Independence had allowed the 'gunman to be the dominant personality', and the country was reaping the reward in civil war. *(National Library of Ireland)*

George Gavan Duffy, then Dáil envoy in Paris: 'things here are very thrilling. I think we are on the eve of momentous happenings. I think, in my own opinion, Ireland is in for the greatest crucifixion she has ever been subjected to'.[106] Later in the year events were even more 'exciting and interesting. Outrages of all sorts on the part of the enemy become worse and worse each day. They are losing the last few friends they had here'.[107] Indeed, the British recourse to auxiliary police, the use of paramilitary forces, the reputation gained by what became the notorious Black and Tans and Auxiliaries, all of the indiscipline, the raids, the reprisals, the shooting of so many civilians who 'failed to halt' by Crown forces of all sorts, all helped Collins to make this type of case. He described the death of Tipperary IRA man Seán Treacy as everything becoming 'more and more lively'.[108] While in London for the Treaty negotiations he sent home the death threats he received at Hans Place: 'Mr Collins thinks value should be made out of this … everything with a view to showing up what the enemy really is'.[109] He took the same approach to Northern Ireland, badgering FitzGerald to get stories of unionist perfidy into the *Daily Mail* and the *Daily Express*; and again during the Civil War, that films should be made of pro-Treaty soldiers' funerals; he wanted cinema goers to see the coffins, to shift uneasily in their seats and to be won over to his side.[110]

In many respects this tactic explains how he was able to carry relatively moderate support in the country with him through the war. Revulsion with his opponents had to be kept at a pitch that inflamed and infuriated more than the actions of his own side. Celia Shaw's diary provides an excellent insight into how the method worked. Already sympathetic, her diary reveals an increasing acceptance of a more radical position, justified at every turn by what was presented to her as the cruelty of Britain's response. After Kevin Barry's execution in November 1920 she confided to her diary: 'we lost all our humanitarian feelings and actually rejoiced when later we heard three English officers would be shot for every Irishman hanged'.[111] 'By Christmas', she admitted, 'we had grown quite callous – when a person was reported shot, we simply asked "which side" & grieved or rejoiced accordingly'.[112] For those unconvinced, the pressure of intimidation, increased social isolation and the fear of speaking out worked their own part. One of the founders of Sinn Féin in Cork, Liam de Róiste, writing in October 1917, already knew that 'I am branded a "moderate", a "compromiser", perhaps a "Griffithite", not a Volunteer, not a republican. "Maybe all right, you know, but …". All of which is amusing to me.'[113] It was a far less amusing position

For many caught in the middle of the tit-for-tat type of warfare the price was high. Standing with what little remained of her worldly goods in January 1921, this woman was left to count the costs of a British reprisal, which followed an IRA ambush led by Sean Moylan in Meelin, County Cork. *(National Library of Ireland)*

To :
Minister for Publicity

A Chara,
          The attached might be of some
interest to you - I don't know whether
there is such a person as W H. Vickers
If there is the thing might be published   Mr.
                                                           f this -
          Do Chara,   says
                                                           it -
                                                            the

3 4 4

5 - OCT 1921

London
4/10/21

Mike the Murderer & Assassion ,

          I thought you would like to
peruse some of the opinions of a few decent
men , I hope we shall have the pleasure of
giving you some of your own dope if you come
to England for Lloyd Georges Surrender.

          Yours, not a murderer

to be in by 1921. But removed from the private wars of small places, confining himself largely to Dublin, Collins never did and never could control that.

The purpose of violence for Collins was to force the British out, if not by winning, then by moral pressure and by terror in its fullest sense. He got what he wanted when Churchill was advised not to linger in the doorways of 'his house, club, office and Parliament' without 'a safety man to cast his eye round before he reaches the pavement', when Maurice Hankey, the Cabinet Secretary, recorded in his diary how much London had changed within just days of Bloody Sunday: 'Great barricades have been erected in Downing St & King Charles St and they want to close the galleries of the House of Commons to all the world … 200 ex-officers have been enlisted & are to roam armed & in plain clothes about the Houses of Parliament and the Govt offices'.[114] Collins wanted General Tudor, Police Adviser to the RIC, to have to 'drive about with a revolver across his knees' because he 'never knew when he might be shot at'.[115] When Lloyd George sometimes stayed in other people's houses 'owing to threats upon his life by the Sinn Feiners', Collins's type of terror won.[116] Whether a Prime Minister tossed restlessly in his bed, whether soldiers loosed off shots at any and every sound in case it might be the coming of their Irish war, the threat did not need to be real for the fear to work.[117] When readers of *The London Magazine* were told 'the Sinn Feiner has the "open sesame" to all doors. It may be the page boy, or it may be a high placed member of the household', in this way at least Collins had won.[118]

This only worked, of course, if actual violence fuelled the fear. He was prepared to have awkward people, as he saw them, those who got in his way, removed: the killing of Alan Bell, a retired magistrate sent to Dublin to find republican money, 'but also acting as undeclared head of intelligence for Dublin Castle', was an obvious case in point.[119] Indeed, it could almost be said he had a rudely functional approach to killing. He stopped Cathal Brugha's scheme to assassinate the British cabinet in early 1921, not because it crossed some ethical line for him as is often thought; he had, after all, suggested kidnapping British MPs as Terence MacSwiney slipped towards death on hunger strike.[120] 'Does he think there is not the makings of a second Cabinet in England' was the reason Seán MacEoin, one of the men Brugha had charged to do it, said Collins gave him, but no doubt he feared too that the pendulum of public sympathy would swing back to London with such an act.[121] For Denis Kelleher, an IRA officer in London, 'Michael Collins was more for the publicity which an undertaking would create': violence had to have an effect; it was violence as spectacle, not just violence for violence's sake. Indeed, Kelleher insisted on distinguishing Collins from other senior IRA men, from Director of Engineering, Rory O'Connor, who, by Kelleher's estimation, just 'did not care about human life'.[122] When it came to killing 'Collins and his assistants were scrupulous, especially when compared to IRA units elsewhere … Collins … may have prevented as many killings as he ordered'. 'The concept of political utility in guiding violence', Hart concludes, 'was uppermost in Collins's mind'.[123] Violence for Collins was not driven by a devouring idealism as it was for some in the revolution. He was pragmatic in this as in all else. Speaking on 5 March 1922 he presented his reflections on war thus:

> War, though necessary and noble, for necessary and noble ends, has terrible effects incidental to it, not only material ruin, but moral effects when prolonged unrighteously; a tendency to lose balance and judgement, to forget or misinterpret the real object of the national struggle, to grow to believe that strife, even fratricidal strife, is noble in itself. Such things must cease as freedom is secured, or the nation will perish.[124]

As he tried to avert a descent into said 'fratricidal strife' his conception of the 'political utility' of violence may well have contributed to this tempered definition of war.

Was he a good leader? Yes, if leadership is measured in a capacity for organisation, in the power to inspire devotion, fear, and authority, if leadership is the trick of combining all the strands that mattered from the essential dreariness of finance to the conspiracies of the IRB. He knew the limits of what could be achieved, and maybe most of all he knew when to stop. He knew 'we had not beaten the enemy out of our country by force of arms', and when he said rejection of the Treaty meant 'a declaration of war until you have beaten the British Empire', it resonated all the more powerfully because he was the one to say it.[125] He was arguably a good leader because the failings of his opponents made him seem far more ominous than he ever really was, and it helped that he was the one they singled out as the embodiment of their Irish fight. It has to be borne in mind that the British forces were never let fully loose in Ireland. Collins even admitted his 'amazement that England had not acted with everything at her disposal', that if it had, 'Ireland would have been paralyzed'.[126] In the words of Clive Wigram, then equerry to the King, the British 'intelligence system over there is rotten', while the Crown forces were slow to improve their propaganda, and worsened their own position with a lack of discipline and restraint.[127] It also took them too long to concede that repressive measures just would not work. But Britain moved to a truce not because Collins forced its hand. Indeed, he was the one to admit in the Treaty debates that the Irish were never 'in the position of conquerors dictating terms of peace to a vanquished foe'.[128] The Truce came because Britain needed the soldiers tied up in Ireland in too many other places, because British public opinion, largely convinced that Britain was a modern liberal state, would not have worn much more of this Irish war, because Ireland was making Britain look bad in American eyes. With a Northern Ireland parliament opened by King George V in June 1921, Britain brokered a truce.

But 'the man who won the war' was also deeply flawed. As Tom Barry alleged, GHQ was detached from the rest of the country, and Collins had at best only flashes of limited control. He was the source of arms and ammunition, of encouragement to act and sometimes of pleas for restraint, but it would be foolish to credit him with powers he never had and never even claimed himself.[129] Ernie O'Malley, on reading Frank O'Connor's biography of Collins written in the 1930s, admitted 'Collins had colour but meant less to fighting Ireland than O'Connor thinks'.[130] But it did not take more than a decade's remove to see that. 'Michael Collins does not appear to be able to control his wild men', Clementine Churchill wrote home to her husband, Winston, from the south of France; the limits of his powers had even reached the Riviera by early 1922.[131] By April it was clear that the actions of some of those 'wild men' were doing him harm. Churchill, exasperated by another of Collins's letters complaining about violence against nationalists in Northern Ireland, was able to snatch away what little scrap of moral high ground Collins tried to establish some footing on: 'When you feel moved to anger by some horrible thing that has happened in Belfast, it may perhaps give you some idea of our feelings in Great Britain when we read of the murder of helpless, disarmed Royal Irish Constabulary and now, this morning, of what is little less than a massacre of Protestants in and near Cork.' While historians may still dispute what prompted the murder of thirteen Protestant men in and near Dunmanway in late April 1922, for Churchill it was just more proof, if proof were needed, of the 'cruel deeds' Collins seemed powerless to restrain.[132] 'His own hands were so red with blood', his own house was by then too disordered, as far as Churchill was concerned, to yield to Collins's pleas for the beleaguered of Belfast.[133]

Bearing an inscription 'Tans glad to have escaped the bombs thrown at their headquarters in Dublin', this photograph was taken at the London and North Western Hotel on the North Wall and includes some Auxiliary officers as well as some Black and Tans. Seemingly unfazed by the explosion, the almost cheery bravura depicted here belies the type of war these forces experienced and fought in Ireland. *(National Library of Ireland)*

These three soldiers of the new National Army, photographed about to enter an unnamed town at some unspecified time during the Civil War, eerily sum up the type of power armed men of all sorts held over the country across the revolution, and a little of the powerlessness of those who claimed to control them. *(UCD Archives)*

As a leader he meddled too much, overstepped too many marks, made enemies when enemies were too easily made, and for an intelligence supremo, as we have seen, he trusted far too easily and exposed himself too often and too readily to unnecessary risks. It was often the good sense of those around him that kept him safe. Some blamed him for indecisiveness when it came to the Treaty split; Seán MacEoin, who by June 1922 was in charge of the National Army's Western Command, was critical that he allowed the anti-Treatyites to build up a 'gigantic force, not only of old Volunteers but what everybody contemptuously called "Trucealeers"...'.[134] Some British reports claimed 'Collins could never escape from this feeling of comradeship with his nominal enemies … that the small number of casualties up to the time of his death is due to his unwillingness to kill his friends of yesterday'.[135] Others were just appalled by what seemed, after the Treaty was signed, to be his double-dealing with all and every side. Lionel Curtis went so far as to suggest that Collins's 'early death alone saved the Treaty' because 'Cosgrave in substance <u>reverted</u> his policy', brought all of the uncertainty of Collins to an end.[136]

Whether Collins ordered the murder of Sir Henry Wilson, the former Chief of the Imperial General Staff and, by the time of his death on 22 June 1922, a Unionist MP and security adviser to Northern Ireland, is still a moot point. Many assume Collins ordered the killing out of his passion to protect the Catholics and nationalists of Northern Ireland; others claim it might have been the fruits of an old order he had issued and had forgotten to rescind. In 1953 P.S. O'Hegarty offered a different view: 'Sam [Maguire] was mad to shoot Wilson' and kept pressing Collins for permission. When he pressed one too many times Collins lost his temper, telling Maguire to '"Get away to hell out of that and don't bother me, and do whatever you like!"', that 'when the thing happened, Mick was in an awful state', not expecting his 'do whatever you like' to be considered his final word. While O'Hegarty dressed it up as 'a sort of Greek tragedy', he remained adamant that nothing could absolve Collins of blame: 'it does not, it cannot, remove from Mick the responsibility for it'.[137] Hart argued that Collins would have needed 'an awfully good reason to arrange such a provocative murder at such a critical time', and while O'Hegarty's explanation might not be an 'awfully good' one, it too casts another doubt over Collins's type of leadership.[138] What is clear is that Wilson's death incensed the British government, and, for one senior figure in London, it raised 'all the doubts I have felt about the whole hateful

Irish business' once again.[139] Churchill announced that he would consider the Treaty broken if nothing was done by the Provisional Government to act against the anti-Treatyites he presumed were to blame. When an order came to put British soldiers back on Dublin's streets, General Macready, the General Officer Commanding in Ireland, who was still in the city, waited for tempers in London to calm and for the order to be thought better of and withdrawn, but for several hours Collins was arguably on the sidelines as the British and the anti-Treatyites almost went to war.[140] The death of Wilson, who was without question for the British side the most significant casualty of these years of Irish troubles, had shocked Westminster to its very core, and it certainly forced Collins's hand. If he had ordered Wilson's death at that point, then it raises very serious questions not just of his attitude to the Treaty, but of his capacity to lead and to strategise at all. If it was his command, then Collins, as we shall see in Chapter 5, may well have started the Civil War he had done so much not to fight.

Once that war began, he threw himself into it with his familiar gusto. As Commander-in-Chief of a new army, he oversaw the effective defeat of the anti-Treatyites in Dublin, the move by sea to Cork, the dramatic expansion of his force. He was lucky, maybe wise, in his choice of senior officers: Richard Mulcahy, Seán MacEoin, Michael Brennan and Eoin O'Duffy brought their considerable skills and Volunteer experience to bear.[141] The meandering to and from the brink of civil war, that looked to London and even to ardent pro-Treatyites like indecisiveness on Collins's part, bought him time to bolster his new force, and he began to tackle the considerable problem of exerting centralised control on what was to be a conventional modern army not just another guerrilla band.[142] His 'Patton-like scourging of unit after unit', suggests discipline, at least his conception of discipline, would be at the heart of this new army, and he settled, as he had before, into a largely managerial conception of the Commander-in-Chief's role. The paper poured forth from his office and his 'solution frequently lay in a properly constructed and filled-out form'.[143] He never took 'command of operations'; he 'spent little time drawing arrows on maps or reading up on the art of war'. If there was an art of war for Collins in 1922 it was to end it fast, and to fight as cleanly as civil war would allow.[144]

It helped that the anti-Treatyites seemed to lack a clear military policy beyond occupying buildings in Dublin and elsewhere in a haunting rerun of Easter week, before drifting back to the by then more familiar type of guerrilla war. But as the

Possibly taken on his last journey south, this photograph evokes something of that 'Patton-like scourging' Collins was undertaking of this new force. *(National Museum of Ireland)*

Civil War wore on through July and into August, it became increasingly clear that Collins, even with his imposing title of Commander-in-Chief, was going to have to conform to the checks and balances of his Provisional Government colleagues, that they were not going to let him run this war with the sometimes patent disregard for the civilian government's will he had been given to in 1920–21. While Collins was keen, even after the bombardment of the Four Courts had just ended, to still encourage 'some avenue or avenues to peace', many of his colleagues, already exasperated with his reluctance to act, wanted a far more aggressive pursuit of the war.[145] 'Decisions were taken in his absence, his wishes were sometimes denied … and he was given orders, which were pressed in spite of his objections'.[146] Powers assumed by him were to be clawed back: the cabinet wanted the power to censor held in civilian rather than military hands, and the Criminal Investigation Department, which was shaping itself into something of a haven for some of his old 'butty men', was no longer to be an unfettered fiefdom, 'the creature of Michael Collins'; rather it was to be put under the tighter rein of the Ministry of Home Affairs.[147] That a committee had reported largely in favour of a reversal of what were said to be his bullish policies on Northern Ireland just days before his death (see Chapter 5), all suggests the Lilliputians, to take Frank O'Connor's view of the world Collins bestrode, had tethered their Gulliver rather well.[148] Given the extent of these attempts to contain and restrain him to the government's will, the hopes that many had, and that some believe still, that the Civil War would have been so very different had he lived, seem, at best, quixotic and naïve. But whether the Civil War would have ended sooner, whether there would or would not have been executions if Collins had lived, well, these are what ifs we can leave for quite another day.

In his memoir, *Guerilla Days in Ireland*, Tom Barry spends three or four pages praising Collins's military and intelligence roles, complimenting his strengths, and recognising the esteem many anti-Treatyites held him in.[149] In private, Cork IRA veteran Florence O'Donoghue remembered Tom Barry expressing a very different view: 'Barry after a while began to discuss Collins … he's no good he said he never shot a man in his life. He was pressing L[iam] T[obin] hard about Collins['s] shooting ability. He thought nothing of the Big Fellow.'[150] And in ways we are almost back where we began. Why in public he was one thing, while in private another, is all part of the quandary of Collins's war. How do we fathom someone who was everything and nothing even to the same man?

If the Free State troops invade that area, of one thing I am certain we cannot be defeated even if Collins and his British Guns succeed in garrisoning every town in Ireland. the Government of the Free State shall not function, as they and their Army and officials shall be treated exactly as the Black + Tans were treated by the I. R. A. Mick has outdone Greenwood his Peelers + Tans raided Dr Endas at 11.30 pm last night and caused Mrs Pearse to break down – Can you understand the mentality of men who are prepared to carry Ireland into the Empire over the bodies of Republicans? The Supreme Council I. R. B. are being rewarded for their treachery by being placed as Military Governors of His Maj. Prisons. Hegarty is Governor of Mountjoy and omeredale is in Command at Kilmainham. – The drunken results of a drunken "Treaty" drunkenly arrived at.

The Dáil has not been convoked as yet and the second Dáil has not been dissolved we expect to hear that there shall

Writing to Joseph McGarrity in the United States on 13 July 1922, Harry Boland, in the Dublin Mountains after the fall of the Four Courts, described his old friend Collins in damning terms. He compared Collins's pro-Treaty forces to the Black and Tans, and rehearsed a popular anti-Treaty accusation that Collins had wined and dined too well in London. Boland's hopes for the future seem all the more poignant given that both he and Collins would be dead within a matter of weeks. *(National Library of Ireland)*

not be another meeting of the old Dáil as England is
very anxious that Dáil Eireann will die and that the Partition
Parliament shall take its place.

I cannot help feeling that every thing will yet work
out right for Ireland, we shall see much slaughter
and desolation ere this unholy strife ceases. yet I am
Convinced that the end will leave Ireland more
determined than ever to push on the road that
leads to Freedom; if it is so ordained that our
Cause goes down in defeat, then the World will say,
(when all the evidence has been weighed) — that Ireland's
latest act of protest against those who would carry
her into the British Empire was the most glorious of
all her glorious history.

Cathal Brugha is Dead! no man is here to replace
him. he was easily the greatest man of his day; what
a wonderful fight he made, with his 15 men against
an Army may God rest his soul and give his Comrades
the Courage of Cathal to fight till the fight is won.
Give my love to all I shall never forget you as
dear to me you whilst I live   Your friend
                                                    Harry Boland

4

'People who are very busy are never so busy that they cannot do something extra':

Collins and the Practice of Politics

Michael Collins, the 'man who won the war', is a very familiar figure. We know him, or at least we've come to think we do. In addition to fighting, however, the separatist movement had to convince the Irish nationalist public. In doing so they found it necessary to create structures with which to win and sustain support. Though political activity was a necessary corollary to the shooting, there were those among Collins's contemporaries who disdained it. They were certain of the superiority of their cause and had been raised to be contemptuous of Irish politicians to a degree that was almost as profound as their desire to expel 'the English'. For them, ideals were pure and fighting virtuous but politics was a compromised plane.

This was not Collins's view and it was not how he behaved. In the weeks leading up to the general election of 1918, as Sinn Féin finalised its slate of candidates, he wrote to Austin Stack, 'I'm having a quiet laugh "within myself" at the political eagerness of some of the "I'm only a fighting man" fraternity. I think I'm entitled to that.'[1] With little hesitation, he sought influence and achieved power across the separatist movement: in the Irish Volunteers and the Irish Republican Brotherhood certainly, but also in Sinn Féin and Dáil Éireann. If he could, he'd most likely have insisted on attending the executive meetings of Cumann na mBan. This has led some, including Batt O'Connor, who worked for him, to present Collins as a singular organising 'genius': 'the movement as a whole,' O'Connor exaggerated, 'was enormously strengthened by the various branches being co-ordinated and directed by a single powerful mind.'[2] On the other hand, there are those, then and now, who would prefer if politicians were as distinct from gunmen as oil from water. For them, Collins is a troubling and confounding figure. They iron out some of the complexity with the morality tale of the gunman who became a politician when the reality was that in 1922 he was still a 'fighting man' and in 1918 he was already a politician. In this chapter and the next we will examine Collins the working politician and attempt to tease out the beliefs that informed his positions.

As we have seen in Chapter 2, Collins was active in seeking to shape the political organisation that emerged after the Rising and, between the spring and autumn of 1917, he promoted political separatism with vigour, campaigning at by-elections and speaking to local Sinn Féin clubs. He was alert to the scepticism that this prompted among some of his republican friends. In the spring he had assured Thomas Ashe, 'for God's sake don't think that Master A[rthur] G[riffith] is going to turn us all into eighty two'ites'. By this he meant to convey that co-operation with Griffith would not involve the abandonment of republicanism and settling for a more restricted form of autonomy, such as that held by the Irish parliament between 1782 and 1800. In early October, as the first post-Rising Árd Fheis of the party loomed, he insisted on the complementary yet distinct value of the IRB and Sinn Féin. He wrote, 'There are many things to be said in favour of Sinn Féin many of whose ideals are but the re-weighed ideals of the IRB. But the things to be said in favour of Sinn Féin do not outweigh the uses of the IRB which is respected and acknowledged by many who will think twice about the prospects of Sinn Féin.'[3]

One of Collins's uses for the IRB was to ensure that republicans achieved maximum representation on the new Sinn Féin executive elected at that Árd Fheis. To this end, the IRB executive organised a ticket of its own 'republican' candidates (in opposition to a moderate ticket being promoted by Darrell Figgis). Using the tactic Collins had deployed for Plunkett's Mansion House convention six months earlier, the IRB tried to guarantee a high attendance of those who shared their views at the Árd Fheis, this time by taking advantage of the Irish Volunteer convention of the following day. As in April, so in October, Sinn Féin had a support and a momentum that Collins found difficult to manipulate. The executive that emerged was 'motley but representative,'[4] leading Bob Brennan to describe it as 'a defeat for Collins'.[5] The historian David Fitzpatrick has characterised Collins's own performance in coming joint last among the 24 candidates elected as a 'humiliation'.[6] Nonetheless, elected he was and other IRB men fared somewhat better, including Austin Stack, Piaras Béaslaí, Diarmuid Lynch, Fionán Lynch and Collins's increasingly close companion, Harry Boland.[7]

At the end of the year, the Royal Irish Constabulary (RIC) reported that a Sinn Féin executive had been elected for the South Cork constituency. Among its members was Collins's brother Seán. One of its first decisions was that Michael Collins would be the 'candidate for a Parliamentary vacancy, should it arise.' No such election was imminent and local executives had not been asked to identify parliamentary candidates but, evidently, Collins was leaving nothing to chance.[8] He was not a prominent participant during the three by-elections that Sinn Féin fought and lost in February and March 1918.[9] His name, however, cropped up in the press due to his role in the Sinn Féin front, the IRPDF, while the RIC in Longford expressed concern at the effects of his efforts in that county.[10] At Ballinamuck, on 17 February, and Legga, on 3 March, he spoke to Sinn Féin meetings attended by several hundred before drilling smaller bodies of Irish Volunteers: double-jobbing as usual.[11]

It was a speech made at the Legga meeting, when he 'incited' Volunteers to raid for arms, which saw Collins arrested outside the Bachelors Walk offices of the INA & VDF on 2 April. The local and national press covered his arrest, initial appearance at a Longford court, refusal to give bail, and consequent remand to Sligo prison (for a July trial).[12] However, the advent of the conscription crisis in the days that followed his arrest not only enhanced Sinn Féin's standing in the country, it altered Collins's path. He was not to spend the late spring and summer on remand in Sligo nor, after conviction, would he pass the autumn and winter of 1918 in Belfast prison with Austin Stack, Joe MacDonagh and several hundred others, killing time in between rioting. Instead, on 20 April, Collins was instructed to accept release on bail.[13] The Mansion House Committee had met two days earlier, and it had agreed that on Sunday 21 April, an anti-conscription pledge would be taken at mass meetings across the country. In this context, all those eligible for bail were considered more useful at liberty, while Collins was needed to help prepare the Volunteers for the resistance in the event of an actual attempt to conscript men. Then, in mid-May, when the authorities responded to the anti-conscription campaign by arresting, and interning without trial, most of the leadership of Sinn Féin, he and Boland avoided capture. So, again, instead of passing the long and crucial months till March 1919 in, for instance, Gloucester prison, talking about the European war with Griffith and Desmond FitzGerald and playing games of handball with Denis McCullough, Collins (and Boland and Michael Staines) became members of the party's Standing Committee.

This was vital because insofar as day-to-day executive control of the party existed, it rested with that body. In any case, prison did not suit Collins. When in Sligo he had complained that the 'inaction is the thing that horrifies me most' and that he suffered from 'the blackest despair' at 'the thought of the work I might be doing.'[14] This compulsion, the necessity, to be busy was noted by others. Years later, the artist Leo Whelan remembered how terrible a sitter Collins proved when he tried to paint him, beginning in late 1921. Collins 'could not manage a moment's quiet,' Whelan recalled. He was 'forever twisting and turning in the chair and liable to dash from the studio without warning to attend to urgent business.'[15] The American journalist Hayden Talbot, who interviewed him some time after that, described a man who 'sprang' and 'strode' and did everything else 'swiftly': 'physically, as well as mentally, Collins was the embodiment of speed.'[16]

During the second half of 1918, Collins and Boland shared a house on Richmond Road, Drumcondra. Beginning with Béaslaí, there has been a tendency in the literature on Collins's career to suggest that at this time they formed an

This head-and-shoulders portrait of Collins shows the young politician rather than the uniformed military man. *(National Library of Ireland)*

influential double-act, with Collins concentrating on the Irish Volunteers and Boland on Sinn Féin.[17] Boland, who was promoted to honorary secretary of the party, replacing the imprisoned Stack, was in a better position to affect Sinn Féin and he was, as Fitzpatrick has shown, a more regular attendee at Standing Committee meetings.[18] It is noticeable, though, that Collins became a consistent and vocal attendee during the crucial weeks leading up to, and in the immediate aftermath of, the December general election: between 14 November and 19 December 1918 he attended five of six meetings. Darrell Figgis's allegation that, even when elsewhere, it was Collins who pulled Sinn Féin's strings for the benefit of the IRB during these months is grounded in Figgis's resentment at his failure to achieve a nomination to contest the election.[19] Figgis was generally unpopular and the implication that Collins, with Boland, successfully manipulated the party's candidate selection is undermined by considerable evidence that the process was often chaotic and, consequently, difficult to control.[20]

It may not, however, be a coincidence that the 14 November meeting was Collins's first in quite a while. It confirmed Richard Mulcahy, a key ally in the IRB and Chief of Staff of the Irish Volunteers, as the candidate for the Clontarf constituency, controversially replacing Kathleen Clarke. Perhaps a more important consideration in his decision to attend on that particular day was a proposal, tabled by George Gavan Duffy, that Sinn Féin should cede labour ten seats at the election. The motion was 'withdrawn after discussion'. At four meetings, between 19 November and 4 December, the major issue confronting the Standing Committee was what to do in those northern constituencies where fielding a Sinn Féin candidate against an Irish Party candidate might see a nationalist majority split, allowing a unionist victory. Collins dominated the discussions on this matter and it was on his proposal that the Standing Committee agreed to a pragmatic compromise brokered by Cardinal Logue. They withdrew their candidates in four constituencies in return for reciprocal withdrawals by the Irish Party in four others.[21] Collins himself was elected to Cork South without a contest.

Writing of the later Treaty split, Frank O'Connor argued that Collins then paid 'the price for the zeal with which years before he had lopped off so many hydra-heads of moderation.'[22] Yet, as the metaphor implies, moderation kept coming back. In August 1918 Collins wrote to Stack about the need to 'unearth and destroy any attempt at compromise' within Sinn Féin and complained that the 'organisation lacks direction at the present moment.'[23] The appointment in

This is a ticket (number 366) to the crucial Sinn Féin Árd Fheis of October 1917. *(National Library of Ireland)*

Many of the accounts of those who knew Collins describe him as boyish or like a big boy, and you can see why in this group photograph, which was taken outside Sinn Féin's offices, *c.* 1918. He is fourth from the left in the second row. *(Military Archives of Ireland)*

GRANARD 4th Apl. 19 18.

I beg to state that Collins lodged at
44 Mountjoy St. Dublin.

A warrant was obtained as directed
and sent to the D.M.P for execution.
Collins was arrested in Dublin on 2nd
Inst. and on the following morning he
was conveyed to Longford, and brought
before Mr Jephson R.M. who took Depositions
and returned the accused for trial to the
next Assizes for the County. The accused,
who was very abusive and insulting,
refused to recognize the court or to give
bail, and was removed to Sligo gaol.
He admitted the truth of the Police
evidence.

Chas. Collins
251.
COUNTY OF Longford
....

County Inspector's Office,
Longford 5 April 1918.

Submitted. I beg to state that I
have informed C.M.A of result of
proceedings so far.

Reynell Sharp

County Inspector,
R. I. Constabulary.

The Inspr. General

Sein Féin Clubs and to get organised and that they could do this in their club Rooms and in their homes. He said that in future they would not be able to have many big public meetings like this, as the days would be getting short. He referred the Sein Féin victories in Roscommon, Longford, Clare & Kilkenny and said when the opportunity offered they would win every seat in Ireland, and then would have the Irish Parliamentary Party, who were so false to the country, banished for ever.

He said the deaths of the late Revd. Ths. Kinkman & Honefoy were a big loss to the Sein Féin movement in this county.

James Oneill C Councillor, addressed the meeting and told how long he was connected with the national movement, and that owing to the meaness treachery of the Irish Parliamentary Party, he became a Sein Féiner and asked that his resignation from the U.I.L. be read to the meeting, which was done by J. Walsh

Capt. Collins, addressed the meeting & spoke at first in Irish. He then referred to the death of the late Thos. Ashe, and said he was there with Ashe the day he made his last speech there, for which he was sent to Gaol and died. He said he would tell them how Ashe was convicted and sent to Gaol & died. He said the first of it was that he made a speech there, which was reported by two Police who were at the meeting. Those Police did (he said) swear the truth truth

These notes, of a Sinn Féin meeting at Ballinalee, County Longford, on 7 October 1917, taken by Sergeant Casey of the RIC, illustrate quite how aggressive Collins's language could be. It was typical that Collins was introduced at such meetings as 'Captain'. *(The National Archives, London)*

Collins's Continued

He said he was present and heard what ashe had said. He said one of the Police contradicted the other, with reference to a statement made by ashe, about the alleged conveyance of a despatch from the late Rebel leader - Pierce - to ashe, before Pierce's execution. He said the cause for which ash died for should be carried on until they had won, and he was sure from what he saw there, that they would carry on the fight. He said that although ash was dead that his spirit remained. He told them are to organise and join the Sein Fein movement, and that their case would be put before the Peace Conference when the war was over. He wound up his speech by quoting from some man who said long ago that "You will not get anything from the British Government unless you approach them with a bullocks tail in one hand and a Landlord's head in the other".

A

J. Finlon addressed the meeting and condemned the Irish Parliamentary Party and their methods, and asked those present to join the Sein Fein movement.

Paul Busach. Appeared in the uniform of the Irish volunteers He said I am glad you all admire my uniform. You should be all wearing the same uniform. Let you all organise and be one body.

Pat McCarthy proposed a vote of thanks to Father markey for presiding at the meeting

meeting

February 1919 of Collins, Boland and Mulcahy to the committee charged with drawing up the agenda for the forthcoming Sinn Féin Executive meeting, giving the IRB a slim three-to-two majority, indicates where the delicate balance of power then lay on the Standing Committee.[24]

In March, however, with the release of the 'German Plot' internees, came the return to freedom of several key moderates. Indeed, the alleged moderation of these men was one of the arguments made in favour of their release during the British cabinet's deliberations on the matter. In the days afterward the possible consequences were quickly revealed. Éamon de Valera had escaped from Lincoln prison, with Collins's help, some weeks before the general release but that general release facilitated his coming out of hiding, and a welcome-home demonstration in his honour was scheduled for Dublin on 26 March. It never happened. When the authorities banned the event, the moderates cancelled it. De Valera thought 'the present occasion is scarcely one in which we would be justified in risking the lives of the citizens' whereas Collins was among those dismayed by this victory for caution.[25] Believing they should have defied the authorities, he wrote, we 'are having our Clontarf today. It may not be as bad, but it is bad and very bad.'[26] This reference to O'Connell's decision not to defy the proclamation banning his proposed monster repeal meeting at Clontarf in October 1843 – a decision seen as fatal to that campaign – is, like his reference to 'eighty two'ites', an example of Collins's tendency to understand and explain contemporary events through historical analogy.

By then Collins had embarked upon what would be his key political role for the next twenty months: domestic fund-raiser-in-chief for Dáil Éireann. This became his official task when he was appointed Secretary for Finance in the new Dáil cabinet. He was nominated by de Valera on 1 April 1919 and confirmed by the Dáil the next day, but he had in effect taken on the job some weeks earlier while still officially holding the post of Minister for Home Affairs.[27] On 13 March it was he who proposed at the Sinn Féin Standing Committee that they begin advertising in the press for funds for the Dáil and, a week later, he replaced Eoin MacNeill, who was still nominally Secretary for Finance, on the relevant Sinn Féin subcommittee.[28] For Daithí O'Donoghue, an accountant employed at the new department, this was a welcome change. He had found MacNeill, during his brief tenure, 'very shy of going into finance matters'. Collins, in contrast, according to Michael Lynch, who also worked closely with him, was eager and quick to learn.[29]

Collins's experience in London may have been an advantage to him in this job: the skills he needed were also very similar to those he had honed during his days at the INA & VDF, although the sums of money were larger. Within days of Collins's appointment to Finance, de Valera, as President, informed the Dáil that they would issue 'Republican Bonds', with the aim of raising £250,000 in Ireland and the same figure in America. Once de Valera arrived in the USA in June, he would become the key agent of the American effort. In Ireland it would be Collins.

After several months of preparation, Collins launched the 'Dáil loan' at the end of the summer, offering for purchase in Ireland bonds ranging in value from £1 to £100. In August he wrote a detailed note, outlining how the purpose of the loan was to be explained by speakers across the country: it was his name and his youthful face that was most associated with the subsequent campaign.[30] Those newspapers that proved willing to carry an initial advertisement for the loan were shut down but the Department of Finance would go on to send out 500,000 copies of the bond prospectus, 2 million leaflets, and 50,000 letters 'to specific people'.[31] Most of these bore Collins's name. He also commissioned a six-minute promotional film, which was shown – willingly or otherwise – at local cinemas, and Collins was its star. Using as his desk 'the block upon which Robert Emmett was beheaded', he greeted the widows and mothers of 1916 martyrs (many of them close associates from the INA & VDF) and Sinn Féin TDs (including Griffith, FitzGerald and Robert Barton). He took their cheques and handed over their bonds with all the efficiency, energy and bonhomie of a particularly effective GAA official. The film projected a combination of revolutionary tradition and effective bureaucracy. It presented Collins and an ensemble cast.[32]

If this was his salesman's face, then his office personality mixed clarity of organisation – he insisted on 'weekly reports and accurate records' – with impatience and charm.[33] He dragooned, hurried, cajoled and bullied his office staff and four paid provincial coordinators as well as TDs and other local organisers to sell the bonds and deliver the money despite consistent harassment from the police.[34] The movement needed it, while his reputation now rested on it. He kept close tally and, like a parish priest enumerating the Easter dues from the altar, he sent out lists in an attempt to shame those constituencies that had not delivered.[35] As late as April 1920, he complained that 'this enterprise will certainly break my heart if any thing ever will. I never imagined there was so much cowardice, dishonesty, hedging, insincerity and meanness in the world, as my experience in

Rec⁰ 21/8/18 5848

a óigire a laoξ

I sent you up a copy of
an toglaċ on Friday last but as
I have been told today that you
asked for copy I suppose it hasn't
reached you or at any rate had
not reached you when your request
was made. Anyway heres another.
          Things have been happening
in S.F. circles that are somewhat
calculated ~~inclined~~ to upset one. Certain well-
know personages in the ~~~~ the movement
officers infact - have been hob-nobbing with
people like Jas O'Connor. The Ard
Coiṁairle - is tomorrow + I shall give
you an account of it. There are certain
resolutions being proposed with a
view to unearth + destroy any attempt
at compromise. The S.F organisation
lacks direction at the present moment.
The men who ought to be directing things

ms 5848/6

This letter from Collins, keeping Austin Stack, who was then in Belfast prison, up to date with developments inside Sinn Féin gives a strong sense of Collins's belief that vigilance was necessary if the moderates in the party were to be kept in line. James O'Connor, whom he believed some of his colleagues to be 'hob nobbing with', had been Attorney General for Ireland until April 1918, when he resigned due to the introduction of conscription. *(National Library of Ireland)* are too lax and spend little or no time at No 6. Unfortunately I cannot go into details — in any case will probably stop the negotiating. In the meantime I am giving you the tip that all is not as well as it might be. — As a result of an interview ∧ I am having tomorrow I may have something important to communicate about conscription.

Would like to have your opinion as to the advisibility of holding an I.V. convention this year? In the ordinary way it is due end of October. The conscription business may intervene but even if it doesn't I don't think we ought have such an assembly for a variety of reasons. Send a note of what you think.

I do hope you have got my letter sent on Friday by this time. That contained the paper. Best wishes to yourself Finn & the other friends. Tell Cady B that we've done something for C Gregory. Yours Mick 19/8/18

26. 3. 19.   17

A ċapa

Well your letter was I think
somewhat prophetic — we are
having our Clontarf today. It
may not be as bad but it is
bad and very bad. The chief
actor was very firm on the
withdrawal as indeed was
Ċiał — I used my influence the
other way and was in a
practical majority of all
minority of one. It may be
that all the arguments were sound
but it seems to me that they have
put up to us a challenge which
strikes at the fundamentals of our
policy and our attitude.
          However that may be, I am

In another letter to Stack, this time on 26 March 1919, Collins expressed his fears about the cancellation of a demonstration to mark de Valera's return from prison. *(National Library of Ireland)* connection with this work has revealed.'[36] In addition to those he criticised for 'not doing their share', there were those who proved both interested and talented. Seán Nolan in mid-Cork, Seán Wall in Limerick and Kevin O'Higgins in Laois were among the latter, while Hart has highlighted Collins's contrasting view of the performances of, and his consequent contrasting attitude toward, two Cork TDs: Terence MacSwiney, who proved a success, and Liam de Róiste, who did not.[37] Once he had collected the money, Collins was prepared to be ruthless in protecting it. As mentioned in Chapter 3, on 26 March 1920, the Squad took Alan Bell, who was employed by Dublin Castle to uncover and confiscate the funds, from a tram at Ballsbridge and shot him dead at the side of the road.[38]

Over the late summer of 1920 Collins closed the 'Dáil loan'. In Ireland, they had raised just over £370,000, roughly 50 per cent in excess of the initial target. The investment in Munster and Connacht in particular marked 'a strong endorsement of Dáil Éireann,' though as Michael Laffan has pointed out, 'not all of the contributions were voluntary.'[39] Taken together with the even larger sums coming in from America, this facilitated 'the immediate and rapid expansion of the Dáil's activities across a broad front.'[40] This was vital because, in addition to waging war on the existing state, it was Sinn Féin's strategy to build a structure that had the appearances, and if possible the realities, of an alternative state. To this end, in June 1919 the Dáil established a 'National Civil Service'. That month it consisted of seven full-time employees, but this would grow to around 300, audited and paid for by the Department of Finance.[41] The growth of Dáil Éireann's infrastructure was therefore a triumph for Collins, cementing his growing political as well as military influence. Indeed, his place in the pecking order became concrete when Griffith was arrested toward the end of November 1920. Then, it was Collins who, on 1 December, succeeded to Griffith's role of deputising for the absent de Valera as President of Dáil Éireann: de Valera returned shortly afterward, relieving him of the task.[42]

In Frank O'Connor's portrait of Collins in the period between the signing of the Treaty and the outbreak of the Civil War we find an erratic man, following, without consultation and in rapid succession, his own contradictory instincts. He was, in short, a nightmare for his colleagues.[43] This tendency may have reached new levels under the stresses of the spring of 1922, but Hart points out that by the second half of 1920 he had already become the bane of many of his cabinet colleagues. He was, Hart wrote pithily, 'a good boss and a fine comrade, but he could be a truly awful colleague.' He then went on to describe a man who

PROCLAMATION!

DAIL EIREANN LOAN.

YOU CAN RECOVER IRELAND FOR THE IRISH

YOU CAN REPEOPLE THE LAND

YOU CAN HARNESS THE RIVERS

YOU CAN PUT HER FLAG ON EVERY SEA

YOU CAN PLANT THE HILLSIDES AND THE WASTES

YOU CAN SET THE LOOMS SPINNING.

YOU CAN SET THE HAMMER RINGING ON THE ANVIL

YOU CAN ABOLISH THE SLUMS

YOU CAN SEND HER SHIPS TO EVERY PORT

YOU CAN GARNER THE HARVEST OF THE SEAS

YOU CAN DRAIN THE BOGS

YOU CAN SAVE THE BOYS AND GIRLS FOR IRELAND

INTERNAL LOAN OF 1919.

DAIL EIREANN LOAN.

ISSUE OF

250,000 5% REGISTERED CERTIFICATES

THE PROCEEDS OF THIS LOAN WILL BE USED FOR PROPAGATING THE IRISH CASE ALL OVER THE WORLD, FOR ESTABLISHING IN FOREIGN COUNTRIES CONSULAR SERVICES, TO PROMOTE IRISH TRADE AND COMMERCE, FOR DEVELOPING AND ENCOURAGING IRISH SEA FISHERIES, FOR DEVELOPING AND ENCOURAGING THE REAFFORESTATION OF THE COUNTRY, FOR DEVELOPING AND ENCOURAGING IRISH INDUSTRIAL EFFORT, FOR ESTABLISHING A NATIONAL CIVIL SERVICE, FOR ESTABLISHING NATIONAL ARBITRATION COURTS, FOR THE ESTABLISHMENT OF A LAND MORTGAGE BANK WITH A VIEW TO THE REOCCUPANCY OF UNTENANTED LANDS, AND GENERALLY FOR NATIONAL PURPOSES AS DIRECTED BY DAIL EIREANN.

PROSPECTUS.   (FOR HOME SUBSCRIPTION.)

ISSUE OF

250,000 5% REGISTERED CERTIFICATES

BEARING INTEREST FROM THE DATE WHEN FULLY PAID, AT THE RATE OF 5 PER CENT. PER ANNUM, PAYABLE HALF-YEARLY ON THE 1st JANUARY AND THE 1st JULY, SUBJECT TO THE RESERVATIONS CONTAINED IN THIS PROSPECTUS.

1.—THE MINISTRY OF DAIL EIREANN IS AUTHORISED BY AN DAIL TO ISSUE THE ABOVE CERTIFICATES TO THE PUBLIC FOR SUBSCRIPTION, AND THE MINISTER OF FINANCE WILL RECEIVE APPLICATIONS UNTIL FURTHER NOTICE.

2.—AFTER THE WITHDRAWAL OF THE ENGLISH MILITARY FORCES THIS LOAN BECOMES THE FIRST CHARGE ON THE REVENUES OF THE IRISH REPUBLIC.

3.—THE CERTIFICATES WILL BE ISSUED IN DENOMINATIONS OF £1, £5, £10, £20, £50, AND £100, AND WILL BEAR INTEREST AT THE RATE OF £5 PER CENT. PER ANNUM. THE FIRST DIVIDEND WILL CONSIST OF INTEREST CALCULATED FROM THE DATE UPON WHICH THE FINAL PAYMENT IS MADE, BUT WILL NOT BE PAYABLE UNTIL A DATE SIX MONTHS AFTER THE IRISH REPUBLIC HAS RECEIVED INTERNATIONAL RECOGNITION, AND THE ENGLISH HAVE EVACUATED IRELAND. THENCEFORWARD, PAYMENT WILL BE MADE HALF-YEARLY, ON THE 1st JANUARY AND 1st JULY.

4.—THE PRICE OF THIS ISSUE IS £100 PER CENT., PAYABLE AS FOLLOWS:—
50 PER CENT. ON APPLICATION.
25 PER CENT. ON 1st DECEMBER, 1919.
25 PER CENT. ON 1st FEBRUARY, 1920.

5.—APPLICATIONS FOR CERTIFICATES, TOGETHER WITH THE AMOUNT PAYABLE ON APPLICATION, MAY BE LODGED ON OR AFTER THE 1st AUGUST, 1919, WITH THE MINISTER OF FINANCE, FOR DEPOSIT WITH THE TRUSTEES.

6.—EVERY APPLICANT WILL BE SUPPLIED AT THE TIME OF PAYMENT WITH A RECEIPT IN WHICH THE AMOUNT OF THE PURCHASE AND THE AMOUNT PAID UPON APPLICATION WILL BE RECORDED. THE REGISTERED CERTIFICATES WILL, WHEN PREPARED, BE ISSUED IN EXCHANGE FOR THIS RECEIPT.

7.—PRINTED FORMS OF APPLICATION AND COPIES OF THIS PROSPECTUS MAY BE OBTAINED FROM THE MINISTER OF FINANCE, DAIL EIREANN; THE HONORARY TREASURERS OF SINN FEIN, AND THE SECRETARY OF ANY SINN FEIN CLUB IN IRELAND.

EAMONN DE VALERA, President.
MICHEAL O COILEAIN, Minister of Finance.

You can restore Ireland's Health, her Strength, her Beauty and her Wealth

SUBSCRIBE TO-DAY TO DAIL EIREANN LOAN.
Or hand it to your local Member of the Dail, or to his representative in your Parish.

This advertisement laid out not only the details of the Dáil Loan, but made a series of extravagant claims for its purposes. *(National Library of Ireland)*

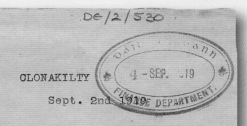

DE/2/530

CLONAKILTY

4 - SEP. 19

Sept. 2nd 1919

A Miceal a Cara,-

I enclose cheque and cash
to the value of £53-10-0, being the amount
subscribed to the Loan at the Dunmanway
meeting, you will also find enclosed the
forms signed.

Miceal O'Coilean	£25-0-0	1st instalment (50%)	
Cors. Hallissey	10-0-0	fully paid up	
J. M. Collins	5-0-0	1st instalment (50%)	
Mrs Collins	5-0-0	do	do
seven children)			
£1= each)	3-10-0	do	do
D. O'Connell	5-0- 0	do.	do
	£53-10-0		

Kindly acknowledge receipt.   I hope you
are in good form after your rather hurried trip
down this way.

Yours sincerely

Joe Lynn

P.S.

Have you sent the copies of the prospectus
to the Executive? There are quite a number of people
awaiting copies. Joe.

Collins himself was at the top of the list when the early Clonakilty subscriptions to the Dáil Loan arrived on his desk. *(National Archives of Ireland)*

This photograph, from the Dáil Éireann file on the loan, projects the image of Collins the dynamic administrator. *(National Archives of Ireland)*

Memo to L.

18th June, 1920.

1.   I acknowledge receipt of no.302, 302a, 302c (note there is no 302b, but the confidential memo is numbered 303b)

2.   CONSULAR PAYMENTS: Noted with thanks.

3.   FOREIGN ACCOUNT: I assume there is no necessity for sending you a Draft on this account yet. I shall be glad to know from you the exact position as you suggest.

4.   LITERATURE: Thanks for note from D.H.

5.   SEPARATE MEMO: With reference to your Confidential Memo, first, let me thank you for sending it. I may say that almost in every regard it bears out the judgment I had formed. Some points arise which I will deal with when I get a moment to spare. Particularly, is the point of having somebody here to attend to foreign matters of importance. We are carrying an absolute dead weight, and when the suggestion that you have made was made at this end, there was an inclination to think that people were being turned down. You know what I mean. To me it is nothing short of being a disaster. For instance, I get many matters through you for other Departments. I tell you I receive them, and hand them over, and there, as a rule, the matters ends. Important communications are left unanswered. Important actions are delayed, with all the consequent disadvantages and dangers.

In this memo to Art O'Brien in June 1920, Collins makes clear his frustration at the ineffectiveness of the Department of Foreign Affairs under Count Plunkett. *(National Library of Ireland)* was 'consistently interfering and insulting, dismissive, critical and undermining of anyone who didn't do what he wanted, wouldn't let him do what he wanted, or didn't meet his standards.'[44]

There is no doubt that regularly Collins failed to make any allowance for, or bite his tongue in the matter of, the failings of his colleagues, perceived and real. FitzGerald, W.T. Cosgrave, Stack and Joe MacDonagh endured critiques that may have been more robust than wise.[45] For example, FitzGerald's propaganda department was, Collins complained to Art O'Brien, 'heart-scalding' in its 'careless-ness'. They had felt the lash of his pen on several occasions but he was now of the view that this was 'a waste of time' as 'These people cannot be taught anything.'[46] On the other hand, certain of his own competence, he rejected any interference with his own autonomy to act. None of his colleagues dared to interfere with how he ran Finance and his famous differences with his cabinet colleague Cathal Brugha were exacerbated by his rejection of Brugha's attempts, as Minister for Defence, to direct Collins's actions in his roles as Director of Purchases and Director of Intelligence at Irish Volunteer HQ. John Regan has written of Brugha being forced to 'suffer the daily humiliation of holding an emasculated portfolio as a sinecure while real power remained outside his influence in GHQ and by inference with the IRB and Collins.'[47] These are hardly unusual characteristics in a driven successful person, or one under profound stress (constantly overworked and never quite safe), but they are not attractive. More dangerously, if a crisis hits, the accumulated resentments and petty enmities created can begin to look like political capital needlessly squandered.

Writing to Art O'Brien of the Department of Foreign Affairs, Collins stated that they were 'carrying an absolute dead weight'.[48] Count Plunkett was, in reality, an absentee minister who failed to develop a department.[49] Instead, the various tasks that would have fallen to a functioning department were picked up by individuals or were simply neglected. In this context, it is surprising how rarely biographers and historians have pointed out that, from early 1920, Collins managed the Dáil's relationship with its representative in London, O'Brien, and with the organisation O'Brien headed up, the Irish Self-Determination League. Collins's correspondence with O'Brien and the London office is perhaps the largest single body of correspondence in the Dáil Éireann files. It covers everything from the actions taken to support hundreds of prisoners, to fostering allies from other British colonies, to exchanging intelligence about potentially important or useful visitors coming to Ireland via London, to supplying questions that sympathetic

MPs might ask in parliament, to assessing the evolving attitudes of the British elites. Maintaining this critical work, which demanded daily attention, consumed a considerable proportion of Collins's energies, particularly during crises.[50] That he did it in addition to his various other functions is remarkable, although the attitude that lay behind his willingness and capacity to do so is hinted at in his comment to Terence MacSwiney that 'it is my experience that people who are very busy are never so busy that they cannot do something extra.'[51] It did, however, create tension when Bob Brennan was appointed under-secretary for Foreign Affairs in February 1921 with the twin purposes of making that department more effective and bringing it under de Valera's control.[52] Brennan, it is clear, became very irritated when O'Brien ignored his correspondence and continued to regard Collins as the appropriate line of communication with Dublin.[53]

It was during the final year of his life, however, that Collins faced the greatest political tests of his short career. By the summer of 1921 he had come to favour a truce and negotiations. Despite an acute awareness of the difficulties in maintaining the conflict (sometimes exaggerated later when defending the Treaty) he was vigilant in insisting that a truce should not be concluded in circumstances that indicated desperation, even weakness, on the part of Dáil Éireann. He believed that 'rushing in' had 'torpedoed' previous truce negotiations.[54] His letters to de Valera in the immediate aftermath of the coming into force of the truce, on 11 July, were informed by an interest in the progress of initial talks about talks but perhaps even more by his concern that the truce should not be understood as a 'surrender' on the IRA's part, that their people should remain vigilant, and that they should prepare for a potential breakdown of the talks.[55]

There has been a certain amount of spurious controversy about Collins's presence on the eventual negotiating team. Collins was a very reluctant plenipotentiary. According to Frank O'Connor, all his friends agreed that the prospect 'produced an acute sense of misery and exasperation'.[56] This led Collins to argue that he should remain at home so that, in his absence, the delegation could present him to the British as a gun-toting bogeyman they would find difficult to placate without a generous deal.[57] The arguments in favour of his going were, nevertheless, overwhelming. He was in the best position to represent militarists, and in particular the IRB faction, at the negotiations. If there was a settlement, he was the individual most likely to be willing and able to convince these groups to accept it. More than that, through four years of striving he had made himself a political figure of substance and had become, after de Valera and maybe Griffith, the most significant and most able operator in cabinet.[58] Indeed, during the negotiation process, he demonstrated practical political skills of a high order by carefully preparing the IRB for the possibility of a settlement on more or less the terms agreed and by giving them the impression that they were being consulted throughout the process.[59]

Becoming dogmatic about our understanding of what influenced or motivated the key actors as they made their choices during those weeks of negotiations and during the months that followed is foolish. That Robert Barton, one of Collins's fellow plenipotentiaries, was taken aback at Collins's announcement that he would sign during the final hours of debate and negotiation on 5 December and that Collins, in turn, was shocked that de Valera rejected that Treaty stands as a warning against any certainty on our part at this remove.

All the accounts of the negotiations agree that Griffith and Collins led the five-man Irish delegation. In doing so they faced considerable disadvantages. Their team was inexperienced and, arguably, it was weak: Lloyd George quickly decided that Griffith and Collins were the only negotiators of substance on it and Churchill's later account confirms that this was a view shared by others on the British side.[60] Crucially, from the beginning, the Irish team, and those at home, were divided as to what would constitute success. This ensured that their preparations for, and conduct of, the talks were disjointed, even incoherent. Collins's tendency to hold himself apart from his colleagues – to the extent of living separately while in London – probably exacerbated these problems but the root cause was the ideological differences between them.[61] Their opponents, on the other hand, were more powerful, were more experienced and, though somewhat divided as to the ideal outcome, had a clearer sense of a shared bottom line.

During the negotiations, Erskine Childers, who was one of the secretaries to the negotiating team, was, on occasion, critical of Collins's knowledge and grasp of particular issues: 'even MC showed complete ignorance of the defence position,' he wrote in his diary on 21 November.[62] On the other hand, in his history of the negotiations Frank Pakenham described Collins's 'assimilative intellect' as an asset. Generally, he seems to have deployed to good effect his grasp of detail during plenary sessions, at subcommittees and when assessing written proposals.[63] His notes on the draft Treaty proposal as it stood on the evening of 1 December illustrate this capacity for close reading. During the final hours of negotiations, he would achieve real improvements to the final text of the Treaty, amendments grounded in these notes. Despite these real successes, neither he nor his colleagues appreciated the dangers in the ambiguous drafting of clause 12 as it related to what would be called the Boundary Commission.[64]

If he could be forensic, he was also prepared, if he thought it useful, to be belligerent and robust, playing the blunt soldier or the simple countryman seeking a straightforward answer. He particularly enjoyed deploying both his knowledge and his reputation in the occasional games of allegation and counter-allegation, bluff and counter-bluff, which arose over reported breaches of the truce. Mark Sturgis, a senior official at Dublin Castle who met him to discuss the maintenance of the truce, recorded the aspects of Collins's personality that he seemed to project when faced by British politicians and elite civil servants. Or, at least, Sturgis recorded the aspects they tended to see: 'He is just the big young pleasant prosperous self-satisfied cattle dealer in a big way of business … But he is undoubtedly quick to understand and I should imagine is twice the man if he is up against you … Strong, brave and quite ruthless.'[65] He provided them with someone they thought they recognised, someone they believed they could deal with, yet someone they would be foolish to take for granted. In this regard it seems likely that there was considerable overlap between what Collins wanted them to see and what they saw.

When it came to the final hours of the talks he was, they knew, the person they needed to convince. It may be that Collins, regarding himself in the same light, tried to position himself both to ensure that there was a deal and to maximise the advantage to be extracted. On 4 December the delegation returned to London after a heated cabinet meeting in Dublin. That meeting confirmed that they had the power to sign a deal but instructed them to return to the Dáil cabinet before doing so. It also faced them with the futile task of continuing to pursue de Valera's idea of external association, rejecting dominion status as described in the draft Treaty the negotiators had brought from London. Dominion status would see the new Irish state exist inside the Empire while having the status and levels of autonomy of Canada, South Africa, New Zealand and Australia. External association would see the state exist outside the Empire but retaining an association with it in areas of common concern. Furthermore, they were to attempt to ensure that if a breakdown came – and the question was surely how quickly rather than whether a breakdown would come if they adhered to external association – that it should appear to happen on the issue of Ulster.[66] A very reluctant Griffith, who would have been content to sign a deal on something close to the terms on offer, tried to carry through the strategy – if it could be called a strategy by then – at a meeting with the British negotiators on the afternoon of 4 December. Robert Barton, Eamonn Duggan and George Gavan Duffy were with him. In contrast, Collins refused to attend this crucial, potentially final meeting: he was apparently unwilling to present a position he knew would be rejected. Hart has described this action as 'bizarre', 'childish', and 'irresponsible', and speculated that Collins, anticipating a complete breakdown, was 'trying to avoid the blame for failure', 'trying to salvage his political reputation.'[67]

It seems just as plausible, however, that Collins was thinking not about the choreography of failing to make a deal but rather the choreography of making a deal. If he expected that the meeting of 4 December would end without agreement, it seems plausible that he gambled that in staying away he offered Lloyd George another chance, after this apparent final collapse. The negotiations did break down on 4 December and Lloyd George did see the opportunity that Collins had afforded him. Following contacts between Griffith and the secretary to the British delegation, Tom Jones, Lloyd George and Collins met in private on the morning of 5 December.[68] If the British realised that Collins's action in staying away had signalled that he did not want the negotiations to fail, then that knowledge, as Joseph Curran argues, probably limited the extent to which Collins could extract further concessions. Yet it might also tempt them into giving just that little bit more to secure Collins for an agreement.[69] On the morning of 5 December both Lloyd George and Collins held out to the other the prospect of sufficient flexibility to suggest that another meeting of the delegations might be worthwhile that afternoon. As Curran has noted, Lloyd George left thinking that Collins might accept a deal based on dominion status and Collins thought he would be able to gain important concessions on the oath, trade and defence.[70]

There were various twists and turns during the negotiations that followed that afternoon and evening but if one concentrates on the text, the upshot was that dominion status remained in place while the oath was amended, full fiscal autonomy was granted to the new state, the prospect of the Irish developing a navy was opened up, the word 'local' was removed from the clause describing the Irish military, and the term 'Governor-General' was removed from the clause describing the Crown's representative in the Irish Free State. At that point Lloyd George's dramatic threat of 'immediate and terrible war' had the effect of ensuring that the plenipotentiaries signed. In doing so they created a Treaty, rather than returning to Dublin with another unsigned draft. Some historians have affected bafflement that the Irish delegation did not call Lloyd George's bluff and insist that they needed time to consult with Dublin. It seems possible, however, that Collins and Griffith could see just as well as Lloyd George, and feared just as much as he, that back in Dublin an unsigned draft would unravel. A signed agreement, on the other hand, might not.

Collins spent the last eight months of his life securing and defending the gains he believed that Treaty represented even as the Sinn Féin movement sundered around him. At first, he did this during the high-level political debates that followed the signing. Then, following the Dáil's approval of the Treaty on 7 January 1922, he took up the position of Chairman of the Provisional Government, the pro-Treaty executive which the British recognised and dealt with as the transition to independence occurred. In that post, during several months of manoeuvrings, he sought to avoid, and yet prepared the pro-Treaty party to win, a military conflict with their opponents. Finally, he led the fight for the Treaty during the two months of the internecine war that he survived. From early July he did this as Commander-in-Chief of a new army. He did not claim that it was the ideal but he argued that the Treaty was the best that could be achieved and that it was pregnant with opportunity.

The thinking that informed this, the case he made, the relationship of his policy on Northern Ireland to that case, and the power he accrued during this period are all discussed in Chapter 5. At this juncture, however, it is worth reflecting a little further on his effectiveness as a politician during that period. Collins had already proved that he could mix it with the best that the revolutionary movement had to offer in the back-room politics of the committee meeting, the office, the Brotherhood, or the would-be government department. Defending the Treaty, however, involved embracing the public theatre of politics in a way that he had not till then. Of his speech during the Treaty debates Frank O'Connor wrote that it was 'good and manly'. Peter Hart has described it as 'easily the best speech of Collins's life, and one of the great statements of political rationality in Irish history.' At the time, Tim Healy wrote that it was 'worthy of a lawyer as well as a politician. It was big enough for a trained statesman. I was surprised by its precision and detail, and rhetoric.'[71] In contrast, having just re-read the Treaty debates in 1963, Lord Beaverbrook was moved to remark in a letter to Cosgrave:

This photograph of Collins, with Arthur Griffith and George Gavan Duffy, was taken in London during the Treaty negotiations in 1921. *(Military Archives of Ireland)*

MR. MICHAEL COLLINS' MINUTE OF HIS INTERVIEW WITH MR. LLOYD GEORGE AT 10, DOWNING STREET AT 9.30 a.m MONDAY, DECEMBER 5th., 1921

----oOo----

Arising out of Mr. Jones' conversation with Mr. Griffith, the latter indicated to me last night that Mr. Lloyd George desired to see me.   This conversation took place subsequent to the official conference held at 10, Downing Street on Sunday evening at 5 p.m.   I did not attend this conference for the reason that I had, in my own estimation, argued fully all points.   This morning Mr. Griffith came to me again and suggested in his official capacity as Chairman of the Delegation that I should have the meeting with Mr. Lloyd George as so much depended on the Delegation at this vital time.   Mr. Jones had suggested the interview for 9.15, but as I had not made up my mind until after speaking to Mr. Griffith this morning I did not see Mr. Lloyd George until 9.30 as stated above.

Acting on the general resumé of points of difference as sketched by me at the Cabinet Meeting on Saturday, 3rd instant, I had my points set out as follows :-

(1) The essential unity of Ireland.   Suggestion that we
      should press for a letter from Craig indicating
      either :

        (a) Acceptance of Conditions, and naming those
             Conditions.

        (b) Rejection.

(2) Oath of Allegiance.   Clause 4 of British Document.

(3) Defence. Clause 6 and Annex A. of British Document
      (29a) - date 1st December.

(4) Trade. Clauses 9 and 10 of ditto.

Mr. Lloyd George opened the conversation indicating that he was having a meeting of his Cabinet at 12 o'clock and was

(1)

The first page of Collins's own minute of his crucial meeting with Lloyd George on the morning of 5 December 1921. *(National Archives of Ireland)*

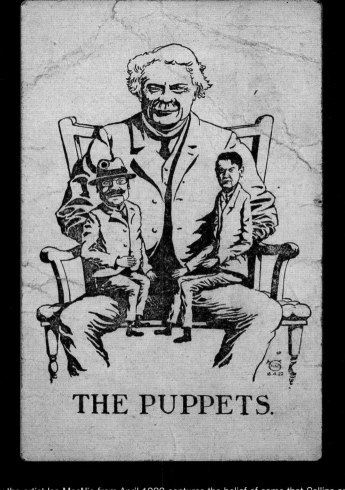

THE PUPPETS.

This cartoon by the artist Isa MacNie from April 1922 captures the belief of some that Collins and Griffith had been, and continued to be, manipulated by the wily puppetmaster Lloyd George. *(National Museum of Ireland)*

This photograph by Joseph Cashman shows Collins leaving Dublin Castle with Kevin O'Higgins and W.T. Cosgrave on the day of its surrender. *(National Library of Ireland)*

'What a confused speaker was Michael Collins. Reading him now, it is almost impossible to understand him. And yet he seemed to me quite a good talker.'[72] He would go on to be a very effective defender of the Treaty in print and on the stump. There was, nonetheless, very little that was statesmanlike in his response to the anti-Treatyites' decision to walk out of the Dáil following their defeat: 'Deserters all! We will now call on the Irish people to rally to us. Deserters all!' and 'Foreigners – Americans – English,' he shouted at them.[73]

In the months between that Dáil vote, in January 1922, and the beginning of the Civil War at the end of June, the Collins who strived to attract people to him seemed regularly at war with the Collins who lashed out at those who opposed him. Given the level of invective that was directed at him, and given his personality, it would be a surprise if he did not return some of the attacks with interest. Despite the strain, his relationship with Harry Boland survived to within days of the end and proved a key channel between those who sought compromise on both sides.[74] All too often, though, even in comparatively minor matters, he seemed almost overcome by not only the constant demands of others but by a profound sense of their ingratitude and disloyalty.

In early February 1922 Tim Downey, the uncle of Pat Harte, an IRA member who had become insane while in prison in England, wrote to Collins reminding him of the family's desire that Pat be transferred to an Irish hospital and enquiring if 'anything had been done about the matter yet?' Collins, who had been attentive to this case since September 1920, to the extent of personally visiting Harte at Broadmoor asylum during the Treaty negotiations, informed Downey that Harte had just been moved to the Richmond Hospital in Dublin before sniping that, given his personal efforts, 'it strikes me as being rather unfair to suggest that a genuine effort has not been made to give Pat Harte a chance of recovery.'[75] When, at the end of March 1922, he achieved the release of fourteen prisoners held in England for offences committed during the truce, Collins wrote to Liam McCarthy in London. He took the opportunity to mark the success but also to lash out at his old friend Art O'Brien. O'Brien, who opposed the Treaty, had used the prisoners' ongoing detention as a stick with which to beat Collins and now Collins complained that O'Brien had known perfectly well that he was doing his 'utmost in season and out of season' on the matter. 'Fair criticism,' he wrote, 'one does not mind, but when people deliberately say the very opposite to what is the truth, one cannot give them credit for the very highest of motives.'[76]

In late April and May Collins engaged in an exchange of tetchy letters with Seán T. O'Kelly. Collins had become aware of third-hand rumours from Rome, where O'Kelly had represented Dáil Éireann, that the latter was telling stories about Collins that Collins regarded as false. The most wounding of these was that Collins was 'a drunkard and spent the time during the Truce boozing with Cope' and 'that Collins himself told Sean T. O'Kelly after signing the Treaty that he could have got Document no.2 [external association] if he liked.' Collins concluded his first letter by stating that 'I don't believe you said those things, and that, notwithstanding the political differences there is, as you said yourself on one occasion, "no coolness."' Nonetheless, he challenged O'Kelly to 'send to me an answer within the next few days.' In ending the correspondence, a fortnight later, Collins described himself as 'thoroughly dissatisfied' and now convinced that if O'Kelly had not said exactly the words reported to Collins then those words 'did convey your meaning.'[77]

The name-calling, the questioning of others' motives and character, the creeping sense of persecution went hand in hand with ongoing efforts at conciliation or, at least, efforts to avoid immediate military conflict. It was the fact that Collins sometimes took these initiatives unilaterally, as much as the efforts themselves, that on occasion irritated both his pro-Treaty colleagues and the British, ever alert to a retreat from the deal. Despite being urged by senior colleagues, who were sure they would win a pro-Treaty mandate, he did not call a quick election. Indeed, in late February he agreed with de Valera that one would not take place for three months.[78] In March, he and Mulcahy rejected the advice of those who urged them to act against republicans as they tried to take effective control of Limerick city.[79] On 17 May he agreed a pact with de Valera (brokered by Boland) to run a joint pro- and anti-Treaty Sinn Féin panel at the upcoming election. Both sides, they decided, would be represented on that panel 'in the same proportion as they were represented in the existing Dáil.'[80] This apparently anti-democratic initiative not only annoyed colleagues in the Provisional Government, particularly Griffith, it prompted a summons to London from Churchill.[81] All the while, Collins encouraged the committee appointed to draft a constitution that they should, to the greatest extent possible, use the language of republicanism, ignoring the Treaty when this proved problematic. In response, the committee provided Collins with two options, and he forwarded to London a version that reflected his original instructions. It was designed both to attract the allegiance of moderate republicans and to mitigate, if not erase, their problems with the Treaty. It may or may not have succeeded in these aims but it was never published.[82] When it reached Lloyd George in late May, he dismissed it as 'a complete evasion of the Treaty and a setting up of a republic with a thin veneer,' insisting that it be revised to conform to the terms of the December agreement.[83]

Several purposes lay behind this pattern of behaviour. There was a genuine desire to preserve unity and reconcile as many as possible to the settlement. There was a real reluctance to enter conflict with his old colleagues: Tom Garvin has characterised this as a 'sentimental sneaking regard' for the 'hard men'.[84] More empathetically, David Fitzpatrick has written of Collins's and Boland's instinct 'to rely upon fraternal goodwill to transcend divisions which, in public politics, seemed to signify irreconcilable differences in principle.'[85] There was calculation. He and Mulcahy were delaying confrontation until they had built the strength to win a military contest, while the pact with de Valera ensured that the republicans allowed an election to proceed, only to see Collins renounce the agreement at the last moment, when it was too late for them to do anything about it. When the British scuppered his plans for a 'republican' constitution, he waited until the morning of the election, 16 June, to publish the final, amended document so as to minimise any negative effects for the pro-Treaty position.[86]

Just as Collins attempted to mete out just enough violence to achieve the ends he desired, so too his actions as a politician give ample evidence of a man constantly calculating. His rhetoric could be aggressive. He was inclined to take criticism personally. He resorted to *ad hominem* attacks more frequently than was either admirable or expedient. Too often, he proved not to be a team player. He had little trust in others' capacities to do a job well. In part because of this, and no doubt in part from ambition, he took on responsibility for too much. He was a little too fond of the plot and the stroke. Yet, behind this he was both strategic and tactical in his thinking. He was discerning and decisive, identifying what he believed could and should be done, while recognising, acquiring and deploying the means to do it. Confidants testified that his decisions sometimes came with ostentatious expressions of angst and melodramatic hand-wringing, but his actions suggest that at the same time he measured out advantage and disadvantage, distinguished the possible from the impossible, and discriminated between the unpleasant and the unwise. He was a formidable politician.

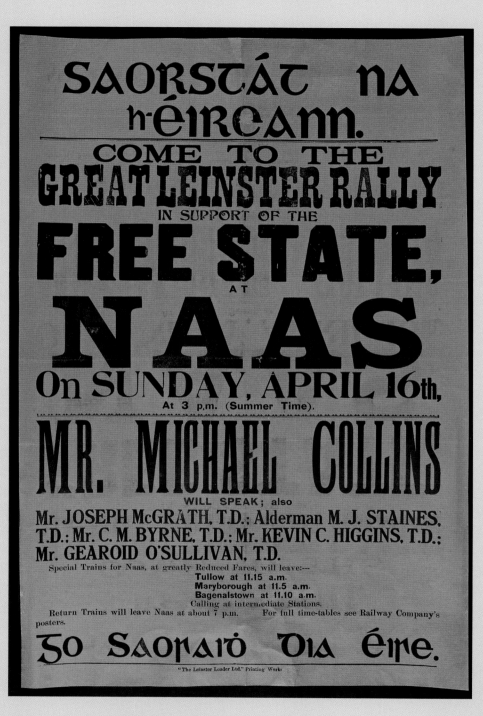

In the early months of 1921 Collins became the most important public advocate for the Treaty, addressing a series of meetings across the country. *(National Library of Ireland)*

15, The Crescent, Clontarf,
Dublin.

30th May, 1922.

Mr. J. McGarrity,
3714 Chestnut Street,
Philadelphia.

My dear Joe,

I delayed writing until I had something to report to
you which would give you pleasure. You will have read of the
"COLLINS DE VALERA PACT" and all I can say is this – that I
worked very hard to secure unity and am quite happy with the
present situation.

The whole game is now in the hands of Mr. Collins. We
shall see how he will act. I, for one, would like to think that
he will direct all his actions towards the Republic. I cannot
say that I doubt him; yet I am uneasy as to his intentions. Our
only safeguard is the Army and I am happy, indeed, to report that
unity has been secured and in so far as it was possible to safeguard the Republic, we have succeeded.

As a result of the union I will be in a position to secure
the return of the money given to the I.R.A. I will have it lodged
in the names of the two members of the S.C. pending a Convention,
after which I will hand it over to the new S.C. I am very proud
of the fact that the Clan money saved the situation and am sorry
that there should have been any uneasiness amongst the members
of the Executive as to my disposal of the money. The money was
raised for the Republic and I felt bound to see to it that the
money was not used to subvert the Republic. Now, that the situation has become clarified we will have our adjourned Convention
and it might be well for you to make another trip as soon as you
possibly can.

I want you to send me a copy of my cable to Luke as it
reached him – the cable in which I asked for the discretionary
power with the money.

I notice that the "Irish Press" has ceased to exist. I
do hope you have recovered some of your losses. One of the
tragedies of this movement is that men who have given their all
to Ireland see their labours and sacrifices gone to enrich many
people who gave nothing and cared less for Ireland's Freedom.

HS 17,424/2/4 (1)

As this letter from Harry Boland to Joe McGarrity demonstrates, as late as the 30 May 1922 there were those
on the republican side who hoped that Collins could rescue the situation using the new constitution. Boland did
not know that Lloyd George had already rejected Collins's preferred draft as 'a complete evasion of the Treaty
and a setting up of a republic with a thin veneer'. *(National Library of Ireland)*

No. 9.

YOU CAN GET TO THE REPUBLIC
—FOR ALL IRELAND—

Through the safe and sure road of the Treaty

or

YOU CAN TRY ANOTHER ROUND

Through the
Alphabet of Miseries

Auxiliaries	Jails	Spies
Black and Tans.	Knoutings	Threats
Commandeerings	Licence	Usurpation
Deaths.	Murders	Vandalism
Executions	Nerve Strain	Wails
Ferocities	Oppression	
Gallows	Persecution	X The final horrors
Harassings	Questionings	Y which words
Internments	Raids	Z cannot describe.

to get

(perhaps)

DOCUMENT No. 2
(or others in later series)

Which way should a
Sane Man or Woman Go ?

NATIONAL
EXTERMINATION

Support the Treaty Candidates.

This Pro-Treaty poster articulates their claims as to the potential of the deal and the dangers of rejecting it.
(National Library of Ireland)

5

'I'm on the side of those who do things, not on the side of those who say things':

What Collins Believed

In the years since his death, Michael Collins has been recruited to countless causes. There have been those who have claimed to know what his attitude would have been in all manner of situations, including – during recent financial crisis – to the arrival of the troika and to the question of burning bondholders.[1] All too often the invited speaker at the annual commemoration at Béal na mBláth has been overcome by the temptation to turn his or her speech into a speculation upon where Collins would have stood on some question of the moment or to remake Collins in their own image. In 2015, for Frances Fitzgerald, then Minister for Justice, Collins was both a champion of women's role in public life and a defender of law and order.[2] In 2011, Ed Walsh, the iconoclastic former president of the University of Limerick, knew that 'Michael Collins, were he around today, would put the fear of God into those who abuse their secure positions and fail to put Ireland first at this time of great crisis. Reforming our public sector and cutting back on public expenditure in order to balance our budget, sooner rather than later, is the priority.'[3]

This unsurprising if ahistorical activity stands in contrast to, though it has no doubt been facilitated by, a notable lack of interest in what Collins actually thought or believed. This has perhaps been copper-fastened by a tendency to present him as a realist who acted rather than an idealist who thought and talked. Collins himself promoted this image, indicating that it was action that he valued. When discussing the appropriate members for a fund-raising delegation to the USA in October 1921, Collins wrote to de Valera, that it was 'practical work' rather than the ability to speak that counted: 'if the speaker is not practical it will be only so much money wasted; at least in my view. The practical people will get the money; the speakers will not.'[4] Six weeks later, he put it even more bluntly in a letter to Kitty Kiernan, 'I'm on the side of those who do things, not on the side of those who say things. And that's that!'[5]

Batt O'Connor, who thought Collins very remarkable indeed, thought the 'most remarkable thing about him' was 'his power to keep his own counsel.'[6] Consequently, building a rigorous and coherent picture of Collins's worldview is hampered by the fact that he was neither a prolific writer nor was he given overmuch to philosophical reflection in his public statements. On the other hand, we do have a collection of articles and speeches, published posthumously as *The Path to Freedom* by the Talbot Press in 1922. This short book has been reprinted several times since then and it offers a good deal of insight into his thinking.[7] Some months earlier, Martin Lester, Limited, had published *Arguments for the Treaty by Michael Collins*, a collection of several speeches made between December 1921 and March 1922.[8] We have other evidence, including his letters, his contributions to Dáil debates, his short prison diary, his actions, and his attitudes as recorded by contemporaries.

ARGUMENTS FOR THE TREATY

By MICHAEL COLLINS
President of the Provisional Government.

MARTIN LESTER, LIMITED
78 Harcourt Street :: Dublin

PRICE SIXPENCE.

The Pro-Treaty party knew that Collins was their most effective weapon in making the case for the Treaty, and they busily associated his image with it and put him into print. This is the front cover of *Arguments for the Treaty*. The pamphlet included the texts of speeches Collins made in Dáil Éireann, and at meetings at Cork, Skibbereen and Waterford. *(The Board of Trinity College Dublin)*

This image of Collins addressing a crowd in Cork conveys the sense of a man straining to ensure that he makes his point. *(National Library of Ireland)*

This Anti-Treaty handbill is less than impressed by Collins's methods of persuasion, showing him stuffing the Treaty down the throat of an unwilling citizen. The deployment of force-feeding as a political metaphor, given its recent real-life use in response to nationalist hunger strikes, is notable. *(National Library of Ireland)*

The Path to Freedom and *Arguments for the Treaty* have to be considered carefully. He wrote most of the material during the immediate aftermath of the Treaty split when he was chairman of the Provisional Government. As such, the texts were unmistakably shaped by the concerns of those months. While it is possible that he was not the sole author of all of both, they do reflect his thoughts, albeit thoughts produced for public consumption, at a particular moment of crisis and controversy. It should also be borne in mind that each letter he wrote during his career was addressed to a precise audience. Similarly, the content of his parliamentary speeches was, on occasion, dictated by the demands of expedience. Sometimes, a man's actions reveal contradictions or development rather than consistency, and when reading what contemporaries recalled of Collins we should bear in mind that they too had agendas and fallible memories. Nonetheless, it seems important to try to sketch out the mind of Michael Collins.

Collins was not, as Bill O'Herlihy, the journalist and public relations consultant, claimed at Béal na mBláth in 2013, 'a visionary, a deep thinker about the future of Ireland'.[9] Even Frank O'Connor, who described a 'bookish' and 'quick-witted' Collins, suggested that his reading 'regularly out-distanced his powers of reflection'.[10] As discussed in Chapter 1, Collins's formation was, in all sorts of ways, wholly typical of separatist activists of the period. Collins may have read more widely than the average but he too consumed, and discussed, the key books and periodicals that his nationalist contemporaries read. His views reflect this formation. As Piaras Béaslaí put it, he was 'a great reaper where others had sown'.[11]

Collins believed, without equivocation, that the Irish were a separate nation and because of this they had a moral entitlement to self-governance. This belief was grounded in a nineteenth-century romantic understanding of the Irish nation, which existed – or, as Collins put it, had 'survived' albeit 'drooped and weakened' – as a 'national spirit' or as 'the soul of the nation'.[12] One of the ways in which Irish-Ireland separatists explained how they differed from the Irish Party was that they were animated by, and servants of, this 'soul'. Their informing consciousness, they insisted, was a spirit-imbued 'nationality' whereas their Irish Party opponents were possessed merely of a pale, zombie cousin named 'nationalism'. The Party was limited to concerns about parliaments and positions (politics alone) while separatists maintained that political freedom must be accompanied by and grounded in the 'essentials': 'language, culture, memory'.[13] When one reads *The Path to Freedom* one finds Collins returning again and again to this conception of 'nationality'. During the Treaty debates he used the compound phrase 'our continued national and spiritual existence'.[14] There is little doubt that Collins believed sincerely in it, although in the context of 1922 the formulation had the potential to perform a particular function for him. We will return to this.

When the German or Russian romantic nationalist of the nineteenth century sought out this 'spirit' in tangible form he turned to 'the people'. He found it in their language, customs and stories. For the Irish-Ireland separatist of the early twentieth century, including Collins, this was both an imperative and a problem. 'Irish nationhood springs from the Irish people,' Collins insisted. Nonetheless, he acknowledged, that though the 'Gaelic soul of the Irish people still lives. In itself it is indestructible … its qualities are hidden, besmirched, by that which has been imposed upon us'. When he considered contemporary Ireland what Collins thought he saw, far too often, was 'English civilization'. He was sure that this was merely an ill-fitting 'alien' garment. Yet, he wrote, it had been worn for so long that the 'external and internal life' of the Irish people had 'become the expression of its unfitness': 'we are soaked, saturated, and stupefied with the English outlook'. Ireland's towns and villages were, he claimed, 'hideous medleys of contemptible dwellings and mean shops and squalid public houses' while, despite 'all their natural intelligence, the horizon of our people has become bounded by the daily newspaper, the public house, and the racecourse'.[15] Similarly, in 1918, he had quoted approvingly Michael Fogarty, the sympathetic Bishop of Killaloe who claimed that 'we had almost ceased to be Irish until Sinn Féin rose and struck the English rust from the soul of Ireland. Unfortunately that rust had eaten deep and spoiled many a good Irish heart'.[16] The 'biggest task', he wrote, was the 'restoration of the Irish language.' 'Irish will scarcely be our language in this generation, not even perhaps in the next,' he continued, 'But until we have it again on our tongues and in our minds we are not free, and we will produce no immortal literature.'[17]

All of this was second-hand thinking. He was repeating ideas that had become orthodoxy within his milieu. P.S. O'Hegarty was, for example, among those who had deployed the adjective 'indestructible' in the same manner in the title of his 1918 text, *The Indestructible Nation*.[18] The passages on the degeneration of modern Irish life contain more than a hint of the influence of D.P. Moran's *The Leader* and J.J. O'Kelly's *Catholic Bulletin*. Collins had read Moran as a youth and he knew O'Kelly, who had founded the Keating branch of the Gaelic League and was one-time treasurer of the INA & VDF (see Chapter 2). Moran and O'Kelly's versions of Douglas Hyde's call for the de-anglicising of Ireland had become the commonplaces of Irish-Ireland rhetoric, the clichés of Gaelic League meeting rooms, the stuffing of many a Sinn Féin speech.[19] It is hardly a surprise that echoes of their journalism found their way into Collins's thought both directly and indirectly. He had probably read similar concerns, expressed in a similar manner, in the pages of 'A Gaelic League Catechism' aimed specifically at members in London.[20] It should be noted, however, that Collins's language is largely free of the Catholic chauvinism that marked out Moran and O'Kelly's writings.

Given the problem of the apparent and willing anglicisation of the Irish people, Collins's belief in the reality of Irish nationality rested on two grounds. These were, again, unoriginal. The first was history. He and those who thought like him were sure that the Irish were a nation (and could govern themselves) because, as Collins asserted, 'Our historians had shown our nationality as existing from legendary ages'. He painted a picture of an ancient civilisation that had once been characterised by 'security, prosperity and national greatness'. This 'Gaelic civilization' was 'quite different' because its strength was 'the democratic basis of its economic system, and the aristocracy of its culture', while 'the people of the whole nation were united, not by material forces, but by spiritual ones.'[21] In making these assertions Collins was drawing upon a vibrant nationalist school of contemporary history writing, both popular and academic. Influential scholarly texts included Alice Stopford Green's *The Making of Ireland and Its Undoing* (1908) and Eoin MacNeill's *Phases of Irish History* (1919).[22] In Collins's case large sections of his essay entitled 'Distinctive Culture: Ancient Irish Civilization: Glories of the Past' were ripped from the 'The Gaels in Ireland', the first chapter of Stopford Green's *Irish Nationality*, an accessible book that she published in 1911.[23]

The second ground on which Irish nationality stood was the collective imagining of the western seaboard as a place where this authentic, non-material, spiritual culture had survived. Collins explained what was, once more, an entirely conventional Irish-Ireland position (most familiar to us now from the poetry, theatre and art of the period) like this:

It is only in the remote corners of Ireland in the South and West and North-West that any trace of the old civilization is met with now. To those places the social side of anglicisation was never able very easily to

This caricature of Alice Stopford Green by the artist V.L. O'Connor depicts her at her desk writing the books that created 'Old Ireland'. When *The Making of Ireland and Its Undoing* was published in 1908, Collins was in the Gaelic League in London. The June volume of its journal, *Inis Fáil*, promoted the book, stating that 'it will probably create a revolution in Irish historical scholarship' and offering it at a discount price of 3s. 6d. to 'Irish-Irelanders'. The journal continued, 'We trust that every patriotic Irish man and woman in London – to say nothing of Ireland – will take advantage of this patriotic offer'. *(National Library of Ireland)*

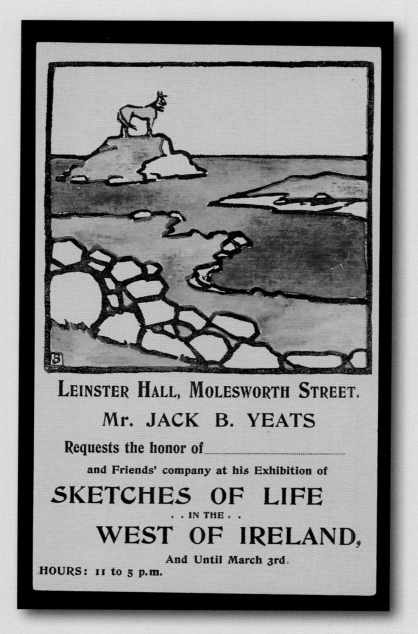

'The West' became a site of enormous cultural consequence and imaginative potential during the period of the Gaelic revival. This is an invitation to a Jack Butler Yeats exhibition 'Sketches of Life in the West of Ireland'. He held a series of exhibitions under that title from 1899, but the March dates suggest that this relates to one in 1900. *(National Library of Ireland and Jack B. Yeats's Estate)*

penetrate. To-day it is only in those places that any beauty and grace in Irish life survive … It is only in such places that one gets a glimpse of what Ireland may become again.[24]

Many romantic nationalists of cosmopolitan backgrounds during this period made a transformative journey to 'the west' or to a Gaeltacht summer school, a journey in search of the authentic Ireland. Collins had not. Instead, his physical journey east (to London) seems to have worked a nostalgic and romantic magic upon his conception of the rural places he left behind. However this came about, for Collins as for others, not only was 'the west' the place where one went to find an authentic Ireland, what one found there provided the model for a renewed Ireland.

Collins conceived of the process by which Ireland would rejuvenate its nationality and assert its freedom in three stages. Again, this was rather typical of his contemporaries. First, the cultural and separatist political movements had to counteract the 'poison of foreign ways', which had 'infected' the nation during centuries of 'foreign usurping government'. The combined efforts of the Gaelic League, Sinn Féin and, to a lesser extent, the GAA had begun this task.[25] When this was sufficiently advanced – when the 'national consciousness was fully re-awakened' – there came a second, and for Collins, a necessary stage. 'Armed resistance,' he insisted, 'was the indispensable factor in our struggle for freedom.' According to Collins, it was no accident that the right of Ireland to decide its own destiny was finally acknowledged when it became 'a nation under arms': freedom could not be a 'gift' asked for and granted by parliament, it had to be won.[26] Once freedom had been achieved, there came the third phase: the effort to 'realize that for which they had fought – a free, prosperous self-governing Gaelic Ireland.' Or, as he put it in August 1922: 'The negative work of expelling the English power is done. The positive work of building a Gaelic Ireland in the vacuum left has now to be undertaken.'[27]

When Collins imagined this renewed Ireland what did he see? During late 1921 and early 1922 the most significant element of that question, at least for many others, was, did he see a republic? Bill Kissane has pointed out that Collins 'studiously avoided' the word 'Republic' in the speeches immediately prior to his death'.[28] Nonetheless, the answer to the question remained, in an ideal world and ultimately, yes: he wanted a republic. From 1909, when he joined the IRB, to December 1921, when he signed the Treaty, he had pinned his colours to that mast. In the aftermath, he remained President of the IRB. During the drafting of the Irish Free State Constitution he worked to ensure that it was as 'republican' a document as possible. As outlined in Chapter 4, he needed to do that in an attempt to placate republican opponents of the Treaty but there is no reason to doubt that he also did so from conviction.[29] In January 1922, James G. Douglas, who sat on the committee tasked with drawing up the new constitution, wrote to Collins arguing that the final document should be approved by the Dáil only, and should not require the approval of the British parliament. To do other, Douglas contended, would imply that the new state occupied 'a position definitively subordinate to Great Britain'. Collins's response was to claim that he was 'fully aware that the procedure is awfully important' but to insist that while he 'entirely agreed' with Douglas that

> we must make our stand on the basis of 'a position of absolute equality, freedom not only among the other States of the Empire but among the other nations of the world.' If we keep this firmly and clearly before our minds we need not worry for the moment whether or not the constitution will eventually have to go through the British parliament.[30]

For Collins, given the circumstances, achieving the greatest level of autonomy possible was more important than worrying about what mere 'procedure' might or might not imply and, crucially, it was more important than cleaving to any particular model of governance. When it had come to making decisions about whether to sign the Treaty and, later, whether to accede to British demands that the new constitution include references to the monarch and the oath, Collins concluded that a republic was not on offer. Given this fact, adhering to a particular mode of governance was, he would claim, a betrayal of that for which separatists had fought.

He made this case again and again, in a variety of ways, during the final months of his life. The key consequence of the Treaty, Collins maintained, was the evacuation of the British and it 'is the evacuation by the British which gives us our freedom'. This was the proof of success, he insisted, 'not the name for, nor the form of, the government we have chosen. If we had still a descendant of our Irish Kings left, we would be as free, under a limited monarchy, with the British gone, as under a Republic.' Elsewhere he made the same point in a different way:

The British form of government was monarchical. In order to express clearly our desire to depart from all British forms of government, we declared a Republic. We repudiated the British form of government, not because it was monarchical, but because it was British. We would have repudiated the claim of a British Republic to rule over us as definitely as we repudiated the claim of the British monarchy.[31]

As he told a crowd in Dublin on 5 March 1922, 'We must be Irish first and last, and must be Republicans or Document Two-ites, or Free Staters, only within the limits which leave Ireland strong, united and free.'[32]

It is unsurprising that if in Collins's view the evacuation of the British, which he equated to the freedom of Irish nationality to flourish, was more important than the achievement of a republic, then this was equally true of any other constitutional formulations, including Document No. 2 in which de Valera outlined external association. The 'essence of our struggle was *to secure freedom to order our own life,*' Collins declared, 'without attaching undue importance to the formulas under which that freedom would be expressed.' And again: 'Fidelity to the real Ireland lies in uniting to build up a real Ireland in conformity to our ideal, and not in disruption and destruction as a sacrifice to the false gods of foreign-made political formulas.' For anyone reading closely the implication was unmistakable: those truly faithful to Ireland had always been concerned with 'nationality' while those obsessed with the 'republic' or 'external association' were guilty of a version of the Irish Party's sin when they thought that Home Rule was the issue. They had been misled into the heresy of thinking of freedom as a merely, or even primarily, a 'political' matter, as a disagreement about constitutional formulations. They had, Collins accused, started to think of a particular form of political autonomy as an end in itself.[33]

When Collins defended the Treaty he stood on the ground of pragmatism: 'If we would only put away dreams, and face realities, nearly all the things that count we have now for our country'.[34] He did so, proposing to move forward step by step: the Treaty provided, he thought, 'freedom, not the ultimate freedom that all nations desire and develop to, but the freedom to achieve it (applause)'.[35] He defended his position as resting on democratic principles, insisting in the Treaty debates on the principle of 'government by the consent of the governed'[36] and later demanding 'allegiance to and support of the National Government, democratically elected'.[37] All of these, however, followed from his position that their ultimate collective purpose was the attainment of this higher plane, 'nationality'. And 'nationality' was every bit as much a commitment of heart over head as Cathal Brugha or Mary MacSwiney's 'republic', if not more so. His pro-Treaty position was, he seemed to argue, every bit as idealistic as the anti-Treaty case. Indeed, more than that, his ideal was the essential one. He, not they, was the bearer of the true flame.

In 1986 Jeffrey Prager argued that the Civil War split could be viewed as one between a pro-Treaty mentality, which he characterised as 'Irish Enlightenment', and an anti-Treaty mentality, which he described as 'Gaelic Romantic'. In this formulation the 'Irish Enlightenment' mentality was non-sectarian and grounded in a belief in parliamentary democracy, while the 'Gaelic Romantic' mentality was dominated by a desire to restore an 'authentic', Gaelic nationality and its adherents were prepared to embrace non-democratic, violent means to this end. In early 1922, Prager suggested, Collins and de Valera constructed 'hybrid political positions' as both sought to find a middle ground that might 'ward off' civil war. In Collins's case, by making an argument that sought to reflect the essential values of both mentalities, he hoped to ameliorate the split. More importantly perhaps, he endeavoured to construct a position through which he could reconcile himself and others, who were in many ways 'Gaelic Romantic' in their outlook, to the 'Irish Enlightenment' reality of the Treaty. As Prager put it, Collins 'came to accept, roughly speaking, Irish Enlightenment values while still holding to Gaelic-Romantic norms'.[38]

The tendency to represent Collins as a lost moderniser ignores the evidence of just how strong the 'Gaelic Romantic' strain of thought was within his mental make-up. When Collins brought to mind the Ireland that he dreamed of, like de Valera, he saw an idealised version of his rural upbringing. In Frank O'Connor's words, he was 'a man possessed of a boyish loyalty; a vision of whitewashed cottages, of old people sitting by the fire, of horses outside the forge on a summer evening'. According to O'Connor, Collins returned to this vision more frequently in the months after the Treaty, the period when he felt 'most uncertain of himself'.[39] De Valera lived long enough for the term 'frugal comfort' – the state he associated with the ideal version of that life – to become the subject of mild derision. If Collins had lived, his equivalent would have been 'fair comfort' or, a little more optimistically but carrying the same meaning, 'moderate luxury'.[40]

THE TREATY
GIVES IRELAND

1. A PARLIAMENT RESPONSIBLE TO THE IRISH PEOPLE ALONE.

2. A GOVERNMENT RESPONSIBLE TO THAT PARLIAMENT.

3. DEMOCRATIC CONTROL OF ALL LEGISLATIVE AFFAIRS.

4. POWER TO MAKE LAWS FOR EVERY DEPARTMENT OF IRISH LIFE.

5. AN IRISH LEGAL SYSTEM CONTROLLED BY IRISHMEN.

6. AN IRISH ARMY.

7. AN IRISH POLICE FORCE.

8. COMPLETE FINANCIAL FREEDOM.

9. A NATIONAL FLAG.

10. FREEDOM OF OPINION.

11. COMPLETE CONTROL OF IRISH EDUCATION.

12. COMPLETE CONTROL OF HER LAND SYSTEMS.

13. POWER AND FREEDOM TO DEVELOP HER RESOURCES AND INDUSTRIES.

14. A DEMOCRATIC CONSTITUTION.

15. A STATE ORGANISATION TO EXPRESS THE MIND AND WILL OF THE NATION.

16. HER RIGHTFUL PLACE AS A NATION AMONG NATIONS.

DUBLIN CASTLE HAS FALLEN !
BRITISH BUREAUCRACY IS IN THE DUST !
IS THIS VICTORY OR DEFEAT ?

SUPPORT THE TREATY

This poster, which makes the case for what was gained by the Treaty, invokes a speech Collins made in Skibbereen on St Patrick's Day, 1922: 'The British game is up. Dublin Castle has fallen … The future rests entirely with ourselves – a new order of things is facing us,' he declared. *(National Library of Ireland)*

He used these terms in an essay 'Building up Ireland: Resources to be Developed'. In it he drew upon the reports of the Commission of Inquiry into the Resources and Industries of Ireland established by Dáil Éireann on 18 June 1919. It underpinned his claim that, once free, the country would be built up economically because the land was fruitful and abundant with 'natural resources'. Citing statistics from the Commission's *Report on Water Power*, published in January 1922, which in turn drew on data from a British Board of Trade report of the previous year, he placed considerable weight on the potential of hydro-electric power: 'white power' he called it, in contrast to the 'black coal' that buttressed British industrialisation. [41] And, in added contrast to Britain, he wrote:

> Our object in building up the country economically must not be lost sight of. That object is not to be able to boast of enormous wealth or of a great volume of trade, for their own sake. It is not to see our country covered with smoking chimneys and factories. It is not to show a great national balance-sheet, nor to point to a people producing wealth with the self-obliteration of a hive of bees.

Instead, the purpose of economic activity was to facilitate the Irish people in reaching out 'to the higher things in which the spirit finds its satisfaction.'[42] There is no mistaking the parallels with de Valera's famous, often ridiculed, speech of twenty years later: 'The ideal Ireland that we would have, the Ireland that we dreamed of, would be the home of a people who valued material wealth only as a basis for right living, of a people who, satisfied with frugal comfort, devoted their leisure to the things of the spirit.'[43]

It is impossible to tell whether Collins would have pursued this ideal in a manner that was markedly different from de Valera. There are, however, signs of the language of protectionism, tillage and self-sufficiency, borrowed from Arthur Griffith, that would sit at the core of Fianna Fáil's economic approach from the 1920s through to the 1950s. During the Treaty debates, on 19 December, for example, he characterised Britain's colonisation of Ireland in economic terms. It had been, he said,

> a story of slow steady, economic encroach by England. It has been a struggle on our part to prevent that, a struggle against exploitation,

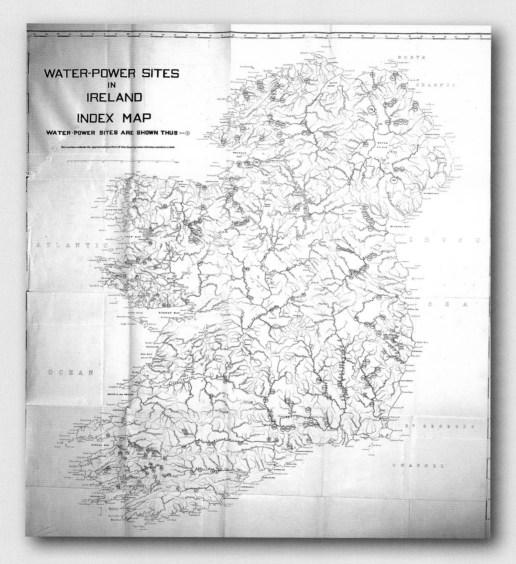

This map comes from Commission of Inquiry into the Resources and Industries of Ireland's *Report on Water Power*. It evidently impressed Collins. *(National Library of Ireland)*

(c)   Picturesque photos showing the braod seas calm, wild etc., with such captions as "The Atlantic Gold Mine"   "Full of wealth for the taking of it"

(d)   Showing the poor, ill-equipped little fleets of the poor people.   Their little canvas coated curraghs.   Show them a whole day's fishing - Their going forth in the morning and their return in the evening with the "Harvest of the Seas"

(e)   This section will show the reason why they are so poor and have to go as harvesters to England and Scotland.   Although great wealth at their doors, not properly equipped tob reap it.

Show them the well-equipped up-to-date Steam trawlers of Great Britain which poach on them.

Show also a portrait of a busy fishing centre like Hull or Grimsby or some Scotch Port.

The end up :

"Fellow countrymen this is one of our problems. It rests with us now to equip these Fishing folk and make them as propperous as the English and Scotch.   To do this we must have Peace and stable conditions in the Country" etc. etc.

B.   Other Pictures could show :

(a)   1.   Our barren Mountain sides as they are.

(Little dissertation here on the terrible de-forrestated condition of the country, compare it in this way with other countries)

2.   Our barren Mountain sides as they should be.

(Photos of Swiss Mountain sides covered with acrea of noble pines and other trees)

(b)   The need for rational drainage. Show the terrible depredation of the water in such scandalously under-drained areas as the Erne, Barrow, Shannon

national

3.   Show what Holland has done to save and reclaim her little land.

(c)   The great question of a national power generator. This will probably be water aided by Peat.

Pictures of what Northcliffe described as the "White Coal of Ireland"   Hundreds of great Waterfalls all over the country going to waste.

o to Desmond FitzGerald of 12 July 1922, Collins proposed various propaganda and pub
ne that would stress the social and economic possibilities for a new Ireland that could

5

On the other hand show the marvellous use
Italy has made of its Water power : nearly every
little village there having its electric engine
to operate light, heat and power.

(d)   Then deal with City and Urban problems.

    1. Photos showing the terrible slums, the long
ranks of unemployed with counter pictures of
the little garden suburbs they will have to
be turned into.

    2. Portraits too, with detailed sections of the
sort of industries which it would be economic for
us to create: Soap works, great Tanneries,
Horn and Bead Factories, Beet-root Sugar
Factories, great Frozen Meat (including potted
meat) Factories. We should point out that we
have all the raw material in the country for
these things.

These are only some of the many problems we
could deal with pictorially and so get the
minds of the people focussed on them and off
such controversial matters as the National
position.

In every picture you could make a direct
plea for peace and stability in order to enable
the Government to carry out these reforms.

I have thousands of other possible films in
my mind, but these will do to illustrate the
line that I think these films should take.

They will have an enormous effect and will
enable you to jamb in little pieces of
pro-Government propaganda amongst purely
educational pictures

I am sure, should these ideas be suggested there
will be a great croaking about expense, but still that
should not prevent us from carrying it out.

It means not only our very life's blood, but the
life's blood and being of the Nation.

I believe the cinema propaganda thus outlined would
largely repay us for expenditure on it.

B.   Posters on Hoardings: This is also a very excellent
and striking means of Propaganda. Lloyd George resorts very
much to it. Mr. Figgis, by his apt employment of it, put
on at least 5,000 votes to his large poll. We should try
it.

Early in his speech at Skibbereen on 17 March 1922, Collins pointed to what he called 'an everyday indication' of the freedom which had been achieved: 'You already see Irish letters on the stamps, which you use every day, and in a short time we will have our own Irish-designed stamps instead of stamps we have been used to from our childhood.' It was James G. Douglas who had proposed to W.T. Cosgrave in January that the existing stamps be overprinted with the new lettering (a surcharge). This was symbolic but it was also practical: 'It has been usual every where in Europe when any change of Government takes place,' Douglas explained, 'to sur- charge the postage stamps, & I think if done here it will help to remind people that they had now got their own Government, & would have the additional advantage of bringing in a revenue from stamp collectors all over the world of some thousands of pounds'. The first such stamps appeared on 17 February. *(National Library of Ireland)*

a struggle against the cancer that was eating up our lives, and it was only after discovering that, that it was economic penetration, that we discovered that political freedom was necessary in order that that should be stopped.

And later in the same speech, he insisted, 'every day some other business concern in this city is taken over by an English concern and becomes a little oasis of English customs and manners. Nobody notices, but that is the thing that has destroyed our Gaelic civilization.'[44] On a train journey to Cork with the writer Clare Sheridan in 1922 he expressed the view that there should be 'less grazing and more agriculture' and that this could be encouraged through taxation. It was 'an easy life,' he said, 'to put your hands in your pocket and whistle a tune while the grass grows and the cattle get fat, but tilling gives employment'.[45] That Ireland should support itself and employ more people on the land through tillage, rather than raising cattle for beef for the English table, was a staple of Irish nationalist economic thought.

Interpreting Collins's attitude to social relations in the new Ireland involves considerable conjecture, though we do have some evidence. Collins, it seems clear, did not subscribe to a particular social or economic ideology. His rhetoric was critical of unrestrained capitalism. As Hart has pointed out, in 1910 he wrote to the *Sinn Féin* newspaper criticising it for appearing to become 'the defender of the landlords – the exponent of the capitalists'.[46] His sister Hannie, with whom he was living then, recorded that as a young man he greatly admired George Bernard Shaw, and though she does not explicitly say so, it seems safe to assume this included Shaw's socialist politics. She wrote, 'No one appreciated Bernard Shaw more than he, and he felt his influence, as all among the younger generation who think at all have come under that same salutary influence.'[47] That influence certainly waned with time, though during the summer of 1920 he was less cautious than others when the establishment of diplomatic relations between Dáil Éireann and the new Bolshevik government in Russia was mooted.[48] Later still, in 1922, he asserted that what 'we must aim at is the building up of a sound economic life in which great discrepancies cannot occur. We must not have the destitution of poverty at one end, and at the other an excess of riches in the possession of a few individuals'. Neither was capitalism mitigated by philanthropy or charity enough. With Andrew Carnegie in mind, he argued that ordinary people should have the resources to 'put together their own local libraries' rather than depending on millionaires to bestow libraries. Capital, he wrote, 'must not be allowed to draw away all the fruits of labour to itself' and labour 'will be free to take its rightful place as an element in the life of the nation.' 'Economically,' he insisted, 'we must be democratic'.

On the other hand, he was definitively not a social revolutionary: the land campaign of Davitt was, to his mind, only justified in that it attempted to reverse the national 'subjection'. 'I think we shall safely avoid State Socialism,' he wrote, 'which has nothing to commend it in a country like Ireland.' In August 1922 Horace Plunkett, who met him at a private dinner, recorded in his diary that Collins said, 'After we get over the present trouble we shall have to fight Bolshevism.' Instead of unfettered capitalism or socialism the 'keynote of Irish revival,' he proposed, 'must be development of Irish resources by Irish capital for the benefit of the Irish consumer in such a way that the people have steady work at just remuneration and their own share of control.'[49]

These were the positions of a man who needed the support of both capital and organised labour (or at least he needed to avoid their active opposition) if his infant state was to survive. In January 1919, he appears to have both participated in meetings that led to the drafting of the Democratic Programme and yet been prepared to see it suppressed when an IRB meeting he convened to vet the Programme, and the 'Declaration of Independence', objected to the contents. The Democratic Programme was not suppressed, but was revised and then passed at the Dáil's first meeting.[50] Conor Kostick did not, it seems to us, prove his case when he argued that Collins was motivated to sign the Treaty 'by the scale of class conflict in Ireland'.[51] Nonetheless, Collins certainly viewed class conflict as a threat to the stability of the post-Treaty state. Class politics was, in his view, a lower form of politics and, beyond centrist sentiment, perhaps influenced by Catholic social thought, there is little sign of a developed philosophy or plan that might create a society that was economically democratic. That said, Collins appears to have been attracted to the co-operative movement. The 'countrysides', he argued, would 'cease to be the torpid deserts they are now' through people 'co-operating in industry, and co-operating and competing in pleasure and in culture.'[52] Indeed, Collins had been supportive of the establishment, with Dáil Éireann funds, of a bank that from December 1919 directed capital to co-operative land societies and to co-operative economic activity in areas such as fishing. This was a mixed success but Collins continued to see potential.[53]

This is a draft of the letter Collins wrote in 1910, titled 'A Wail of Regret', complaining that Sinn Féin had become 'the defender of the landlords – the exponent of the capitalists'. *(UCD Archives)*

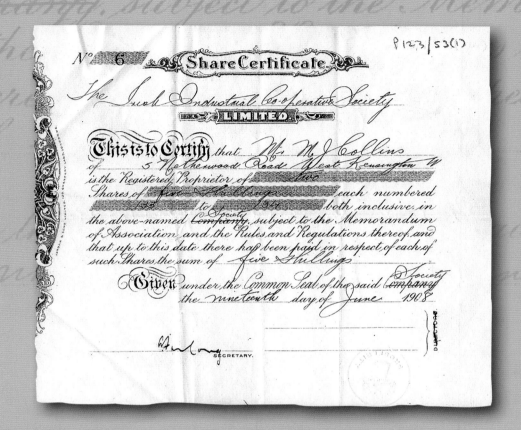

In 1908 Collins bought shares in the Irish Industrial Co-operative Society, and he had the certificate to prove it. *(UCD Archives)*

Despite the trying circumstances of his time as a cabinet minister, Dáil Éireann's authority, funds and number of employees grew. In his positions Collins found himself ideally placed to influence the manner in which the money was managed and how appointments should be made. In distinguishing themselves from the Irish Party, separatists had for many years loudly decried their opponents' alleged corruption – the place-hunting, the nepotism, and the localism.[54] Collins has been praised for his 'meticulous concerns for financial probity' in his role as Minister for Finance and his austere demands of his staff and colleagues, while in May 1921 he took a firm line in the matter of perceived jobbery.[55] Then, Kevin O'Higgins at the Department of Local Government wrote wondering whether two of that department's inspectors, George Nicholls and Lorcan Robins, could be retained in their posts although they had recently been elected to the Dáil. O'Higgins acknowledged that 'the present is a time of fruitful precedent that may be quoted hereafter' but replacing these men, he argued, would be disruptive and he was inclined toward expediency. In his reply, Collins was unequivocal:

> It occurs to me that if we institute the practice of having members of DAIL also officials of Departments we shall be doing a thing which will be leaving us open to charges of jobbery, and with good reason, I believe. There could be no impartial criticism by an official of the Local Government Board who was a member of the DAIL. He would have no liberty in debate, and he would have no standing with a Local Body.

He was just as, if not more, blunt in a letter to de Valera on the same matter on the same day.[56] As we have seen, however, he worked to ensure that members of the IRB and close associates occupied key posts. If he recognised this as a form of jobbery, then it was jobbery that was justified. In March 1922, for example, he was instrumental in the appointment of Michael Staines, close ally and Pro-Treaty TD, to the position of commissioner of the new Civic Guard. When one appoints one's own friends, it seems, one is simply picking the best person for the job, when someone else does it, it is, of course, jobbery. As it turned out, Staines was not the best person for the job and he resigned within months, following a mutiny. Ironically, the official reason given for his departure was the necessity of keeping politicians out of policing.[57]

As this postcard illustrates, Sinn Féin's self-image was that of the nemesis of the venal and corrupt Irish Party, which had put a parliamentary salary, place-hunting and jobbery above the national interest. (The Board of Trinity College Dublin)

Extract from D244/

<u>AL. No.17</u>

24th May, 1921.

<u>PRESIDENT</u>

. . . .

A letter is submitted from Local Government
Department to which is attached a copy of my to same.
My view differs from the view of the Local Government
Dept. as I think it would look very much like jobbery
if we had Members of the DAIL serving as officials
in DAIL Departments - would it not break down all
confidence? I am afraid the suggestion is
indefensible - there are so many obvious points against
it, that there is no need to detail them.

. . . .

[M. Collins]

In this memo to de Valera in May 1921, Collins appears a firm opponent of jobbery or even the appearance of
jobbery. *(National Archives of Ireland)*

Collins appears to have been consistently interested in the fate of northern nationalists.[58] In Chapter 4 we noted his role in brokering the deal on nationalist candidates for Ulster constituencies at the 1918 general election, and he was himself elected to represent South Armagh in May 1921. Despite this, Collins was entirely typical of southern nationalists in his incomprehension of northern unionists. 'The tendency of sentiment in the North-East, when not interfered with,' he wrote, 'was national, and in favour of freedom and unity.' This led him to assert that, once the British were gone, unionists could be won over: 'We have the task before us to impregnate our northern countrymen with the national outlook.' It was, he maintained, a matter of time before the 'North-East' learned to 'revolve in the Irish orbit and get out of the orbit of Great Britain'. This certainty was underpinned by an apparent confidence that the Boundary Commission would 'deprive "Ulster" of Fermanagh and Tyrone' and in these circumstances 'union is certain'. The only question was 'how soon?'[59] Persuasion, politics, economics and time were to be the forces that brought about unification.

That, at least, was his public position. In parallel, during the first half of 1922, and despite signing peace pacts with Sir James Craig, Prime Minister of Northern Ireland, on 21 January and 30 March, he sanctioned a policy of military activity along and across the border. It contributed to widespread violence and included raids, the taking of hostages and shootings in the border counties. These actions were promoted by key figures within the Ulster IRA, carried out by that body, and approved by GHQ in Dublin. IRA offensives in February, March and May fed, and were in turn fed by, sectarian violence in Belfast. During these months 73 Protestants and 147 Catholics were killed in Belfast alone.[60] In April Collins complained to Craig that Catholics in his 'territory' were 'harassed and persecuted in the most appalling fashion by armed mobs' and that this was 'apparently not interfered with in any way by your police and military' but he did not acknowledge that his actions were exacerbating the situation.[61] In describing this as Collins's 'personal crusade against partition' the historian of the northern IRA Robert Lynch stretched a point, but there is no mistaking Collins's crucial authorising role.[62]

As early as January 1922, Collins had established within the IRA, what Lynch describes as, a 'shadowy body' called the Ulster Council or Northern Command. The February offensive began just days after Collins – perhaps responding to criticism of the first Craig–Collins pact by northern nationalists – issued a hard-line public statement which threatened that without the transfer of those counties where there were nationalist majorities, there would be a 'resumption of the old disturbances, the old conflicts, the old animosities'.[63] There were, Collins told a delegation of northern nationalists, 'only two policies – peace or war. He and his colleagues were going to try the peace policy first.'[64] Reflecting on these threats, in a letter to the conservative politician Leo Amery on 7 February, Craig suggested that when Collins returned to Dublin

> he got alarmed that he would not be able to obtain a majority of the Dail if his representatives in the north came out against him, and that consequently he completely changed his view on that question and decided to be anti-Ulster made a stronger case than to try and conciliate moderate opinion.[65]

That very evening, the IRA launched the first serious raids across the border. The pretext was to pressure Craig's government to reprieve three men who were due for execution on 9 February for their part in the deaths of two RIC constables during an attempted escape from Derry prison four days before the Treaty was signed. While Craig saw double-dealing and aggression on Collins's part, Collins saw intransigence and a lack of generosity on Craig's. Explaining the events of 7 February, and the further violence that followed, to the northern nationalist Louis J. Walsh, Collins wrote, 'the reprisals' had occurred because the British and the Northern Ireland government had 'shilly shallied and would not give me an assurance that the Derry prisoners would be reprieved'.[66]

Despite the terrible effects for the Catholic community and the poor prospects for success, there were those within the northern IRA who believed,[67] and historians who have argued since,[68] that at the time of his death Collins remained intent upon an aggressive northern policy. Others have been less certain. John Regan has reasoned that in supporting aggression on the border during these months Collins pursued the short-term aims of, first, not ceding the initiative on the north to anti-Treatyites and, second, securing the northern IRA for the pro-Treaty position or at least some form of neutrality.[69] Marie Coleman has also emphasised that attempting to 'retain republican unity' was a key consideration in Collins's thinking, contending that when the rift within the IRA worsened in March 1922 this 'heightened Collins's efforts to use the north as a ploy'.[70] Further,

McGarry and Kissane have argued that Collins's cabinet colleagues were, in the weeks before his death, moving to shut down any further provocative actions and instead impose 'a policy of peaceful do-nothingness', a phrase coined by Kevin O'Shiel, a legal adviser to the Provisional Government who was originally from Omagh, County Tyrone.[71] This was the policy they adopted once Collins was gone; whether, and how quickly, they would have succeeded in achieving that policy shift if Collins had lived is open to speculation.

Collins's relationship to his cabinet colleagues, as well as his status and actions during these months, raise the subject of his commitment to democracy. Regan, a historian who has repeatedly suggested that others in the profession have been too willing to take the case for the legitimacy of the Irish Free State at face value, posed this question starkly when he asked whether the Irish Free State experienced 'a military dictatorship' under Collins in July and August 1922. In January, Collins may have instructed his committee to draft 'a true democratic constitution'[72] but he showed scant regard for democratic norms and institutions in the months that followed. Prior to the general election of June the 'southern parliament', of which the Provisional Government was the theoretical executive, met once, for an hour.[73] Then, as Regan points out, the Civil War was launched on 28 June, prior to any meeting of the new parliament elected on 16 June 1922. Subsequently, the Dáil did not meet at any point up to Collins's death. Indeed, Regan argues, somewhat speculatively, that if Collins had lived and had his way the Dáil would not have met till the war was over. As long as the new Dáil did not sit, the Provisional Government was not accountable to a democratic body, and there is no doubt that Collins was the dominant figure in that government.

In making his case, Regan paints a picture in which Collins's cabinet colleagues wielded very little authority, individually or collectively. He observes that, a fortnight after the beginning of the war, Collins became 'General, Commander-in-Chief' of the army, heading a 'War Council of Three' with his close IRB allies Mulcahy and O'Duffy. Laffan notes that Collins 'announced' this development to the cabinet 'as a *fait accompli*'.[74] Subsequently, a great deal of power that one might expect to reside with civil government passed into the hands of Collins and his 'War Council'. Others argue it was temporarily ceded; Regan suggests it was taken with little certainty that it would be returned. Further, Regan stresses the potential of the IRB, under Collins's control, to act as a non-democratic force manipulating these circumstances. Taken together, this evidence led Regan to

As this poster indicates, Collins and Frank Aiken contested the Armagh constituency for Sinn Féin in the election to the new Northern Ireland parliament which followed the Government of Ireland Act, 1920. Collins took the second of four seats, winning 12,656 votes. Aiken came a distant fifth. *(National Library of Ireland)*

OIFIG AN UACHTARAIN.

A.L

20th February 1922.

L.J. Walsh, Esq, B.A.
Solicitor,
The Cross,
Draperstown,
Co. Derry.

A Chara,

First of all, let me correct a little inaccuracy
in my letter of the 7th February, in the third paragraph
on page 2, I see "solid anti-conscription party" - this
should read "anti-partition". "Anti-Conscription" was a
typist's error. It sounded rather foolish but I expect
you understood.

Many thanks for yours of the 16th. So far as I am
concerned I am in wholehearted agreement with what you
say about Peace - that is really the vital thing, and we
must not be halfhearted when we make our efforts for
Peace, any more than we must be halfhearted when we make
efforts for War. My attitude is very simple in this
regard. If we make Peace at all let us make it in a
generous way. It is no use forcing Peace upon people any
more than it is any use forcing War upon them. That is
the way I look at it, and at the present time I am trying
to get a mutual amnesty rather than mutual punishment.
I made it quite clear both to the British and to the North
East representatives that if the Derry Prisoners were not
reprieved such a revenge would be executed as was unknown
in Ireland. They all shilly shallied and would not give
me an assurance that the Derry Prisoners would be reprieved.
The result was as I forecasted, and it was only by herculean
efforts on the part of some of the men responsible here
that greater reprisals were not taken. As you are probably
aware it was only at the last moment I heard of the reprieve,
and the men here, knowing the fears which existed in the
North, at once set to work to avoid any disturbance and
sent special messengers to the North East with the news.

(1)

insist that 'applying the term "dictatorship" to the treatyite regime under Collins is neither misplaced nor excessive' and to suggest that 'Only when Collins was dead did power begin to devolve to an embryonic parliamentary democracy.'[75]

Under the Civil War conditions of July and August 1922 Collins held extraordinary levels of power and was apparently disinclined to answer to any person or body. One can readily see that this might have posed a danger to the democratic development of the Irish Free State. However, Collins's colleagues were not unaware of the dangers. In the days before Collins's death, for instance, Cosgrave voiced his concern that the repeated decisions to postpone the convening of the Dáil might prompt allegations that 'the Govt & Army are closing the mouths of Parliament.'[76] Also, Regan downplays the evidence that Collins saw himself and his pro-Treaty colleagues as defenders of democracy. Admittedly, that was, at least to some extent, a rhetorical pose, grounded in the fact that the democratic credentials of their opponents were weak. On the other hand, the pro-Treatyites had a better, if not unassailable, case for arguing that they possessed a democratic mandate.

Regan's is a question worth posing. Whether his answer is more credible than the alternatives is a matter of judgment. If possession of a democratic mandate did not necessarily make Collins a democrat then neither did possessing extraordinary powers at a moment of crisis necessarily make him a dictator. J.J. Lee, for instance, asserted that 'Collins behaved more like a democrat than would many a man of his temperament in the circumstances.'[77] For Laffan, Collins's 'actions in the last weeks of his life were undoubtedly high-handed and autocratic, but in wartime there is nothing unusual in heads of government arrogating to themselves exceptional powers. Such patterns have not always endured after the restoration of peace.'[78] Sometimes, on the other hand, they have.

Collins's personal relationships with women have been the subject of much interest.[79] In contrast, less attention has been afforded to Collins's attitude toward one of the great 'democratic' questions of his day: the participation of women in public life, particularly in politics. Frances Fitzgerald's recent efforts to suggest that Collins would have proved an advocate of women's place in the post-independence public sphere brought a sharp rebuke from Diarmaid Ferriter in August 2015. Having reviewed some of the evidence, he concluded: 'The path to freedom for Irish women? I don't think so.'[80] It is hard to disagree. The testimony of several admiring female witnesses suggests that not only were his close political associates all men but he did not regard it as worth his while to discuss political matters with women. This prompted Hart to suggest that Collins may have seen female activists as 'the servant class of the revolution, rarely as colleagues or comrades, more often as landladies, maids or cooks', while anyone reviewing the correspondence between Collins and Kitty Kiernan will surely, like Tim Pat Coogan, be struck by 'the want of intellectual communication between them.'[81]

In 2007 Mary Kenny drew on the same correspondence in a discussion of Collins and religion. She pointed out, accurately, that in his letters to Kiernan during the Treaty negotiations Collins appeared devout, if not pious, reassuring Kiernan as to his daily attendance at Mass.[82] This may, in part, have been about impressing, or bonding with, his fiancée. Yet he was attending Mass on a daily basis and this seems to have been of value to him then. In apparent contrast, if the young Collins was not anti-clerical then he was of the definite opinion that the clergy had no business meddling in politics. Béaslaí wrote of him giving a paper in London during which he denounced 'the clergy in an unmerciful fashion'. No doubt with an audience of 1926 in mind, Béaslaí implied that Collins grew out of this youthful pose.[83] It was, however, an attitude shared by many republicans, who took a dim view of clerical condemnations of the IRB.

As noted earlier, Collins was prepared to challenge Denis Kelly, the Bishop of Ross, when Kelly obstructed INA & VDF collections in his diocese during the summer of 1917. Reportedly, his response to the issuing of a decree by Daniel Cohalan, the Bishop of Cork, on 12 December 1920, which excommunicated those who 'organise or take part in an ambush or in kidnapping' was to declare 'if I had my way, that ___ bishop would be shot'.[84] On the other hand, also in December 1920, he was willing to meet with Patrick Clune, the Archbishop of Perth, who was then attempting to broker a truce with the British, while he made prominent use of Bishop Fogarty as a trustee of the Dáil Loan.[85] It seems likely that Collins's attitudes varied quite naturally depending on the audience and across time. Not only does he appear to have been capable of separating his personal faith from his attitude to the institution, the clergy and the hierarchy, but his view of a bishop's intervention in politics no doubt depended on whether he agreed with the particular intervention.

Kenny also speculated that Collins would have created a more secular Ireland than that which emerged under de Valera.[86] This seems doubtful. De Valera's constitution of 1937 reflected the influence of Catholic social thinking in a way that the Irish Free State Constitution did not but Cumann na nGaedheal was every bit as, if not more, deferential to the Roman Catholic Church than Fianna Fáil. Even if Collins had lived, there is little reason to think that the circumstances of the Civil War would not have drawn the pro-Treaty elite and the Catholic Church into close alliance. Neither does it seem likely that, with Collins at their head, his pro-Treaty colleagues would have proved any less pliable in the face of the forceful clerical and lay Catholic lobbies of the 1920s. If nothing else, the pragmatist in Collins indicates otherwise. The sparse evidence of the Dáil record also suggests that Collins was impatient with sermonising and was prepared to resist, at least to some extent, calls to use parliament as a force for social control. In particular, this emerged in resistance to calls for an inquiry into the manufacture and sale of intoxicants and calls for the closing of public houses on St Patrick's Day in 1922, calls that had followed lobbying by Catholic abstinence associations.[87] There are also fragments of evidence to suggest that Collins may have acted as a reassuring presence for the minority populations in the new state. Though it was almost certainly as much a matter of pragmatism as principle, he told a delegation from the synod of the Church of Ireland on 22 May 1922 that 'Ireland required the services of all her sons of every class and creed' and condemned recent attacks on members of their community.[88]

Why do so many commentators imply that Collins would have shaped an independent Ireland that would have differed fundamentally from what emerged in his absence? The first cause is, of course, their dissatisfaction with that Ireland, and their own need to imagine an alternative. If Collins becomes a candidate for the lost leader of that alternative it can only be because we concentrate on his evident abilities, his pragmatism and his capacity for change. Collins, the champion of a different, better, new Ireland, begins to look rather more threadbare when his beliefs and thought are examined. He had hopes and aspirations for the country that would emerge after the departure of the British but these were informed by assumptions that were widely shared rather than by any distinctive or developed plan for the future.

10th April 1922

My Dearest Kitty

No letter again today —
I got back from Wexford late last
night but it was only this morning
I got your wire. — There was
a very good meeting at Wexford
and a very good reception all along
both going and coming. No
interruption at all at the meeting.

What has happened to you
though seriously not to have written
for three days I suppose you've
been enjoying yourself too well or
something — staying up at night
and in bed at day. Is that it?
How did the hunt go on?
Honestly I do think it a shame

In this letter of April 1922 to his fiancée, Kitty Kiernan, Collins expresses his fears that 'the country has before it what may be the worst period yet' while stressing that 'As God knows, I do not want to be worrying you with these things'. (National Library of Ireland)

2

You haven't written — but then
I may be hard on you there
may be a real reason and if
I said anything — but then I
don't say anythings that I
have to regret afterwards.

Things are rapidly becoming
as bad as they can be and
the country has before it what
may be the ~~first~~ worst
period yet. A few madmen may
do anything. Indeed they are
just getting on the pressure gradually
— they go on from cutting a tree
to cutting a railway line, then
to firing at a barrack, then to
firing at a lorry, and so on.
But God knows I do not want

to be worrying you with these
things.

Are you going to Nobber for
Easter? Or are you going anywhere
I'm most awfully anxious to see
you quickly and this week is
going to be a bad week with
me by the look of things. Any
improvement in the Connemara
plans yet? Kitty do please
hurry with making that definite
but I am anxious about you.
I wonder if you're writing even
to day — Yes? No?

May God bless you
Fondest love Micéal

That 'As God knows' may just have been a turn of phrase but it probably signified more than that: Collins's weariness just then, an apology, belief. Here Collins is pictured in Free State uniform, kissing a bishop's ring, probably that of Archbishop James Duhig of Brisbane at Arthur Griffith's funeral. *(National Library of Ireland)*

6

"Most "Wanted" Man in the World":

Collins and Celebrity[1]

On 21 January 1922 James Crabtree entered the Worsthorne annual fancy dress contest. A doughty competitor in the under-eight category he was only a little fellow, probably a truculent little fellow having come a no doubt surly second to a girl called Florence Powell. Gripping his consolation prize, he, or at least whoever rigged him out for the contest, may well have decided to try a different tack next time – Charlie Chaplin, Lawrence of Arabia, even Lloyd George if he was still in charge – certainly not that Michael Collins fellow who had cost little James first place this year.[2] But in an odd way James Crabtree was a measure of far more than his own disappointment that day. A small boy in a small village on the outskirts of Burnley, Lancashire, dressed up in whatever amounted to a Michael Collins costume, was a strange measure of what Michael Collins had become. James Crabtree was proof of just how famous Michael Collins was in January 1922.

It is unlikely young Crabtree would have risked such a costume even months before; a small English child in a small English village dressed up as the notorious head of 'the murder gang' in Ireland, as many newspapers called Collins, might well have tested the mettle of Worsthorne's village matrons.[3] Certainly, it would not have secured him a respectable second place in 1921. Something had changed, something that is much more striking to see in the places where Collins was so clearly once reviled, in the *Burnley News*, and the *Daily Mirror*; in the *News of the World*, in the *Yorkshire Post*, in the many, many newspapers from Dundee to Devon that fuelled and fed a public fascination with Collins in 1921 and 1922. Infamy had turned into a kind of fame, and Michael Collins while certainly famous, celebrated and feted at home, while certainly fodder for the fascination of the Irish public and press, became a kind of celebrity abroad. And it was there to see in the small things most of all. Odds of four-to-one could be got on Michael Collins in August 1921, on Michael Collins the whippet, that is, racing in the 130 yards £10 whippet handicap at Stockton.[4] 'Mick Collins' the racehorse was one of many that prompted the *Yorkshire Post* to muse on how the names of thoroughbreds are 'a by no means negligible index to our history', are 'a reflex of our causes célèbre'.[5] But Frank Blewitt's entry of a 'Michael Collins monument' in a Penzance sandcastle contest just days after Collins's death maybe says it best of all. Frank Blewitt was a nine-year-old boy, not from Cork but from Cornwall, and he clearly knew enough about Michael Collins to carve his name in the sand.[6]

But why should Collins's celebrity matter? Why piece back together the patchwork of gossip and tittle-tattle that makes for an exaggerated or just a superficial sense of him? Why look when it goes so directly against the grain of recent biographies which have forsworn the 'story nearly fantastic in its details' for 'the real' Mick?[7] The answer might lie in what we mean by 'the real' Mick or whose 'real' Mick we are thinking of. For most people the Michael Collins of the newspapers and the newsreels was the only 'real' Collins they knew. Most did not have the luxury of the writer Signe Toksvig's choice, choosing not to meet him 'for I like to keep a few heroes intact', and they relied on the daily diet of news

Something of the public fascination with Collins is caught in this still from a British Pathé newsreel. *(British Pathé)*

the papers served up.[8] He was the Collins they constructed from their belief or bemusement with what they had heard or read. They made him piecemeal from rumours and gossip columns and second- or third-hand news.

Equally, the impulse to mythologise or idolise can still say something about the kind of Collins many people needed to have. Whatever the 'real' Collins did or did not do, it was often only judged or understood according to the kind of Collins people wanted him to be. And how and why and when he became the focus of so much adulation or revulsion can tell us a lot, as we saw in Chapter 3, about the kind of war he fought, the kind of peace he made. His celebrity can even explain why so much could be said of him by so many for so long after his death. The journalist C.H. Bretherton said Collins was 'scarcely cold in his grave before he became the hero of as many mythical adventures as Fionn'.[9] But Bretherton got this, as many other things, wrong: Collins had become whatever Fionn the public wanted long before that point. Most of the myths were already in place before Béal na mBláth did its dark work. Death simply removed the remaining restraints. But his celebrity is also important because of his keen awareness of it. How he used it, how it was used against him, how it helped and how it hindered him, are all part of the Collins that cannot be separated from the kind of scrutiny under which he found himself. Living up or down to reputations and expectations was part of what strengthened and weakened him; in the end it may have even cost him his life.

If these are not reasons enough then another remains: his celebrity, and the extent of its reach, sets him apart from almost all of his comrades. Many were written of, many were reported on locally, but none, possibly with the exception of the far less photogenic de Valera, fascinated as Collins did. While some were satisfied to be legends in their own townlands, only Collins made the headlines from San Francisco to Sydney and in most places between. As 'the most famous of all the IRA leaders', this celebrity gave him power over his colleagues in life and this celebrity has been remorseless to them in death.[10]

And that celebrity was a particularly modern one. Peter Hart describes him as 'the first example of that twentieth-century phenomenon: the guerrilla celebrity', and then more heavy-handedly, as 'the revolution's Princess Diana'; but however fittingly or awkwardly characterised, Collins's fame was in a large part the creation of the sensational and the increasingly popular press.[11] Growing steadily since the 1860s, but flourishing through and in the wake of the Great

THE BAD MAN OF IRELAND.

MICHAEL COLLINS AND THE MURDER GANG.

By "R. I. C."

Michael Collins, the head of the Irish murder gang, is slowly assuming the importance of a symbol. He is to the British Tommy engaged in the Irish war a figure of speech and legend just as in the great war "Old von Kluck," Hindenburg, and Tirpitz typified the opposition. Apart from this fleeting phase of canteen popularity, it is not fair to class Collins with men who, after all, were of some importance

MICHAEL COLLINS.

in history. Mike is a relatively young man, and is the son of a small farmer near Clonakilty, in the wilds of Co. Cork. Just before the war he came over to England, and after a period of undistinguished service as office-boy and clerk to a commercial concern, he found employment as a temporary sorter of letters in the G.P.O.

It was the brutal tyranny of Lord Derby that drove Collins into the ranks of the revolutionists. The Derby scheme, with its hidden innuendo that fit and robust young Irishmen who were good enough to accept the jobs and salaries of Englishmen who were fighting Germans should also be asked to fight Germans, was enough for him. He fled back to Ireland and adopted Irish patriotism as a profession.

At the moment the ranks of professional patriotism were full and salaried billets scarce, so Mike became a clerk in the employment of a small firm of Dublin accountants. In the intervals of being an Irish Volunteer and talking he mastered the intricacies of international finance, or at least so much of it as came his way, considering his relatively unimportant position in the outer office of his employers. Then came the rebellion of Easter 1916, and Mike was one of the survivors.

This photograph, used by the *Daily Express* to illustrate their 'Bad Man of Ireland' article of 17 March 1921, was already in circulation for many months, and, as the next document suggests, had already appeared in a number of publications in 1920. (Daily Express, *17 March 1921, Daily Express/N&S Syndication*)

A.O'B.   Memo to L.

No 508   17. 12. 1920.

1.   I acknowledge receipt of memos nos.753,754,755,756,757,
also, one memo not numbered and signed "F".

2.   CORRESPONDENCE (753): This does not call for any further
remark from me

3.   COVERING ADDRESSES (753) I told the Propaganda Dept. I
assumed your note was a temporary thing. They have been sending
all sorts of complaints about the London Office not functioning
as far as they are concerned, etc..I suppose they are carrying
on the the usual way again. It is impossible, I'm afraid, to
prevent these difficulties so far as that Department is concerned
        I note also what you say about my own covering addresses.
The Propaganda Department did not convey to me the message that
came from you evidently. Quite obviously you could not have
said that all your covering addresses were raided.
        I have written a note to the Propaganda Dept. about this
question of addresses.

4.   "DAILY SKETCH (753) That photograph is the ordinary one
which they have distributed broadcast to their agents here in
Ireland. It is taken out of the Dail group which was photographed some time early last year. The same photograph has
appeared in several other English papers. I have no idea of
who "W.M." might be. There was a Willie Murphy of Shepherds'
Bush, who was connected with a firm of Chartered Accountants
who audited for the "Daily Mail". There was a W. McInerney"
also of Shepherds Bush, connected with the "Daily Herald" long
ago, and prior to that, with Northcliffe papers. I don't think
it would have been either of these.

5.   Seoirse (754) I hope you have got something definite since
you wrote your memo about his location. I am rather anxious
about this as I'm afraid he will be running short of funds, and in
his precarious circumstances this would be a serious matter for
him. I should not like to think of him doing a "hold-up"
somewhere on the Continent. Please advise me as soon as you hear
anything.

6.   R.I.C. Auxiliaries (755) Thanks for sending me the advertisement. I have sent it on to the Propaganda Dept with a note of my
own.

7.   "OBSERVER" (756) Thanks for sending me this cutting. I
had not been told it was an article by Stephen Gwynne Evidently
he is in close communion with certain of the Castle authorities
here.
Par. 8 attached to D453.   1.

9.   Two enclosures for Sean T. (one letter contains draft for
£500)

10.   Letter for D. Hales.

In a letter to Art O'Brien on 17 December 1920 Collins noted the use of the same photograph, this time by the *Daily Sketch*. The photograph had been taken at an early meeting of Dáil Éireann in 1919, and certainly challenges the idea that Collins was a faceless and mysterious figure. *(National Archives of Ireland)*

War, a thoroughly modern media fed a growing public appetite for gossip and scandal and sensational news.[12] Popular newspapers had long recognised by Collins's time that 'human drama' could 'generate more reader interest and enthusiasm' than traditional news, and with photographs to stir the sense of glamour and excitement even more, celebrity became entangled with the news.[13] And Collins seemed ideal fodder for the popular press to feast upon. He became a way to explain what the troubles in Ireland amounted to, a way to put a face to the violence the newspapers sometimes seemed at a loss to name. Just as the American press characterised much of the Mexican Revolution by their portrayal of Pancho Villa, the British newspapers crafted Collins as the elusive IRA leader bringing off yet another hair's-breadth escape.[14] There were rumours of his death in battle, and always the rush for the 'first picture' claimed proudly in September 1921 on the *Daily Mirror's* front page.[15] Never mind that the *Daily Express* had carried his picture and a quite precise biography of him back in March; the clamour of yet another first was always enough in itself.[16]

As early as October 1920 papers were reporting on 'the notorious Michael Collins'; by November 1920 it had become the 'Mystery of Collins'; by January 1921 some were 'beginning to wonder if there is such a man', such were the powers of the elusive 'mystery man of Ireland'.[17] And this coverage seemed to set the tone far beyond Fleet Street. By February 1921 he was already 'A man of mystery' to the *Derby Daily Telegraph*, the 'Irish De Wet' to the *Western Gazette*.[18] A month later the *Dundee Evening Telegraph* called him the 'MOST "WANTED" MAN IN THE WORLD' with all the urgency that upper case letters and inverted commas could bring. 'Romance of Elusive Michael Collins. Troops Who Did Not Look for Him in a Coffin', 'A Master of Disguise' with 'about half-a-dozen doubles' followed fast upon these capitalised words and suggests much of how this man was written about.[19] The *Yorkshire Post* was even quicker off the mark. '"Mysterious Mike" Evades Arrest' read the headline in early October 1920; and gripping his revolver, he came off the page as 'a desperate man', 'the "Moriarty" of the Irish Republican Brotherhood', swearing 'he will never be taken alive'.[20] By 1921 his notoriety was such that an American journalist quipped back to his editor, 'No interview with Collins. Did not find the man. Found a god.'[21]

While journalists often had stories syndicated to more than one newspaper, and while this may explain why paragraphs and headlines found their ways into all sorts of titles all over the world, whether in France or America, in China or in

India, this type of sensational tone crossed the newspaper genres. *The North China Herald and Supreme Court and Consular Gazette* called him 'The Sinn Fein Field Marshal' in November 1920.[22] The *Manchester Guardian* surmised that 'when the horror and the misery of the present years are forgotten', tales of Collins's exploits would provide 'episodes of high romance as realistic as anything in Dumas and Stevenson'.[23] It was quite a benign response for March 1921. The sober London *Times* noted that Collins was Christmasing in Cork almost as they would a titled gentleman in a society column and later photographed him accepting flowers from 'the poorer children' of Cork city.[24] It called him 'the people's hero and darling' when he died.[25] The *Financial Times* ran a 'human interest' piece on the 'popular hero of the hour', and remarked he was once a transfer clerk for a well-known firm of London Stock Exchange brokers.[26] Gossip, it seemed, could be tailored for every taste. Even the hard-line *Morning Post*, conceding that he was 'the Free State idol', admitted, however much it reviled him and what he stood for, that he 'was at any rate a brave man'.[27]

Full of photographs, firm views and sensational headlines, the *Daily Mirror* was read by more than a million people every day in 1921. In the same year the *Daily Mail* made it into more than 1.7 million homes, while nearly two million took their Sunday helping of scandal from the *News of the World*.[28] Although 1918 saw the tide just about turn in Britain from the local press to the national Sundays and dailies, the local and regional press still held their own, and for the purposes of measuring Michael Collins's fame in this chapter they show just how far and how broadly it could reach.[29] The London *Times* may have sold just over 110,000 copies each day, the *Morning Post* for all its bluster and vitriol, with a mere 50,000, may have prided themselves on forming more discerning opinion, but their more popular counterparts, along with an increasingly popular illustrated press, defined what celebrity was, and, for many, defined what Michael Collins meant.[30]

A journalist from the *Gloucester Citizen*, in London to cover the arrival of the Irish plenipotentiaries, watched as the cheering crowds welcomed the Irishmen to Downing Street and was duly challenged to consider what this celebrity was. He stood with a colleague from the French press and was struck by what he saw as the Frenchman's cynicism, by the Frenchman's contempt for the crowd. 'This could happen in no other country', the French journalist said, 'unless they believe Michael Collins is a Dick Turpin they have no use for him … what interest do

Typical of a softening of Collins's image in the British press, this photograph, used in a number of newspapers, was taken in April 1922 after a speech by Collins in Cork city. While *The Times* described him receiving 'a beautiful bouquet from the poorer children of Cork', this well-dressed pair were clearly meeting Collins in their Sunday best. *(National Library of Ireland)*

they take in Mr Arthur Griffith?'[31] The *Daily Mirror* was soon to prove his point. By February 1922 the paper complained that 'Mr Michael Collins' now had none of the power he 'possessed as the "mystery" leader of a desperate guerrilla war, he has a sadly diminished influence as a peaceful and prosaic Minister'.[32] The paper's interest in him was only really restored when news came through of him leading a new army, when he became a man of action again: 'Mr Collins will look quite an imposing young general', and once more they rushed him to the front page when the first photographs of Collins in uniform came in.[33] There were plenty of prosaic politicians; the *Daily Mirror* needed Collins to be more than that to satisfy their readers' demands.

Collins himself knew the power and the fickle nature of this kind of fame. 'I would not matter very much to anybody were it not for the things the English are saying about me', he admitted in May 1921, and, if we can believe Hayden Talbot's 'own story' of Collins, the value Collins placed on his own 'legend' was clear.[34] Talbot records him making the following case as to why de Valera should not have sent him to London to negotiate:

> for several years – rightly or wrongly makes no difference – the English had held me to be the one man most necessary to capture because they held me to be the one man responsible for the smashing of their Secret Service organisation and for their failure to terrorise the Irish people with their Black and Tans. Brugha has spoken of this English legend as having been altogether of newspaper manufacture. What difference does that make? The important fact was that in England, as in Ireland, the Michael Collins legend existed. It pictured me a mysterious active menace – elusive, unknown, unaccountable. And in this respect I was the only living Irishman of whom this could be said. If and as long as the legend continued to exert its influence on English minds, the accruing advantage to our cause would continue. Bring me into the spotlight of a London conference and quickly would be discovered the common clay of which I am made! The glamour of the legendary figure would be gone forever.[35]

Collins may well have been turning an old argument of de Valera's against him. Back in January 1921, when de Valera was trying to convince Collins to come to

THE STAR, TUESDAY, OCTOBER 11, 1921.

"Mysterious Mick" Collins.
(Wearing his best smile for Low.)

'"Mysterious Mick" Collins wearing his smile for Low' quite deftly punctured the figure of 'mysterious active menace' Collins described. Low, best known for his creation of the figure Colonel Blimp in the 1930s, had been critical of Lloyd George's policy in Ireland in a number of cartoons in *The Star*. In January 1921, for example, he compared the behaviour of the British forces in Ireland to that of the German army in Belgium in 1914. *The Star*, founded by the nationalist MP T.P. O'Connor in 1888, was liberal in outlook and had been staunchly opposed to the Boer War. *(David Low/Solo Syndication, British Cartoon Archive)* the United States, he appealed to Collins on those very terms: 'you probably do not appreciate, as I do, what your presence will mean there for the cause, if only you will not be too modest to exploit your fame, or notoriety if you prefer it'.[36] But de Valera did not listen, just as Collins had not listened then. On 11 October 1921 David Low drew his cartoon '"Mysterious Mick" Collins' for *The Star*, and, rather simply, proved Collins's point.[37] He was not very menacing or mysterious any more.

Whether evading the press by travelling separately from the rest of the delegation or delaying another day in Dublin as a way to heighten the newspapers' expectations of his arrival, whether giving interviews to the popular British and American papers at key points to make his case, Collins certainly knew the power of the medium and realised the value of the character the press had turned him into throughout 1921. All those years living in London must have taught him much about the nature of the British press. His much-publicised joke when he came upon a rifle in 'Number 10' and called on the Prime Minister to get a photographer quickly to capture him in that place with rifle in hand suggests he knew very well what he had become to the newspapers that went on to lap up this very anecdote.[38] He played the dangerous rebel for them when he could, allegedly noting to journalists on his arrival in London in October 1921 that 'I have held up the British Empire and richly have I enjoyed … [the] adventures', intimating that he had been over to the city secretly in the summer, and that he had been able to move freely around in spite of all the money on his head.[39] Carl Ackerman, the American journalist, managed to meet him in August 1920, and in an interview that was paraphrased as far afield as the *Times of India* and beyond, Collins was happy to play the Scarlet Pimpernel for him. Ackerman was told in no uncertain terms, 'I know you better than you know me'.[40] Noting the clandestine nature of the meeting, the sequences of secret knocks before doors were opened to let him in, it maybe suited Ackerman's syndication numbers to play along.

Other contemporary accounts confirm his prominence. Churchill's cousin, Clare Sheridan, who was writing then for the *New York World*, recorded a train trip she took with Collins from Dublin to Cork in June 1922. She noted the interruption 'at every station by people who opened the carriage door for a sight of him, apologising, asking for a handshake or throwing in a word of welcome. Some wanted to show him to their children', so the child could at least grow up to boast that they had met that Collins fellow once. Sheridan left him at

Dáil Éireann.

8. 10. 1921.

I don't know at the moment
whether there is a special financial
arrangement made for the remainder
of the party. Please send me £50
which I'll account for separately.
It can be incorporated in the
general accounts later on. At the
moment I have about £3 in my pocket.
It would be serious if I could not
give a porter a tip at Holyhead.

M O C

G.M.

Sent £50.
5.00.
8/7/21

£ 15 6cod

Deeply conscious of how he would be perceived, Collins wrote to the Department of Finance just after his arrival in London to request a loan of £50. In much the same way that the delegation was seen to arrive at the opening sessions of the negotiations in Rolls-Royce cars, appearances mattered even down to the amount of the porter's tip. *(National Archives of Ireland)*

Pictured here with one of his older constituents in Cork just before the June 1922 election, Collins tried to exploit media interest in him to the greatest possible effect. With far greater access to the media than any of his anti-Treaty opponents, he used that advantage as much as he could. *(National Library of Ireland)*

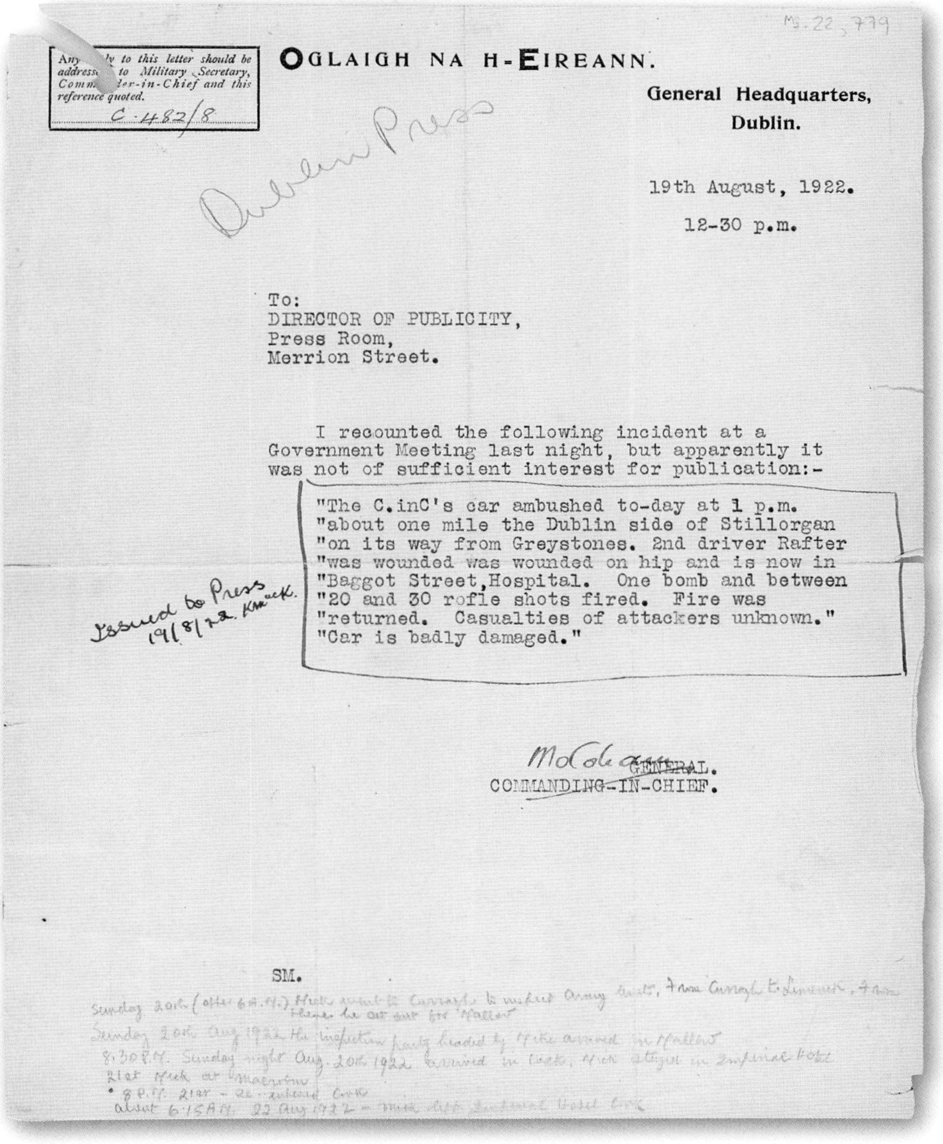

Any reply to this letter should be
addressed to Military Secretary,
Commander-in-Chief and this
reference quoted.

C. 482/8

ÓGLAIGH NA H-ÉIREANN.

Dublin Press

**General Headquarters,
Dublin.**

19th August, 1922.

12-30 p.m.

To:
DIRECTOR OF PUBLICITY,
Press Room,
Merrion Street.

I recounted the following incident at a
Government Meeting last night, but apparently it
was not of sufficient interest for publication:-

*Issued to Press
19/8/22. Kavanagh.*

"The C.inC's car ambushed to-day at 1 p.m.
"about one mile the Dublin side of Stillorgan
"on its way from Greystones. 2nd driver Rafter
"was wounded was wounded on hip and is now in
"Baggot Street, Hospital.   One bomb and between
"20 and 30 rifle shots fired.   Fire was
"returned.   Casualties of attackers unknown."
"Car is badly damaged."

M. Collins ~~GENERAL.~~
~~COMMANDING-IN-CHIEF.~~

SM.

[handwritten notes:]
Sunday 20th (after 6 P.M.) Mick went to Curragh to inspect Army ... from Curragh to Limerick, ...
... he set out for Mallow
Sunday 20th Aug 1922 the inspection party headed by Mike arrived in Mallow
8.30 P.M. Sunday night Aug. 20th 1922 arrived in Cork, Mick stayed in Imperial Hotel
21st Mick at Macroom
* 8 P.M. 21st - 22 entered Cork
about 6.15 AM. 22 Aug 1922 — Mick left Imperial Hotel Cork

Collins's huffy rebuke, sent just days before his death to the Director of Publicity, Desmond FitzGerald, shows just how conscious he was of the power of his own public persona. It was another weapon to draw on in civil war. *(National Library of Ireland)*

Cork station, watching as he 'disappeared' into 'a cheering crowd'; welcomed as 'the people's idol' just as the *Daily Telegraph* said he was.[41] Nankivell and Loch, two writers who had come to Dublin to see troubled Ireland for themselves, called him 'the man whom public imagination had lifted highest of all', and they measured his elevation by the money on his head: £4,000 they heard.[42] The sum grew to £10,000, to £20,000, to £40,000, just as Chinese whispers magnified his exploits and escapes.[43] Brigadier General Crozier felt obliged to write to the *Times* in 1924 to settle the point. It was never more than £1,000.[44] But this public Collins had an odd effect even on those charged with capturing him. While Nevil Macready felt sure that 'to all soldiers … Collins was, and must for ever be, the embodiment of a campaign of ruthless murder', others were not so certain and seemed swept up in the wider fascination with him.[45] Private J.P. Swindlehurst, having read about him in the press, noted in his diary on 9 January 1921: 'He must be famous, £500 is being offered dead or alive for his capture, but all the Black and Tans … and CID men from Scotland Yard, can't get hold of him.' The entry of 28 February noted that Collins was still at large: 'I was going to say I hope he keeps free, but someone might see this before I get it home so that is better left unwritten.'[46] Because Swindlehurst forgot or never got the chance to un-write the written, we have some sense at least of how Collins's celebrity may have seeped in and affected the other side.

In some respects, the fourth estate had done the British government some service. By crafting Collins into 'the elusive Michael Collins', by making him a dastardly Moriarty, 'the genius of fighting Ireland', it seemed understandable, reasonable almost, that such a man should never be caught.[47] Equally, the smiling, charming Collins that emerged in the gossip columns in October 1921, or the gallant, heroic Collins that surfaced by December, 'the coolest man on board' helping to launch lifeboats when the Dublin mail boat he travelled on collided with another boat, countered the vigorous criticism that the Prime Minister was sitting down to deal with a murderer, something Lloyd George had felt the public could not accept or countenance just months before.[48] Back in the summer of 1921 Lloyd George set out his problem thus: 'the question is whether I can see Michael Collins … whether the British people would be willing for us to negotiate with the head of a band of murderers … it would be rather like the Prime Minister of the day seeing Kelly, who was engaged in the Phoenix Park murders'.[49] The softening of Collins's image in the British press, the kind of

Collins who had romantic adventures and escapades, may bear some relationship to Lloyd George's need to prepare the British public for the thought of such a man in Downing Street. Just days after the negotiations began Churchill's private secretary, Edward Marsh, wrote to the *Morning Post* to deny the allegation that 'Mr Churchill … listened with interest to Mr Michael Collins' "adventures"'; in October 1921 it was as delicate for Churchill and his colleagues as that.[50] While the *Edinburgh Evening News* was confident that 'the fighter has become friend', the *Manchester Guardian* provided its readers with a slightly more sceptical insight: 'the success of England … is largely due to her bad memory', in knowing when it was expedient to forget.[51]

While wariness of Collins and of the act of negotiation certainly remained, many in Whitehall also seem to have been beguiled by Collins's fame. On the day negotiations began, 'the dignified windows of the Foreign Office, facing the Premier's residence, were filled with official heads, intently watching the scene, and high officials may have caught the cry "Up the rebels!" from the crowd beneath … Of course all eyes were eager for a glimpse of the redoubtable Sinn Fein Commander-in-Chief, the elusive Mr Michael Collins, whose athletic form and pugnacious features were soon picked out'.[52] The civil servants in the Foreign Office were as curious as all the rest. The British negotiating team and those in its inner circle seemed familiar with the myths as well, seemed to have been led to expect someone far more impressive than the man they encountered. Many of those close to the negotiations recorded a private disappointment on their first meeting with him that suggests something had led them to believe he would be made of more. Although the *Manchester Guardian* insisted that 'British ministers who had accepted Dublin Castle's theory of Collins as the blood-thirsty chief of a murder gang' found themselves instead 'confronted with a severely practical politician, tenacious in his demands', it seems expectations were not met for quite different reasons.[53] Macready called him 'a great disappointment, flippantly trying to get out of corners by poor jokes in bad taste'; Lloyd George referred to his 'simple sort of mind', the mind 'found in a great military commander' but a simple one nonetheless.[54] 'Collins was an uneducated rather stupid man' according to *Manchester Guardian* editor C.P. Scott, although Scott still maintained he liked him with the next breath.[55] Most seemed so struck by his ordinariness that they must have come to take the newspaper version of him at least somewhat to heart.

Gossip columns lapped up and dished out the anecdotes from the negotiations: the two houses rented by the Irish delegation, the 'army of pretty Irish girls … at work there', Mrs Folkard the 'jolly Irishwoman' brought over to 'rule the kitchen' at Hans Place, Lloyd George playing mother and pouring out the tea; cigars all round at Number 10; 'Conference Gossip' wondering what could have kept 'Mr Churchill' and 'Mr Michael Collins' chatting together for so long.[56] It all fed into the appetite for news of him. Frank O'Connor would go further: Collins was the only point of popular interest in the negotiations at all. He was the only member of the otherwise 'rather colourless delegation' that the 'photographers, pressmen and gossip writers' were interested in; that 'his presence' and his presence alone 'assured the negotiations a good Press'; that the media simply 'delighted in him'.[57] Indeed, the *Times of India* later called him 'the idol of the street crowds'.[58] But coming out into the open had changed the kind of celebrity he was. The mysterious mastermind of murder, the elusive figure became the hero of popular romance. For the *Hull Daily Mail* this 'modern outlaw' proved romance could still thrive in a world grown 'hopelessly humdrum'.[59] Stress on his fine figure, his 'raven's wing' black hair, his 'typically Irish blue' eyes, gathered more and more interest to him as a 'rollicking figure of dare-devil Irish romance'.[60]

The crush of women the press described sending him off from Euston Station in early December 1921 also confirmed him as a celebrity in a very modern sense. More than a dozen police were reported necessary to save him from 'the wild stampede', and even so, one young lady still managed to break through the cordon and to catch him in a hearty embrace, planting 'kisses upon his cheeks with wonderful rapidity'.[61] By then he may well have been used to it; he was reportedly 'mobbed by scores of colleens, who wished to kiss him' when he appeared at a reception in October at the Albert Hall.[62] Although the *Sunday Pictorial* was among the few to admit that 'the real Mike was as little like a film hero as Winston Churchill', that 'in his later days' he acquired 'a rather rotund figure and double chin', most newspapers remained blind to his expanding curves (they were not to know that Collins had to return his new uniform for alterations because 'it is too tight in the waist and neck').[63] It helped that he was photogenic, that he periodically played up to the cameras, that he was the only one to cut a subdued but nonetheless smiling dash in the Pathé newsreel filmed after the signing of the Treaty.[64]

But it was a very modern kind of celebrity in all sorts of other ways too. Tom

Collins was certainly the chief figure of interest when British Pathé filmed the two negotiating teams on the announcement of the signing of the Treaty. *(British Pathé)*

Jones, secretary to the British delegation, later wrote of the 'girls who pursued him for favours'; while the travel writer H.V. Morton remembered the fierce competition among society hostesses 'to produce "Mick" Collins at a dinner-party', that having him to dinner became 'the dream of many of a foolish woman's life' in late 1921. Collins, Morton wrote, had to fight hard against becoming 'a social sight'.[65] The 'Sinn Fein delegation' even admitted to the *Yorkshire Evening Post* that 'quite a number of extraordinary individuals call with the object of being photographed with Mr Michael Collins'.[66] His engagement, '"Mike" Collins' marriage' plans – to wed at Tara 'during the revival of the ancient Tailtean [*sic*] Games' apparently – brought scrutiny further into his private life.[67] Although Kitty Kiernan seemed amused by this type of coverage, teasing him 'that in *The Sketch* there are lovely pictures of the pretty girl secretaries', and that 'no doubt you will have a word with them!!', her own bereavement became the stuff to add to the sensation of his death.[68] The *Daily Mail* claimed that but for Griffith's death the couple would have married on the day Collins was killed at Béal na mBláth. It carried photographs of Kiernan, and cast her an all the more pathetic figure as the woman who 'had already purchased her trousseau'.[69] The *Daily Mirror's* 'Today's Gossip' column kept up with Kitty Kiernan even after his death: 'she has been staying a fortnight in Paris' and 'leading a very secluded life'.[70] The wedding of her sister also merited remark.[71]

'Danny boy', his Kerry blue terrier, did not escape attention either. British Pathé filmed his dog winning the puppy class in a dog show in November 1921, while 'Michael Collins Owns a Dog' exclaimed the headline in *The Freeman's Journal*, as if a precious and unknown secret had suddenly come to light.[72] When the dog competed at Crufts the following February it made the British press, described as 'a sort of doggish ambassador from the Irish Free State'; it probably helped that King George V was showing his Labradors there the same year. Journalists clucked that Collins had set a new 'Fashion in Dogs' given the number of Kerry Blues at the Kennel Club show at the Crystal Palace just a month after his death in September 1922. 'Everybody is for that little fellow just now, some from sentimental reasons as well as from a desire to be in the vogue. Michael Collins made the Kerry blue his particular favourite'.[73] It was modern celebrity, indeed.

What Peter Hart calls 'Collinsmania' possibly expressed itself at its grasping best in the rush to get exclusive rights to the story of his life.[74] 'Will you consider

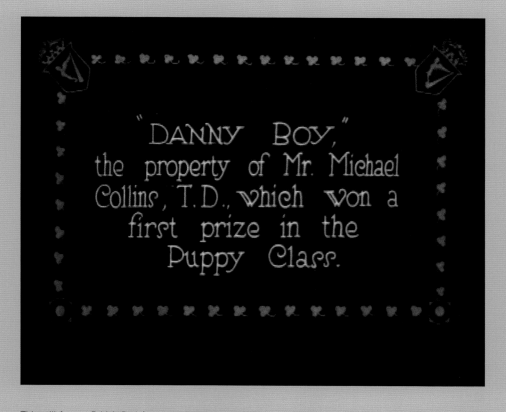

This still from a British Pathé newsreel suggests something of the level of interest in all aspects of Collins's life by the end of 1921 and throughout 1922. While nothing seemed too trivial, this type of media attention concocted a Collins with a deeply human side. *(British Pathé)*

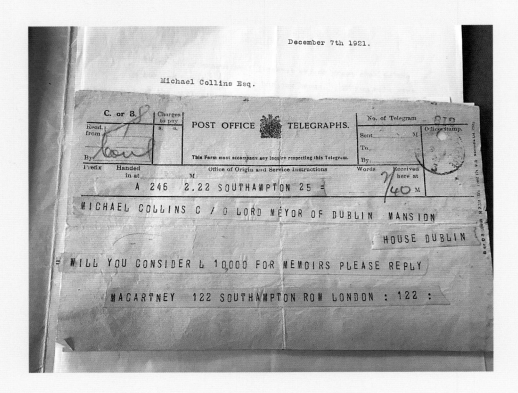

One of many offers, the amount is suggestive of how lucrative Collins's life story had become by the summer of 1921. The competition to publish an authorised account of his life only increased after the Treaty was signed.
(National Library of Ireland)

L[£]10,000 for memoirs. Please reply' was the telegram sent to Collins from W.H.S. Macartney, a London agent, in July 1921.[75] The Truce was just days old. While his refusal of this offer simply gave the press something else to marvel at, other offers followed: $25,000 from the *New York World*, a mere £2,000 from the *Daily Despatch*, and £10,000, again from Macartney, all in January 1922.[76] While most agents and journalists were just eager to get him to agree, the *Daily Despatch* did specify its readers' interests: 'They do not want "political revelations" so much as the human story'; romance and derring-do should be at the forefront of his mind.[77] To put the offers in context, Winston Churchill received a variety of amounts from British and American agents and publishers on the strength of his forthcoming book, *The World Crisis*. The sums were similar to those offered to Collins: £3,000 from a US agent, £9,000 from a British publisher, another £10,000 from various syndications and rights. Churchill spent part of his first cheque on a new Rolls-Royce.[78] T.E. Lawrence was paid £2,000 by the *Daily Telegraph* for the 1926–7 serialisation of *Revolt in the Desert* and a £3,000 advance for an abridged *Seven Pillars of Wisdom* from Jonathan Cape.[79] Newspapers remarked 'the smallness of the amount' Collins left when he died, a mere £1,950, particularly when 'tales of his exploits' could 'have brought in £50,000'.[80]

Although Collins refused the prospect of a million-dollar speaking tour of the United States when it was dangled before him by the American journalist Hayden Talbot, Collins met with him and clearly contributed to Talbot's story of his life.[81] Talbot, knowing an interview with Collins 'was patently what newspaper readers most wanted', promised him access to 'my fifteen million readers in America', and it was obviously an opportunity Collins felt he could not pass up.[82] Piaras Béaslaí, as Director of Army Publicity, and, in practice, chief press censor during the Civil War, used his position to attempt to block the *Sunday Express* serialisation of what he termed Talbot's 'bogus' work.[83] He called on the *Irish Independent* to do all it could to 'expose the forgery', 'a forgery founded upon current gossip mostly misinformed'. Nonetheless, Talbot's work, whether 'too much hero-worship and distinctly too little history', became the first lengthy published account of Collins's life.[84] Béaslaí again led the charge against a series of articles carried in *The World's Pictorial News* in September 1922.[85] 'The Secret history of Michael Collins by one of his bodyguard' was deemed sensational and in very bad taste published so shortly after Collins's death. While most claim Béaslaí objected to the type of overblown stories of Collins riding around on a white horse, the nature of the publication might have had something to do with it as well. The three issues which carried his 'Secret history' had Collins jostling with stories of 'The ex-Kaiser's love intrigue', the 'Rooking of Film Struck Girls', and the quaint story of 'Three men, a Eurasian girl, and the call of the east'.[86] Collins's life was on the level of scantily clad film stars and poisoning stories, and Béaslaí just couldn't have that.

It should be remembered that even before these articles went to press Béaslaí was eagerly pushing for his own appointment as Collins's official biographer: 'If this is not done you will have some chancer "on the make" butting in and dealing with our dead hero in a way that none of us would like.' He complained that 'the English papers' were already 'publishing rubbish and fables about him' and such lies simply had to be put right.[87] A cynic might suggest Béaslaí was moved to use his powers to censor by less honourable motives: he was privy to the various offers made to Collins (they are now archived in his papers after all), and certainly Hayden Talbot believed Béaslaí's motives were no better than his own.[88] He wrote, 'For a year past Beasley [sic] has been trying to negotiate in these quarters (i.e. with the London correspondents of American newspapers) for the publication of inside stuff about Michael Collins.'[89] Béaslaí, of course, refuted this allegation when it appeared in the *Sunday Express*, but Michael Collins was quite a commodity in 1922.

When R.D. Blumenfeld, editor of the *Daily Express*, tried to convince Collins to 'write the story of your adventures' for the paper in December 1921, he offered to 'pay generously for them', but he also tried to lure Collins in with the prospect that his words, in Blumenfeld's paper, would 'remove the false impression that exists in this country' about him and about Ireland, that his story would 'do great good in the new and happier era that has now begun'.[90] Although the ink was barely dry on the Treaty when Blumenfeld made this suggestion, and although signing the Treaty marked another shift in Collins's celebrity, the main British newspapers predictably continued to reflect the ups and downs of the official view. They questioned and criticised Collins in the early months of 1922, and called him 'pigeon-livered' and 'powerless' because of the de Valera pact.[91] They scorned him for his inaction in Dublin when Sir Henry Wilson was killed, but within days of firing on the Four Courts, he was 'the "Big Fella"' once again.[92] He was the 'Idol of his Troops', and 'no cheap novel … can compete with the real truth of his fighting life'.[93] And so went the ebb and flow of coverage of his

15th September, 1922.

To:
The Editor,
"Sunday Express".

Sir,

    In a letter by HAYDEN TALBOT in the "Sunday Express" of September 10th the following statement is made about me:-

    "For a year past Beasley has been trying to negotiate
    "in these quarters (i.e. with the London Correspondents
    "of American newspapers) for the publication of 'inside
    "stuff' about MICHAEL COLLINS."

    The statement is a lie. I have never at any time tried to negotiate with anybody for the publication of 'inside stuff' about the late General Collins.

    Yours etc.

Piaras Béaslaí

COMMANDANT GENERAL.

Piaras Béaslaí was deeply protective of his position as Collins's biographer. As this letter suggests he was prepared to battle hard to defend, what Peter Hart called, his position as 'the Big Fellow's Boswell'. *(National Library of Ireland)*

THE LONDON EXPRESS NEWSPAPER LTD.

TELEGRAMS:
"EXPRESS, FLEET, LONDON."

TELEPHONE: HOLBORN 6688.
(PRIVATE BRANCH EXCHANGE).

**The
Daily Express**

EDITORIAL OFFICES:
8, SHOE LANE,
FLEET ST., LONDON,
E.C.4.

December 7th 1921.

Michael Collins Esq.

Dear Sir:

Mr. Wright has informed me of his communications
with you yesterday on our behalf when you stated that you
might be willing to write the story of your adventures in
Ireland prior to the truce. We shall be very glad if you
will do this for us. Mr. Wright tells me that you are
hesitating over the question of accepting remuneration. Of
course we shall be only too glad to pay you at special rates,
and if you will write for us at your convenience the story of
the great hunt — how through many months of strife you
evaded capture — we think it will make a first rate story
that ought to be told to the public and thus remove the false
impression that exists in this country. The story told by
your pen, giving the facts without political bias would, we

This appeal by R.D. Blumenfeld, editor of the *Daily Express*, to Collins, written on the day after Collins signed
the Treaty, is suggestive of the political capital Blumenfeld assumed Collins could make from his own life story.
It also reveals what *Daily Express* readers now wanted of Michael Collins. *(National Library of Ireland)*

GRESHAM HOTEL.

JANUARY 8th. 1922.

THE LONDON EXPRESS NEWSPAPER LTD.

TELEGRAMS:
"EXPRESS, FLEET, LONDON."

TELEPHONE: HOLBORN 6688.
(PRIVATE BRANCH EXCHANGE).

The Daily Express

EDITORIAL OFFICES:
8, SHOE LANE,
FLEET ST. LONDON,
E. C. 4.

2.

think be of exceptional interest and do great good in the
new and happier era that has now begun. If you will give
us the exclusive copyright of half a dozen articles of not
more than 1500 words each we shall be prepared to pay generously
for them. Possibly the calls on your time are so great that
you cannot manage to write them yourself? In this case we
shall be only too pleased to send to any place at any time you
may fix a first rate journalist and stenographer who will take
them down from your dictation and put them into form for your
approval.

With heartiest congratulations on the settlement.

Yours faithfully,

R. D. Blumenfeld
Editor.

last weeks and days. The more sober London *Times* was sceptical, though, even to the last: 'it remains, however, to be seen whether he has the spirit to be something greater than a popular idol'.[94] The *Times* never got its answer. It published these reservations on 23 August 1922: too late with the news of his death to stop the presses, but maybe uncannily prescient with a question we seem to ask of Collins still.

An arguably more dramatic shift in his portrayal came with his death. The more sensational papers took an obvious tack: 'Amazing Tales of How Collins Tricked Pursuers', 'Man of Daring who Laughed at Death', 'Devotion of Girl he Loved', while the *Daily Express* recorded his spectral appearance to an Irish soldier in a vision, the lost hero was found more broadly still.[95] The *Times* reviewed his 'Romantic Career' and his 'Hairbreadth Escapes', while the *Manchester Guardian* wrote of his 'picturesque and daring exploits', that 'he looked at all events a man of high heart who would wage a merry war'.[96] For the *Sunderland Daily Echo* he had even become 'a kind and chivalrous gentleman'; the *Daily Telegraph* now thought he 'was of the stuff of which great men are made'.[97] They all clearly had the same sort of 'bad memory' for which the *Manchester Guardian* once chided England.

Such was the shift that the author G.K. Chesterton used the treatment of Collins to indict the vacuity of the British press at a debate at the London School of Economics: 'Did the British public learn anything from the press about the extraordinary events that caused the change of front towards Ireland? All the press did was to call Michael Collins a murderous assassin on the Monday and a noble national hero on the Tuesday.'[98] Chesterton waited until 1923 to air this view, but this point had already been made, vigorously throughout 1921 and 1922 by the *Morning Post*, and somewhat more subtly by the *Yorkshire Post*'s Harold Owen, who with a north-of-England disdain for his London counterparts, was already mocking the same fawning journalism just days after the Treaty negotiations began. An article entitled 'Begorrah!', written in a stage-Irish brogue, lampooned the Collins of 'the London Dail-y papers'. Gentle by and large, it still managed to bare its teeth: 'Mike Collins shot out of his car right through the doorway of Number 10 at a bound – for all the world to remind you of a gunman entering a Dublin hotel early on a Sunday morning, before the officers were out of bed!'[99]

When it came to the florid outpourings on Collins's death many letter writers to the editor of the *Morning Post* could take no more. One writer, identified only as 'G.S.', was 'nauseated by the fulsomeness of the majority of the Press reports of that event – more especially in those newspapers lately supporting Unionism. Collins died the death he had planned only too successfully for British soldiers and members of the RIC', while J.M. Power of Tunbridge Wells condemned 'the slobber poured forth by a section of the London Press'. 'An Englishman', 'speaking as one who fought in Ireland under this government', was revolted that 'his death is more grieved over – even by the Prime Minister – than those of the Britons who died fighting against anarchy, murder and Bolshevism in Ireland'. 'An Irishwoman' fumed: 'let it not be forgotten that two years ago Michael Collins was leading those bands of cowardly assassins in those brutal and uncivilized ambushes'. She reminded the readers of all those 'columns about Collins's virtues and heroic deeds' that he had been killed close to Kilmichael: 'What ye sow that shall ye also reap', she wrote. For her, Collins got what he deserved.[100] The southern unionist peer, Lord Oranmore and Browne, was staying in a hotel in the German spa town of Godesberg when he read the newspaper coverage of Collins's death. While convinced by the journalists that Collins had 'died bravely', he was keen that his diary should record that Collins 'murdered Frank Brooke in the Chairman's room at Westland Row Station with his own hand', that he was to blame for 'the foul murder of 28 officers in Dublin on that dark November Sunday morning less than two years ago'.[101] John St Loe Strachey, editor of *The Spectator*, took the same press forcefully to task in his editorial of 25 August 1922. He admitted Collins was 'brave', that he had 'wonderful boldness and cunning', 'but when all has been said we must confess that we are dismayed by the uncritical praise of Mr Collins's character'. It would lead people to 'think lightly and easily of murder', and Strachey did not want anyone to 'think lightly and easily' of that.[102] In private he admitted, 'I am sorry for his murder', but he sought evidence he could use to show Collins's own involvement in the 'assassinations of individuals': 'I want to know the facts, and the whole of the facts, in regard to his career before I indulge in the kind of panegyric which the *Times* prints today.'[103] Indeed, there were similar complaints about the press from other quarters. Major General Sir Hugh Jeudwine, General Officer Commanding the 5th Division of the British Army in Ireland, grumbled that 'Michael's funeral was really a frost, *pace* the press'.[104] The former Director of Intelligence and Deputy Chief of Police, Ormonde de l'Épée Winter, put it more plainly still: 'the fuss the English papers make about him makes me vomit.'[105]

COLLINS KILLED IN FIERCE FIGHT WITH 200 REBELS

The Daily Mirror

NET SALE MUCH THE LARGEST OF ANY DAILY PICTURE NEWSPAPER

No. 5,869. | Registered at the G.P.O. as a Newspaper. | THURSDAY, AUGUST 24, 1922 | One Penny.

GEN. MICHAEL COLLINS SHOT DEAD

General Collins and Mr. Arthur Griffith, who recently died, leaving Downing-street.

Miss Kitty Kiernan, the fiancée of General Collins. They were to have been married shortly, the wedding being delayed by renewed fighting.

Portrait of Michael Collins taken at the age of six.

Another photograph that shows his sunny, ever-ready smile.

Recent portrait of General Michael Collins taken just after he took command of the Free State forces. He had lately shaved his moustache.

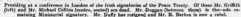

Presiding at a conference in London of the Irish signatories of the Peace Treaty. Of these Mr. Griffith (left) and Mr. Michael Collins (centre, seated) are dead. Mr. Duggan (between them) is the sole remaining Ministerial signatory. Mr. Duffy has resigned and Mr. R. Barton is now a rebel.

The death of General Michael Collins, shot during an ambush at Bandon, Co. Cork, has robbed Ireland, within a few days of the death of Mr. Arthur Griffith, of the second "strong man" of the new Free State Government. Mr. Lloyd George has telegraphed to the Acting-Chairman of the Provisional Government that "the Free State has lost a fearless soldier and a leader of great energy and devotion." Only last week a bomb was thrown at General Collins' car, but he was not in it. (Other pictures on pages 8 and 9.)

The front page of *The Daily Mirror* on 24 August 1922 typified the type of coverage that upset Winter so much. The prominent place given to Kitty Kiernan, and the exaggerated report of his death in a 'fierce fight with 200 rebels', could be found in many of the popular British newspapers. (The Daily Mirror, *24 August 1922, Trinity Mirror Publishing Ltd*)

The newspapers' larger-than-life Collins, as we saw Seamus Robinson protest in Chapter 3, clearly prodded at sullen jealousies at home. It reduced Collins to a caricature of himself, made him a far more divisive figure when writ so large in the newspapers' trenchant black and white. It allowed Countess Markievicz to try for silly victories in the Treaty debates, because he had become someone silly stories stuck to: 'I also heard that … the Princess Mary is to be married to Michael Collins'.[106] It made sense to throw that kind of allegation at him alone. With so much attention he had far less room for manoeuvre, at least in all the ways he might have liked. If the newspapers said he was weakening, being too friendly or too fierce with Craig or Churchill, with de Valera or whoever else they reported him meeting with, the newspapers certainly coloured the views of those who read only the headlines and were never privy to Collins's own plans or views. Sir Henry Wilson certainly took Collins at the *Daily Herald*'s word back in October 1921. Wilson noted in his diary: 'in today's *Daily Herald* Michael Collins openly boasts that he has, and will again, hold up the British Empire. It is <u>true</u>.'[107] While nothing was going to change Wilson's mind about Collins, it is suggestive that even he shaped his sense of Collins from what the newspapers had to say. In the same way that the 'massed photographers' must have made Collins's task in London more difficult, positive and negative newspaper reports, even if they did not impinge on his own position, must have made it harder to convince his allies and opponents that he was not only the sum of what the newspapers said he was.[108] And in 1922 convincing others was a considerable part of the battles he fought on all fronts.

Collins played, or at least tried to play, the British newspapers' game. He used their columns to snap back at adversaries old and new. In February 1922, he wrote an article for the *Illustrated Sunday Herald* to take de Valera very sharply to task, while he later chose the *Sunday Express* to put Erskine Childers in his place.[109] Despite being keen to reach a wide readership, he knew, no doubt from his own London days, which titles held the greatest sway. When Collins criticised James G. Douglas, then serving on the committee charged with drafting a constitution, for his excessive haste in publishing an article on the status of the Irish Free State in April 1922, the rebuke was almost as stinging about Douglas's lack of discernment about where he published as much as it was about what he chose to write: 'I was much more sorry that it appeared in the *Daily News*. This is a paper that has no real influence and has no real public backing it.'[110] Although the paper's pedigree must have impressed Collins (Charles Dickens was its founding editor; the title was an early supporter of Irish home rule, and a sometimes-sympathetic reporter of events in Ireland before the Truce), its flagging sales clearly counted to him more. For his message to be popular he knew he had to court the genuinely popular press. 'Am arranging for some interviews now and there are many press correspondents waiting – the weather is sweltering & so I am completely out of sorts': so he wrote in passing to Kitty Kiernan from London in June 1922.[111] By then, obliging the press had become just as commonplace for him as the weather; interviews were just more wearying obligations contributing to his often bad moods. But all this obliging mattered as can be seen by the measure of his opponents' scorn. One anti-Treatyite handbill sneered that even though Collins had 'given 65 press interviews, and written 48 newspaper articles' since he signed the Treaty, none of his words would change their views.[112] That they kept such close count, that they used such scant resources to criticise what might seem a relatively ephemeral thing, probably suggests just how important they perceived those 65 interviews and 48 articles to be. Playing the newspapers' game, giving all those interviews, writing, or at least having all those articles written, gave Collins a clear advantage over the other side. While his celebrity may have clouded and complicated things for him in certain contexts, celebrity certainly gave him more column inches to make his point. Even a retired Scarlet Pimpernel was always going to be worth a newspaper's while.

A promotional tour for *The Kid* took Charlie Chaplin to London in the autumn of 1921. There were even reports of a special showing of *The Kid* for Lloyd George at Gairloch, where he holidayed in the Scottish Highlands, just before the Treaty negotiations began.[113] Shortly after Chaplin left, Collins arrived and may well have done something to sate the hunger for scandal in Chaplin's wake. One journalist noted how 'the interviewers [are] all after him now Charlie Chaplin has gone'.[114] Collins must have known that this interest was a fleeting, dangerous sort of thing; that someone else would just as quickly take his place. He did not need to cast even a cursory glance at the latest London newspapers and magazines that he sent home to Kitty Kiernan to know the kind of deal he might be making with this particular devil.[115] Celebrity had helped and hindered him already: made him more ominous, more mysterious, more illustrious than he ever was; made it harder for him to hide, and harder for others to accept the limits of what he amounted to. When he showed himself, celebrity made him

Since he Signed the Treaty

Michael Collins

has made 95 Speeches, given 65 Press Interviews, and written 48 Newspaper Articles

———————

If he made 135 million Speeches and wrote 48 million Newspaper Articles, he could not alter this fact:

That under the Treaty

The King of England is King of Ireland

The anti-Treatyites were acutely aware, as shown by this handbill, of the extent of Collins's access to national and international media and the advantage this gave the pro-Treaty side. The disparity between the two sides became more acute as the anti-Treatyites were denied access to the mainstream media. *(National Library of Ireland)*

His opponents were also quick to point out just how much Collins seemed to play up to the British press. Here, on Harry Boland's death, the view of the die-hard *Morning Post* is alleged to be the thing that matters most to Collins. *(National Library of Ireland)*

human, made him frivolous, made him respectable according to certain lights. Celebrity made him palatable for others who before had dismissed him wholly out of court. With it, fame brought a reputation beyond country or county or parish; fame made his successors seem more pallid than was fair. Fame set him very clearly a revolutionary apart. Why look at his celebrity? Celebrity is the reason we know so much about him; celebrity is the reason 'the real' Mick is so obscure.

Here, photographed talking to a journalist, Collins gives one of the many interviews that had become part of his daily round. *(Military Archives of Ireland)*

Michael Collins

However much Collins tried to control his persona, the newspapers would always conjure up plenty of caricatures of their own. This image, drawn by 'Matt' (Matthew Sandford), appeared in the *Illustrated Sunday Herald* on 12 February 1922. *(National Library of Ireland)*

7

'If he **had ever** been in a **scrap** he'd have **learned** to **stay** down':

Collins's Death[1]

The ending wouldn't do. The hero died and the audience didn't like it. So the ending wouldn't do. United Artists took back the reels of *Beloved Enemy* and made it over. And so, *Beloved Enemy* came to have a happy ending in 1936.[2] Shot, but this time not killed, its Irish rebel protagonist pulls through; he lives to fight another day with Merle Oberon doe-eyed by his side. *Beloved Enemy* changed his name to Dennis Riordan but even the *Times of India* knew that the actor Brian Aherne was 'playing Michael Collins', that the 'Michael Collins character' just could not die.[3] Almost 60 years later while wandering around looking for Béal na mBláth, Neil Jordan and Liam Neeson came upon something of the same dilemma: 'so his life ends in nondescript absurdity', Jordan wrote, 'in an ambush that was almost called off'.[4] When it came to filming the fatal scene 'the actors are stunned. It seems to them almost too peremptory, too casual.' Although Jordan tried to reassure them 'that that is how it was, a casual bullet in an ambush that felled him while nobody was watching; that any glorious death … would be inappropriate,' Liam Neeson remained 'plagued by nagging doubts'.[5] After so much life, the audience would never be satisfied with such a small and 'nondescript' sort of death. Once more, it seems, the ending wouldn't do.

While films might have him live or die according to directors' wiles and cinemagoers' whims, the rest of us must surely be bound by what was, rather than by what might have been. Except, it has never really been so. His death is mystery, conspiracy; it is parlour game and whodunit. It is all rumour and allegation, claim and accusation, and our unease and our fascination with it is there in all the raking over of old rumours, in all the names that have been named, in all the fingers pointed at long-dead men who might have, and could have, and must have, killed Collins after all. Books and documentaries have aired a variety of theories, and while the fervour that needed a second edition of *The Shooting of Michael Collins* within a month of its first publication has abated since most have settled on Sonny O'Neill as the man who fired the shot, there is something in the death of Michael Collins that troubles and intrigues us still.[6] Whether sitting in a darkened cinema or not, the ending wouldn't do. It just won't do.

It is a bit of a disappointment really. He dies in 'one of the most ill-prepared ambushes of the entire period', maybe drunk, and certainly in a fight that the Commander-in-Chief of a national army should have had the sense to avoid.[7] But Béal na mBláth has to be seen first for what it was, not for the larger-than-life thing it has become. Collins's decision to go to Cork was in keeping with his movements in the days and weeks before his death. He had undertaken inspections through the midlands, in Limerick; 12 August took him from Dublin to Kerry, so 'there was nothing remarkable' about his tour of Cork. The risks to his life there may have been no greater than in any other place: an attempt had been made on his life in Dublin, although he was not in his car when it was ambushed on 16 August. The temptation to 'shroud his journey in foreboding' is perhaps too much for many writers, but he had 'visited other liberated areas from Dundalk to Tralee in the last few weeks in exactly the same way'.[8] He spent 21 August in one meeting after another – 'meeting with local representatives, setting up an intelligence network … and recovering money seized by the IRA from banks and customs offices'.[9] He went to Macroom, where he is said to have met the neutral IRA man Florence O'Donoghue, then back to Cork city, to see his sister Mary and her son.[10] The next morning he left Cork shortly after 6am: Collins in his touring car, with a scout on a motorcycle, a Crossley tender and an armoured car. There was more inspecting to be done. He went back to Macroom, then on to Bandon, stopping to ask what turned out to be an anti-Treaty sentry the way near a place called Béal na mBláth. He met Sean Hales at Bandon, while Sean's brother Tom, an officer on the other side, took his part in preparing the ambush at Béal na mBláth. On Collins went to Rosscarbery, but stopped first to go home, to see Woodfield for the first time since June. Then on to Skibbereen, more inspections and discussions, before heading back out on the road for Cork. Back he came through Clonakilty, another stop at Bandon, but turning for Macroom, not the straight and shorter road for Cork.[11] At about 8pm or 8.30pm he arrived at Béal na mBláth. Most of the ambush party had gone, had given up hope that Collins would return by the same route he had travelled out, assumed they were thwarted as they were when they laid an ambush for him at Farran the day before, but six men were still in their positions and three more managed to get back when they saw the convoy halt at their barricade set out on the road below.[12] Fire was opened on the vehicles as they stopped. The shooting lasted maybe 30 minutes, no more than an hour, and there was one fatality only: the Commander-in-Chief.[13]

Little can be said of this, if even this much, without dispute, and there is much that has been read into the motives and the movements of that day. John Feehan, like many before him, was adamant in his book, *The Shooting of Michael Collins*, that Collins was in Cork to make peace, citing Collins saying, not once but twice, 'I will not leave Cork until the fighting is finished', and 'I'm going to put an end to this bloody war'.[14] Feehan reads all sorts of things into Collins's many visits to Macroom, that the key to it all lies there. But Collins's own words on 21 August suggest this might all have been rumour and conjecture and hoping for the best. 'The people here want no compromise with the irregulars', Collins wrote. And he ended, 'The people are splendid'. He was not, it appears, in any way at odds with their mood.[15] The war was going well from his point of view,

After a difficult journey back from Béal na mBláth to Cork, Collins's body was examined and laid out in Shanakiel Hospital. His own instincts to photograph the funerals of dead pro-Treaty soldiers for propaganda purposes were put into action here, as this and other images of the dead leader were widely circulated, particularly those taken when his body came back to Dublin where it lay in state. *(National Museum of Ireland)*

Cork city had been secured, so why would he offer a compromise now when he rejected efforts of peace before; why would he assume the anti-Treatyites would listen when nothing had convinced them by that time?[16] Other rumours, other interpretations, of course, abounded and abound, about why he met with Florence O'Donoghue, who was by then a neutral, but who had, between March and June 1922, been Adjutant General of the anti-Treaty IRA. For some, such a meeting suggested Collins wanted to make peace, that he wanted to appeal to the anti-Treatyites before the war went too far, that with Cork city taken now was a fitting time to bring it all to an end. Others prefer to believe peace was on his mind because he had had a change of heart, that 'he was fed up with how things had developed' in Dublin, that 'the O'Higgins-Cosgrave element had got a grip on the majority', that 'the Unionist cum pro-British elements in the Government … were replacing all the IRA men with ex-British soldiers', and somehow allying with the anti-Treatyites would put it all to rights. Some even blame his death on older enemies still, that British intelligence, possibly in cahoots with those same 'pro-British elements in the Government', finally managed to kill him after all.[17] And, of course, amongst other rumours, there is the persistent suspicion as to what de Valera was doing near Béal na mBláth.[18] It all remains speculation and a good story still.

Two days after Collins's death the *Westminster Gazette* called it 'a paltry skirmish', far from a fitting end for 'the first young man in living memory to disturb the Imperial counsels … to turn back the Imperial tide'.[19] Peter Hart writes of 'the banality of his death', that 'in personal terms, there is no reason to see Collins's death as any more tragic than any of the others that took place during the Civil War', that it 'was a lot cleaner and made a lot more sense than many of those that followed', that as he was 'one of those responsible for starting the war and ordering the men into combat, his killing was more justified than most, according to his own understanding of violence'.[20] But saying or writing or even knowing these things does not make them sit any more readily for some, does not make them seem any less harsh, any less callous at first sight. It goes beyond propriety, beyond not speaking ill of the dead; it hits to the very core of what J.J. Lee calls 'our own silent assumptions' about Collins.[21] What we think he was, what we choose to see in what he did, maybe more what we hope he might have been, what we assume he would have done, how different, how better we imagine the Free State would have been, it all craves a better death for him than this haphazard, foolish one in the coming darkness on the side of a west Cork road. The hope and the expectation of him will not let him die as inconsequentially as that.

There had to be more to it. Early reports exaggerated the size of the anti-Treaty party: maybe 200 men, with a number of casualties inflicted on the ambushers' side.[22] While the first official reports referred to it as a 'battle' not some mere ambush, there followed more detailed, stirring accounts of Collins's gallant fight.[23] 'Although mortally wounded, [he] still fired from the ground and encouraged his men'; he fell 'rifle in hand' uttering the Christ-like words 'forgive them' or a variety of instructions for his burial, depending on which newspaper was read.[24] The act of contrition Commandant Sean O'Connell whispered in his ear, while he gripped O'Connell by the hand more tightly to thank him for the words, these solemn and sentimental things were made into the last and increasingly romantic moments of his life.[25] While for Neil Jordan Béal na mBláth was 'nothing spectacular, special only in its air of non-consequence', for O'Connell it would always be 'a desperate, deadly looking place' where he watched Michael Collins die.[26] Denis Hurley, reading of Collins's death in the United States, wrote home to Cork capturing the way his death was quickly changing: 'Too bad that Michael Collins' young life should be extinguished in a petty ambush', he wrote, but reading about it in the press Hurley knew this life was 'more romantic' than any of the rest.[27] The petty became romantic in the space of one sentence in Hurley's letter, and the romantic went on pushing the petty out of sight.

As an elusive Pimpernel figure, no one could catch him or kill him. 'He had dared death so often in the struggle with England that men felt he could run all risks and emerge unharmed.'[28] That an Irishman finally killed him made it 'a tragedy too deep for tears'; it summed up the futility of civil war.[29] But to accept this is to accept a very particular version both of Collins and his death. It subscribes to the myth of him, to making his death more than it was, to accepting Collins as the kind of military figure, as we saw in Chapter 3, he arguably never was. His death throws the notion of the great military figure into disarray. John Regan has been saying so for many years; J.J. Lee said it long before.[30] '[H]e had no need to stop to fight at the ambush site', he was 'behaving more like a cowboy than a head of government'.[31] To Charles Townshend, 'there was nothing to stop the car he was travelling in from driving through to safety – nothing except

23rd. August 1922
9.20.p.m.

An account of the ambush in which the Commander-in-Chief was killed, issued from Army Headquarters, states:-

The Commander-in-Chief of the National Army – General Michael Collins, with members of the Headquarters staff left Cork on tuesday morning, in continuation of his visits to various military positions in the South, and was wounded on Tuesday night at Bealnablath, midway between Macroom and Bandon- and expired in a short time. The party were proceeding to Bandon by bye-roads, in consequence of the obstacles on the main roads, accompanied by a Whippet armoured car, when they were ambushed by a large party of Irregulars. The battle lasted for close on an hour, and it was in the very last stage of the fight that General Collins was killed. The steady careful, fire of the ambushed party took a heavy toll during the fight – a very large number of the Irregulars being killed or wounded. For threequarters of an hour the only casualty on the side of the troops was the wounding of a despatch Rider. And then occurred the terrible calamity which has plunged the whole Nation into grief and mourning. The battle was nearly over and the Irregulars were on the point of retreating- defeated in spite of their overwhelming numbers, their better positions and other advantages. The firing had become much less intense. Suddenly the Commander-in-Chief collapsed and fell prone struck in the head by a bullet. From the very first it was obvious that the wound was fatal. But the Commander-in-Chief, though mortally wounded, still fired away from the ground, encouraging his men by his magnificient bravery. In a feeble voice he asked for Major-General Dalton, and this Officer and Comdt. Sean O'Connell went to the dying National Leader. Although sorely stricken with grief, they whispered a few prayers and recited the Act of Contrition before General Collins breathed his last.

The Commander-in-Chief's last works, when he lay dying on the roadside, when he knew he had only a minute ot two to live, revealed his greatness if nothing else could have done. "Forgive Them" were the last words that escaped his lips before Michael Collins died. The body was removed under fire to the armoured car. The Irregulars were by this time in full retreat, having sustained very heavy casualties and leaving several dead and wounded on the field. The troops were obliged to leave the Leyland Touring Car, and it was in the armoured car that the remains were brought to Cork- being conveyed to Shankill Hospital. The sad procession reached the city between midnight and one o'clock on Wednesday morning.

This account, issued by Army Headquarters on 23 August 1922, set the tone for many of the early and quite exaggerated newspaper accounts of Collins's death. Keen to make a 'battle' out of this ambush, it described a Collins brave and messianic to the end. *(National Library of Ireland)*

12 Pages

12 Pages

Le Petit Journal

illustré

HEBDOMADAIRE
61, rue Lafayette, Paris

PRIX : 0 fr. 30
3 Septembre 1922

(au dos) Papuelot

Les convulsions sanglantes de l'Irlande

Au cours d'une tournée d'inspection dans le sud du Comté de Cork, Michaël Collins, chef du gouvernement provisoire de l'île libre, est attaqué par des rebelles en embuscade et, après une véritable bataille entre ceux-ci et les troupes de l'escorte, est tué d'une balle au front.

For the cover of its 3 September 1922 issue, the French illustrated paper *Le Petit Journal* produced this perhaps his desire to demonstrate that he was truly a fighting man, not a pen-pusher', that he was the Commander-in-Chief of an army after all.[32] Smiling for exclusive pictures for British Pathé newsreels in his new general's uniform, he was the symbol of what the National Army ought to be, but 'he seems to have behaved like a caricature of his own glamorised image', he seemed to know very little indeed about the kind of warfare with which he had been associated for so long.[33] Emmet Dalton, who travelled and fought with him at Béal na mBláth, claimed he told the driver to 'Drive like hell!' when the firing started, but that it was Collins who insisted they should 'Stop! Jump out and we'll fight them' instead.[34] Dalton, a former British Army officer, knew more than most at Béal na mBláth what war was made of; he was awarded the Military Cross at nineteen for bravery at the Somme. In private and in later years, he was said to have admitted: 'Mick wouldn't keep down. If he had ever been in a scrap he'd have learned to stay down … and so Mick was killed standing up.'[35] Not the position to be in when opponents have the advantage, when they are firing down upon you from above. It said little for this new army that it could not protect him, but it said less of him because he seemed to die so foolishly, because he did not seem to know how to fight.

The *Sunday Pictorial* said 'his death is one more proof that "generals" should keep out of the firing line … he had exactly the same weakness as Mr Winston Churchill for running about instead of staying in his office. A minister with a taste for the adventurous ought to give up his job.' It was a sentiment, like the paper's pronouncement that 'the only pathway to peace in Ireland is the way of Maxwell and the way of Cromwell', that might only be expressed at London's remove in August 1922.[36] But in 1954 the Fianna Fáil Minister for Defence, Oscar Traynor, gave a more charitable, official interpretation, certifying as part of a dependent's allowance application by Collins's sister, Mary Collins Powell, that Collins's 'death was not due to any serious negligence or misconduct on his part.'[37] With a bit more feeling, and admittedly published only in 1982, the anti-Treaty leader Liam Deasy put Collins's death down to 'the foolhardy act of a brave man.'[38] Even though he accepted that Collins was still 'the greatest leader of our generation', everything about the nature of Collins's last day, the route taken, the arrangements made, were 'inexplicable' to him, 'baffling', to Deasy, 'in military terms.'[39] While the *Pictorial*'s view of the Irish Civil War as 'a series of furtive scuffles between corner-boys, masquerading in smart uniforms' is rather harsh, it is hard to make any kind of military hero out of the man who died at

ROINN COSANTA.

Certified that the late General Michael Collins
was a member of the Irish Volunteers and of the National
Army, that he was killed on the 22nd August, 1922, in
the course of his duty while on active service and that
his death was not due to any serious negligence or
misconduct on his part.

Minister for Defence.

3rd May, 1954.

As part of an assessment of a dependent's allowance application by Collins's sister, Mary Collins Powell, this appraisal of Collins's death was produced by the Department of Defence. *(Military Archives of Ireland)*

Béal na mBláth.[40] But military hero is what, for many, he remains. While dying in uniform, dying in action, dying as General rather than just Minister or President or Mick, serves only to confirm some in their sense of him as a soldier most of all, the nature of his death makes something of a mockery of that. It implies he was much more of all the other things: the administrator, the schemer, the accountant, that maybe he was the arch pen-pusher after all.

For all that, every movement of his last days has been scrutinised and analysed. Why risk such a route through west Cork, why drive so ostentatiously through the territory of men who had seen some of the War of Independence's tougher fights, of men who wanted 'to have a go at the Dublin crowd', of men who were bruised by Cork city's recent loss?[41] Why sit so openly in his touring car; why so brazenly with the top down, making 'himself very prominent' as the anti-Treaty IRA reported back to their Chief of Staff?[42] Why such an inadequate convoy; why so little protection? Why return by the same route as he went out, a mistake British patrols stopped making back in 1921 for fear of IRA attack?[43] Why was a son of Woodfield so lost on the roads of west Cork? Liam Deasy could understand a Dublin man making those kinds of mistakes, but not Michael Collins.[44] Some blame his death on his own arrogance. 'No one is going to shoot me in my own county', 'Ah, whatever happens to me, my own fellow countrymen won't kill me', other similar phrases are recorded by various people in Dublin, in Bandon, and elsewhere, who told him it was too dangerous, who told him which roads not to take, who told him not to go at all.[45] Allaying others' fears, and perhaps his own, he may well have had a 'suicidal lapse of judgement' if he thought any of it was true, as J.J. Lee has said.[46] That so many recall him expressing this kind of sentiment maybe says more of their own sense of responsibility for letting him go; remembering him saying it proves they warned him; his saying it might make it all his own and not their fault. Joe McGrath, one of Collins's old 'friends and loyalists', insisted he wrote Collins a letter begging him not to go south; insisted he wrote it, adamant in red ink, not in any ordinary black or blue.[47] There comes a certain comfort in knowing he had himself to blame.[48] Even those whose sympathies were closer to the anti-Treaty side recounted the same kinds of sentiment. Florence O'Donoghue later told Ernie O'Malley that when he met Collins on that trip 'he was really talking big': "'I've been all over this bloody county but no one has said a bloody word to me'"; more of his own arrogance, his own fault, whether pro- or anti-Treaty, whether neutral in between.[49]

Almost every book that deals with his death ascribes to him some level of precognition, almost clairvoyance about his own demise. Even Churchill could not resist referring to Collins's 'presentiment of death': 'I shall not last long; my life is forfeit'.[50] Authors read his sense of his impending doom in asides and overheard conversations. Asking Joe O'Reilly, 'his personal courier and dogsbody', or Sinead Mason, his 'personal secretary', if they fancied a new boss; wondering to W.T. Cosgrave if he would make it through this civil war – they have been read like signs in the tea leaves that in these and other ways he knew of, and even wished for, his coming end.[51] His curiosity about the shooting of his namesake, a young Michael Collins, a new army recruit, his writing 'Michael Collins shot' in his diary just days before he died, easily fuels this kind of superstitious surmise.[52] Because he was found wandering around Newcestown graveyard, reading the inscriptions on the headstones, when his convoy had to make an impromptu stop, it does not necessarily follow, as it seems to for some, that he had premonitions of his own demise or that he longed, like some tubercular Romantic poet, for the embrace of death.[53] The graveyard might well have been one of the few things worth seeing in Newcestown in August 1922. He was known to be a maudlin type when the mood took him, and maybe he had seen enough death, been to enough funerals, felt he was in enough danger for death to prey heavily on his mind.[54] By the end of August 1922 such rumours already circulated: 'I heard from people close to him … that he was desperate and welcomed the end', but that authors still return again and again to such presentiments is perhaps the telling thing.[55] They make his death more tragic, more romantic; they instil it with maybe something more dramatic than it deserves. The flat ending becomes a better story for all the mysterious omens and portents; the pages turn faster as our hero moves on to his inexorable doom.

We have blamed his own arrogance, the curse of his indomitable fate, but then there is his misplaced pride as well. The bravado of his last day has been contrasted with the businesslike behaviour of the first two days of his tour. There were still inspections to be made, but this day was the day for going home. Hart calls it 'the Big Fellow's victory lap', while John Regan dismisses it as Collins's 'personal vanity'.[56] Equating him with 'many a returning "Yank" or ne'er-do-well from "beyont in England"', Regan claims 'Collins took the cliché of the returning emigrant to its zenith and bathed joyously in his reflected glory'. 'No other returning local boy made good could park his own army outside and claim without pretence that he was both Commander-in-Chief and the undisputed leader of the new state.'[57] Coogan admits Collins 'would not have lasted a day had he been so unguarded' in 1920–21, but he at least allows that 'it was human' if not quite 'wartime behaviour': 'forget the war, relax, take a drink, have a chat and a joke'.[58] Hindsight is a po-faced thing. Pride, hubris, arrogance, recklessness, it offers these kinds of words in explanation, but without much empathy. Maybe he just wanted to go home, to see his brother, his family, old friends, to be away from the struggles of Dublin, the strain of the weeks and the months past, to put all the death away from him, Boland, Griffith, even Brugha, to be somewhere where less might seem wanted of him, somewhere like old times again.[59] Prisoners had thrown the debris of their cells at him when he last visited Limerick Jail; in Cork he faced the slogans on the walls: why weren't his troops marching into Belfast instead of Cork.[60] He was tired, sick, overworked; his marriage postponed, 22 August might have been his wedding day.[61] Pride, hubris, arrogance – maybe; reckless – certainly; but in the weary and the worn there is a powerful instinct for home.

Along the way people came out to see him, to cheer him, to fete him. Drink was taken. How much, like many other things about that day, is still in dispute.[62] He may have stood rounds wherever he stopped; there may have been a fight in a pub because Jock McPeak, the machine-gunner of the convoy's armoured car, tried to take a bottle of whiskey without paying; Collins was said to have run, to a chorus of cheers, carrying a barmaid up the stairs of the Williams Hotel.[63] Emmet Dalton admitted to drinking but he always denied publicly that the convoy was drunk. Privately he was said to have acknowledged 'we were all arseholes' that day.[64] His problems with drink in the 1920s and 1930 maybe make it easier to assume that drunkenness, his own, Collins's, the convoy around them, contributed to Collins's death.[65] When Tim Pat Coogan cited an admission from Billy Powell, the IRA Captain from Lissarda, that Collins's convoy were 'in no shape for fighting. They'd been on a bit of a spree all day', he added to the speculation about drink's part.[66] Why was Joe Dolan slumbering over his rifle as they drove into Béal na mBláth?[67] Was he drunk or just tired from being on the road since after 6am? Drunkenness is just another one of the imponderables of 22 August 1922.

But drunkenness is not really good enough. It makes it squalid, careless, ordinary. It does not satisfy the instinct that insists, and has insisted since 1922,

X

3. The people here want no compromise with the irregulars

4. It is wise to postpone the Dail meeting as already suggested.

5. You might get before you minds 'e three persons under par 1, but don't announce anything until I return

6. It would be a big thing to get Civic Guards both here and in LIMERICK. Civil Administration urgent everywhere in the south. The people are splendid.

Miceál Ó Coileáin
21/8/22

Writing to W.T. Cosgrave on the day before his death, Collins showed little of the foreboding often alluded to, and, given his reference to the people wanting 'no compromise', little of the instinct for peace many subsequently claimed he had come to Cork to make. Reminiscent of Sir Henry Wilson's last diary entry – 'A lovely day' – Collins ends here on a poignantly upbeat note. W.T. Cosgrave kept this copy in his private papers. *(Royal Irish Academy)*

Photographed here outside Lee's Hotel in Bandon on the day of his death, this recently discovered image is believed to be the last picture taken of Collins alive. That a young Agnes Hurley had her Box Brownie to hand reinforces the sense that his visit was quite a spectacle. *(National Museum of Ireland)*

that there had to have been more to his death than that. With so much lost, someone had to be to blame; he had to have been betrayed, shot by a British spy, shot by one of his own, shot before he could make peace and end the Civil War, shot because he was about to – and you can finish this sentence any way you choose. While the deaths of many were contested and remain contentious through and beyond 1919–23, no other death has prompted such wondering, such conspiracy, such intricate machinations as Collins's demise. Some of the rumours that he was shot at close range, even shot by a poisoned bullet, shot in the back as well as the head, might have been silenced or satisfied by an inquest, or if Oliver St John Gogarty's post-mortem report had survived.[68] Its disappearance, of course, only fuels the fire. That there was fire to fuel, that some of the conspiracies surrounding Collins's death could manage to fly so high, goes quite some way to show how set apart he had become from all the rest. Ordinary deaths could be believed of others, but not of Michael Collins at Béal na mBláth.

George Bernard Shaw's certainty that 'Collins himself would be horrified at the idea of trying to seek out a man who shot him in battle' has been blithely ignored.[69] Coogan thought he would 'make it clear once and for all how [Collins] came to be killed'.[70] He rejected the old familiar conspiracies, those concocted and well-rehearsed about Emmet Dalton or the machine-gunner of the armoured car, Jock McPeak, and settled, as Colm Connolly's documentary had before him, on Sonny O'Neill, an ex-RIC man, a former soldier, a 'marksman', as Coogan called him, in the anti-Treaty party, as the man who probably fired the fatal shot.[71] That it took a 'marksman' to kill Collins might be thought a type of tribute in itself. Coogan put the silence O'Neill observed for many years, the never admitting it was him, down to a decent kind of 'West Cork reticence'. He claims that members of the Collins family were told, certainly within a year of Collins's death, that not talking about it was a mark of O'Neill's respect for Collins and for them.[72] Given that O'Neill remained active in the IRA, that he was still on the run in 1926, self-preservation probably made silence the most sensible choice, but O'Neill remained tight-lipped nonetheless.[73] When his Military Service Pension application was released in 2014, national newspapers noted he made no reference to the part he played in Collins's death. They deemed it 'telling', but arguably more telling were the newspapers' attempts to add yet another layer of mystery to Collins's demise.[74] Even though we think we know 'whodunit' the residual passion for conspiracy can be stirred quite easily still.

The heyday of conspiracy belonged to the 1960s, the 1970s and the early 1980s. In 1972 John Hickey published his thoughts in the *Limerick Weekly Echo*, findings from an investigation he undertook when he was a Garda in the 1920s, but kept under wraps until that point. Other elderly men also began to speak out and became more likely to be heard. Although one New Yorker, Richard Lucid, was prompted to write to Florence O'Donoghue about Collins's death in 1964 by 'the recent assination [*sic*] of President John Fitzgerald Kennedy', most were prompted to speak by the treatment of Collins's death in a sequence of books, newspaper articles and later television programmes, to which they objected.[75] The anti-Treatyites at the ambush became concerned when it looked like Eoin Neeson was to publish a book on the Civil War with the Mercier Press in 1964. 'What is the use of adding another half-baked account to [Rex] Taylor's and others already known to be unreliable? … Neeson has not the instinct or humanity to treat it as it ought to be treated', Florence O'Donoghue wrote.[76] So stirred by the prospect of the book, the six 'surviving members of the republican forces who participated in the engagement' at Béal na mBláth, 'Liam Deasy, Tom Kelleher, Tom Crofts, Pete Kearney, Jim Hurley, Dan Holland' assembled with Florence O'Donoghue at the Metropole Hotel in Cork on a Tuesday evening in February 1964 'to record what could be established as the truth'.[77] The Mercier Press had promised them not to publish the book until 'we were satisfied that the part of it dealing with the death of Collins was in accordance with the facts', at least their understanding of the facts, itself a remarkable demonstration of old men protecting their own position, and in turn being taken at their word.[78] These men were adamant that there was no order to kill Collins, that the first they had known of his presence in the area came on the morning of 22 August when his convoy stopped and asked directions at Béal na mBláth.[79] They insisted that they did not know for several hours after the ambush that he was dead.[80] Some of them later met with Neeson, disputing his view that they planned to kill Collins all along, demanding he remove the phrase 'the object was to kill him' from the text: 'we told him it was wrong, and told him why, and told him it could not appear again to which he agreed'.[81] 'We' may have been Liam Deasy and O'Donoghue, persuasive if for no other reason than that they were formidable old-IRA men after all. They had a similar message for the editor of the *Sunday Review* in April 1964 when they 'went into the editor's office … [and] told him who we were'.[82] He printed a withdrawal at their request. There was no pride in

UACHTARÁN NA HÉIREANN
(PRESIDENT OF IRELAND)

ÉIRE

BAILE ÁTHA CLIATH
(DUBLIN)

16th October, 1964

A Liam, a chara,

I duly received your letter of the 20th ultimo but thought it better postpone a reply until you had returned home.

The "Sunday Review" article, which you quote, is not accurate. There was no such 'meeting' of officers as is suggested. There were a few officers in the house at which I called as I passed through the village of Ballyvourney on the first stage of my journey from Gougane Barra to Dublin: a meeting of the Dáil had been announced for September 9th and I was on my way back so as to be close at hand.

I do not remember any remark having been made such as that attributed to "Sando" and Mick Murphy. I did not know many of the Cork Officers personally and am indeed not sure that "Sando" and Mick Murphy were amongst the officers I then met at Ballyvourney.

Neither have I any recollection of having made such a remark as that attributed to me. I did not regard Collins as being really in any serious danger in Cork. He knew the area and would, I believed, have information as to the routes which would be dangerous, and, in any case, would have seen to it that any route he proposed to take would be well scouted in advance.

Ambushes were, of course, the tactics used by Republicans against the Free State troops at that period and any talk about ambushes would not have surprised me. My belief, however, is that the story that has been commonly accepted is the true one - that no deliberate or specific ambush was laid for the Collins party; that an ambush had been laid for some Free State troops who had been accustomed, or were expected, to pass in the neighbourhood of Béal-na-Bláth; that when the Free State trooøps did not come, the ambush was called off and the main body withdrew; that a few of the ambushers did not retire in the direction taken by the main body and that these seeing, later, a Free State convoy passing, fired on it. The common belief is that it was by one of the shots fired at a distance by this small group that Collins was killed.

Mise, do chara,

Éamon de Valera.

Mr. Liam Deasy,
47, Kimmage Road West,
Dublin.

Blamed in many of the conspiracy theories surrounding Collins's death, and implicated for another generation by Neil Jordan's portrayal of Collins's death, de Valera was a quite careful guardian of his own reputation when it came to Collins. Deasy's note of a telephone conversation with de Valera, which took place after Deasy received this letter, claimed that de Valera's memory of 22 August 1922 was somewhat unclear. What is clear is the common insistence that there was no deliberate plan that Collins should die. *(National Library of Ireland)* having killed Collins, or at least in being thought to have killed him in some mean and underhand type of way; there was no pride in knowing that the Civil War may have been prolonged because they killed him, that it may have changed into something more ruthless and more vicious because he was gone.[83] While they had made the decision to wait for him in ambush, they wanted it known that they had not set out to kill him and they wanted that to be accepted as undisputed fact.[84]

The same instinct moved Con Crowley to take a libel action against the *Sunday Express* almost a decade before. He had been named and implicated by an article in the newspaper by Rex Taylor in February 1956. The High Court heard that he had been 'greatly injured in his credit and reputation … had been held up to and brought into hatred, ridicule, or contempt'. The *Sunday Express* settled. The newspaper paid 'a substantial sum of money for the injury', published an apology on its own pages, but also in the *Cork Examiner* so Crowley could be sure that those he lived among knew he did not bear any guilt.[85] A farmer and a council worker, Crowley took on the might of the Beaverbrook Newspaper Empire for the sake of his good name. Such was the slur, as he saw it, of being blamed.

Although blaming de Valera might make for a good story and appeal to the visceral nature of the division between the pro- and anti-Treaty sides, the more persistent rumour was that Collins was shot by one of his own men, with Emmet Dalton emerging as the chief suspect. There seems to be no consensus as to when the suspicion began, but it certainly cast a long shadow across Dalton's life.[86] Suspicion settled on him for all sorts of reasons. His British Army past was enough for some; his successes in Cork against the anti-Treatyites before Collins's death might have prompted the bitterness of others, while more read guilt into his resignation of his commission in December 1922, or into the problems of his later years.[87] Regret, even guilt, might be assumed from the blank picture postcards of Collins's funeral that Dalton kept for the rest of his days, though they might more prosaically denote his heartfelt loss and grief.[88] Regardless of the cause, the rumours took on a pernicious and a wayward type of life. Allegations that Brigadier Sean Hales was shot, not by the anti-Treatyites on 7 December 1922 as we have long assumed, but rather by the British Secret Service to cover Dalton's tracks, because Hales did not believe Dalton's account of Béal na mBláth, were perhaps as far-fetched as the supposed motive for Collins's death – that Collins was about to expose Tim Healy, who would become the Free

State's first Governor General within months of Collins's death, as a long-time British spy. But the reasons why Dalton might have killed Collins seemed a far less important part of the conspiracy than trying to establish that he was the one who fired the fatal shot. Robert Flynn made a statement under oath in 1975 claiming to have been part of Collins's convoy, claiming that he saw Dalton shoot Collins in the back of the touring car, claiming an officer silenced him with 'none of you knew this happened', that he was stopped from speaking up 'or you'll get the same'.[89] He suspected that a 'man in civilian clothes tried to kill me in a Dublin theatre' to keep him quiet when he got home.[90] Mistakes about dates and places, maybe even his assertions that Kitty Kiernan 'was the fiancée of many and was playing for high stakes', meant that Flynn's account was dismissed with the words 'no credibility' written later across the top.[91]

When an interview with Dalton by Cathal O'Shannon was broadcast on RTÉ in 1978, it stirred the memories of many more like Flynn, many more who wanted to blame him for Collins's death.[92] The urge to blame him may well say more of the desperate need of others to absolve themselves, to find something more ominous in Collins's rather straightforward death. Bill McKenna, part of the Collins bodyguard, claimed in 1981 that he heard '[Oliver St John] Gogarty saying that Collins must have been shot at very close range'.[93] When asked who he thought had killed Collins, he said, 'I do not know but I am quite sure, as were most of my fellow soldiers, that he was not shot by an IRA bullet.'[94] Dan Ryan wrote to John Feehan in November 1981, presumably like the others, in the course of the preparation of Feehan's book. He alleged that while walking with Desmond FitzGerald in Government Buildings many years before, FitzGerald stopped and asked him if he wanted to know who had killed Michael Collins. 'It was Emmet Dalton who shot him', and on they walked side by side.[95] Hearsay also came to Feehan from a Fr O'Donoghue of Rockwell College. O'Donoghue claimed his father told him that Collins always knew Dalton was a British spy.[96] From a Fr Redmond of New York came a story from his aunt; a matron at Shanakiel Hospital, she said she took the bloodstained rags from Collins's head, but there was a singed bullet hole on the back of his tunic as well. He wrote that she knew what bullet holes looked like; she had served as a nurse through the Great War.[97] He counselled Feehan to have the body exhumed so everyone would know what had happened once and for all.

In the late 1980s Dalton was found in the frame once more. His nephew, Joe

The Funeral of General Michael Collins.

Mr. Sean Collins & his sister, Miss Johanna Collins.   D.4. 909.

These two postcards, produced in the wake of Collins's death, show aspects of both public and private grief. That there was a commercial market for such items is revealing in its own right. Because both postcards are to be found in a collection of Emmet Dalton's papers they might fan the flames of conspiracy for some, but they might more likely be just keepsakes of a lost friend. *(National Library of Ireland)*

Dalton, signed an affidavit in 1987 attesting that before his death Emmet Dalton admitted to him that 'he shot Michael Collins at point blank range with a luger [*sic*] pistol', that de Valera was supposed to die on the same day as part of a pact to remove the most prominent figures on both sides of the divide, but that the anti-Treaty leader Liam Lynch had failed to play his part.[98] When Joe Dalton died soon after making this claim, his solicitor, Larry Murphy, said he did not know what to do.[99] As well as the affidavit, Joe Dalton entrusted Murphy with what he claimed was his uncle's diary, a diary allegedly recording Emmet Dalton's part in Collins's death amongst other supposedly sensational things.[100] Murphy spoke to Michael Keating, then Fine Gael TD, about what he purported to possess, but the unease he seemed to have with his knowledge soon gave way to something else. He admitted Joe Dalton was 'vindictive against his uncle over the fact of what he saw in the diaries', but asserted that Joe Dalton was 'a daily communicant' and 'a very honourable man' in the very next breath.[101] But his interview with Keating then took on a sourer note. Murphy objected to Colm Connolly's documentary about Collins's death: 'there was so much bulshit [*sic*]. Everyone saying someone did this and someone did that. There was old people saying this happened and that happened. I knew what happened.'[102] 'I knew what happened': just me alone. Although Keating quickly wrapped up the interview, 'we will leave it at that', he still brought the tale of it all to a *Sunday Independent* journalist, still brought the story to Neil Jordan as he set about making his Collins film.[103] Keating had no answer when Jordan wanted to know why he was bringing him this yarn.[104] A letter from Collins's nephew, Liam Collins, in 1993 seems to suggest at least some purchase for the Emmet Dalton story within the Collins family. Recalling Dalton's interview with Cathal O'Shannon, back in 1978, he wrote: 'a brother of mine has down through the years and still accuses Dalton as the man who shot Michael Collins … one man residing in Dublin assures me that he knows a man to whom E.D. admitted he had done the deed'.[105] While Liam Collins conceded in the same letter that 'it is of no real consequence whose bullet ended my uncle's life', not knowing clearly nagged away at him still. 'I would naturally prefer it had not been "one of his own"' was how his letter ended.[106]

For others, Jock McPeak, the machine-gunner of the armoured car in Collins's convoy at Béal na mBláth, or the 'Scottish mercenary', as Calton Younger rather disparagingly termed him, was the more likely culprit.[107] When it emerged that he had stepped in at short notice to fill another's place on the convoy, when the gun he manned jammed during the ambush, when he went on to steal the armoured car and defect to the anti-Treaty side, when de Valera was said to have paid him a secret service pension in later life, it was enough for some pro-Treatyites to suggest McPeak was to blame for Collins's death.[108] For those on the anti-Treaty side McPeak was instead a victim of what he had seen at Béal na mBláth, that he alone knew that it had all been a British or a Free State plot to dispose of Collins all along, that anti-Treatyites were not to blame, and the Free Staters hushed him up with threats and torture and punishment. His time in prison, the troubles of his later life, took on portentous meanings to reflect the conspiracy. It was alleged that he was beaten in prison, 'held incommunicado by the Military Authorities for almost two years'.[109] He spent five years in Portlaoise prison, went back to Glasgow, where 'jobless and penniless … he decided to change his name'.[110] He claimed he changed it in order to get a job, but, of course, this has a far more sinister aspect for those who wish to see far more sinister reasons for his choice.

It took John Brennan until 1983 to come forward to write to Collins's nephew, Michael. 'I have read some books about the shooting and I have to laugh.'[111] Brennan wanted it known that Collins was not shot by anyone in his escort, that the shot had certainly come from the other side. He wanted no publicity, but at the same time felt frustrated and ignored: 'None of these bookwriters [sic] ever asked us about the ambush … I wrote to Brian Farrell RTE and told him what happened. No one ever came to us, maybe because they considered we had not enough intelligence as soldiers.'[112] He spoke up again in 1984, another elderly man wanting to claim authority over the mystery, wanting to be heard, wanting to be listened to while there was still a tale to tell.[113]

Even when it seemed that the secret was finally out, that Sonny O'Neill was probably the man who fired the fatal shot, there were moves to release an interview with a man called Tom Foley which had been conducted by a priest in 1989.[114] Whether driven by a wish to protect O'Neill's reputation, to protect his descendants from the curiosity and the pointing fingers once that name had been named, Foley wanted to exonerate O'Neill. Foley said he was fetching and carrying for the anti-Treaty IRA at Béal na mBláth, that all the talk of Sonny O'Neill being guilty was 'a bad story', 'worth nothing', that Jim Kearney who said it to Colm Connolly was not even at the ambush at all, that Sonny O'Neill had already left before the firing started, that 'any man that claimed to be in the ambush they wouldn't know who shot who'.[115] It clearly still mattered; it still made a difference who got to say 'who shot who'.

In some respects, this is a pointless and only partial recitation of accusations, unsubstantiated theories and, sometimes, just sheer spite. They are not here to prove any case; instead, they go to show just how much a straightforward death simply would not do. While clearly some enjoyed being mixed up in making Collins's death 'one of the great Irish whodunits of the century', the perseverance of the rumours, the persistence of the instincts to conspire and connive, suggests something of how much many felt was lost.[116] The notion of 'the lost leader' is a powerful thing, and the rush to find something more significant in Collins's passing says much of all that was expected of him, much of what many assume he might have been.[117] That an ordinary death just would not do shows how extraordinary he had become.

While many have clearly struggled and struggle still with causes and explanations and even blame for Collins's death, all of this reflects just how significant his loss was, and how deeply that loss was felt from the very start. Loss expressed itself in many ways as all sides tried to make their own sense of his demise. For the British government, there was certainly disquiet at his death; the prospect of the Treaty smashed, of being pulled further into Irish troubles just as the prospect seemed to be improving for getting out. Early reports back to London from Major General Boyd in Dublin were convinced that Ireland needed a strong hand in Collins's place, that Cosgrave was not adequately warlike, had not the stomach for the task at hand, that in the wake of Collins's death the Irish might even 'implore the English to come back'.[118] For Major General Sir Hugh Jeudwine, the General Officer Commanding the 5th Division of the British Army in Ireland, it was 'a case of "when" not "if"' that would occur.[119] It is an irony, Bill Kissane has skilfully pointed out, that the 'eminently civilian' politicians who followed Collins went on to pursue a much more ruthless civil war than Collins ever conceived of, but it was far too soon for Major General Boyd to suspect that.[120] Other reports, however, began to take a type of solace in his demise. A report on the position of the Provisional Government confirmed to London that 'Cosgrave with his administrative experience upon the Dublin Corporation would be much more likely to overcome [administrative] difficulties than Collins with his cinema and star turn attitude'.[121] 'Cosgrave who is now at the head of the Free State Government seems inclined to run straight', a welcome alternative from Collins 'the "corner boy" in excelsis'.[122]

In the weeks after Collins's death Boyd was even franker still: 'The present Parliamentary Session is distinctly encouraging. The Provisional Ministry have stated their determination to uphold the Treaty. There are no signs of double-dealing at present, a feature noticeable with the preceding Ministry.'[123] There was the prospect of something more biddable and more pliant, and Boyd was not alone in weighing up the virtues of him being gone. Writing privately to Henry Rawlinson, the Commander-in-Chief in India, Edward Stanley, the soon-to-be Secretary of State for War, saw other merits to his loss: 'This murder of Collins, however, has done one thing, if it has done nothing else, it has shown the world generally what Ireland is, and that we were not the brutal and overbearing British nation that we were pictured'; for Stanley there was always 'a bright turn' to be found.[124]

Beyond their concerns for what Collins's death might mean for their own political positions and for the fledgling Provisional Government, British politicians paid predicable, but seemingly heartfelt tributes; messages came privately and publicly, Lloyd George accepted an invitation to attend High Mass for him in Southwark within days of his death.[125] Under direction from Andy Cope, Assistant Under Secretary, still in Dublin Castle, the politicians generally followed the Provisional Government's preferred line: 'The P.G. ministers are most anxious that we shall not show any excitement or anxiety about Treaty. They want us to regard the death as a fortune of war and it is in this way they are putting the death to the Irish people. They are most anxious to prevent their people getting despondent.'[126] Certainly, we should not underestimate just how precarious the position of the Provisional Government was or must have seemed, not least because Collins's death followed so closely after Griffith's demise. Indeed, the size and spectacle of Collins's funeral may have been as much a show of resolve and strength on the Provisional Government's part as it was an expression of loss. While Lionel Curtis commiserated with Collins's colleagues on how they 'will miss his bright presence terribly', while he empathised that 'a good many of us would feel like this if Mr Lloyd George were cut off', for the British government the security of the Treaty took precedence over such sentiment.[127] Within two days of Collins's death Churchill warned Cope in Dublin in quite stark terms: 'the danger to be avoided is a sloppy accommodation with a quasi-repentant De Valera. It may well be that he will take advantage of the present situation to try to get back from the position of a hunted rebel to that of a political negotiator.'[128] Churchill wanted the death of Collins to become, above all else, a

To Cope

Prime Minister to Cosgrave ✓

Deeply grieved to hear of death of
Commander-in-Chief. In his death the
Free State has lost a fearless soldier,
a leader of great energy & devotion, &
a man of remarkable personal charm.
Please convey to members of your government
my profound sympathy with them in their
loss of one of Ireland's most brilliant sons, at
a moment when Ireland most needed
his special qualities of courage
& resolution

271

Acting on Cope's advice about a muted response, this is the first draft of a private message from Lloyd George to W.T. Cosgrave. *(Parliamentary Archives, London)* private, sentiment for other reasons too. Clementine Churchill had counselled her husband not to send a wreath for Griffith's funeral just over a week before, not wanting to show, as she put it, that Griffith was 'too much in with us'.[129] While similar sensitivities may have tempered Churchill's public gestures on Collins's death, he bought Collins's sister, Hannie, her passage on the boat train home.[130]

But further down the ranks with orders to stand to attention, to fly flags at half mast, how do we gauge the response to Collins's death by the British forces ordered to act? Nevil Macready claimed in his memoir that the soldiers of the Field Artillery resented their horses and gun carriage being given to bring the murderer Collins to his grave.[131] One of those soldiers, Sergeant Harold William O'Riley, left an unpublished and quite different account:

> In the 17th Battery was my sub-section's wagon team of six black horses. These were handed to the Irish Free State together with a coffin board, and drew the gun carriage at Michael Collins's funeral. All the equipment for the horses was handed over with them: harness, horse rugs, saddles, blankets, grooming kit, nose bags, stable head collars, log chains and logs – everything. It was handed over in immaculate condition, log chains and logs burnished, stable head collars leather soaped and buckles polished. Of course, the horses were trimmed out, manes hogged, heels clipped, tails pulled – all spit and polish, as it should be. Esprit de Corps is the basis of discipline, and we were really proud to hand them over in that condition.[132]

'Esprit de Corps' may well imply that this was about his Battery, his army showing the old enemy how it should be done, but 'all spit and polish', 'as it should be'. There is something in these words more than Macready allows, something given willingly, one army to another, given with respect and pride.

The anti-Treaty response was more complex still. Killing the leader of your opponents' army, the most iconic and arguably the only charismatic figure they had, should have been a moment for celebration, but for some it was always a death to regret: some of those involved in the ambush claimed they parted in silence when they finally heard the news that Collins was dead.[133] It was not only that he might have been more likely to make peace with them, or that 'it would

27. 8. 1922

A Seoraisín a éara,

         I think I shall not have time this evening to write you more than a few lines. Perhaps I may have an opportunity to deal with matters more fully within the next couple of weeks. If so, I shall do so. But, at any rate, I have not much to say to you that the bearer cannot communicate verbally. Of the big happenings, such as the regrettable end of our old friend Mick, you have knowledge thro' the press. Personally I am extremely sorry about Mick. You know the hopes I entertained when in America that he might make everything right by procuring an acceptable Constitution. There was very ground for this hope. Even at the Ard Fheis on 23ᵈ May (immediately after the Pact) he spoke in such a way that it seemed he was about to throw over the English. But in a couple of weeks he had changed again. And then came the attack on the Four Courts and the War which has continued to date. May God rest him. He did great work for Ireland up to the Truce - no man more.

Austin Stack, writing to Joseph McGarrity on 27 August 1922, describes the deep sense of loss felt by some on the anti-Treaty side. 'I am more than sorry – I am heartbroken. I fail to see how it is all to end', suggests a sense of disillusionment that went beyond the pro-Treaty side. (National Library of Ireland)

I am more than sorry. I am heartbroken. I fail to see how it is all to end. Perhaps others of us go down. If it were to serve I should gladly accept it for myself tomorrow but the Republican position must be saved if possible. The country must never be counted as having given up its independence.

Whatever else happens to others I trust to see DeValera spared. Ireland is bound to want him again - and soon. He is head and shoulders over all the would-be leaders. He was always so. I cannot understand why he should be regarded otherwise than as a great patriot and leader even by those Republicans who have changed their coats, unless it be that the latter are bitter instead of being ashamed. The attitude of the Press - always pro British - is comprehensible. In spite of them all however DeValera, dead or living, will come into his own yet. He is and has been quite consistent.

Our people have decided to send out a delegation consisting of J. J. O'Kelly (Sceilg) and Joe O'Doherty. I am sure you will take them in hands and be a great pity if Collins were killed because he might be succeeded by a weaker man'; he counted for more than that with many of these men.[134] De Valera's tears after he heard the news, whether crocodile or not, Tom Barry's account of the prisoners in Kilmainham Jail dropping spontaneously to their knees to say the rosary for him, are well known, well-rehearsed examples of the ways he was mourned and missed.[135] Tom Hales was said to have 'cried his eyes out over the killing'; Jim Hurley, also at Béal na mBláth, asked in despair of Michael's brother Seán in 1923, 'How could we do it? We were too young – I was only nineteen.'[136] He had come to regret it, it seems, by twenty. Even Dorothy Macardle, the supposed 'hagiographer royal to the Irish Republic', only tersely noted of his death that 'there was little joy in such achievements, for the Republican side'.[137]

But the anti-Treaty response was not as coherent as that, not as straightforward as some of the later memoirs might imply. While one anti-Treaty handbill from late 1923 tried to make the best of it for propaganda purposes, claiming that Collins at least got to die 'fighting gun in hand among his friends in daylight', unlike young republicans 'murdered friendless and unarmed in the dead of night', in private letters some expressed themselves more freely than in more guarded public statements, than in more sober published writings in later life: 'Congratulations on having killed off the two infamies Griffith & Collins'; 'how does little Jack feel about M. Collins? Glad I suppose.'[138] It might have been easier to celebrate for younger women and men, for those who did not know him through the earlier fight. Francis Stuart recalled prisoners cheering in Portlaoise prison, but claims he stood aloof from them, 'I just watched'.[139] Frank O'Connor remembered the joy of it, that he 'rejoiced', that 'it was only later I remembered how Childers slunk away to his table silently' to write an article in praise of Collins.[140] O'Connor made his own kind of amends, his 'act of reparation', with his biography of Collins in 1937.[141] For some the sense of it changed with age and experience. Marie Comerford explained this best: 'I didn't know enough at the time to have been sorry about it … I suppose I might even have been glad'.[142]

Ernie O'Malley was taciturn in his comments at the time, while his colleagues in the IRA, the Chief of Staff, Liam Lynch, and the Adjutant General, Con Moloney, still followed Collins's name with the respect of an RIP.[143] But for all that deference, even though he admitted that 'it is indeed a regrettable National Position', Lynch still could not resist remarking that the ambush 'was a splendid achievement from military point of view', that 'Collins' loss is one which they

Harry McEntee was found dead on the side of a road in Dublin almost a year after Collins's death. The anti-Treatyites' reluctance to make earlier and more explicit use of Collins's death for propaganda purposes is suggestive in itself. *(National Library of Ireland)*

TO. Richard Mulcahy.

Now dare you insult the memory of Terence MacSwiney, a dead Soldier of the Republic by coupling his name with that of a man that died fighting to drive Ireland into the British Empire, and to force down the threats of Republican Soldiers an oath of allegiance to the King of England.

Terence MacSwiney rests in a Republican Grave, faithful to the oath he took to the Irish Republic. He cannot answer your insults. Do not slander the dead. He had no British Representatives to walk in his funeral, no messages of poignant sympathy from England's king and ministers, no fulsome eulogies from Ireland's enemies to dishonour his memory among his Race. These things are the marks of those who have surrendered to England. Terence MacSwiney had their hate to the end, as had every Irish Patriot that they could neither break or bend.

The Pageant you arranged for Michael Collins will fill the picture papers, and picture theatres, but History will place the man himself in his rightful place among these who died serving England against the Republic. Truth always prevails. Scenic displays captivate the mind at the moment but they fade before the truth in man's soul. 'Michael Collins will be the legend of Ireland.' You say. 'Are you mocking the man or mocking Ireland, Has she survived 750 years of oppression and treachery to make a legend of a man - the first in her History - who used his position as a sworn Soldier of the Republic to betray the Republic and advocate an oath of allegiance to the EnglishKing. Truth is the basis of a legend and truth has nothing in common with the breaking of lawful oaths and the taking of flase ones, Michael Collins is dead, may his soul and all others rest in peace. But he will never be a hero in Irish History. The side on which he fought condemns him. Because he was once a member of the I.R.A. every Republican is glad that he met a soldier's death, fighting bravely - they grudge him his pageantry as little as they envy himEngland's tears and from both they turn with pride to view the passing of Cathal Brugha - Hero of the Irish Republic. Such has been always the passing of the Republican Dead. Such will it always be till treachery is defeated.

Two separate bands of your Imperial Army have been raiding thro' Terence MacSwiney's home to-day - preceded by a drunken ex-soldier who burst into that home and threatened to shoot whoever moved, and informed us as he burst out again that he was going to fetch others. Sure enough others came, two separate bands of them within twenty minutes of each other, with their English talk of "murderers" and "Looters" - the very words used by English raiders in the homes of Republicans. When asked for their warrant they answered none was necessary, we did not expect it would be considered so, one can hardly be surprised at these raiders when the man who sent them - Mr. Dalton - is responsible for the tale that a bag of money was taken from Miss MacSwiney's house and stored in a Convent. Mr. Tobin gave Mr. Dalton as his authority for this very English piece of news. We knew of the tales of our wonderful wealth-the continuation of the German Gold story - but we are glad to be able to trace these to their avowed source.

Fresh from this and from the pain of seeing men wearing the uniform of Pearse carrying on the work of English Tommies in our home. I took up the paper that has always been the fawning agent of England here and find you - the man who stands for the breaking of a Sacred oath to the Republic, and the taking of an unholy oath to the enemy of the Republic- using the name of Terence MacSwiney in your peroration. You mentioned other Dead Soldiers of the Republic too, but I can only speak for one, and for him emphatically I do speak. If he were living to-day you would be turning England's big guns on him as you are turning them on his brothers. He died a soldier of the Republic, and you insult him by coupling his name with those who betray the Republic. When you eulogise those who have been false to their trust refrain from including in your eulogy those whose honour is unsullied.

From the 12th August to 25Th October is an anniversary with

cannot fill'.[144] O'Malley was far less equivocal in his memoirs, recalling that 'many republicans were in high spirits. The two men more than any others responsible for the treaty were dead. Religious ladies nodded heads in significance. "Yes, it was a judgment of God". He was now on our side'.[145] He caustically contrasted the pomp of Collins's funeral to the men buried quietly on his side.[146] Todd Andrews argued with his uncle Christy about Collins's death, and only made peace with him about it in the summer of 1924. As a prisoner in Cork Jail, Andrews was puzzled that the Cork men did not share his resentment of the Free State, that they frequently expressed their regret at Collins's death, that they were convinced it all could have been different if only Collins had lived. Unlike the Kerry men in the same jail who had no admiration or regret for Collins, not least because their county saw some of the worst excesses of the Dublin Brigade, Andrews found the Cork men 'suffered from a sense of collective guilt' for Collins's death.[147] Unlike other old anti-Treatyites Andrews felt no need in his memoirs to try and put any of this to right. Liam Deasy, on the other hand, was keen to refute that anti-Treatyites ever took pleasure in Collins's death. Deasy denied that an anti-Treaty officer, Sean Lehane, ever said 'we got your friend Mickeen'. He took various authors to task for citing this, these 'strangers', as he called them, who 'caused much pain', who 'did not help in what they wrote'.[148] 'I plugged Mickeen', 'Micheen was not much of a fighter', were what the anti-Treatyites were said to have taunted Seán Collins with when he was held up by them on his way to his brother's funeral in Dublin.[149] This was widely reported at the time and obviously still preyed on Deasy's mind.

It is easy to attribute this anti-Treatyite ambivalence to the fog of civil war through which they remembered Collins's death, to the type of war it became after and maybe because of 22 August 1922. It is easy to understand those instincts in purely political or strategic terms, to overlook that, for some, Collins's death meant that on a very personal level they could never reconcile with him. Some were simply grieving an old pal who happened to be on the other side. When interviewed in 1968 Dan Breen admitted: 'Collins' death was the sadness of my life … I reacted like you react when you hear of the death of your mother. I cried. I didn't cry when [Seán] Treacy was killed. Collins was the only one who moved me to tears. In Collins' death 'twas the sadness of a civil war when a fellow you like very much, but didn't agree with, is killed. That makes it very sad. I cried. I never remember crying before or since, except when I got a hammering at school'.[150] The anti-Treatyite, Martin Walton, described the loss in even more visceral terms: 'Stab. Absolute pain. I fell back in the bed. Unbelievable. Utterly unbelievable.'[151] Others even brought their children up to mourn: Máire MacEntee was inculcated by her republican parents to mourn Collins and to mourn Tom Kettle alike, 'however mistaken they might each have been.'[152]

The grief of those who loved him, those who lost him as a colleague, as an ally, as a friend, maybe makes an easier, more natural kind of sense. Our obsessions with war and politics hide that for many soldiers and politicians, this was also a very private kind of loss. Our cynicism may not trust the tears of politicians any more, but it would be churlish to dismiss them out of court. There are many examples of soldiers seemingly bereft: 'he was everything', 'I can't bear it', 'Dear God! Our Mick dead … I can't write any more, Tom. This paper is swimming before my eyes. Strong, brave lads all around me are sobbing like kids, lads who faced death a score of times'; 'I loved him as I never loved a girl in my youth'; 'Comdt Sean O'Connell was crying like a child'.[153] For Joe Dolan, 'we knew that there was nothing left, that everything was gone'.[154] For the pro-Treaty TD, Patrick McCartan, it was just as bad: 'I'm really too sad and too sick to write. If all belonging to me were dead I'd not feel half so sad'.[155] Joe O'Reilly was blindly convinced 'he could have saved Collins's life' if only he had been there.[156] For others there was anger more than disillusionment to be found. Emmet Dalton stopped that anger working itself out on the prisoners in Cork Jail on the night Collins died, but Richard Mulcahy's plea for no reprisals was not enough for the men who killed Alfred Cole and Sean Colley, and then Bernard Daly on the angry, possibly drunken Saturday evening after Collins's death.[157] Vinny Byrne, one of the Squad, confessed that, in the days after Béal na mBláth, 'I'd have shot any bloody Die-hard I came across'.[158] Charles Dalton has long been suspected of involvement in the killings, a little over a month after Collins's death, of Edwin Hughes, Joseph Rogers and Brendan Holohan, aged seventeen, sixteen and seventeen respectively.[159] Dalton, a younger brother of Emmet, had joined Collins's Squad at a similar age to these three boys and he may have marked Collins's passing by taking three more young lives. He had been among the first to hear the news of Collins's death when it reached Portobello Barracks; he wrote of the 'profound grief' he felt, and the grief of the men around him, when he recalled his 'memories of a tragic time in Irish history' for the *Sunday Independent* in 1946. The sad 'dumbfounded' teenager of 22 August was the man consumed by fury by early October 1922.[160] Often used to serve different

This image by Shemus (Ernest Forbes) from *The Freeman's Journal* of 24 August 1922 portrays the overwhelming sense of loss felt in the immediate aftermath of Collins's death and how quickly he was incorporated into a pantheon of nationalist heroes. *(National Library of Ireland)*

Some of those who considered themselves closest to Collins are pictured here carrying his coffin into Glasnevin Cemetery. *(National Library of Ireland)*

Return to me immediately

26th August, 1922.

Sean Collins, Esq.,

A Chara,

    I am desired by the members of the staffs of
the Government to convey to you their sincere
sympathy in the terrible tragedy which has deprived
you and your brother and sisters of a noble brother,
and Ireland of her most brilliant statesman and
bravest soldier.

        Mise le meas,

    Acting Secretary to the Provisional Government.

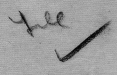

Here the Provisional Government writes officially to inform Seán Collins of his brother's death. *(National Archives of Ireland)*

purposes in different places, the sadness and the savagery belong together; they both serve on the same page.

But what can we ever really know or understand of grief? Much of what we can make of the measure of the loss of him comes from how the newspapers recorded and conceived of it, how grief was written up as a spectacle on show. Although Emmet Dalton furiously rejected Hearst newspapers' offer of $1,000 for the gory details of Béal na mBláth within a matter of hours of Collins's death, the newspapers were there at every turn to tell us just how much he was missed: a journalist followed Hannie Collins home to her lodgings in London just as she heard about his death, scribbled avidly for the readers her heartbroken realisation that 'there are lonely years ahead of me', even described the look on her face as she found out.[161] The *Daily Mail* described how Seán Collins broke down on seeing his brother, the *Illustrated Sunday Herald* how he 'kissed the general's brow and shook his hand'.[162] The details followed how the 'grief of the women was unrestrained', sparing little detail, the more heart-wrenching the better to satisfy the newspapers' readerships.[163] Because of the hunger for photographs we can see Kitty Kiernan's single lily on his coffin, we can see his brother bent over him in tears.[164] When the funeral was over and all the journalists had gone, we can only imagine his brothers and sisters trying to fathom why the youngest of them had gone, we can imagine Kitty Kiernan's anger at the life she and he never led.

The wider sense of his loss is a complex, difficult thing that fuels so much of what this chapter has shown. The grief of those who never even knew him expressed itself in all sorts of ways. You might fathom it in the picture of a young woman falling to her knees in the street to pray at the sight of the newspaper headlines bringing word of his death, in the cries of another, desperately imploring 'why did you leave us?', in the words of a mother berating her anti-Treatyite son for associating 'with the murderers of General Collins[,] the best and bravest Ireland ever had'.[165] It might be counted in the record number of words transmitted by telegraph at the time of his death, in how far and how foreign went the reach of the news.[166] It might be measured in all the reported tears of the 'men … seen weeping in the streets of Irish towns', in the reproduced portraits bought, in the many Masses and services for the repose of his soul.[167] It might be there in the relief of the Dublin builders whose wage cuts were postponed for a week out of respect for his death.[168] We might catch it in the hours people spent queuing to file past his body in City Hall, in those who kissed his brow, in the 'one woman

ENGAGEMENT
—AND—
WEDDING RINGS
A SPECIALITY

1, CRAMPTON QUAY, AND ASDILL'S ROW,

DUBLIN, *Feb 1st* 1922

M. Collins Esq, T.D.

TO **J.J. KELLY**, DR. PROPRIETOR F.A.REDDY.

MANUFACTURING JEWELLER, DIAMOND SETTER & SILVERSMITH,

DEALER IN PRECIOUS STONES.

To Single stone Diamond Ring £60 · 0 · 0

This receipt for Kitty Kiernan's engagement ring captures, perhaps by its very brevity, something of the magnitude of her loss. *(National Library of Ireland)*

This still from a British Pathé newsreel shows part of the queue of people waiting to pay their respects to Collins as he lay in state in Dublin's City Hall. Young and old are seen queuing here while one lady reads the newspaper coverage of his death. *(British Pathé)*

who kissed the dead lips'.[169] It was why parents brought their children to see him so one day they could say they had been brought.[170] We might count it in all the wreaths, one even from the flower sellers at Nelson's Pillar, in the nine unbroken hours of people filing past his body as it lay in state, in the time it took his funeral to pass one spot. From the highest honours paid by a new state, to his picture pinned to a dirty flag flying from a tenement window, his death was marked and, in all sorts of ways, mourned.[171] And while some may have been swept along by the sense that there should be grief, there still seemed to be a widespread sentiment that 'Ireland's one hope' was gone.[172] People may well have been grieving for an imagined Collins, for a character if not quite a real man, for the Collins they had made out of headlines and hearsay, but their sense of what was lost might just have been all the greater because it was so. For good or ill, the ending wouldn't do. The ending just wouldn't do.

LONDON GIRL'S PRAYER FOR COLLINS.

The first news of the assassination of Michael Collins created a deep impression in London. Picture shows a City girl kneeling before a poster announcing the Irish leader's death, on her way to business.

Photographed on a street in London, this young 'City girl' depicts something of the shock of Collins's loss.
(Birmingham Daily Gazette, *24 August 1922, Trinity Mirror Publishing & British Library*)

Better known for his painting of the dead Collins in 'Love of Ireland', Sir John Lavery also painted this more formal portrayal of Collins's funeral at the Pro-Cathedral in Dublin. *(Hugh Lane Gallery)*

8

'He'd have hated the idea of being a bloody martyr':

Collins's Afterlives[1]

In September 1931 Dr Heffernan was leaving Francis Street and Ballina for good. He was going to America, never coming back. Before he left there was an auction in his well-appointed home; two shillings in to keep the gawking riff-raff out. Every stick of claw-footed furniture, every handwoven rug, the beds, the bath, the boot-rack, everything must go; he rid himself of the remnants of an old life in the old world he was soon to leave behind. Among those remnants, one of the lots, was a picture on his dining room wall, a sketch by John Lavery, an early draft, not some cheap mass-produced reproduction mind, of Lavery's portrait of Michael Collins. Appropriate American heroes might watch over the doctor's dinner table when he reached the new world, but there was no room for Collins in the doctor's packing case.[2]

There is no way of knowing how or why Collins had come to adorn the doctor's wall: the choice might speak of some admiration for the man, for what he stood for, or at least for what the doctor wanted him to mean. The picture might say something of the doctor's politics; that he was on one side and certainly not the other, or it might have meant nothing beyond the snobbery of boasting there was a Lavery, any Lavery, on his tastefully decorated wall. What Heffernan thought of Collins when he looked up from his plate, or when he decided to sell his picture in 1931, may always be beyond our ken. Nine years since Collins's death, the ardour that moved him to hang such a picture may just have waned, or time and the tide of things since 1922 may well have soured admiration to indifference, to hate: Heffernan was leaving the state Collins was credited with creating, after all. Alternatively, American streets were not paved with much of anything in 1931, so a picture of Collins might just have been quite lucrative to sell. But between the picture hung and the picture sold, in the mights and maybes of just one auction lot, there is something of the challenge of what could be called Collins's afterlife. We can assume all sorts of things because Lavery thought Collins fit to paint, but the picture by itself can only take us so far. The challenge of an afterlife is in trying to fathom what it might have meant, what maybe came into the doctor's mind when he stopped to look up at that face.

The tangible markers of a Collins afterlife are quantifiable and clear. There are biographies and books in abundance, enough memoirs claiming a clawing kind of closeness to him, and then, of course, there are the films, novels, plays, poems, songs and so on. Each mete out a Collins to the measure of their own times. He has been in the language of politicians' promises since 1922, and he has long suffered the certainty of those who profess to know exactly what he would have done. What is clear is that he has been kept in various guises before the public view. What is harder to discern is why. Why did he, more than others, capture the popular imagination of those revolutionary years? Why did he become so great a part of the myths we have wanted to tell to others and needed even more to tell ourselves?

The quality of an afterlife, if we can call it that, might be measured in terms

Michael Collins
Chairman Provisional Government

Collins was painted by Sir John Lavery while in London for the Treaty negotiations. Lavery's paintings of Collins, particularly because cheap copies became quickly available, helped to keep the image of the lost leader before the public mind. While there may be more interest in Collins's relationship with Lavery's wife, Hazel, it is worth considering how the attention of such a significant painter contributed to Collins's afterlife. *(National Museum of Ireland)* of popular resonance. While Cumann na nGaedheal governments certainly told the citizens of the new state that Collins would be remembered 'forever', they swore the same perpetual promise to every National Army casualty of civil war, the same to Arthur Griffith and, again, the same to Kevin O'Higgins, when five years later IRA men took his life. However heartfelt the sentiments, none secured a place in the public's affections to rival Collins. Indeed, the resilience of affection for Collins could be said to exist almost in spite of official efforts. Collins lay in an unmarked grave until 1939, when de Valera finally allowed Collins's brother, Seán, to erect a cross. De Valera stipulated no marble, no ostentation; he prescribed the wording of the inscription, and nothing was to cost more than £300. The modesty of de Valera's own grave might suggest he saw more sincerity in the humble and the plain, but a priest, a gravedigger and an altar boy were the only people there to see the cross erected over Collins's grave. A photograph taken by a passing tourist shows Seán Collins at the grave, a lonely witness to what is too easily perceived as a Taoiseach's petty and damning spite.[3] A temporary wood and plaster cenotaph was erected on Leinster Lawn in 1923 to honour Collins and Griffith, to establish them as heroes of this new Free State, but promises of something permanent befitting the state's esteem fell foul of penny pinching and politics just as the wood and plaster edifice succumbed to the wind and rain. Taken down just before it fell down in 1939, it was only replaced in 1950.[4] Béal na mBláth was marked with a cross by the government in August 1924. Replacing a wooden memento put there by his family and friends, it was a way to rebuke the army officers who had mutinied months before in Collins's name; the speeches at the unveiling ceremony left no doubt of that.[5] The cross itself came free, a donation from an anonymous 'Irish lady in New York', which just left a trail of unpaid bills for the ceremony.[6] Only the arrival of solicitors' letters eventually forced the government to pay.[7] In much the same way, the gravedigger was left waiting for his fee; it took almost two years for the government to pay for the wreaths laid on Collins's grave.[8] The inadequacies of government efforts to commemorate Collins have certainly been pointed out, but fine physical expressions of commemoration should not be so readily equated, as they have frequently been, with the evidence of a vibrant afterlife. The fate of the memory of the Great War dead in the Irish State should make us question any easy faith we place in expensive displays in mortar and stone. In the first decade of the Irish Free State the government set aside £25,000 to spend on the care of

Unveiled in August 1923 in a quite lavish ceremony by Free State standards, attended by all sorts of dignitaries and notables, from the tenor John McCormack to a Syrian archbishop, the cenotaph on Leinster Lawn was the site of annual commemorations until the change of government in 1932. *(National Museum of Ireland)*

TELEPHONE: DUN LAOGHAIRE 449

INVOICE NO.356.

TMC
TERRAZZO-MARBLE-CONCRETE
PRODUCTS, LIMITED

Factory and Works:
WEST PIER
DUN LAOGHAIRE

Accounts strictly monthly

Registered Offices:
WEST PIER
DUN LAOGHAIRE

Sean Collins, Esq.,
"Inchidoney",
Booterstown Road,
Dublin.

4. 8. 39.

To erection of Monument in Glasnevin Cemetery to the Late General Michael Collins	£200.	0.	0.
" Foundation Fees, as per receipt attached	£18.	15.	0.
" Cemetery Fee, as per receipt attached	£1.	0.	0.
	£219.	15.	0.

Paid With Thanks 4th August, 1939.

As this invoice shows, Seán Collins kept well within his £300 limit for work on his brother's grave. *(National Library of Ireland)*

British military graves, and contributed £50,000 to the National War Memorial at Islandbridge, yet it has taken the best part of a century for us to acknowledge fully how much that war shaped this island, what that war did to Irish lives.[9] All that money spent, particularly by the Free State's rather miserly standards, a fine Sir Edwin Lutyens memorial, but only decades of what some have called official 'amnesia' as reward.[10] It is easy, maybe too easy, to complain about the honours that governments failed to pay to Collins, when official honours maybe signify so little in terms of popular resonance, so little in terms of all the many ways that remembrance works.

Alternatively, successive governments saw no need to spend on Collins because Collins seemed so prevalent or pervasive still. When a civil servant asked for Collins's grave to be 'properly dressed' for the anniversary of his death in 1924, he admitted more than his attempt to save the government's blushes over the unkempt grave.[11] His letter acknowledged that large numbers had made their pilgrimage to Collins's grave since his death in August 1922, even though, as Collins's brother Seán had complained as early as February 1923, there was no way to distinguish Michael's grave from any other in the National Army plot.[12] And this letter anticipated that more pilgrims would come: the Tailteann Games of August 1924 were expected to bring 'a large influx of visitors' to the city, 'many of whom will, no doubt, visit Glasnevin' and would go to Collins's grave.[13] Seeing Collins's grave was now part of what a visitor to Dublin was supposed to do. No grandiose monument was needed to compel people to that mound of earth. Whether they went to look, pray or pay their respects, even if they went just to say they had been there, they speak of an afterlife far more explicitly than the sum of all the books written, the pictures painted, the monuments erected and a government playing its official part. The history of any government's commemoration of Collins might tell us much of political twists and turns, even something of the nature of the state, but the essence of his afterlife is in whatever drove those people to go, even when going was to an unkempt grave; it is in all the reasons why his grave is the most visited in Glasnevin still.[14]

The decades since Collins's death have not seen seamless continuities of commemoration though, and, for all the public fascination, his commemoration inevitably ebbed and flowed according to very clear political tides. With Fianna Fáil in government in 1932 the army was no longer sent to the annual ceremonies at both Béal na mBláth and Leinster Lawn, and naturally the Blueshirts made

S/3913

Reg.
Have we any papers regarding
the acquisition of the plot where Genl Collins
is buried?

DEPARTMENT OF THE PRESIDENT
IRISH FREE STATE

saorstát éireann

Secy. Yes. File S.3913
16/4/31   9ᵗʰ April 1931

Re Plot where General Collins is
buried in Glasnevin.

Mr Sean Collins desires to know
how the plot is held. & whether
Mr Sean Collins is at liberty to
put up a Tombstone to his brother.

My own impression is that it is
not advisable but now
That if a monument were put
up it should be a good one & in
some degree worthy of the dead.
The selection of a suitable monument
and its erection would in my opinion
be a matter which should be left to
consideration in the future when
the subject can be solved free
from the heat of the conflict which
occasioned the death.

Writing on 9 April 1931 in response to a query from Seán Collins, W.T. Cosgrave outlines his reticence about erecting a 'tombstone' over Collins's grave. Worried that the grave should be marked with something 'worthy of the dead', his view that it should be left to the future 'when the subject can be considered free from the heat of the conflict that occasioned his death' is a revealing concern given the date of this note. *(National Archives of Ireland)*

The grave of Michael Collins in Glasnevin Cemetery is surrounded by the National Army plot. (*National Library of Ireland*)

official commemorations of Collins even more unlikely through the 1930s and beyond.[15] While Fianna Fáil claimed to be a broad republican church, the threat of extreme republicanism within the state was always such that de Valera, whatever his own view of Collins, could never risk open concessions to the memory of such a prominent pro-Treatyite.[16] While the first inter-party government sent the soldiers back to Béal na mBláth, on Fianna Fáil's return to power the soldiers were ordered home.[17] There was a predictable type of déjà vu in 1954 and 1957 worthy of the grand old Duke of York.[18] The local Collins Commemoration Committee, which had come together in Cork because it feared the appetite for the Béal na mBláth ceremony seemed to be waning, simply welcomed the publicity this political playacting brought, and set about widening the road around the monument to cater for the growing crowds.[19] In the mid-1960s the Michael Collins Commemoration Committee came together because it feared 'present day affluence' might make a new young generation indifferent to the principles and sacrifices of Collins and his times, but events in Northern Ireland quickly replaced these worries with worries of a very different kind.[20] When it came to Collins, no more than any other figure from the Irish revolution, the Troubles left some too certain, and others more uncertain still, of what they ought to say and write. In the 1980s and 1990s, Collins came to serve all sorts of ends; cast as fighter-turned-negotiator, he has flourished in the post-Good Friday agreement peace.[21] Compared to the commemorative fate of others from the revolution, the vigour of his survival is unparalleled. Police reports from the 1940s recount the five, eight, twelve and twenty-one people in attendance at ceremonies to remember the anti-Treatyites killed at Benbulben in 1922, and most of those five, eight, twelve and twenty-one were well known to the police as members of the IRA.[22] Collins's afterlife experienced its share of peaks and troughs, but the peaks were always higher, and the troughs were never so low as all the rest.

Peter Hart's biography of Collins was criticised for not tackling Collins's afterlife because without it the reader could not grasp why Collins had managed to mean so much to so many for so long.[23] Hart specifically wanted to avoid it, to move 'beyond fandom and the story of his life' as Collins and 'his claque wanted it told'.[24] John Regan shared Hart's wish 'to scrape away the layers of mythology and idolisation that have encrusted his reputation', taking as a given that we long to find the authentic Collins underneath.[25] Regan is offended by the 'grossly unanalytical' affection that persists for the image of Collins the General, the man of action, by the posters of him in uniform that sell alongside 'Kurt Cobain, and other, altogether more modern icons' in 'the trendy poster shops of [Dublin's] Temple Bar'.[26] For Regan it is as if we have been hoodwinked by the cheap heroics of some sort of second-hand Errol Flynn; we have fallen for 'the story of Michael Collins' that began to be told long before the end of his life.[27] But in pursuit of 'the real Michael Collins', the instinct seems to be to drive the story out of sight, not to concede its value, or to admit that many still wanted to hear it even though they knew it exactly for what it was.[28] There are appetites which only stories satisfy and heroisms that persist even when we have all the evidence to discredit them. Sometimes the point is in the passion for the myth.

In 1939 *The Times of India* published an interview with the Hollywood actor George Brent. Brent claimed he had been 'a dispatch bearer for the celebrated insurrectionist, Michael Collins, during the Irish rebellion'.[29] While Brent was not a terribly talented actor, indeed, one critic quipped that for Brent characterisation amounted to whether he chose to play a part 'with or without a moustache', he was then at the very height of his Hollywood powers, having starred opposite Bette Davis in *Jezebel* the year before.[30] Nonetheless, both actor and newspaper believed Collins added to the glamour of George Brent's life. Maybe more striking still was that neither actor nor newspaper needed to explain; it was assumed the readers knew exactly who Michael Collins was. We can attribute this easy familiarity, this sense of Collins as daredevil rebel, to long memories of the news reports that had circulated in India back in 1921 and 1922, or it may well have owed much to the romantic figure of Collins that emerged from *Beloved Enemy*, his first Hollywood outing, produced by Samuel Goldwyn back in 1936.[31] It might also have had something to do with the kinds of Collins that had already emerged, even so far afield, from the popular biographies of his life. Hayden Talbot's sensationalist *Michael Collins' Own Story* of 1923 was succeeded by Piaras Béaslaí's two-volume biography published in 1926.[32]

Initially, Béaslaí had government and family backing for the work, for what would be an official biography, or at least, as Béaslaí phrased it, 'a worthy monument to the life-work of a Great Man'.[33] Relations with the government soured when Béaslaí mentioned serialisation, but Collins's family supported Béaslaí's ambitions, not least because Béaslaí promised 'that the lion's share of the money' would go to them.[34] When Seán Collins threatened to withdraw his

Possibly marking the first anniversary of Collins's death, a military chaplain says Mass at a wooden cross at Béal na mBláth. A more elaborate cross was erected in 1924 and unveiled by W.T. Cosgrave with a speech framed very explicitly in the context of the army mutiny. *(National Library of Ireland)*

family's co-operation the government gave in.[35] By March 1924 Cosgrave wrote: 'we can scarcely justify having on the payroll of the Army a "General" whose only occupation is writing the life of the late Commander in Chief'.[36] Béaslaí was demoted and resigned from the army, taking his manuscript with him in disgust.[37] Although Béaslaí failed to get the £12,000 he hoped from an American publisher, the book sold well when it was published in Dublin in 1926.[38] Reviewed and advertised widely, certainly in Britain, America, India, China and Australia, and serialised in the *Manchester Guardian*, it was clear from the far-flung places from which Béaslaí received his fan mail, that his Collins had considerable resonance and reach.[39] Indeed, Béaslaí, 'the Big Fellow's Boswell', played a key part in shaping the nature of the Collins myth.[40] According to Roy Foster, 'the book began a venerable and often mawkish tradition of celebrating Collins's glamorous image and early death'. It was 'often inaccurate as well as pietistic', but it certainly set a very clear tone, not least because Béaslaí, as we have seen in Chapter 6, was desperately possessive of his subject and his own position as chronicler-in-chief.[41]

Indeed, Béaslaí brooked no rivals of any kind: Kitty Kiernan did not merit a single mention in the 942-page work.[42] When Seán O'Faoláin dared to write of Collins, to tell 'the true story of a great Irishman' over a series of articles in the *Sunday Chronicle* in 1932, Béaslaí threatened recourse to the law. 'The *Sunday Chronicle* buckled to the legal threat' and O'Faoláin's 'true story' came to an abrupt and sudden end.[43] Béaslaí published a condensed version of his book in 1937, under the title *Michael Collins: Soldier and Statesman*.[44] It was meant as a retort to Frank Pakenham's *Peace by Ordeal*, which was published two years before.[45] Like Dorothy Macardle, who published *The Irish Republic*, also in 1937, Pakenham, some felt, 'was recruited to write de Valera's version of Treaty history', and Béaslaí was determined to thwart them all.[46] But in 1937 Béaslaí was also tackling a challenger for his own crown. Frank O'Connor's biography of Collins, *The Big Fellow*, was published that year and most of all it wanted to undo the myth of Collins Béaslaí had long fostered and fattened on.[47]

But however sentimental Béaslaí might have been, Frank O'Connor would have to grapple with appetites for syrup and gush that even Béaslaí could not satisfy. For the British travel writer H.V. Morton, Béaslaí's book was cold: 'it does not give me a picture of the man so vivid as that which comes through now and then in less pretentious and more portable reminiscences of the time.' Morton much preferred Batt O'Connor's 1929 book, with its descriptions of 'the superb coolness of Michael Collins in the face of danger; and danger in those days meant a firing squad'.[48] Morton believed that Collins would eventually become the 'Bonnie Prince Charlie of Ireland', that 'romance will in the generosity of time claim him'.[49] Although Morton had been given tours of some of the dank spare rooms of Dublin in which Collins was said to have stayed, he presumed this was just the beginning of a fascination that would grow.[50] By the 1930s Frank O'Connor knew that the 'generosity of time' was already long past; Collins had already fallen victim to romance. For Collins's sake O'Connor wanted to bring the sentimentality to an end. He wanted to remind readers that Collins was still 'a human being, that he took a drink, swore and lost his temper' just like everyone else. He saw the need for this flawed and fallible kind of Collins for a coming generation who had no memory of 'the great story that began in Easter 1916'. He feared that generation would tire of the 'utterly unhuman shadows we have made of its heroes', would 'have no time to spare for this cloudy pantheon of perfect and boring immortals' it was being presented with.[51] But even O'Connor gave into it in the end: with the loss of Collins 'the greatest oak in the forest had crashed'.[52] Arguably, by the second edition in 1965 the things that made Collins human by O'Connor's lights were the source of his heroism now.[53] O'Connor's drinking, swearing Collins was a man apart from what were, by the 1960s, increasingly old rebels with their medals. For all that Collins was very much a product of his own generation, as we have seen in Chapter 5, he represented none of the hoary pieties about the revolution which the coming generation might wish to kick against.

Just over two decades after the publication of *The Big Fellow,* in 1959 Emmet Dalton produced a film about the erection of a monument to a dead IRA man.[54] It ended with an explosion, with the grotesque statue blown up by the 'blessed patriot's' 'illegitimate' son. Based on Louis D'Alton's 1954 play, *This Other Eden* usually merits attention because of Emmet Dalton's involvement, seen as some sort of coded admission of what might have been his part in Collins's death. Given that Collins and Dalton are mirrored in the film's main characters, with the patriot ambushed and the companion later suspected of complicity in his death, the film can certainly be read through that particular lens. But the film tells a more interesting tale than that: a tale of small-town worthies happy to turn a blind eye to the awkward truths, eager to erect a monument because it

Óglaiġ na h-Éireann.

PUBLICITY DEPARTMENT,

ÁÐÐ-OIFIS, ÁT CLIAT.

Reference No..............................

General Headquarters,

Dublin.

7th. November 1922.

RE LIFE OF THE LATE GENERAL COLLINS.

To:-
The President.
————————————

A Chara,

      I enclose copies of a letter addressed by me to the Secretary to the Ministry and his reply.

      I may point out that the proposals put forward on behalf of the Government in the latter letter are so preposterous as not even to afford a basis of discussion. Summarised they amount to this - that I am to toil for the next twelve or eighteen months at a work of the utmost importance and most exacting nature, living on my Army pay of £ 25 a month - a junior clerk's salary - that the work of my head and heart when completed is not to be my property but that of the Government - that the work of a literary man of reputation will be liable to be overhauled and revised by a committee of little or no literary experience - and that, as a great condencension, "the question of royalties will be considered." Was the like ever heard of ?

      First let me say that neither I nor Sean Collins (who asked me to do the work) dreamed till now that the Government contemplated undertaking the publication themselves. In all my conversations with yourself and other Cabinet Ministers on the subject, with Mr MacGann and even last week with Mr MacDunphy an entirely contrary impression was given to me. Had I known that such was their intention I would at once have registered my strong dissent from such a course.

      I have made inquiries from literary men and I have been approached by publishers and I am informed that any big publisher will pay £1000.or more and royalties on subsequent editions for the copyright of the life of Michael Collins. Secondly- I have it direct from representatives of the Hearst Newspapers and the " New York World " that the Hearst people or any big syndicate will certainly pay at least £5000 for the serial rights of the book.

Writing on 7 November 1922, Béaslaí elaborates on his grievances with the government and on his own hopes for his book. It was clear from this early point that his ambitions for the book were at odds with the government's views. *(National Archives of Ireland)*

Óglaiġ na h-Éireann.

PUBLICITY DEPARTMENT,

General Headquarters,
Dublin.

(2)

It was my intention that the lion's share of this money --
all the profits above bare remuneration for the work - should go to
the Collins family and this was agreed to by Sean Collins.

Now I am expected to do work which I can sell for six or
seven thousand pounds and give it to the Government to do what they
like with, to sub-edit and censorise and spoil, in return for a weekly
salary of £ 5. 17. 0. or thereabouts, and abandon an opportunity of
benefitting the Collins family to the extent of several thousand
pounds of English and American money.   Was anything more prepos-
terous ever heard of ?.

I may tell you that I intend to write a life of Michael Collins
with or without Government approval or assistance because I want to
put on record my memories of a great man I know intimately and raise
a worthy monument to his memory.

If the Government want a book written by a literary man to
be their property they must do what the private publisher does, they
must buy it from the author.   If the Government sets up as a publishing firm they must deal with the author like any other publisher.

So much for the matter as far as it concerns myself. Now to
deal in detail with the points in the letter

(1) Government as publishers.   I think it would be a fatal
    mistake for the Government to undertake the publication of
    such a book. There is no instance on record, so far as I
    know, of anything of the sort being done by a Government.
    A Government has not the machinery at its disposal which is
    required for such a work. It cannot advertise, push or boom
    a book like a private publisher can.   It cannot operate
    effectually outside its own teritory.   The public will
    regard the work in the light of a Blue Book, a dry official
    record or mere pro-Treaty propaganda. The demand for it
    will be correspondingly small and its statements will be
    discounted and discredited as the official pronouncements
    of a vested interest.   It seems undignified for a Govern-
    ment to undertake such a work at all.   It leaves them open
    to competition in which the private publisher will beat them
    hollow.   Some outsider with a good readable style will
    produce a popular " life" which will cut out the official
    committee-controlled book as far as the public are concerned.

'would do the town a power of good', 'because the tourists will be flocking here … cramming your hotel, hiring your cars, buying your horrible souvenirs'.[55] It is a tale of men desperate to maintain the myth of the martyr, adept at exploiting the legend, but incapable of acknowledging the more brutal realities of his war, unwilling to admit to his flaws, to the existence of his inconvenient son. Like O'Connor's book, but in all sorts of much blunter ways, it was another plea to see the past for what it was, to see Collins all the richer for his faults, to see him free of the pieties of those who had 'embalmed him in words'.[56]

But the words kept coming, keeping all make and measure of Collins in the public mind. Rex Taylor's biography of 1958, reprinted through the 1960s, was republished in 1970 just before the release of Margery Forester's *The Lost Leader* the following year, its title alone summing up all of that sense of what might have been.[57] Another edition of Forester's book came in 1989, following the many reprints in the 1980s of León Ó Broin's life of Collins, but arguably Tim Pat Coogan's *Michael Collins* trumped them all in 1990, making Collins a staple of airport book shops ever since.[58] Neil Jordan's film in 1996 no doubt reinvigorated the market for more books still: there have been books on the women in his life, the nature of his death, on Collins and intelligence, Collins and the Treaty, Collins and de Valera, Collins and the Civil War, and, of course, another biography by Peter Hart in 2005.[59] This is not to even touch upon all the Collinses of all the other books that have tried since the 1920s to bring the nature of the revolution to light. Almost a century-worth of words have certainly sustained the ardour of his afterlife.

Although Mary Banotti, Collins's grand-niece, could still complain in 1998 that 'there was no mention of him in the history books', J.J. Lee was quick to contradict her when he wrote in the same book, within a page of Banotti's protest, that 'it cannot be credibly claimed that Michael Collins has been neglected by historians and biographers', that instead he 'has attracted intense biographical attention by Irish standards', far more than any other figure from the revolutionary time.[60] It is maybe why the popular conception of the period is so shaped by the accepted impression of his life, why so many are so willing to reduce a complex period to a caricature of one man. He has an advantage that his contemporaries do not share: so many central and walk-on parts in so many other people's books. His appearances in Irish memoirs, of whatever form, are many, whether published in the first flush of remembrance or in later

6 St. Helen's Road,

Booterstown,

Co. Dublin.

Dear ········ ···

I have received your letter dated ....
and in reply may I say that as discussion of
Michael Collins, or of his affairs, would
appear to me a breach of the confidence placed
in me during the period (April 1919-August 1922)
I was privileged to act as his personal secretary,
I have felt myself obliged to refuse requests
for interviews such as you suggest. Therefore,
I hope you will kindly excuse me in the present
instance and believe that I do not wish to be
discourteous to you.

Yours faithfully,

Sinéad O'Deirg.

Refusing to give an interview about her work as Collins's personal secretary from 1919 to 1922, Sinéad Mason bucked the trend and kept her counsel about Collins. Taking an anti-Treaty position in 1922, she married the Fianna Fáil TD Thomas Derrig in 1928. *(National Library of Ireland)* life with all the benefit of other books and jaundiced hindsight. Authors seem to conjure him up almost as a sort of talisman to prove that they themselves were there, because knowing him may well assert their authority to write, or give credence to their version of events. Even when Collins appears only in passing, he often comes as a character, as a type the author imagines the readers ought to want. Some of the most obvious and enthusiastic were Batt O'Connor and David Neligan. O'Connor set the tone with his title, *With Michael Collins in the Fight for Irish Independence*, whereas David Neligan established the connection in the very first line: 'This is the story of my service with Michael Collins at the time of the Black and Tans', from the beginning basking in the assumed light.[61] Enough books were casting Collins as a heroic figure for Seán Moylan to warn Florence O'Donoghue not to make the same mistake when he set about writing the life of Liam Lynch, the former anti-Treaty chief of staff. O'Donoghue was counselled to beware of making Lynch 'a whale among minnows' as those writing of Collins had done before.[62]

Indeed, Tom Barry wrote from a similar instinct in his own book. Barry reminded his readers rather abruptly that any 'appreciation of Collins should not in any way suggest … that Collins was a giant among pygmies'.[63] To Barry, Collins was in need of perspective most of all. While, in public at least, Barry was relatively conciliatory for an old anti-Treatyite (he even unveiled a monument to Collins in Cork in 1965), Ernie O'Malley was still unflinching when he wrote of Collins decades after 1922, still angry at all the kind words heaped on Collins's reputation since.[64] To him, Collins was no better than the rest of the pro-Treatyites, and, worse still, none of them could 'compare with the Easter Week men': O'Malley had had his fill.[65] For Robert Brennan, Collins remained what Gerry Boland had once called him – 'a braggart and a bully'. 'I could not bring myself to like him', Brennan wrote, which still at least implied that he had tried.[66]

But it would be too straightforward to see this as old anti-Treatyites taking literary potshots just to settle old political scores. Frances Flanagan has traced suggestive strains of ambivalence towards the revolutionary period in the work of many authors in the new Free State, and the dissenting voices she has identified can clearly be heard among pro-Treatyites when it comes to the depictions of Collins as well.[67] It is there in page after obsessive page of Richard Mulcahy's notes on Béaslaí's book, in the refutations of all the myths and inaccuracies, which Mulcahy assembled but never published, which he continued to add to and worry away at even into the last years of his life.[68] It is there even more notably in the work of P.S. O'Hegarty, who like Mulcahy, was deeply critical of Béaslaí's biography, but leaves us a much more challenging prospect in his own 1924 book, *The Victory of Sinn Féin*.[69] As Flanagan writes, O'Hegarty presents his readers with a story of 'heroic triumph' but then he recounts the revolutionary period as 'a physical and moral slaughterhouse' as well.[70] And in ways his treatment of Collins in this book reflects his dilemma. He praises Collins certainly, effusively, but it is a decidedly ambivalent type of praise, given O'Hegarty's distaste for the nature of the Irish war.

> His was the brain that conceived the war policy, and his the courage and determination and capacity that maintained it, and that never faltered in it … right through it Mick Collins was its eyes and ears, its push and its determination, its support, its corner-stone.[71]

However, just a few pages before, O'Hegarty starkly reckoned the fruits of Collins's type of war:

> with the vanishing of reason and principle and morality we became a mob, and a mob we remained. And for the mob there is only one law – gun law. So the gunman became supreme; and the only thing which counted in Ireland, in anything, was force; for the spirit of the gunman invaded everything not politics alone … As the war lengthened, it became more brutal and more savage and more hysterical and more unrelievedly black.[72]

O'Hegarty did not draw Collins directly into these descriptions, but when he asked his readers to remember Collins 'as the greatest soldier, the greatest man of action of the time of the Terror', on O'Hegarty's terms, this was no easy straightforward type of praise.[73]

But for all who damned Collins with praise, ambivalent, faint or otherwise, there were always others quick to banish any doubts. Indeed, the flattery had flown foolishly high. While Lady Fingall saw Collins's face in death take on 'an almost Napoleonic cast', Oliver St John Gogarty saw a fully-fledged 'Napoleon who knew no Waterloo'.[74] Signe Toksvig went further; she wrote of a Collins with the handsome face of a Caligula.[75] The Irish revolution produced few to rival raptures like that. But hyperbole alone did not set Collins apart; while many Irish revolutionaries saw their reputations soar, Collins was among the very few of that period to register an international part. Whether in collections of unpublished British soldiers' letters or diaries or in the few published memoirs of those in the British forces who spent some time in Ireland, while figures such as de Valera get a periodic passing reference, only Collins appears with regularity and is referred to explicitly by name. Douglas V. Duff, who was a Black and Tan before he later turned his hand to writing boys' adventure books, always included a brush with the infamous Michael Collins, when his writings took an autobiographical turn.[76] Duff knew an adventure with Collins was the very thing his readers expected him to have.

More obviously, though, Collins is there in the books of many British politicians of that time, in most biographies of Lloyd George, in all the reminiscences of Birkenhead with the unlikely friendship they were said to have struck up.[77] He is there in the diaries of the press baron Lord Riddell, in those of the editor of the *Manchester Guardian*, C.P. Scott, even in a cartoon version of the life of Churchill in an Australian newspaper in 1949.[78] And, of course, there were far more than that.[79] Some reconciled themselves to a fondness for him; F.P. Crozier, the one-time head of the Auxiliaries, who wrote of a quite stirring interview with him, was a dramatic, albeit not a typical, case in point. However, for others, Collins remained the murderer Nevil Macready thought him, remained the villain of Macready's *Annals of an Active Life*.[80] Quite apart from that, Collins was reflected in the glow of others, recorded passing briefly through lives far more illustrious than his own. Brief and slight encounters with T.E. Lawrence, with J.M. Barrie, with George Bernard Shaw, reflected on the fame of him as well.[81] But it was probably Winston Churchill who counts in this context most of all. *The World Crisis* muses critically, but often almost lovingly, on the Collins it creates: 'he was an Irish patriot, true and fearless ... Successor to a sinister inheritance, reared among fierce conditions and moving through ferocious times, he supplied those qualities of action and personality without which the foundation of Irish nationhood would not have been established.'[82] Of course, Churchill was not beyond using Collins to reflect well upon himself: 'he sent me a valedictory message through a friend for which I am grateful. "Tell Winston we could never have done anything without him".'[83] But then

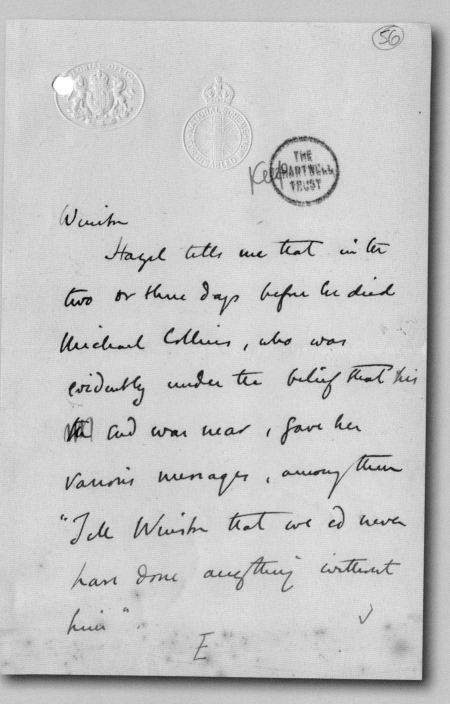

Winston

Hazel tells me that in the two or three days before he died Michael Collins, who was evidently under the belief that his end was near, gave her various messages, among them

"Tell Winston that we cd never have done anything without him".

E

Here Churchill's private secretary, Edward Marsh, passes on a message he received from Hazel Lavery, recounting Collins's final salutation for Churchill. Churchill went on to quote it in his book, *The World Crisis*. (Churchill Archives Centre, The Papers of Sir Winston Churchill)

K.

I think the description of what happened after the Craig Collins Pact is a little unfair to Collins. I have said above that Craig sometimes over-estimated his power to control his own followers. This, I think, was a case in point. Immediately on his return to Ireland, he found himself compelled to make an explanation in terms against which, I am sure, his better nature must have rebelled. As published, it was to the effect that he and Collins had agreed that the boundary and other questions were to be settled amicably, and his followers could be sure that he would not give away an inch of Ulster soil. All this

appeared under flaming headlines in the Dublin newspapers, and it is not to be wondered at that Collins whose nerves, I knew from personal observation, were not very good at that moment, should have made a violent outburst.

If I can be of any further service, by personal description or otherwise, I need hardly say entirely at your disposal.

Yours sincerely,

John Anderson.

The Right Hon.
Winston S. Churchill, C.H., M.P.

John Anderson, joint Under-Secretary for Ireland from 1920–22, sent extensive comments to Churchill on the Irish section of his book. This extract gives some impression of how Anderson recalled Collins by November 1928. *(Churchill Archives Centre, The Papers of Sir Winston Churchill)* modesty was not one of Churchill or the book's strongest points: Arthur Balfour claimed it was 'Winston's brilliant autobiography disguised as a history of the universe'.[84] What mattered in terms of Collins's afterlife was Churchill's reach. In multiple serialisations and editions, in the range of his readership, Churchill set his Collins upon the world.

Perhaps because that reach was so wide and the author so influential, it mattered how Collins was portrayed. Churchill knew the damage he might inflict on the Free State by what he wrote and so had various allies read the Irish parts. John Anderson, who had been joint Under-Secretary for Ireland from 1920–22, felt the text 'is a little unfair to Collins … Collins, whose nerves, I know from personal observation were not very good'.[85] On reading the Irish chapters Lionel Curtis wrote to Churchill in November 1928 in case Churchill was still in any doubt about what his book could do: '[Nevil] Macready's disclosures seem to [have] been measured at the author's unimportance, & to have passed unnoticed. Yours cannot. They must provoke controversy, attract wide-spread interest and gravely embarrass Cosgrave & his followers'. He ended his letter by reminding Churchill of the assassination of Kevin O'Higgins; 'that some of your paragraphs may cost people their lives'.[86] A month later Churchill replied that 'I have asked Cosgrave if he will let me send him the Collins & murder parts', which is a telling association of terms in itself.[87] There is no record of Cosgrave's reply, but his response in 1952 to a draft of Padraic Colum's biography of Arthur Griffith and to a reference it contained to Collins is very clear. Colum had referred to 'Churchill's comment that Collins looked like he wanted to shoot himself after signing the treaty' and Cosgrave simply could not tolerate that: 'This should not be quoted of a man with the religion and courage of Collins'.[88]

Lives might not have been at stake, as Lionel Curtis believed in the late 1920s, but clearly it still mattered what was said about the Treaty and more so what was written of this man. For Cosgrave a version of him had to hold: God-fearing probably, fearless certainly, but confirmed in support of the Treaty most of all. When Cosgrave wrote Collins's entry for the *Dictionary of National Biography* back in 1937 that was precisely the type of Collins he described, and now, into the 1950s, with some old Cumann na nGaedheal friends, Cosgrave encouraged Colum to write a book on Griffith for the very same cause.[89] Wanting to control what was said of Collins, whether it was Béaslaí's attempts to silence Hayden Talbot in 1922, whether it was Béaslaí stymieing Seán O'Faoláin in 1932, suggests that Collins mattered, that he had a popular currency still.[90] When the Irish-American novelist Constantine Fitzgibbon applied for Irish citizenship, Richard Mulcahy tried to convince the Minister for Justice to refuse.[91] By page 15 of Fitzgibbon's 1969 novel, *High Heroic*, a Collins character was found stroking a 'long, strong back', 'her white body against his white body', and although Fitzgibbon still got his Irish passport, his 'foul penmanship' as Mulcahy saw it, was almost enough to jeopardise that.[92] There would have been none of the fuss if Collins was not worth the fight.

This competing for Collins is suggestive, but so too are the various uses to which he has been put. The army mutineers felt a need of him, as did the government that thwarted them; the Blueshirts claimed him in their boisterous Collins walking and cycling clubs, but more worryingly in what was feared to be their version of Mussolini's March on Rome in August 1933; it was Collins's revolver Eoin O'Duffy claimed the police took from him, or at least it was reported so, and it was in Collins's memory this shirted, saluting movement was assembling to march.[93] The use of him to these and many later disparate ends suggests that Collins was malleable enough to champion all sorts of causes, and more, he could prod where prodding hurt. That he could be turned to serve so many ends might suggest he stood for everything and nothing, almost like the man who was not there. And this vagueness suited many who evoked him, as Lee implies: his allies did not 'probe too closely in case their hero turned out to be all too human … in case their connection with him might be exposed as one more of convenience than conviction'.[94] It suited all sorts of purposes if it was never really clear what Michael Collins was.

Yet his imprimatur mattered, and it always has, not just for the army mutineers or for O'Duffy's brand of Irish fascism. Simple searches in the records of Dáil and Seanad Éireann debates find him supporting and opposing a myriad of things, from compulsory tillage in the late 1930s to a criminal justice bill in 1981.[95] He was to hand for those who wanted to make war in Northern Ireland; he came just as readily as a shining example of how to make peace there in its place.[96] Even the *Financial Times* regularly reminded Martin McGuinness and Gerry Adams of all the lessons Collins's example might teach.[97] In the depths of economic crisis, Brian Lenihan became the first serving Fianna Fáil minister to address the commemoration ceremony at Béal na mBláth; the significance of that was not wasted on Lenihan, but his speech

The dead who died for An "EMPTY FORMULA"

WAS IT WORTH IT ?

VOTE FOR CUMANN NA nGAEDHEAL.

Issued by Cumann na nGaedheal and Printed by McConnell's Advertising Service, 10 Pearse Street, Dublin.

The death of Collins is blamed here on de Valera in a Cumann na nGaedheal election poster in 1932. Blaming de Valera for the deaths of Rory O'Connor, Liam Mellows and Erskine Childers was a much more problematic campaign strategy. *(National Library of Ireland)* still drew the obvious contemporary parallels as the economic challenges faced in 2010 blended into the economic hardships of 1922.[98] In 2013 the then Minister for Agriculture, Simon Coveney, claimed that Collins would have been proud of the budget of that year: the politician, the noun, the year, they barely matter, but Collins is the constant still.[99] It is easy to mock the uses and misuses of him to selfish and to seemingly contradictory ends, to snigger at the type of slip Enda Kenny made at Beál na mBláth in 2012 when he claimed that Collins had brought Lenin to Ireland, to sneer along with newspaper opinion pieces which point out how limited this generation's politicians are when they try to conjure a great like Collins to their side, but it is the politicians' perseverance that matters most of all.[100] In his first leader's address to the Fine Gael Árd Fheis in November 2017, it was with Collins that Leo Varadkar chose to end.[101] Something in Collins resonates still, enough to make the pointed references to him worth the speechwriters' while.

But Collins has a popular appeal that goes beyond any formal commemorative process, beyond any particular group's attempt to control or contain him, and that appeal was there from the start. While he was by no means the only revolutionary figure advertisements encouraged newspaper readers to buy pictures of, while the phrase 'every Irish home should possess copies of these great pictures' still applied to Kevin Barry just as it did to Michael Collins well into 1923 and 1924, Collins remained, and remains with us, in forms we could not imagine of many of his peers.[102] *Michael Collins – A Musical Drama* premiered in Cork in 2006.[103] When it ran in Kilkenny in 2014 advertising hoardings were routinely vandalised, maybe saying something in and of itself of Collins's continued notoriety or fame.[104] While the internet prompts and provides home to wondrous types of Collins discussions, it has also brought all sorts of Collins items to buy.[105] Michael Collins mugs, all manner of T-shirts, key rings and hats; Michael Collins blankets, pictures, jackets and statuettes.[106] There have been Michael Collins tours since 1997; there is now a Michael Collins House Museum in Clonakilty's Emmet Square.[107] Auctions regularly come and go, selling anything that amounts to memorabilia of him, things long kept as relics perhaps, now inherited across generations, and, which became, in the run-up to the centenary of the Rising, quite lucrative to sell.[108] Auctions peddle anything with his initials or his signature, anything with the mark or the hint of him, for considerable amounts.[109] A revolver that may or may not have been

Photographed by Carl Mydans for *Life* magazine in 1954, de Valera works under a copy of the medallion of Collins from the cenotaph on Leinster Lawn. *(Carl Mydans, The Life Picture Collection, Getty Images)*

with him at Béal na mBláth sold for €72,000 in 2009; his bible, a British Post Office-issue King James Bible, went under the hammer for €1,800 the very same day.[110] Even brass buttons, found in his uniform pocket when he died, fetched a quite considerable €4,250.[111] In 2012 an attempt to sell a cloth used to wipe his dead face, and a lock of his hair, clipped from his head as a keepsake after his death, was abandoned after the couple who hoped to sell them for an expected €3,000 to €5,000 eventually acknowledged, after public pressure, that selling these items was really in quite poor taste. They donated them to the National Museum instead.[112] This instinct to consume and to commodify him is far older than this recent rush to auction houses with his most intimate and his more tangential effects. As early as May 1923 an 'American collector' came upon Collins's copy of Oscar Wilde's 'De Profundis' in a London bookshop. Collins had signed his name in Irish on it, and assiduously recorded when he bought it. The find made the newspapers because 'relics of Michael Collins have been fetching high prices in the United States, and the lucky American is expecting to make a substantial profit on his purchase', the 'lucky American' having bought it for just 'a few pence'.[113] Collins, it seems, could always command a considerable price.

Without question that price has inflated since Neil Jordan's *Michael Collins* was released. Much has been said of the film's representations of violence, about the kind of Collins it personified, about the historical inaccuracies that might pass for artistic licence, but whatever its faults or failings, there were notable markers of its appeal and its success. The film won the Golden Lion at the Venice Film Festival in 1996, it broke Irish box office records in its first eight weeks and was released with a General certificate because the Irish film censor considered its 'great significance' outweighed concerns about the violence it contained, that 'it was so important that Irish parents might want to bring their children to see it'.[114] For one critic, 'Collins was dead as a character as soon as [Liam] Neeson was cast … since a Neeson hero cannot be bad', that with Neeson the moral ambiguities a Collins character needed were all gone.[115] Neeson did bring the shadow of Schindler and Rob Roy, and with Alan Rickman, best known as the dastardly Sheriff of Nottingham, as Hans Gruber, the persecutor of Bruce Willis in *Die Hard*, playing opposite him, it was equally clear that de Valera's villainous die was cast.[116] When Neeson was invited to unveil a new statue of Collins six years after the film's release, itself perhaps indicative of the film's enduring effect, it was not clear any more if the sizable crowd came for Neeson or Collins or if the line had blurred between them.[117] If you take graffiti at the Collins home in Woodfield as a measure, curiously all the 'I woz 'eres' seemed to date from after 1996.[118] And the film's effect has certainly remained. Tourists are still encouraged to travel the 'Michael Collins drive' through the various sites where scenes were filmed, while in 2012 a group of students took a life-size cardboard cut-out of Collins in his general's uniform on their summer trip round the United States.[119] They took pictures of all the places where their Collins had been; they took him to the coast, brought him to the ball game, to the bright lights of Times Square in New York: it was their odyssey to find Liam Neeson, the real Michael Collins, after all.[120]

But this type of notoriety is not all because of Neeson and Jordan; there have been many other Collinses, lofty and popular alike: Cecil Day Lewis's Collins, Denis Devlin's Collins, Tom Paulin's Collins, Seamus Heaney's one; he is there in the shadows of Sebastian Barry's *The Steward of Christendom*, his *Boss Grady's Boys*, even in *Cooking for Michael Collins* a 2006 BBC4 radio play. Michael Fassbender brought Mary Kenny's vision of him to the Edinburgh stage, while Roddy Doyle and Dermot McEvoy followed Constantine Fitzgibbon's fictional attempts to bring him back to life.[121] Graphic novels, Mick O'Dea's art, Vincent McDonnell's book and Gerard Whelan's children's stories, Brendan Behan's 'Laughing boy', even a Gavin Friday album cover, all, amongst others, have kept a Collins before their own particular audiences' eyes.[122] And there are many more Collinses to find, not least the Collinses that might have been: David Puttnam, Michael Cimino, Kevin Costner, and Robert Redford were beaten to it by Jordan and Neeson, though all had their own Collins films in mind.[123] Whether it is art, consumption or kitsch, it all reveals the constancy of his appeal, and how each generation shapes something of their fascination with him in turn. No doubt when the then Manchester United manager, Alex Ferguson, and rugby player Ronan O'Gara admitted their admiration for Collins, they confirmed, if confirmation were necessary, that Collins was very much a man for their own times.[124] Frivolous or not, these are still measures of Collins's vibrant afterlife.

That more interest has been taken in Collins's private life in recent decades, more concern given to the women in his life, that in 2012 David Norris claimed Collins was gay, all suggests quite bluntly just how far we mould Collins according to the measure of our own times.[125] We fashion him, just as every other

131, Morehampton Rd.,
Donnybrook.

22nd Nov., 1937.

Piaras Béaslaí, Esq.,

A Chara,

The first instalment of your new work on the
late Micheál Collins, published in the "Sunday Dispatch"
recalls to me, in its reference to "his life on the
bicycle," something which I thought would be of interest
to you.

When Micheál was staying at 9, St. Mary's Rd.,
Haddington Rd. - which I rented for him - he decided to
buy a new saddle for the bicycle. The old saddle was
taken by me when leaving the house and remains in my
possession to this day.

I may add that in a recent conversation with
Mrs. O'Connor, Eglinton Road, we agreed that the
saddle should be presented to the National Museum.

Mise, le meas mór,

Mary F Woods

Writing to Piaras Béaslaí in November 1937, Mary Woods expresses some of that fascination with Collins that sustains his afterlife as she recounts how she came by his old bicycle saddle. *(National Library of Ireland)*

Collins souvenirs began to appeal immediately after his death, including this china plate produced in 1922. One of these plates, along with one depicting Arthur Griffith, sold at auction in 2009 for €1,000. *(Imperial War Museum)*

period has, to suit whatever our current definitions of heroism require. Hart argued that all of the many Collinses along the way have always just conformed to whatever amounted to 'appropriate and attractive behaviour by a male hero', with, for instance, his 'virginal disregard for women' befitting the proprieties of the 1920s, and his 'oo7esque seizing of sexual opportunities' satisfying the 1990s' significantly more salacious demands.[126] When Moya Llewelyn Davies was known to be in the process of writing her version of Collins in the 1930s, old IRA men sent her an anonymous death threat and none of what might have been her juicy revelations came out; by 2007 her letters and diaries sold for a considerable price, such was how our appetites for the scent of scandal had changed.[127] The daughter of nationalist MP, James O'Connor, and a relative of Collins's ally Batt O'Connor, Moya Llewelyn Davies was married to Crompton Llewelyn Davies, an adviser to Lloyd George and Solicitor General to the British Post Office. Radicalised by the Rising, she came to live in Dublin with her children in early 1920, and stored guns and gathered information for Collins until her arrest in March 1921. She later claimed to have been Collins's mistress, and rumours spread in some anti-Treaty quarters that Collins was the father of her son, Richard, and that he was blackmailed into signing the Treaty in order to stop this becoming known.[128] And the flights of fancy might go on. The sniff of what might have been Collins's colourful private life, whether a romance with Dilly Dicker or more sensational affairs with Llewelyn Davies or Hazel Lavery, was for a while just more proof, if such suspect proof was needed, that Collins's Ireland would have been a different place from de Valera's one.[129] His letters to his fiancée, Kitty Kiernan, suggest a seemingly gentle courtship. With the promise of a pilgrimage to Lough Derg in her last letter to him, it is a correspondence of scolding and hints and teasing; there is little racier in their letters than that.[130] Whether his wild oats had already been sown by 1922, is, like the rest of his private life, just that – private, and deciphering his dalliances from his passions is far too dependent on those who carried a torch for him to comfortably discern anything more than their own hopes or heartbreaks. The rise of our gossipy interest in this side of his life probably says far more about the turn our history has taken than it does of Collins, says more about how we define our historical figures to ourselves, and not only in the context of their personal lives. On the publication of Hart's Collins it was called 'a Collins for the Celtic Tiger cubs', and with chapter titles such as 'manager', 'player',

Thousands responded to such calls for extras for the crowd scenes in Jordan's film. Indeed, the director recorded his shock at the numbers who wanted to be in his film. *(National Library of Ireland)*

of that white holly with pink tips to the white leaves. ~~that a born~~ ~~he~~ ~~was~~ looked at it as if it were some rare jewel, & when I came up to him he said "What do you think of it?" Tobin gave a guffaw of disgust, as if a weak effeminate side of Mick were being revealed which should be kept hidden if he had it. He did, in fact, love beautiful things, had a hunger for them; knew he had not had them and that it was a loss to him that he had not. That house of ours was old, spacious and beautiful, the most beautiful house I have ever seen, and he loved to come out to spend an hour or two in it. It was quiet, serene and peaceful, and he came for that peacefulness more than for anything else, because we had nothing to give him of the riotous pleasures he was said to be addicted to. ~~We~~ We were a quiet family, fond of books and ideas. I never drank a glass of wine with him ~~only~~ during all those visits. I have a liking for the door of a house to be open, so that a friend will not have to wait while a maid adjusts her cap; so ~~when~~ when Mick used to come out he could walk straight in, and often I would find him in one of the rooms with a book from one of the bookshelves in his hand. He was one of the most humble of men, did not know, so far as I could see, what a great man he was. You know how much he liked to have a child on his knee. He always treated a child with respect, took their questions seriously, and gave them serious answers. One of his mental qualities which fascinated Crompton and me was the quickness with which he seized on the essential point, and dealt with it in one short telling sentence which left nothing more to be said. This gift made what he said remain fixed in the memory. He was of course anything but a talker, but I think I could repeat nearly every word I heard him say, as you remembered him saying "Get a bike".

Kitty Kiernan belonged to his rowdy past & you are right in saying that if they had married he would have destroyed himself with drink. She was herself a heavy drinker - she began tossing down the brandies from early in the day. "I saw her only once - after his death - one night in the Gaiety theatre (she was taking 'a quick one' in the interval) when somebody told me who she was. I could not believe my eyes - plain-looking, flash and vulgar. The strange thing is that Mick knew she was this. He once annoyed me for two hours, asking me to take her under my wing - she had "had no advantages";- in a word, to put it vulgarly, I was to show her how to be

Over two letters to P.S. O'Hegarty, written shortly before she died in September 1943, Moya Llewelyn Davies presents some of the problems of navigating the interior world of Michael Collins. Dismissed by some as a woman obsessed by Collins, are her comments in these letters about Kitty Kiernan and Hazel Lavery reliable impressions or the outpourings of a woman scorned? *(National Library of Ireland)*

a lady. Pretty cool and pretty offensive, wasn't it? Anyhow, that
is how I took it, (it was ~~that~~ a soon after the engagement, and I
had never met her.) And when he told me that she was brainless, I
said "then why on earth are you marrying her?". He laughed,
answering 'Because she is a girl'.

Well, perhaps you can understand all that. I have my own
explanation. He was intensely shy, had no experience of women,
and the drinking, rollicking Kiernan girls were easy company,
as easy as the drinking, practical-joking young men he chose for
his companions. Such company enabled him to keep his inner
self unmolested. I believe he had never had any sexual experience. I got the impression that he was still virginal.

When Frank O'Connor was going to write his book, I was
one of the persons he came to see. But he made a mistake at the
very beginning of our interview. I mentioned Arthur Griffith's
name. He shook his head. Turned him down with his thumb,
in fact. I almost literally showed him the door. I was boiling
at a little whipper-snapper, who became a 'Republican' after the
fight was over, daring to belittle a man, a giant of a man,
who was the most single-hearted, the most selflessly-devoted, of
any patriot Ireland ever had.   So I told him nothing I knew
of Mick. He was not particularly friendly to him then either,
and so judging by his book he must have learned better afterwards, and if so it is to his credit to have expressed his altered
views.   And of course he was young, and may have
corrected his opinion of Griffith also (we did let the other side
put out their story almost unchallenged).

Please tell me frankly if what I write is of no use to you.
Yours sincerely
Moya Llewelyn Davies.

'CEO', Hart possibly left himself open to that.[131] It seems Hart, like all the others before him, and no doubt like us too, cut his Collins from a very contemporary cloth.

This chapter has not been about the way he stayed in the hearts and minds of those who knew and who loved him most. The button from his coat Kitty Kiernan never threw away; the lock of his hair Joe O'Reilly kept; the son Emmet Dalton named after him; the son that Kitty named Michael Collins Cronin just the same, are not part of what is meant here as an afterlife.[132] It is his resonance beyond his family, his own circle, his own time; it is in the fact that he persists and seems to mean something heroic to us still. What this choice of heroism suggests for our sense of the revolutionary period is certainly open to question, but we seem largely content with the Collins story as it is. He was Irishman of the century in a 1999 *Irish Times* poll, and he was voted Britain's second 'greatest foe' when the British National Army Museum had a public vote in 2012. Losing out to George Washington, he easily beat Napoleon Bonaparte.[133] There have been dissenting voices certainly, some from his own side, some who warn against any easy reading of a complex period and a difficult man, but his popular appeal seemed and seems to outlive these largely political and historiographical points of view. Collins captured the public imagination in life and certainly in death, and understanding the possible influence and effect of him cannot be attempted without trying to fathom the nature of his afterlife.

In January 1926 Sir Horace Plunkett wrote to the Countess of Fingall about a medium who claimed to have 'done a good deal of talking with Michael Collins', that when he first saw the automatic writing it 'seemed to be that Michael Collins alone could have concocted the message'.[134] Whether Collins did or did not move the medium's hand is a quandary for a very different book, but that there was want enough of Collins for a medium to build a reputation for reaching him, that even a little bit of Plunkett seemed tempted to believe, hits to the heart of what we might mean here by an afterlife. An afterlife is the fascination with him that expressed itself in many and varied, and, with some like Plunkett, even in quite mysterious ways. We might never know what Collins meant, or who he meant it to, beyond impressions of individual opinions or echoes of some unrelated points of view; in this we may not be as far from Plunkett and his medium as we might like. But we can be sure that he prevailed, that he flourished and abounded, that Collins endured in all the ways we wanted him far more than any other figure from that time.

Photographed, probably on the first anniversary of Collins's death, his sister Mary Collins Powell visits a temporary memorial at Béal na mBláth. Erected by some of his old comrades, the cross joined the makeshift crosses already left to mark his loss. *(National Library of Ireland)*

Conclusion

'We want something more than that'

On 11 September 1922 W.T. Cosgrave made his first statement as President to the Third Dáil. He reflected on the state of things, on what had happened and, as he saw it, why. He apportioned praise where he felt it due, and blamed all there was to blame on the perfidious and misled anti-Treatyites. Arthur Griffith came in for honourable mention, while Collins, 'the most hunted man by the British during the late war', was cast in his by then familiar heroic role. When it came to what lay ahead he had very little to say: vague mumblings about 'the Gaelic spirit', empty encouragements about the nation's 'upward and onward march towards the achievements of its highest hopes'.[2] In civil war it may have been unwise to promise more. But for the Labour TD Cathal O'Shannon, none of this was good enough and he said so straightaway. He wanted a president who would 'face the future on the strength, courage, resolution and authority of this Dáil', not one who only 'rattled the bones of the dead in our faces' for want of anything better to say. He wanted a president who 'when questions as to the future policy are put' did not hide behind Collins and Griffith and the 'many brave and courageous things they did'. For O'Shannon it was simple: 'we want something more than that'.[3] It was just twenty days since Collins's death but already 'we want something more than that'.

In a book such as this it is easy or maybe expedient to assume that the protagonist had a legacy worthy of all the words. We know Collins had an afterlife made and shaped in the image of whatever seemed necessary to make a point or win an argument, that he has been a fitting hero, a suitable villain, depending on the books you read, the politics you inherit, or how readily you reduce the revolution to a neat and straightforward tale. But 'we want something more than that', and the rather indecent haste with which it was said, should give us pause for thought before we accept fine words and flowery funeral sentiments for the actual measure of the man. Biographies do not tend to take account of how the bereaved adapt, how quickly the gaps are filled, how the missed are nonetheless replaced. And Collins was replaced remarkably quickly and relatively easily for the idea that 'none except Collins was irreplaceable' still to hold, or at least to hold as firmly as it does.[4]

The speed with which the Provisional Government reneged on many aspects of what seemed fundamental to Collins's approach was striking, whether immediately instituting the principle of collective cabinet responsibility in the face of his more idiosyncratic style, or divesting itself sharply of the commitments he had made to undermine the Northern Ireland state. That the Dáil met at all in September 1922, that O'Shannon got the opportunity to air his views, was directly at odds with Collins's wishes, because on the day before he died he had written to postpone the meeting of the Dáil yet again. We can interpret, as John Regan does, that all of this change was 'a conscious reaction to Collins's style of leadership', an undoing of the 'dictatorial powers within the new regime', which, Regan argues, Collins had taken upon himself.[5] Regan goes further: 'if no crisis followed his death, it may well be because by 22 August 1922, Collins was the crisis'.[6] Alternatively, it can be read in a much more benign light: the speed with which his policies were overturned might instead suggest the machine was more powerful than the man, that he was only ever the sum of the systems and organisations that he had come to manipulate or had helped to put in place.

Pictured here leaving Earlsfort Terrace after the vote on the Treaty, Collins seems an oddly solitary figure, despite his shadow, at the end of the debate.
(National Library of Ireland)

Photographed here with his fellow pro-Treaty TDs, Collins makes little sense without the context of the people who surrounded him at this and at every other point in his career. He may have been important, but he was only ever one of many. *(National Library of Ireland)*

Given the sizable Collins-shaped gap left by his death there were, certainly, winners and losers with him gone: Cosgrave won, albeit reluctantly, and that it was him might well have been a comment on Collins's recent type of leadership. Liam de Róiste wrote by 29 November 1922 that 'Cosgrave, more even than others, shows the reaction from the high posturings and heroic moods of the last four years'.[7] 'Cosgrave is not a big man', but some clearly felt the time for 'a big man' had passed.[8] Kevin O'Higgins, who immediately left the army and returned to take such a key role in civilian life, certainly won. Collins had labelled him 'the balls' for his 'if we go into the empire … we go in with our heads up' of the Treaty debates, and Richard Mulcahy certainly believed Collins would have stymied O'Higgins's later 'intrusion into army affairs', would have kept O'Higgins in, what Mulcahy thought, was his proper place.[9] Mulcahy himself got to come out from Collins's shadow, albeit only for a brief while, until the army mutiny, arguably another of Collins's legacies, brought his time in charge of the army to an undignified close.[10] The IRB with its 'somewhat inglorious end', the Northern IRA, the military ambitions of Eoin O'Duffy, the list might go on; it is all subjective still who won and lost.[11]

That some could, indeed, win, supports Peter Hart's view, that even by 1921 it was clear that Collins 'could be replaced', that 'once Collins had his departments up and running in 1920, they would probably have survived without him'.[12] Even though he had concentrated considerable amounts of power within himself in the months before he died, and while he may have assumed that there was no job he could not do better himself, 'that he alone was competent, or at least, best equipped to lead', we overestimate him and underestimate his structures and his colleagues at our peril.[13] One of those colleagues, Michael Hayes, contrasted 'when Parnell died in 1891 … it took nearly ten years to appoint a successor' with 'our situation, in 1922, all-important replacements were accomplished in as many hours': it was meant to compliment Collins, but it seemed to serve his colleagues just as well.[14] As we have seen throughout this book, for all the focus on Collins and his unique abilities, his voracious appetite for work, his capacity to juggle multiple positions and organisations, he only really makes sense as part, or at the head, of a crowd. He was never more than a product of, and for a while a channel for, larger forces. While he may have seemed the obvious inspiration for much of what passed for the revolution, he was actually very little without all those people who kept the cogs of the revolution going. In all sorts of ways we have never really seen Collins straight; he is out of proportion, exaggerated beyond our capacity to focus, and so we miss much of why 'we want something more than that' made sense to so many in September 1922.

During the 1920s and 1930s the Free State was one of the most stable democracies in Europe. Of the 22 democratic polities enumerated in the 1920s, the Free State was one of the few to survive the interwar period.[15] And while this stability may have looked more like stasis when read back through the economic despair of the 1950s, and again through the dispiriting lens of the 1980s, the Collins we have indulged ourselves with makes it almost impossible to see independent Ireland on its own terms. Detached, even coldly critical analyses of Collins's life slip seamlessly into speculation as to what he would have done, how it might have been different, better, more dynamic. He would have ended the Civil War earlier, he would never have allowed extrajudicial or any other type of executions, he would have ended partition, made the state prosperous, liberal, secular, or, indeed, insert the adjective, phrase or prejudice of your choice. A parallel, idealised Free State is there to find with Collins as high priest of your own chosen progress, with very little if any basis in what Collins actually said or did or believed. Those still harbouring the notion that Collins could have been a bulwark against what many identify as 'de Valera's Ireland' might pause to reflect on Collins's *The Path to Freedom* as this book has done. While J.J. Lee wondered if Collins might have 'founded something like Fianna Fáil himself', we can only be certain that Collins was very much a man of his time and he shared the values of the revolution that produced him.[16]

That said, to understand Collins is also to accept that the imagined Collins matters as much as 'the real' Mick, that he became whatever people thought he was. Far-fetched notions attached themselves to him, they took hold, made him recognisable around the world as no other Irish revolutionary was known. Indeed, the *Times of India* sulked in 1925 that the Irish Free State 'has become a bore' because no single exciting figure had been inflated by the media to take his place.[17] Collins benefited from 'mysterious Mike' and encouraged the 'Scarlet Pimpernel' in some contexts, and we have to fathom the sense people made of him precisely because often they saw him through this sensational lens alone. But accepting the role the imagined Collins played does not mean it is the only role we should value. Neil Jordan presented a 'man-of-action' Collins to a new generation, gave us a tragic narrative of terrorist or freedom fighter (well,

Seen here with Arthur Griffith on his way to Sean MacEoin's wedding in June 1922, Collins was the one who became 'the lost leader', the embodiment of what might have been. *(National Library of Ireland)*

Do <u>YOU</u> stand for the Free State and <u>THIS</u>?

This anti-Treaty handbill pointed to some of the excesses on the National Army side during the Civil War, but it also describes something of the nature of the violence unleashed more broadly across the revolutionary years.
(The Board of Trinity College Dublin)

you can take your pick) turned peacemaker, sundered from his friend Boland, losing his life as tragic heroes often do. We got what we had come to expect: the violence, the spying, the adventure story that sets the pulses racing; we got a character, a persona, not the complex nuanced life. Despite all of the scholarship that has traced the many parts he played, the many sides to his life, Collins the Minister for Finance, Collins the administrator, Collins the letter-writer remains somehow a less appealing figure still; book after book (as this one may too) falls into the same trap as Jordan's life; maybe the pages just turn quicker that way. But even when Collins the man of action gives way to Collins the politician and the peacemaker, that straightforward narrative arc misses the most significant point: Collins was always all and none and most of these things at once. He was always the politician, always the fixer, the negotiator; he was far less of the spy and the soldier the pictures in uniform and the sensational depictions might suggest; he was much more the wrangler and the accountant, and most of all the writer of letters, the man who hatched a revolution by post. In John Le Carré's novel *Tinker, Tailor, Soldier, Spy*, when George Smiley tried to fathom why his old colleague had become a Russian spy, one motive would not do: 'he settled instead for a picture of one of those Russian dolls that open up, revealing one person inside the other, and another inside him'.[18] It might make sense to think of Collins with always yet another doll inside.

Although his role and his capacity to control the revolution's violence has been questioned in this book, his recourse to a certain kind of violence and its ramifications present a challenge to us still. He could be callous in his use of violence, ruthless in terms of disposing of enemies as he saw them in his way, and he may well have realised that the legacy of that violence would be a troubling one. He knew many of the young men closest to him in the Squad and in the Dublin Brigade were increasingly consumed by the kind of violence they practised. He nonetheless put some of them to work in the Criminal Investigation Department in Oriel House in 1922, and many of the worst excesses of the Civil War in the south of the country bore the mark of those who had fought what could be called his kind of war. As Peter Hart wrote, 'the Squad and the Intelligence Department have often been lionised as Collins's men in the triumphant struggle against British intelligence, but any real accounting of their history – and his – must include their murderous campaign against republicanism in 1922–3'.[19]

The problem is as much with our capacity to read and maybe even revel in tales of Collins and his Squad almost as a type of *Boy's Own* adventure, with plucky underdogs using cunning and ingenuity against the might of the British Empire during the War of Independence, as it is with our willingness to see the same violence in a very different light during civil war, if we are prepared to acknowledge it at all. But the problem goes beyond that. The celebration of the kind of violence associated with Collins, there even before Griffith described him as the 'man who won the war', and surviving and thriving long after Jordan's film, leaves questions to be asked of how we respond to and frame the violence of that period of Irish history more broadly. The echoes of what he, and those he associated with, unleashed are there to hear in the army mutiny of 1924, in the men who still wanted to use old methods to get their way; they are there in the enquiry into the same mutiny, in the testimony that 'if such a disease as shell-shock existed in the IRA prior to the Truce, the first place to look for it would be amongst' the men who had served in his Squad.[20] We can hear the echoes in the early 1930s, this time mocked up in blue shirts and giving a one-armed salute. If violence is one of the ways Collins is to be understood, then hold him squarely and unflinchingly to account.

Our understanding of the Irish revolution has changed considerably since the 1970s. New sources are still emerging, different questions are being asked, which all confirm that the history of the revolution cannot be told through the life of one man any more, great or otherwise. It is a history of combatants and civilians of every kind and sort, of lives changed considerably and of lives barely interrupted at all. It is a history conscious of broader contexts, that takes the influence of the Great War as a given now, that is alive to the comparisons that come from the much more violent wars and revolutions that Europe endured after 1918. It is the history of society, culture, politics, with questions and conclusions reflecting all of the variety of experience with which this period boldly confronts us. Collins was certainly part of it, an important part, yes, but just a part nonetheless. Heroic, exceptional, unique are attributes for your own judgement, but this book would like you to consider that maybe he was just hungrier, luckier, more brazen, more tenacious, more written about and, eventually, more photographed than many of the rest. Make a great man of him if you wish, but at least ask why we still need him to be great.

Collins is the best man we have to my mind, on the whole those working now seem very capable the odds against them are tremendous, and the country is going through worse than 98, the stories of every kind of devilish cruelty practised on our people don't bear telling, in spite of it there is no sign of break, the spirit seems to be, its our last stand, we must win, we can suffer longer, if you knew of the bravery & heroism of men & women here day in, day out you say thanks God I belong to such a people, such a change in less than 15 years, when we came home that time, it seemed a hopeless task

without help. garden to be attended to +
meeting, I find it hard to get the time
but. I mean to do it, though I have so
little experience I fear I shall make a
hash of it.

I quite agree with you about Griffith
+ Collins, though Collins in his sphere
was a capabale, energetic man, but.
if he had all the qualities in the world
his two weaknesses would have off
set them, drink + vanity,

Re. Wolfe Tone Memorial foundation
stone. Just before receiving your letter
I had written to J. D. on the question,

The idea of that site was abandoned
by the old W. T. M. Com, as the Arch at
the entrance to St Stephens Green Park when
faces it, would overshadow it, The
Commissioners in removing placed the
choise of two or three other sites at the dis
posal of the remaining members of that
Com, Of course the general public only know

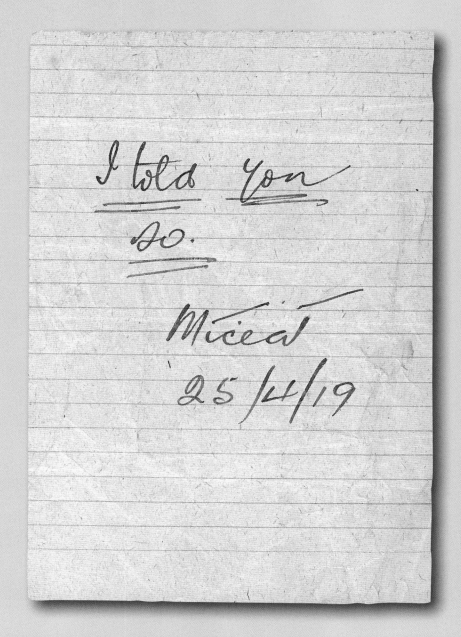

Written on 25 April 1919, and sent to an unknown recipient, this note shows Collins at his most adamant.
(National Library of Ireland)

Collins, seen here on a public platform, at some point between the Truce and the June 1922 election. *(National Library of Ireland).*

Notes

Introduction

1   *Dáil Éireann Official Report: Debate on the Treaty between Great Britain and Ireland* (Dublin, 1922), 7 January 1922, p. 326.

2   *Michael Collins* (1996), directed by Neil Jordan.

3   Hayden Talbot, *Michael Collins' Own Story* (Dublin, 2012; 1st ed. 1923), p. 4 & p. 9; Piaras Béaslaí, *Michael Collins and the Making of a New Ireland* (Dublin, 1926), p. ix.

4   Peter Hart, *Mick: The Real Michael Collins* (London, 2005); Frank O'Connor, *The Big Fellow: A Life of Michael Collins* (London & New York, 1937); Margery Forester, *Michael Collins: The Lost Leader* (London, 1971); Tim Pat Coogan, *Michael Collins: A Biography* (London, 1990).

5   Alan Forrest, *Napoleon* (London, 2011), pp. vii–viii.

6   Hart, *Mick*, p. xxi.

7   Frank O'Connor, *The Big Fellow* (Dublin, 1996; 1st ed. 1937), p. 10; Hart, *Mick*, p. xiii.

8   Collins to Art O'Brien, 28 May 1921, National Archives of Ireland (NAI), Dáil Éireann papers (DE) 2/330.

9   *Dáil Éireann Official Report: Debate on the Treaty*, 7 January 1922, p. 326.

10   For aspects of his role as holder of various purse strings see Nicholas Ridley, *Michael Collins and the Financing of Violent Political Struggle* (London, 2018); Ronan Fanning, *The Irish Department of Finance, 1922–58* (Dublin, 1978).

11   See for example, Coogan, *Michael Collins*; Tim Pat Coogan, *De Valera: Long Fellow, Long Shadow* (London, 1993); T. Ryle Dwyer, *Michael Collins and the Treaty: His Differences with de Valera* (Dublin, 1981); T. Ryle Dwyer, *Big Fellow, Long Fellow: A Joint Biography of Collins and de Valera* (Dublin, 2006).

12   For example, see Meda Ryan, *Michael Collins and the Women in His Life* (Cork, 1996); Sinead McCoole, *Hazel: A Life of Lady Lavery, 1880–1935* (Dublin, 1996); Meda Ryan, *Michael Collins and the Women who Spied for Ireland* (Cork, 2006).

13   See for example, Frank Pakenham, *Peace by Ordeal: An Account, From First-hand Sources, of the Negotiation and Signature of the Anglo-Irish Treaty, 1921* (London, 1935); A.T.Q. Stewart (ed.), *Michael Collins: The Secret File* (Belfast, 1997); Vincent MacDowell, *Michael Collins and the Irish Republican Brotherhood* (Dublin, 1997); T. Ryle Dwyer, *The Squad and the Intelligence Operations of Michael Collins* (Cork, 2005); T. Ryle Dwyer, *'I signed my death warrant': Michael Collins and the Treaty* (Cork, 2006); Michael Foy, *Michael Collins's Intelligence War: The Struggle Between the British and the IRA, 1919–1921* (Stroud, 2006); T. Ryle Dwyer, *Michael Collins and the Civil War* (Cork, 2012); Tim Pat Coogan, *The Twelve Apostles: Michael Collins, the Squad and Ireland's Fight for Freedom* (London, 2016); Dominic Price, *We Bled Together: Michael Collins, the Squad and the Dublin Brigade* (Cork, 2017).

14   Peter Hart, *The IRA at War 1916–1923* (Oxford, 2003), p. vii.

15   Comment by Bishop Fogarty at the unveiling of portraits of Griffith, Collins and O'Higgins, Dáil Éireann, 21 January 1944, University College Dublin Archives (UCDA), Cosgrave papers, P285/190.

16   *Dáil Éireann Official Report: Debate on the Treaty between Great Britain and Ireland*, Arthur Griffith, 19 December 1921, p. 20.

17 *Irish Press*, 18 March 1943; Maurice Moynihan (ed.), *Speeches and Statements by Eamon de Valera 1917–1973* (Dublin, 1980), p. 466.

18 Nancy Brandt, 'Pancho Villa: the making of a modern legend', *The Americas*, 21:2 (1964), p. 146.

1: Making Michael Collins

1 Béaslaí, *Michael Collins*, pp. ix & 2–5.

2 R.F. Foster, *Vivid Faces: The Revolutionary Generation in Ireland 1890–1923* (London, 2014); Fearghal McGarry, *The Rising. Ireland: Easter 1916* (Oxford, 2010), pp. 8–43; Peter Hart, 'The social structure of the Irish Republican Army' in Peter Hart, *The IRA at War 1916–1923* (Oxford, 2003), pp. 110–40; Joost Augusteijn, 'Motivation: why did they fight for Ireland? The motivation of Volunteers in the revolution' in Joost Augusteijn (eds), *The Irish Revolution, 1913–1923* (Basingstoke, 2002), pp. 103–20.

3 Thomas Mann, *The Magic Mountain* (London, 1983; 1st ed. 1924), p. 32.

4 David Fitzpatrick, *Politics and Irish Life 1913–1921: Provincial Experience of War and Revolution* (Cork, 1977), p. 169; Hart, 'The social structure of the Irish Republican Army', pp. 120–2.

5 Tom Garvin, *Nationalist Revolutionaries in Ireland 1858–1928* (Oxford, 1987), p. 50.

6 Hart, *Mick*, pp. 12–14; 1901 census returns for Woodfield, Coolcraheen, County Cork; An Foras Talúntais, *West Cork Resource Survey* (Dublin, 1963), p. C-20.

7 'An account of Collins' life in London', Johanna Collins to Béaslaí, 25 September 1923, Dublin, National Library of Ireland (NLI), Béaslaí papers, Ms 33,929 (19).

8 https://tfl.gov.uk/corporate/about-tfl/culture-and-heritage/londons-transport-a-history/london-underground/a-brief-history-of-the-underground (viewed on 1 May 2016).

9 Leif Jerram, *Streetlife: The Untold History of Europe's Twentieth Century* (Oxford, 2011), pp. 182–3.

10 Matthew P. Llewellyn, 'A British Olympics', *International Journal of the History of Sport*, 28:5 (2011), pp. 669–87.

11 Luke McKernan, 'Diverting time: London's cinemas and their audiences, 1906–1914', *The London Journal*, 32:2 (2007), pp. 125–44.

12 John Physick, *Victoria and Albert Museum: The History of its Building* (London, 1982).

13 Deborah S. Ryan, 'Staging the imperial city: the Pageant of London, 1911' in Felix Driver and David Gilbert (eds), *Imperial Cities: Landscape, Display and Identity* (Manchester, 1999), pp. 117–35.

14 Hart, *Mick*, pp. 26–8.

15 P.S. O'Hegarty, *The Victory of Sinn Féin* (Dublin, 1998; 1st ed. 1924), p. 15.

16 *Inis Fáil*, February 1909.

17 Coogan, *Michael Collins*, p. 15.

18 McGarry, *The Rising*, p. 33.

19 Foster, *Vivid Faces*, pp. 1–30, p. 24.

20 Hart, *Mick*, p. 6.

21 Coogan, *Michael Collins*, p. 7.

22 Hart, *Mick*, p. 10.

23 Coogan, *Michael Collins*, p. 11.

24 McGarry, *The Rising*, p. 34.

25 Quoted in Coogan, *Michael Collins*, p. 10.

26 David Fitzpatrick, 'Knowledge, belief and the Irish revolution: the impact of schooling' in James Kelly and Susan Hegarty (eds), *Schools and Schooling 1650–2000: New Perspectives on the History of Education* (Dublin, 2017), p. 130.

27 Béaslaí, *Michael Collins*, pp. 7–9.

28 Johanna Collins to Béaslaí, 25 September 1923, NLI, Piaras Béaslaí Papers, Ms 33,929 (19). For interesting commentary on late Victorian and early Edwardian boyhood, respectability and reading material see Kate Summerscale, *The Wicked Boy: The Mystery of a Victorian Murderer* (London, 2016), pp. 108–14, and Geoffrey Pearson, *Hooligan: A History of Respectable Fears* (London, 1983).

29 Íosold Ó Deirg (ed.), 'Oh! Lord the Unrest of Soul: The Jail Journal of Michael Collins' in *Studia Hibernica*, 28 (1994), p. 14; Tom Clyde, *Irish Literary Magazines: An Outline History and Descriptive Bibliography* (Dublin, 2003), pp. 161–2.

30 Collins to Stack, 6 September 1918, NLI, Stack papers, Ms 5,848.

31 Joe Good, *Enchanted by Dreams: The Journal of a Revolutionary* (Dingle, 1996), p. 6.

32 Talbot, *Michael Collins' Own Story*, p. 25.

33 'Examination composition by Michael Collins', 1906, London, The National Archives (TNA), CSC 11/63.

34 John Hutchinson, *The Dynamics of Cultural Nationalism: The Gaelic Revival and the Creation of the Irish Nation State* (London, 1987), pp. 259–65.

35 *Westminster Gazette*, 30 August 1922.

36 Hutchinson, *The Dynamics of Cultural Nationalism*, pp. 266–76.

37 Ernest Gellner, *Nations and Nationalism* (Ithaca, 1983), pp. 51–62.

38 *Dáil Éireann Official Report: Debate on the Treaty*, 10 January 1922, pp. 393–4.

39 Hart, *Mick*, pp. 75–6.

40 Talbot, *Michael Collins' Own Story*, p. 25.

41 Giulia Ní Dhulchaointigh, 'The Irish population of London, 1900–14' (PhD thesis, Trinity College Dublin, 2013), pp. 8, 17, 184–6.

42 Hart, *Mick*, pp. 55–7.

43 *Inis Fáil*, April 1908; Minutes of Geraldines Gaelic Athletic Club, 6 March 1908, Dublin, GAA Archive, GAA/GER/01.

44 *Inis Fáil*, June 1908.

45 Minutes of Geraldines Gaelic Athletic Club, 12 January 1910, GAA Archive, GAA/GER/01 (Also available at www.gaa.ie/centenary/administrative-docs/minute-book-the-geraldines-gaelic-athletic-club-1909-1915/).

46 Hart, *Mick*, p. 48.

47 Minutes of Geraldines Gaelic Athletic Club, 8 January & July 1910, GAA Archive, GAA/GER/01.

48 Marcus de Burca, *The GAA: A History* (Dublin, 1991; 1st ed. 1980), pp. 70–1.

49 Report of the GAA Annual Convention, 1911, GAA Central Council Minute Book, 1911–1925, GAA Archive, GAA/CC/01.

50 Minutes of half yearly meeting of Geraldines Gaelic Athletic Club, 5 January 1909, GAA Archive, GAA/GER/01.

51 León Ó Broin, *Michael Collins* (Dublin, 1980), p. 5; Hart, *Mick*, p. 65.

52 Brian A. Cusack, Bureau of Military History (BMH), Witness Statement (WS) 736.

53 *Lincolnshire Echo*, 26 January 1909; *Aberdeen Daily Journal*, 3 July & 18 August 1909.

54 Martin Pugh, *The Pankhursts* (London, 2001), pp. 234–98.

55 Essay completed for homework at King's College, http://digital.ucd.ie/view/ivrla:10999 (viewed on 12 May 2016).

56 Joseph Conrad, *The Secret Agent* (Oxford, 2004); Joseph Conrad, *Under Western Eyes* (Oxford, 2003).

57   M.J. Kelly, *The Fenian Ideal and Irish Nationalism, 1882–1916* (Woodbridge, 2006), pp. 182–4.

58   Béaslaí, *Michael Collins*, pp. 18–19; Notes on interview with Sam Maguire, NLI, Béaslaí papers, Ms 33,929 (14).

59   Hart, *Mick*, p. 65.

60   Hart, *Mick*, pp. 65–73; Jeremiah O'Leary, BMH, WS 1108; Joe Good, BMH, WS 388.

61   Catriona Pennell, *A United Kingdom: Popular Responses to the Outbreak of the First World War in Britain and Ireland* (Oxford, 2012), p. 30 & pp. 47–60.

62   *Ibid.*, pp. 204–9; Adam Hochschild, *To End All Wars: How the First World War Divided Britain* (London, 2011), p. 153; Michael McDonagh, *In London During the War* (London, 1935), p. 93.

63   Fergus FitzGerald (ed.), *The Memoirs of Desmond FitzGerald, 1913–1916* (London, 1968), p. 80.

64   Notes on interview with Sam Maguire, NLI, Béaslaí papers, Ms 33,929 (14).

65   *Irish Volunteer*, 16 October 1915, cited in Hart, *Mick*, p. 68.

2: The Collins Method

1   Allan to Collins, 14 February 1917, NLI, INAA papers, Ms 23,464.

2   For an insightful account of the INA & VDF's workings see Caoimhe Nic Dháibhéid, 'The Irish National Aid Association and the radicalization of public opinion in Ireland, 1916–1918', *The Historical Journal*, 55:3 (2012), pp. 705–29. See also William Murphy, *Political Imprisonment and the Irish, 1912–1921* (Oxford, 2014), pp. 73–4.

3   Minutes of the Dublin, INA & VDF, 1 July 1918, NLI, INA & VDF papers, Ms 23,469.

4   Peter Hart, 'What did the Easter Rising really change?' in Thomas E. Hachey (ed.), *Turning Points in Twentieth-Century Irish History* (Dublin, 2011), p. 19.

5   *New Ireland*, 24 June 1916.

6   Minutes of the Executive Committee of the INA & VDF, 29 August 1916, NLI, INA & VDF papers, Ms 23,469.

7   *Official Report of the Ill-treatment of the Irish Prisoners of War Interned at Frongoch Camp* (Cork, 1916).

8   Minutes of the Games Committee, Frongoch, NLI, O'Mahony papers, Ms 44,038/1; Seán O'Mahony, *Frongoch: University of Revolution* (Killiney, 1987), p. 66.

9   David Fitzpatrick, *Harry Boland's Irish Revolution* (Cork, 2003), p. 92.

10   Murphy, *Political Imprisonment*, pp. 60–5.

11   James McDermott, *British Military Service Tribunals, 1916–18: 'A Very Much Abused Body of Men'* (Manchester, 2011), p. 14.

12   Ann Matthews, *The Kimmage Garrison, 1916: Making Billy-can Bombs at Larkfield* (Dublin, 2010).

13   Patrick Belton would also be on the INA & VDF committee when it appointed Collins.

14   Honor Ó Brolcháin, *Joseph Plunkett* (Dublin, 2012), pp. 336–7.

15   Lawrence William White, 'Joseph Mary Plunkett' in Lawrence William White and James Quinn (eds), *1916: Portraits and Lives* (Dublin, 2015), pp. 261–70.

16   O'Mahony, *Frongoch*, pp. 124–5.

17   Collins to O'Brien, 13 October, 19 & 21 November 1916, NLI, O'Mahony papers, Ms 44038/4.

18   Eamon T. Dore, BMH, WS 392.

19   Heygate Lambert to Edward Troup, Home Office, 9 December 1916, TNA, HO 144/1456/ 313106(278–661).

20   Michael Staines, BMH, WS 944.

21   Collins to Staines, 22 March, 2 & 9 May 1917, NLI, INA & VDF papers, Ms 23,464 & Ms 23,465.

22   Collins to Nicholas Stack, 16 June 1917, NLI, INA & VDF papers, Ms 23,465.

23   Collins to Mulcahy, 16 & 20 March, 17 May 1917, NLI, INA & VDF papers, Ms 23,464 & Ms 23,465.

24   Collins to O'Donovan, 10 April 1917, NLI, INA & VDF papers, Ms 23,465.

25   Collins to Traynor, 6 March 1917, Collins to Boland, 5 April 1917, Collins to Good, 27 April 1917, Collins to Béaslaí, 2 October 1917, NLI, INA & VDF papers, Ms 23,464, Ms 23,465 & Ms 23,466.

26   Eamon T. Dore, BMH, WS 392; Laurence Nugent, BMH, WS 907.

27   Béaslaí, *Michael Collins*, p. 161.

28   Marie Coleman, *The Irish Revolution 1916–1923* (London, 2014), p. 77. Joseph E. A. Connell Jnr, *Michael Collins: Dublin 1916–22* (Dublin, 2017), pp. 74–113.

29   Collins to Thomas Kelly, Enniscorthy, 7 December 1917, NLI, INA & VDF papers, Ms 23,466.

30   Hart, *Mick*, p. 127.

31   Michael Laffan, *The Resurrection of Ireland: The Sinn Féin Party 1916–1923* (Cambridge, 1999), pp. 90–1.

32   Collins to Alphonsus Kivlehan, 5 April 1917, Collins to Thomas Kelly, 5 April 1917, Collins to J.J. Clancy, 12 April 1917, NLI, INA & VDF papers, Ms 23,465.

33   Laffan, *The Resurrection of Ireland*, p. 94.

34   *Roscommon Herald*, 25 August 1917.

35   *Longford Leader*, 14 April 1917.

36   Collins to Liam McCarthy, 18 April 1917, NLI, INA & VDF papers, Ms 23,465.

37   Michael Staines, BMH, WS 944.

38   *Longford Leader*, 28 April 1917.

39   Laffan, *The Resurrection of Ireland*, p. 100.

40   Murphy, *Political Imprisonment*, p. 78; Collins to Bishop Denis Kelly, 18 July 1917, NLI, INA & VDF papers, Ms 23,465.

41   Collins to de Lacy, 30 August 1917, NLI, INA & VDF papers, Ms 23,466; Shaun Boylan, 'Stephen O'Mara' in James McGuire and James Quinn (eds), *Dictionary of Irish Biography: From the Earliest Times to the Year 2012* (9 vols, Cambridge, 2009), VII, pp. 689–90.

42   Collins to Kivelehan and Collins to Daly, 30 August 1917, NLI, INA & VDF papers, Ms 23,466.

43   John O'Callaghan, *Revolutionary Limerick: The Republican Campaign for Independence in Limerick, 1913–1921* (Dublin, 2010), pp. 63–5.

44   Hart, *Mick*, p. 179; he was replaced by Peadar Dunne: see Military Service Pension Application, Peadar Dunne, http://mspcsearch.militaryarchives.ie/docs/files//PDF_Pensions/R1/MSP34REF2414 PeadarDunne /WMSP34REF2414PeadarDunne.pdf (viewed on 15 Feb, 2017).

45   Collins to Cosgrave, Dublin, RIA, Cosgrave Papers, P285/302/1.

46   Collins to Mackey, 19 October 1917, NLI, INA & VDF papers, Ms 23,466.

47   León Ó Broin, *Revolutionary Underground: The Story of the Irish Republican Brotherhood 1858–1924* (Dublin, 1976), pp. 176–8.

48   Pauric Travers, '"Our Fenian dead": Glasnevin cemetery and the genesis of the republican funeral' in James Kelly and Uáitéar Mac Gearailt (eds), *Dublin and Dubliners: Essays in the History and Literature of Dublin City* (Dublin, 1990), pp. 52–72.

49   Collins to Daly, 31 July 1917, NLI, INA & VDF papers, Ms 23,465.

50   Murphy, *Political Imprisonment*, p. 89.

51   Seán Ó Lúing, *I Die in a Good Cause* (Tralee, 1970), p. 189.

52 Minutes of Sinn Féin Standing Committee, 6 March 1919, Dublin, NLI, p. 3269.

53 Minutes of INA & VDF, 27 November 1917, NLI, INA & VDF papers, Ms 23,468.

54 'A Further Appeal', NLI, ILB 300,12 [Item 77].

55 *Irish Independent*, 10 December 1917.

56 Collins to Corr, 6 December 1917, NLI, INA & VDF papers, Ms 23,466.

57 Statement attached to Application Form under the Military Service Pensions Act, 1934, 27 June 1945, p. 6, MA, MSP, http://mspcsearch.militaryarchives.ie/docs/files//PDF_Pensions/R5/MSP34REF 60559%20Kitty%20O'%20Doherty/MSP34REF60559%20Kitty%20O'%20Doherty.pdf [viewed on 12 January 2018].

58 Minutes of INA & VDF Committee, 1 July 1918, NLI, INA & VDF papers, Ms 23,468.

59 Minutes of Sinn Féin Standing Committee, 28 November and 19 December 1918, NLI, p. 3269; See a significant file of correspondence on prisoners between Collins and O'Brien, Dublin, NAI, DE/2/453.

60 Hart, *Mick*, p.172.

61 *Freeman's Journal*, 19 June 1917.

62 Frank Thornton, BMH, WS 510.

63 Collins to McCabe, 20 June 1917, NLI, INA & VDF papers, Ms23,465.

3: Collins at War

1 Rev. Patrick J. Doyle, BMH, WS 807.

2 *Ibid.*

3 Clare Sheridan, *In Many Places* (London, 1923), p. 28.

4 *Dáil Éireann Official Report: debate on the Treaty between Great Britain and Ireland*, Arthur Griffith, 19 Dec. 1921, p. 20; Frank Pakenham, *Peace by Ordeal: The Negotiation of the Anglo-Irish Treaty 1921* (London, 1992; 1st ed. 1935), pp. 81–2.

5 Robinson had been involved in the ambush at Soloheadbeg, Co. Tipperary, on 21 January 1919.

6 *Dáil Éireann Official Report: Debate on the Treaty*, Cathal Brugha, 7 January 1922, pp. 325–8 & Séamus Robinson, 6 January 1922, p. 290.

7 *Ibid.*, pp. 290–1.

8 Hart, *Mick*, p. 425.

9 John Regan, 'Looking at Mick again: demilitarising Michael Collins', *History Ireland*, 3:3 (Autumn 1995); John Regan, 'Michael Collins: the legacy and the intestacy' in Gabriel Doherty and Dermot Keogh (eds), *Michael Collins and the Making of the Irish State* (Cork, 1998).

10 See, for example, Andrew McCarthy, 'Michael Collins – Minister for Finance 1919–22', in Doherty and Keogh (eds), *Michael Collins*. The various chapters in Peter Hart's biography include 'Athlete', 'Manager', 'Player', 'Director', 'Minister', 'CEO', Hart, *Mick*.

11 Michael Hopkinson, 'Michael Collins' in McGuire and Quinn (eds), *Dictionary of Irish Biography*, II, pp. 678–82.

12 Eunan O'Halpin, 'Collins and intelligence 1919–1923: from brotherhood to bureaucracy' in Doherty and Keogh (eds), *Michael Collins*, p. 69.

13 *The Word*, December 1968, Dublin, Trinity College Dublin Manuscripts Department (TCD), J.R.W. Goulden papers, Ms 7,379.

14 Ernie O'Malley, *On Another Man's Wound* (Dublin, 1994; 1st 1936), p. 82.

15   Frances Flanagan, *Remembering the Revolution: Dissent, Culture and Nationalism in the Irish Free State* (Oxford, 2015), p. 21.

16   Béaslaí, *Michael Collins*; *Michael Collins* (1996), directed by Neil Jordan.

17   Flanagan writes that Ó'Faoláin was earning £4 a week for his column on Collins from the *Sunday Chronicle*. Flanagan, *Remembering the Revolution*, pp. 21–2 & p. 42.

18   John Horne, 'Ireland and the wars after the war, 1917–23' in John Horne and Edward Madigan (eds), *Towards Commemoration: Ireland in War and Revolution, 1912–1923* (Dublin, 2013), p. 59.

19   Copies and clippings of articles, c. July 1961, Dublin, University College Dublin Archives (UCDA), Mulcahy papers, P7/D/101.

20   'Time to remember … 1922', British Pathé, film id 617.01; *The Word*, December 1968, TCD, J.R.W. Goulden papers, Ms 7,379; Oliver St John Gogarty, *As I Was Going Down Sackville Street* (London, 1954; 1st ed. 1937), p. 187 & p. 195.

21   Hart, *Mick*, p. 421; The Earl of Birkenhead, *Frederick Edwin Earl of Birkenhead: The Last Phase* (London, 1935), p. 151.

22   J.J. Lee, 'The challenge of a Collins biography' in Doherty and Keogh (eds), *Michael Collins*, p. 22.

23   Risteárd Mulcahy, *Richard Mulcahy (1886–1971): A Family Memoir* (Dublin, 1996); Report by Major W.E. de B. Whitaker, King's Regiment and special correspondent of the *Daily Express*, circulated to Cabinet Situation Committee on Ireland, 19 September 1922, TNA, CO 739/16.

24   This was further sensationalised after his death in *The World's Pictorial News*, 9, 16 & 23 September 1922, NLI, Béaslaí papers, Ms 33,915(3).

25   O'Halpin, 'Collins and intelligence 1919–1923', p. 80.

26   See, for example, typescript of manuscript by Seán Ó Murthuile, n.d., UCDA, Mulcahy papers, P7a/209; Hart, *Mick*, pp. 224–43.

27   Byrnes and Molloy were both killed in March 1920, while Quinlisk was shot a month before by the IRA in Cork. See Hart, *Mick*, pp. 224–39 & p. 238.

28   Hart, *Mick*, pp. 238–9.

29   A fifteenth died within weeks of these fourteen. See Jane Leonard, '"English dogs" or "poor devils"? The dead of Bloody Sunday morning', in David Fitzpatrick (ed.), *Terror in Ireland 1916–1923* (Dublin, 2012), p. 102.

30   'Account of IRA intelligence by Captain Frank Thornton to army units', c. 1940, Military Archives of Ireland (MAI), A/0800/IV.

31   Some of the fourteen died later from their wounds. Conor Clune, who was killed with McKee and Clancy, was visiting Dublin on business from Clare. He was taken in a raid on Vaughan's Hotel on the night before Bloody Sunday, where he was visiting a fellow language enthusiast, Sean O'Connell. Clune knew nothing of the plans of the Dublin Brigade. See Michael Foy, *Michael Collins's Intelligence War* (Stroud, 2006), p. 152, pp. 165–8.

32   Hart, *Mick*, p. 242.

33   Robert Kee, *Ireland: A History* (London, 1995; 1st ed. 1980), p. 187.

34   Copy of letter from Kate MacCormack to Mulcahy, 23 March 1922, NLI, Collins papers, A/0535X. [The name was transcribed by Mulcahy as MacCormack.]

35   Collins to Mulcahy, 7 April 1922, NLI, Collins papers, A/535X.

36   Typescript of manuscript by Seán Ó Murthuile, n.d., UCDA, Mulcahy papers, P7/a/209.

37   List of persons suspected of complicity in the murder of police, military and civilians, October 1919, TNA, CO 904/229.

38   Frank Thornton, Ernie O'Malley notebooks, UCDA, O'Malley papers, P17b/100(117).

39 G.W. Albin, 'Bill Albin's England', London, Imperial War Museum (IWM), Albin papers, PP/MCR/192; Private J.P. Swindlehurst diary, 9 January 1921, IWM, Swindlehurst papers, P538.

40 Clipping from *The Morning Post*, 16 September 1922, IWM, Jarvis papers, 98/11/1.

41 Joice M. Nankivell and Sydney Loch, *Ireland in Travail* (London, 1922), pp. 288–9.

42 C.H. Bretherton, *The Real Ireland* (London, 1925), p. 23.

43 Sir William Y. Darling, *So It Looks to Me* (London, 1952), p. 211.

44 Collins to Art O'Brien, 21 May 1921, NAI, DE/2/330; Joe Vize to Collins, 11 March 1921, NLI, Ms 33,916 (2). Vize was interned in the Curragh at the time of writing.

45 Epitome of seized material no. 2567, n.d., London, Liddell Hart Centre for Military Archives (LHC), Foulkes papers, 7/24.

46 *Ibid.*

47 Collins to de Valera, 1 June 1921, NAI, DE/2/244.

48 Collins to de Valera, 20 July 1921, *ibid.*

49 Peter Young, 'Michael Collins: a military leader' in Doherty and Keogh (eds), *Michael Collins*, pp. 89–90.

50 See, for example, 'General Michael Collins 1922', British Pathé, film id 276.28.

51 Gogarty, *As I Was Going Down Sackville Street*, p. 185.

52 Memo by Governor Greenway, Wormwood Scrubs, 20 October 1921, London, Parliamentary Archive (PA), Lloyd George papers, LG/F/45/6/39.

53 Trevor Wilson (ed.), *The Political Diaries of C.P. Scott 1911–1928* (London, 1970), pp. 405–6.

54 Smyllie to FitzGerald, 24 March 1922, UCDA, FitzGerald papers, P80/42(26).

55 FitzGerald to Smyllie, 30 March 1922, UCDA, FitzGerald papers, P80/42(27).

56 Celia Shaw diary, 11 February 1922, NLI, Ms 23,409.

57 *Ibid.*, December 1921.

58 Bretherton, *The Real Ireland*, p. 23.

59 Lee, 'The challenge of a Collins biography', p. 22; Statement by Michael Noyk, n.d., NLI, Noyk papers, Ms 18,975; Typescript of manuscript by Seán Ó Murthuile, n.d., UCDA, Mulcahy papers, P7/a/209.

60 Notes of interview with Sam Maguire, n.d., NLI, Béaslaí papers, Ms 33,929 (14); comment by Sean McGrath quoted in Hart, *Mick*, p. 69.

61 Notes of interview with Pat Brennan, n.d., NLI, Béaslaí papers, Ms 33,929 (14).

62 W.J. Brennan-Whitmore, *Dublin Burning: The Easter Rising from Behind the Barricades* (Dublin, 1996), pp. 32–3.

63 Hart, *Mick*, p. 93.

64 *Ibid.*, pp. 93–4.

65 Good, *Enchanted by Dreams*, p. 46.

66 Hart, *Mick*, p. 94.

67 *Ibid.*, p. 95.

68 Collins to Kevin O'Brien, 6 October 1916, quoted in Coogan, *Michael Collins*, p. 54; Michael Hayes, 'Michael Collins', *Capuchin Annual* (1972), p. 285.

69 Geraldine Club reports, 1909, NLI, Ms 13,329 (4).

70 *Ibid.*

71 Anna Geifman, *Thou Shalt Kill: Revolutionary Terrorism in Russia, 1894–1917* (Princeton, 1993), pp. 31–2; *Marin County Tocsin*, 11 February 1905.

72 Darling, *So It Looks To Me*, p. 212.

73 F. P. Crozier, *Ireland For Ever* (Bath, 1971; 1st ed. 1932), p. 217. Crozier had resigned as Commanding Officer of the Auxiliary Division of the RIC in February 1921 over issues of indiscipline in the force.

74 *Ibid.*

75 C.S. Andrews, *Dublin Made Me* (Dublin, 1979), p. 155.

76 Rex Taylor, *Michael Collins* (London, 1964; 1st ed. 1958), p. 106.

77 William Shakespeare, *Julius Caesar* (Paris, 1850), II:1, p. 74.

78 Crozier, *Ireland For Ever*, p. 219.

79 A sixth man who had been captured with a weapon and ammunition was also executed with the five men taken at Godfrey's Cross, County Cork.

80 Crozier, *Ireland For Ever*, p. 220.

81 *Irish Times*, 7 July 1921.

82 *Irish Times*, 17 October 1978; Peter Hart, *The IRA and its Enemies: Violence and Community in Cork, 1916–1923* (Oxford, 1998), p. 308.

83 Hart, *The IRA and its Enemies*, p. 308; Crozier, *Ireland For Ever*, p. 220.

84 Curtis to Churchill, 19 August 1924, Oxford, Bodleian Library (Bod.), Curtis papers, Ms 89.fp. 76–83.

85 Statement by Major General Paddy O'Daly, n.d., UCDA, Mulcahy papers, P7/D/8.

86 Talk with Lieut. Gen. Joseph Sweeney, 28 January 1964, UCDA, Mulcahy papers, P7/D/43.

87 Lecture by Joe Leonard, 9 March 1948, UCDA, Mulcahy papers, P7/D/101; Statement by Major General Paddy O'Daly, n.d., UCDA, Mulcahy papers, P7/D/8.

88 *Ibid.*

89 Crozier, *Ireland For Ever*, p. 221.

90 *Dáil Éireann Official Report: Debate on the Treaty*, Richard Mulcahy, 22 December 1921, p. 143.

91 See, for example, William Stapleton, BMH, WS 822; James Slattery, BMH, WS 445.

92 *Michael Collins* (1996), directed by Neil Jordan. In the screenplay it was 'Ned Tannin's hand, Neil Jordan, *Michael Collins Film Diary and Sreenplay* (London, 1996), p. 104.

93 Vincent Byrne, BMH, WS 423.

94 'Skinner' O'Reilly, Ernie O'Malley notebooks, UCDA, O'Malley papers, P17b/95(117–119).

95 Dr P. Daly, Ernie O'Malley notebooks, UCDA, O'Malley papers, P17b/136.

96 Collins to Nunan, 30 September 1920, NAI, DE/2/292.

97 Coogan, *Michael Collins*, p. 168.

98 J.P. Duggan, 'Poltergeist pistol', *History Ireland*, 3:3 (Autumn 1995); *Evening Herald*, 20 November 1924.

99 Churchill to Collins, 12 April 1922, Cambridge, Churchill Archives (CA), Churchill papers, CHAR 8/241.

100 Sean Hegarty was OC of the Cork No. 1 Brigade. Memoir of Connie Neenan, n.d., Cork, Cork Archives Institute (CAI), Neenan papers, PR7/7. There are echoes here of Collins's response to Séamus Robinson when Collins suggested that the Soloheadbeg ambush participants should leave for America. When Robinson refused on the basis that to leave would suggest their actions amounted to murder, that they wanted to 'fight it out' instead, Collins, according to Robinson, 'strode off with the faintest of smiles on his lips but with a big laugh in his eyes: "that's all right with me"'. Statement by Séamus Robinson, BMH, WS 1721, copy at NLI, Ms 21,265; Hart, *Mick*, pp. 217–18.

101 Memoir of Connie Neenan, n.d., CAI, Neenan papers, PR7/7.

102 Eunan O'Halpin, 'Problematic killing during the War of Independence and its aftermath: civilian spies and informers' in James Kelly and Mary Ann Lyons (eds), *Death and Dying in Ireland, Britain and Europe: Historical Perspectives* (Sallins, 2013), pp. 328–9. Thanks to Professor Eunan O'Halpin for the updated figure of 2,159 for 1920–21.

103 Foy, *Michael Collins's Intelligence War*, p. 82.

104 Michael Collins, *The Path to Freedom* (Cork, 1995; 1st ed. 1922), pp. 85–6.

105 *Ibid.*, p. 86.

106 Collins to Gavan Duffy, 18 May 1920, UCDA, Gavan Duffy papers, P152/151.

107 Collins to Nunan, 30 September 1920, NAI, DE/2/292.

108 Collins to Nunan, 15 October 1920, *Ibid.*

109 Memo to Director of Publicity, 5 October 1921, NLI, McKenna Napoli papers, Ms 22,613.

110 Collins to FitzGerald, 20 March 1922, UCDA, MacEoin papers, P151/96; Collins to FitzGerald, 12 July 1922, NAI, Department of an Taoiseach (DT) S595.

111 Celia Shaw diary, November 1920, NLI, Ms 23,409.

112 *Ibid.*

113 Liam de Róiste diary, 18 October 1917, NLI, O'Donoghue papers, Ms 31,146(1).

114 Curtis to Marsh, 8 December 1922, CA, Marsh papers, vol. 3; Maurice Hankey diary, 28 November 1920, CA, Hankey papers, HNKY1/5.

115 Lord Riddell, *Lord Riddell's Intimate Diary of the Peace Conference and After 1918–1923* (London, 1933), p. 202.

116 *Ibid.*, p. 202 & p. 238.

117 John Ramsden (ed.), *Real Old Tory Politics: The Political Diaries of Sir Robert Sanders, Lord Bayford, 1910–35* (London, 1984), p. 156; Anne Dolan, 'The British culture of paramilitary violence in the Irish War of Independence' in Robert Gerwarth and John Horne (eds), *War in Peace: Paramilitary Violence after the Great War* (Oxford, 2012), pp. 202–8.

118 Shaw Desmond, 'Sinn Fein secrets', *The London Magazine*, xlv:120 (October 1920), p. 126.

119 Hart, *Mick*, p. 196; O'Halpin, 'Problematic killing during the War of Independence and its aftermath: civilian spies and informers', p. 322.

120 Hart, *Mick*, p. 222.

121 Answers to a series of questions, possibly for a radio broadcast, n.d. [1960s], UCDA, MacEoin papers, P151/1791(2); Foy, *Michael Collins's Intelligence War*, p. 208.

122 Hart, *Mick*, p. 222.

123 *Ibid.*, p. 222 & p. 223.

124 Michael Collins, *Arguments for the Treaty* (Dublin, 1922), p. 18.

125 *Dáil Éireann Official Report: Debate on the Treaty*, Michael Collins, 19 December 1921, p. 32 & p. 34.

126 Sheridan, *In Many Places*, p. 32.

127 Wigram to Hoare, 13 June 1921, Cambridge, Cambridge University Library (UL), Templewood papers, i, 12, 34.

128 *Dáil Éireann Official Report: Debate on the Treaty*, Michael Collins, 19 December 1921, p. 32.

129 Tom Barry, *Guerilla Days in Ireland* (Cork, 1997; 1st ed. 1949), pp. 182–5.

130 O'Malley to Gallagher, 31 December 1948, NLI, Gallagher papers, Ms 18,353.

131 Clementine Churchill, Cannes, to W.S. Churchill, 10 February 1922, CA, Churchill papers, CHAR 1/158/18–19.

132 Churchill to Collins, 29 April 1922, CA, Churchill papers, CHAR 8/241. These thirteen deaths may have been linked to the death of IRA officer Michael O'Neill on 26 April.

133 Lionel Curtis to Churchill, 19 August 1924, Bod., Curtis papers, Ms 89.fp. 76–83.

134 Notes by Seán MacEoin on the Civil War, n.d. [1960s], UCDA, MacEoin papers, P151/1812(3).

135 'Position of the Irish Provisional Government', 21 September 1922, UL, Templewood papers, i, 13, 26.

136 Curtis to Churchill, 19 August 1924, Bod., Curtis papers, Ms 89.f.76–83.

137 P.S. O'Hegarty, BMH, WS 897.
138 Hart, *Mick*, p. 397.
139 L.S. Amery, Parliamentary and Financial Secretary to the Admiralty, Diary entry, 23 June 1922, CA, Amery papers, AMEL 7/16.
140 *Ibid.*
141 Young, 'Michael Collins: a military leader', p. 86.
142 According to John A. Pinkman, Collins was planning to send a delegation of National Army officers to Switzerland 'for the purpose of studying that country's military system with a view to re-organizing the Irish army'. John A. Pinkman, *In the Legion of the Vanguard* (edited by Francis E. Maguire) (Cork, 1998), p. 176.
143 Hart, *Mick*, p. 407, p. 403, p. 405.
144 *Ibid.*, p. 402 & p. 403.
145 Memo by Michael Collins, 2 July 1922, UCDA, Mulcahy papers, P7/B/28; Hart, *Mick*, pp. 403–4.
146 Hart, *Mick*, p. 404.
147 Discussion between Risteard Mulcahy and his parents, 23 December 1961, UCDA, Mulcahy papers, P7/D/100; Eunan O'Halpin, *Defending Ireland: The Irish State and its Enemies Since 1922* (Oxford, 1999), p. 3.
148 O'Connor, *The Big Fellow*, p. 214.
149 Barry, *Guerilla Days in Ireland*, pp. 182–5.
150 Florence O'Donoghue, Ernie O'Malley notebooks, UCDA, O'Malley papers, P17b/96(2).

4: Collins and the Practice of Politics

1   Michael Collins to Austin Stack, 28 November 1918, NLI, Ms 5,848.
2   Batt O'Connor, *With Michael Collins: in the Fight for Irish freedom* (London, 1929), p. 110.
3   Ó Broin, *Revolutionary Underground*, p. 178; Taylor, *Collins*, p. 88.
4   Laffan, *Resurrection of Ireland*, p. 120.
5   Robert Brennan, *Allegiance* (Dublin, 1950), pp. 154–5.
6   Fitzpatrick, *Harry Boland's Irish Revolution*, p. 103.
7   *Irish Independent*, 27 October 1917.
8   Memo, Crime Special, RIC, 24 December 1917, London, TNA CO 904/196/65.
9   Vincent White, BMH, WS1764. White was Sinn Féin's candidate at the Waterford by-election in March.
10 *Irish Independent*, 12 January and 23 February 1918.
11 Memos by County Inspector, Longford, 20 February and 5 March 1918, London, TNA, CO 904/196/65.
12 Hart, *Mick*, pp. 159–68
13 Ó Deirg, '*Oh! Lord the Unrest of Soul*', pp. 7–34.
14 *Ibid.*, pp. 19–21.
15 *Irish Independent*, 10 November 1945; Brendan Rooney, *Creating History: Stories of Ireland in Art* (Dublin, 2016), p. 121.
16 Talbot, *Michael Collins' Own Story*, p. 13.
17 Beaslaí, *Michael Collins*, p. 196.
18 Fitzpatrick, *Harry Boland's Irish Revolution*, pp. 104, 359.

19   Darrell Figgis, *Recollections of the Irish Irish War* (New York, 1927), pp. 219–20.

20   Laffan, *Resurrection of Ireland*, p. 153.

21   Minutes of Sinn Féin Standing Committee, 14 November – 9 December, NLI, p. 3269.

22   O'Connor, *The Big Fellow*, p. 241.

23   Collins to Stack, 19 August 1918, NLI, Stack Papers, Ms 5,848.

24   Minutes of Sinn Féin Standing Committee, 6 February 1919, NLI, p. 3269.

25   De Valera to Art O'Brien, 25 March 1919, NLI, Art Ó Briain Papers, Ms 8,426/41.

26   Collins to Stack, 26 March 1919, NLI, Ms 17,090.

27   Memo, Michael Collins's Ministerial Career, NAI, DE/2/371.

28   Minutes of Sinn Féin Standing Committee, 13 and 20 February 1919, NLI p. 3269.

29   Daithí O'Donoghue, BMH, WS 548 and Sean McCluskey, BMH, WS 511.

30   Collins to the Director of Organisation, Sinn Féin Standing Committee, 25 August 1919, NAI, DE Papers, DE/2/530.

31   Francis M. Carroll, *Money for Ireland: Finance, Diplomacy, Politics and the First Dáil Éireann Loans, 1919–1936* (Westport, 2002), p. 8.

32   https://www.youtube.com/watch?v=5CfrkvE7_hs (viewed on 21 February 2016).

33   Carroll, *Money for Ireland*, p. 6.

34   Daithi O'Donoghue, BMH, WS 548; Patrick Hegarty, BMH, WS 1606; Kevin O'Sheil, BMH, WS 1770, Section V.

35   Mitchell, *Revolutionary Government in Ireland*, p. 56.

36   Andrew McCarthy, 'Michael Collins – Minister for Finance 1919–1922', p. 57.

37   Collins to MacSwiney, 29 January 1920, NAI, DE/2/530; Patrick J. Ramsbottom, BMH, WS 1046; John M. McCarthy, BMH, WS 883; Hart, *Mick*, pp. 192–3.

38   Pádraig Yeates, *A City in Turmoil: Dublin 1919–21* (Dublin, 2012), pp. 103–8. Bell was also tasked with investigating the attempted assassination of Lord French, Lord Lieutenant, on 19 December 1919.

39   Mitchell, *Revolutionary Government in Ireland*, p. 65; Laffan, *Resurrection of Ireland*, p. 319.

40   Ronan Fanning, *The Irish Department of Finance, 1922–58* (Dublin, 1978), p. 22.

41   Martin Maguire, *The Civil Service and the Revolution in Ireland, 1912–38: 'Shaking the Blood-stained Hand of Mr Collins'* (Manchester, 2008), pp. 96–8; Mitchell, *Revolutionary Government in Ireland*, p. 156.

42   Memo, Michael Collins's Ministerial Career, Dublin, NAI, DE/2/371.

43   O'Connor, *The Big Fellow*, p. 256.

44   Hart, *Mick*, pp. 256–61.

45   Michael Laffan, *Judging W.T. Cosgrave: The Foundation of the Irish State* (Dublin, 2014), p. 74.

46   Collins to O'Brien, 29 September 1920, NAI, DE/2/324.

47   John M. Regan, *The Irish Counter-Revolution 1921–1936* (Dublin, 1999), p. 9.

48   Collins to O'Brien, 18 June 1920, NLI, Ms 8,426/2.

49   Mitchell, *Revolutionary Government in Ireland*, p. 105.

50   See two runs of Collins/O'Brien correspondence in the Dáil Éireann Papers, NAI, DE/2/321–332 and DE/2/451–453.

51   Collins to MacSwiney, 29 January 1920, NAI, DE/2/530.

52   Michael Kennedy, 'Robert Brennan' in James McGuire and James Quinn (eds), *Dictionary of Irish Biography, 1* (Cambridge, 2009), pp. 814–5 or (dib.cambridge.org/viewReadPage.do?articleId=a0934).

53   Brennan to O'Brien, 22 March 1921, NAI, DE/2/328.

54   Collins to Griffith, 26 January 1921, NAI, DE/2/242.

55   Collins to de Valera, 16 and 20 July 1921, NAI, DE/2/244.

56   O'Connor, *The Big Fellow*, p. 219.

57   Forester, *Michael Collins*, p. 218.

58   Hart, *Mick*, pp. 287–8.

59   Regan, *The Irish Counter-Revolution*, p. 30.

60   Frank Pakenham, *Peace by Ordeal* (London, 1935), pp. 130–6; Joseph M. Curran, *The Birth of the Irish Free State 1921–1923* (Alabama, 1980), pp. 81–2.

61   Hart, *Mick*, pp. 291–2.

62   Chiders' Diary, 21 November 1921, Dublin, TCD, Childers' Papers, Ms 7,814.

63   Pakenham, *Peace by Ordeal*, pp. 130–1.

64   Draft of Treaty, 30 November, with Collins's notes, NAI, DE/2/304/1. See online at www.difp.ie/docs/1921/Anglo-Irish-Treaty/208.htm.

65   Michael Hopkinson (ed.), *The Last Days of Dublin Castle: The Diaries of Mark Sturgis* (Dublin, 1999), p. 222.

66   The clearest exposition of these confused conclusions is to be found in Curran, *The Birth of the Irish Free State*, p. 119.

67   Hart, *Mick*, p. 313.

68   Memorandum by Collins on meeting with Lloyd George, 5 December 1921, NAI, DE2/304/1. See online at www.difp.ie/docs/1921/Anglo-Irish-Treaty/212.htm.

69   Curran, *The Birth of the Irish Free State*, p. 121.

70   *Ibid.*, p. 123.

71   O'Connor, *The Big Fellow*, p. 256; Hart, *Mick*, p. 337; Coogan, *Collins*, p. 301.

72   Beaverbrook to Cosgrave, 1 July 1963, RIA, Cosgrave Papers, P285/94/4.

73   Hart, *Mick*, p. 339.

74   Fitzpatrick, *Harry Boland's Irish Revolution*, pp. 7–9 & 264–325.

75   Tim Downey to Michael Collins, 7 February 1922, and Collins to Downey, 18 February 1922, NAI, DE/2/453.

76   Collins to Liam McCarthy, 5 April 1922, NAI, DT S1,795.

77   Collins to O'Kelly, 28 April, 2 May, and 13 May 1922, and O'Kelly to Collins, 1 May and 4 May 1922, NAI, DE/2/514.

78   Bill Kissane, *The Politics of the Irish Civil War* (Oxford, 2005), pp. 67–8.

79   Michael Hopkinson, *Green Against Green: The Irish Civil War* (Dublin, 1988), pp. 62–6.

80   Kissane, *The Politics of the Irish Civil War*, p. 70.

81   Owen McGee, *Arthur Griffith* (Dublin, 2015), pp. 326–7; Ronan Fanning, *Fatal Path: British Government and the Irish Revolution 1910–1922* (London, 2013), p. 327.

82   Brian P. Murphy, 'Nationalism: The Framing of the Constitution of the Irish Free State, 1922 – the Defining Battle for the Irish Republic' in Joost Augusteijn (ed.), *The Irish Revolution 1913–1923* (Basingstoke, 2002), pp. 135–50; Jeffrey Prager, *Building Democracy in Ireland: Political Order and Cultural Integration in a Newly Independent Nation* (Cambridge, 1986), pp. 67–91.

83   Fanning, *Fatal Path*, p. 329.

84   Tom Garvin, *1922: The Birth of Democracy* (Dublin, 1996), p. 133.

85   Fitzpatrick, *Harry Boland's Irish Revolution*, p. 278.

86   Murphy, 'The Framing of the Constitution of the Irish Free State', pp. 141–2.

5: What Collins Believed

1   Johnny Fallon, 'What would the ghost of Michael Collins have to say about the troika and the bondholders? You might be surprised', *Irish Independent*, 22 August 2012.

2   www.francesfitzgerald.ie/2015/08/oration-by-frances-fitzgerald-td.html (viewed on 1 March 2016).

3   www.edwalsh.ie/beal-na-mblath-address/ (viewed on 1 March 2016).

4   Collins to de Valera, 15 October 1921, NAI, DE/2/244.

5   Collins to Kiernan, 30 November 1921 in León Ó Broin (eds), *In Great Haste: The Letters of Michael Collins and Kitty Kiernan* (Dublin, 1996), p. 77.

6   O'Connor, *With Michael Collins*, p. 190.

7   Michael Collins, *The Path to Freedom* (Cork, 2011).

8   *Arguments for the Treaty by Michael Collins* (Dublin, 1922).

9   *Irish Independent*, 25 August 2013.

10 O'Connor, *The Big Fellow*, pp. 22–3.

11 Béaslaí, *Michael Collins*, p. xii.

12 Collins, *The Path to Freedom*, pp. 3–4.

13 P.S. O'Hegarty, *Sinn Féin: An Illumination* (Dublin, 1919), p. 5. Separatists such as O'Hegarty and Collins were not the only people to distinguish between 'nationality' and 'nationalism' in similar terms. Horace Plunkett had written that 'It is this expansion of the sentiment of nationality outside the domain of party politics – the distinction, so to speak, between nationality and nationalism – which is the chief characteristic of the Gaelic movement.' See Horace Plunkett, *Ireland in the New Century* (3rd. ed., London, 1905), p. 154.

14 *Dáil Éireann Official Report: Debate on the Treaty*, 19 December 1921, p. 32.

15 Collins, *The Path to Freedom*, pp. 37, 49, 99 & 101–2.

16 Ó Deirg (ed.), *'Oh! Lord the Unrest of Soul'*, p. 16.

17 Collins, *The Path to Freedom*, p. 105.

18 P.S. O'Hegarty, *The Indestructible Nation* (Dublin, 1918).

19 Patrick Maume, *D.P. Moran* (Dundalk, 1995); Brian P. Murphy, 'O'Kelly, John Joseph ("Sceilg"; Ua Ceallaigh, Seán)' in McGuire and Quinn (eds), *Dictionary of Irish Biography*, VII, pp. 603–8.

20 Foster, *Vivid Faces*, p. 53 & p. 343.

21 Collins, *The Path to Freedom*, pp. 11, 63, 99.

22 Alice Stopford Green, *The Making of Ireland and its Undoing* (London, 1908); Eoin MacNeill's *Phases of Irish History* (Dublin, 1919).

23 Alice Stopford Green, *Irish Nationality* (London, 1911), pp. 14–15.

24 Collins, *The Path to Freedom*, pp. 101–2.

25 *Ibid.*, pp. 4, 107, 127–9.

26 *Ibid.*, pp. 4, 53 and 58. Collins's use of and attitude to violence have been discussed at some length in Chapter 3.

27 Collins, *The Path to Freedom*, pp. 12 & 20.

28 Kissane, *The Politics of the Irish Civil War*, pp. 62–3.

29 Murphy, 'Nationalism: The framing of the constitution of the Irish Free State', pp. 135–50.

30 Douglas to Collins, 25 January 1922, NLI, James Green Douglas Papers, Ms 49,581/7; Collins to Douglas, 28 January 1922, NLI, James Green Douglas Papers, Ms 49,581/74.

31 Collins, *The Path to Freedom*, pp. 54, 58 & 91.

32 *Arguments for the Treaty*, p. 15.

33 *Ibid.*, pp. 6 & 21.

34   *Ibid.,* p. 95.

35   *Dáil Éireann Official Report: Debate on the Treaty,* 19 December 1921, p. 32.

36   *Ibid.,* p. 35.

37   Collins, *The Path to Freedom,* p. 21.

38   Prager, *Building Democracy in Ireland,* pp. 58–62.

39   O'Connor, *The Big Fellow,* p. 27.

40   Collins, *The Path to Freedom,* pp. 110–1.

41   Commission of Inquiry into the Resources and Industries of Ireland, *Report on water power* (Dublin, 1922), p. 3.

42   Collins, *The Path to Freedom,* pp. 109–22.

43   Maurice Moynihan (ed.), *Speeches and Statements by Eamon de Valera 1917–1973* (Dublin, 1980), p. 466.

44   *Dáil Éireann Official Report: Debate on the Treaty,* 19 December 1921, pp. 32–3.

45   Sheridan, *In Many Places,* p. 31.

46   Hart, *Mick,* p. 72.

47   Johanna Collins to Béaslaí, 25 September 1923, NLI, Piaras Béaslaí Papers, Ms 33,929(19).

48   Mitchell, *Revolutionary Government in Ireland,* p. 191.

49   Collins, *The Path to Freedom,* pp. 47, 104, 111–12 & 115; Diary of Sir Horace Plunkett (1922), 19 August 1922, NLI, Plunkett papers, Ms 42,222/42.

50   The Democratic Programme was a short statement of social and economic aspirations, declaring an intent to promote economic development while declaring that the country would be 'ruled in accordance with the principles of Liberty, Equality and Justice'. Emmet O'Connor, 'Neither democratic nor a programme: the Democratic Programme of 1919', *Irish Historical Studies,* XL:157 (2016), pp. 98–9.

51   Conor Kostick, *Revolution in Ireland: Popular Militancy 1917–1923* (Cork, 2009), pp. 4–5.

52   Collins, *The Path to Freedom,* p. 105.

53   Mitchell, *Revolutionary Government in Ireland,* pp. 85–92.

54   James McConnel, *The Irish Parliamentary Party and the Third Home Rule Crisis* (Dublin, 2013), pp. 71–93.

55   Elaine A. Byrne, *Political Corruption in Ireland 1922–2010* (Manchester, 2012), pp. 27–8; Fanning, *The Irish Department of Finance,* pp. 26–8.

56   O'Higgins to Collins, 18 May 1921, Collins to O'Higgins, 24 May 1921, and Collins to de Valera, 24 May 1921, NAI, DE/2/443.

57   O'Halpin, *Defending Ireland,* pp. 4–9.

58   Éamonn Phoenix, 'Michael Collins – The Northern Question 1916–22' in Doherty and Keogh (eds), *Michael Collins,* p. 94.

59   Collins, *The Path to Freedom,* pp. 80–2.

60   Michael Hopkinson, 'The Craig–Collins Pacts of 1922: two attempted reforms of the Northern Ireland government', *Irish Historical Studies,* xxvii:106 (1990), p. 145.

61   Collins to Craig, 27 April 1922, NAI, DT S1,801A.

62   Robert Lynch, *The Northern IRA and the Early Years of Partition 1920–1922* (Dublin, 2006), p. 3.

63   Lynch, *The Northern IRA,* p. 100; Fanning, *Fatal Path,* p. 319.

64   *Irish Times,* 2 February 1922 as quoted in Paul Bew, 'The Political History of Northern Ireland since Partition: the prospects for North-South Co-operation', *Proceedings of the British Academy,* 98 (1999), p. 408.

65 Craig to Amery, 7 February 1922, Churchill Archive, L.S. Amery Papers, AMER 2/1/5.

66 Collins to Walsh, 20 February 1922, NAI, DT, S9,241.

67 McGarry, *Eoin O'Duffy*, pp. 103–4.

68 Tim Pat Coogan, *De Valera: Long Fellow, Long Shadow* (London, 1992), p. 319.

69 Regan, *Irish Counter-revolution*, p. 63.

70 Marie Coleman, The Irish Revolution 1916–1923 (Abingdon, 2014), pp. 110–11.

71 McGarry, *Eoin O'Duffy*, p. 103; Kissane, *The Politics of the Irish Civil War*, pp. 82–3.

72 Laura Cahillane, *Drafting the Irish Free State Constitution* (Manchester, 2016), p. 7.

73 Laffan, *Judging W.T. Cosgrave*, p. 107.

74 *Ibid.*, p. 113.

75 'Michael Collins, 'General Commanding-in-Chief, as a historiographical problem' in John Regan, *Myth and the Irish State* (Dublin, 2013), pp. 113–43.

76 Laffan, *Judging W.T. Cosgrave*, p. 115.

77 J.J. Lee, *Ireland, 1912–1985: Politics and Society* (Cambridge, 1989), p. 68.

78 Laffan, *Judging W.T. Cosgrave*, p. 114.

79 See Brendan Clifford's introduction to O'Connor, *With Michael Collins*, p. 17; Coogan, *Michael Collins*, pp. 285–6 & 288–9; McCoole, *Hazel*, pp. 86–9; Hart, *Mick*, pp. 341–54.

80 *Irish Times*, 29 August 2015.

81 Hart, *Mick*, p. 256; Coogan, *Michael Collins*, p. 282.

82 Mary Kenny, 'Michael Collins's religious faith', *Studies: An Irish Quarterly Review*, 96:384 (2007), p. 425.

83 Béaslaí, *Michael Collins*, p. 10.

84 Tim Pat Coogan, *Ireland Since the Rising* (London, 1966), pp. 229–30.

85 Anne Dolan, 'Patrick Joseph Clune' in McGuire and Quinn (eds), *Dictionary of Irish Biography*, II, pp. 602–3; Dáil Loan literature, undated, NAI, DE/2/358.

86 Kenny, 'Michael Collins's religious faith', p. 424.

87 *Dáil Éireann*, S2:1 (28 February 1922), 104–6 & S2:3 (2 March 1922), 221.

88 Brian Walker, *A Political History of the Two Irelands: From Partition to Peace* (Basingstoke, 2012), p. 48.

6: Collins and Celebrity

1 *Dundee Evening Telegraph*, 31 March 1921.

2 *Burnley News*, 25 January 1922.

3 *Daily Express*, 17 March 1921.

4 *Yorkshire Post*, 21 August 1921.

5 *Ibid.*, 7 January 1922.

6 *Cornishman*, 30 August 1922.

7 Hart, *Mick*, p. xiii.

8 Lis Pihl (ed.), *Signe Toksvig's Irish Diaries 1926–1937* (Dublin, 1994), p. 376.

9 Bretherton, *The Real Ireland*, p. 2.

10 *Hull Daily Mail*, 2 July 1921.

11 Hart, *Mick*, p. 348.

12 Edward Berenson and Eva Giloi (eds), *Constructing Charisma: Celebrity, Fame, and Power In Nineteenth-Century Europe* (Oxford, 2010), p. 6 & p. 17.

13   Adrian Bingham and Martin Conboy, *Tabloid Century: The Popular Press in Britain, 1896 to the Present* (Oxford, 2015), p. 97.

14   Nancy Brandt, 'Pancho Villa: the making of a modern legend', *The Americas*, 21:2 (1964), pp. 149–54.

15   *Daily Mirror*, 8 February 1921 & 7 September 1921.

16   *Daily Express*, 17 March 1921.

17   *Yorkshire Post*, 18 October 1920; *Western Daily Press*, 30 November 1920; *Daily Express*, 22 November 1920 & 23 January 1921; *Manchester Guardian*, 29 November 1920.

18   *Derby Daily Telegraph*, 9 February 1921; *Western Gazette*, 11 February 1921. Christiaan de Wet commanded the Boer forces in the Anglo-Boer War. He was sometimes referred to as the Boer Pimpernel due to his capacity to evade capture.

19   *Dundee Evening Telegraph*, 31 March 1921.

20   *Yorkshire Post*, 11 October 1920.

21   *Times of India*, 9 November 1958.

22   *North China Herald*, 20 November 1920.

23   *Manchester Guardian*, 29 March 1921.

24   *The Times*, 28 December 1921; 15 March 1922.

25   *Ibid.*, 29 August 1922.

26   *Financial Times*, 14 December 1921.

27   *Morning Post*, 24 and 25 August 1922.

28   Adrian Bingham, *Family Newspapers? Sex, Private Life, and the British Popular Press, 1918–1978* (Oxford, 2009), pp. 19–22. Thanks to Elspeth Payne for insights on circulation figures.

29   *Ibid.*, p. 16.

30   Tom Jeffrey and Keith McClelland, 'A world fit to live in: the *Daily Mail* and the middle classes 1918–1939' in James Curran, Anthony Smith and Pauline Wingate (eds), *Impacts and Influences: Media Power in the Twentieth Century* (London, 1987), p. 29.

31   *Gloucester Citizen*, 12 October 1921.

32   *Daily Mirror*, 20 February 1922.

33   *Ibid.*, 18 July 1922 & 1 August 1922.

34   Collins to George Gavan Duffy, 17 May 1921, quoted in Hart, *Mick*, p. xiv.

35   Talbot, *Michael Collins' Own Story*, p. 106.

36   De Valera to Collins, 18 January 1921, NAI, DE 2/448.

37   *The Star*, 11 October 1921.

38   For example, *Daily Express*, 15 October 1921; *News of the World*, 16 October 1921.

39   *Western Morning News*, 11 October 1921.

40   Maurice Walsh, *The News from Ireland: Foreign Correspondents and the Irish Revolution* (London & New York, 2008), p. 145; *Atlantic Monthly*, April 1922.

41   Sheridan, *In Many Places*, pp. 32–3; *Daily Telegraph*, 24 August 1922.

42   Nankivell and Loch, *Ireland in Travail*, p. 288.

43   £10,000 in Douglas V. Duff, *May the Winds Blow! An Autobiography* (London, 1948), p. 80; £20,000 in IWM, Vinden papers, 96/36/1; £40,000 in *Derby Daily Telegraph*, 9 February 1921.

44   *The Times*, 17 January 1924.

45   Nevil Macready, *Annals of an Active Life* (2 vols., London, 1924), p. 663.

46   Diary of Private J.P. Swindlehurst, 9 January 1921, 28 February 1921, IWM, Swindlehurst papers, P538.

47   *Sunday Express*, 9 October 1921 & 27 February 1921.

48   *News of the World*, 4 December 1921; *Sunday Pictorial*, 4 December 1921.

49 Riddell, *Lord Riddell's Intimate Diary*, pp. 288–9.

50 Marsh to the editor of the *Morning Post*, 17 October 1921, CA, Churchill papers, CHAR 2/116/126.

51 *Edinburgh Evening News*, 10 December 1921; *Manchester Guardian*, 11 July 1921.

52 *Exeter and Plymouth Gazette*, 12 October 1921.

53 *Manchester Guardian*, 24 August 1922.

54 Hopkinson (ed.), *The Last Days of Dublin Castle*, p. 219; Riddell, *Lord Riddell's Intimate Diary*, p. 330.

55 Wilson (ed.), *The Political Diaries of C.P. Scott*, p. 405.

56 *Daily Mirror*, 8 October 1921; *News of the World*, 9 October 1921; *Daily Mail*, 10 October 1921; *Daily Express*, 11 &12 October 1921; *Daily Mirror*, 22 October 1921; *News of the World*, 23 October 1921; *Yorkshire Post*, 15 October 1921; *Exeter and Plymouth Gazette*, 15 October 1921; *Derby Daily Telegraph*, 13 October 1921.

57 O'Connor, *The Big Fellow*, p. 160.

58 *Times of India*, 19 April 1922.

59 *Hull Daily Mail*, 17 October 1921.

60 *Manchester Guardian*, 24 August 1922; *Western Morning News*, 11 October 1921; *Exeter and Plymouth Gazette*, 7 December 1921.

61 *Lancashire Evening Post*, 8 December 1921.

62 *Yorkshire Evening Post*, 27 October 1921.

63 *Sunday Pictorial*, 27 August 1922; Collins to Messrs Callaghan & Son, Ltd, Dame Street, Dublin, 5 August 1922, NLI, Béaslaí papers, Ms 33,929(15).

64 British Pathé, 12 December 1921, film id 250.08.

65 Thomas Jones, *Lloyd George* (Cambridge Mass., 1951), p. 191; H.V. Morton, *In search of Ireland* (2nd ed., London, 2000), p. 21.

66 *Yorkshire Evening Post*, 19 October 1921.

67 *Dundee Courier*, 7 June 1922; *Daily Mirror*, 10 June 1922; *Sunday Post*, 16 April 1922.

68 Leon Ó Broin (ed.), *In Great Haste: The Letters of Michael Collins and Kitty Kiernan* (Dublin, 1996 edn), p. 34.

69 *Daily Mail*, 24 & 25 August 1922; *Westminster Gazette*, 25 August 1922.

70 *Daily Mirror*, 16 October 1922.

71 *Ibid.*, 19 October 1922.

72 British Pathé, 5 December 1921, film id 248.40; *Freeman's Journal*, 28 November 1921.

73 *Manchester Guardian*, 6 & 9 February 1922; 26 September 1922.

74 Hart, *Mick*, p. 349.

75 Macartney to Collins, [?] July 1921, NLI, Béaslaí papers, Ms 33,916 (1).

76 His refusal of the £10,000 offer was carried in a number of papers. See, for example, *The Times*, 16 July 1921; *Manchester Guardian*, 16 July 1922; *The Ulster Herald*, *The Derry People*, *The Nenagh Guardian*, *The Connaught Telegraph*, *The Kilkenny People*, *The Fermanagh Herald*, 23 July 1921; *Gloucester Citizen*, 16 July 1921. J.M. Tuohy, *New York World*, to Michael Collins, 8 January 1922; F.D. Long, *Daily Despatch*, to Michael Collins, 9 January 1922; Cahills & Co. on behalf of W.H.S. Macartney to Collins, 17 January 1922, NLI, Béaslaí papers, Ms 33,916 (1).

77 Long, *Daily Despatch*, to Collins, 9 January 1922, NLI, Béaslaí papers, Ms 33,916 (1).

78 Keith Alldritt, *Churchill the Writer: His Life as a Man of Letters* (London, 1992), p. 77; Martin Gilbert, *Churchill: A Life* (2nd ed., London, 2000), p. 443.

79 Michael Korda, *Hero: The Life and Legend of Lawrence of Arabia* (2nd ed., London, 2012), pp. 602–3, p. 617.

80 *Hartlepool Mail*, 4 October 1922; *Aberdeen Journal*, 5 October 1922.

81 Talbot, *Michael Collins' Own Story*, p. 114. See Hart, *Mick*, p. xv.

82 Talbot, *Michael Collins' Own Story*, p. 1.

83 Patrick Maume, 'Piaras Béaslaí' in McGuire and Quinn (eds), *Dictionary of Irish biography*, I, pp. 386–9.

84 Béaslaí to the editor, *Irish Independent*, 5 September 1922, NLI, Béaslaí papers, Ms 33,915 (7); *Dundee Courier*, 11 May 1923.

85 Clippings of *The World's Pictorial News*, NLI, Béaslaí papers, Ms 33,915 (3).

86 *The World's Pictorial News*, 9, 16 & 23 September 1922.

87 Béaslaí to Gearoid [O'Sullivan], 4 September 1922, NLI, Béaslaí papers, Ms 33,915 (7).

88 For the various offers to Collins see NLI, Béaslaí papers, Ms 33,915–33,916.

89 Talbot's accusation quoted in Béaslaí to the editor, *Sunday Express*, 15 September 1922, NLI, Béaslaí papers Ms 33,915 (7).

90 Blumenfeld to Collins, 7 December 1921, NLI, Béaslaí papers, Ms 33,916 (1).

91 *Times of India*, 3 June 1922; *Daily Mirror*, 20 February & 24 June 1922.

92 *Daily Express*, 3 July & 23 June 1922; *Daily Mirror*, 24 June 1922.

93 *Daily Express*, 3 July 1922.

94 *The Times*, 23 August 1922.

95 *Daily Mirror*, 24 August1922; *Daily Express*, 31 August 1922.

96 *The Times*, 24 August 1922; *Manchester Guardian*, 24 August 1922.

97 *Sunderland Daily Echo and Shipping Gazette*, 23 August 1922; *Daily Telegraph*, 24 August 1922.

98 *Manchester Guardian*, 16 May 1923.

99 *Yorkshire Post*, 15 October 1921.

100 All from the *Morning Post*, 28 August 1922.

101 John Butler, 'Lord Oranmore's journal, 1913–27', *Irish Historical Studies*, xxix, 116 (November 1995), p. 589.

102 *The Spectator*, 25 August 1922.

103 Strachey to Mrs Menzies, 24 August 1922, PA, Strachey papers, S/21/4/14.

104 Jeudwine to Judy, n.d., IWM, Jeudwine papers, 72/82/2.

105 Winter to Menzies, 28 August 1922, PA, Strachey papers, S/21/4/14.

106 *Dáil Éireann Official Report*, 3 January 1922, p. 184.

107 Diary of Sir Henry Wilson, 13 October 1921, IWM, Wilson papers, 73/1/6 – emphasis in original.

108 O'Hegarty, *The Victory of Sinn Féin*, p. 47.

109 *Yorkshire Post*, 11 February 1922; *Sunday Express*, 27 August 1922; *Daily Express*, 2 September 1922.

110 Collins to Douglas, 6 April 1922, NLI, Ms 49,581/74.

111 Collins to Kiernan, 10 June 1922, British Library (BL), RP3040.

112 Anti-Treaty handbill, n.d., NLI, ILB 300 P13, piece 124.

113 *Sunday Pictorial*, 25 September 1921.

114 *Yorkshire Post*, 15 October 1921. Kitty Kiernan, based on newspaper photographs of him, even ribbed Collins for what she called his 'Charlie Chaplin moustache'. Ó Broin (ed.), *In Great Haste*, p. 49.

115 *Irish Times*, 14 May 2011; Ó Broin (ed.), *In Great Haste*, pp. 33–4, p. 42, p. 49, pp. 65–6.

7: Collins's Death

1   Florence O'Donoghue's account of Emmet Dalton's views of the ambush at Béal na mBláth, Florence O'Donoghue, Ernie O'Malley notebooks, UCDA, O'Malley papers, P17b/95.

2   *Variety*, 31 December 1935; *New York Times*, 26 December 1936. *Beloved Enemy* (1936), directed by H.C. Potter.

3   *Times of India*, 2 January 1937.

4   Jordan, *Michael Collins Film Diary and Screenplay*, p. 17.

5   *Ibid.*, pp 58–9.

6   *Sunday Independent*, 6 September 1981; John M. Feehan, *The The Shooting of Michael Collins: Murder or Accident?* (Cork, 1981). The book was first published in June 1981, again in July, with a revised edition in April 1982. There were further reprints in 1987, 1988, 1989 and another revised edition in 1991. See also, Gerard Murphy, *The Great Cover-up: The Truth About the Death of Michael Collins* (Cork, 2018).

7   Coogan, *Michael Collins*, p. 409.

8   *Ibid.*

9   Hart, *Mick*, pp. 408–9.

10   John M. Feehan, *The Shooting of Michael Collins: Murder or Accident?* (3rd ed., Cork, 1991), pp. 50–1; Coogan, *Michael Collins*, p. 402.

11   See Feehan, *The Shooting of Michael Collins*, pp. 52–9; Hart, *Mick*, pp. 410–11.

12   See A/G, 1st Southern Division, to Chief of Staff, 24 August 1922, UCDA, Twomey papers, P69/93(177); James Mackay, *Michael Collins: A Life* (Edinburgh, 1996), p. 285.

13   Accounts differ as to the length of the ambush: the IRA account states one hour, others recount a shorter time. See A/G, 1st Southern Division, to Chief of Staff, 24 August 1922, UCDA, Twomey papers, P69/93(177); Liam Deasy, *Brother Against Brother* (Dublin & Cork, 1982), p. 82.

14   Quoted in Feehan, *The Shooting of Michael Collins*, p. 56; letters from various sources suggest a similar reason for Collins's trip, for example, Frank Thornton to Sean T. Ó Ceallaigh, 25 February 1965, NLI, Deasy papers, Ms 43,556 (1–3); Report on the death of Collins, n.d., NLI, O'Mahony papers, Ms 44,102 (5); Copy of statement by Séamus Robinson about John Joe Hogan claiming Collins wished to meet Deasy, n.d., NLI, Ms 18,470.

15   Memo by Collins to Cosgrave, 21 August 1922, or it is described as a diary entry of Michael Collins, 21 August 1922, NLI, Collins Jr papers, Ms 40,420 (12); also, Royal Irish Academy, Cosgrave papers, P285/307.

16   Hart, *Mick*, pp. 409–10.

17   Copy of statement by Séamus Robinson about John Joe Hogan claiming Collins wished to meet Deasy, n.d., NLI, Ms 18,470; suspicion that Collins was being sidelined by the Provisional Government, moved into the Army, to stop his aggressive policy towards Northern Ireland, or that he was killed by British intelligence in revenge for his attacks on intelligence agents during the War of Independence, or even that the British Secret Service killed him to protect their agent, Tim Healy, were put forward by Seán Mac Bride, n.d., NLI, O'Mahony papers, Ms 44,104 (7); Coogan, *Michael Collins*, pp. 389–94.

18   Account of de Valera's movements on 22 August 1922, 26 March 1990, NLI, O'Mahony papers, Ms 44,104 (5).

19   *Westminster Gazette*, 24 August 1922; Pakenham, *Peace by Ordeal*, p. 270.

20   Hart, *Mick*, pp. 411–12.

21   Lee, 'The challenge of a Collins biography', p. 37.

22 Account of the ambush issued from Army HQ, 23 August 1922, NLI, O'Duffy papers, Ms 48,281 (6); *Daily Mail*, 24 August 1922.

23 Account of the ambush issued from Army HQ, 23 August 1922, NLI, O'Duffy papers, Ms 48,281 (6).

24 See, for example, the account in *The Freeman's Journal*, 24 August 1922; 'Forgive them. Bury me in Glasnevin with the boys', *Manchester Guardian*, 24 August 1922; Account of the ambush issued from Army HQ, 23 August 1922, NLI, O'Duffy papers, Ms 48,281 (6).

25 *Freeman's Journal*, 22 August 1923.

26 Jordan, *Michael Collins Film Diary*, p. 17; O'Connell quoted in Calton Younger, *Ireland's Civil War* (Glasgow, 1990; 1st ed. 1968), p. 437.

27 Denis Hurley to John Hurley, 18 September 1922, CAI, Hurley papers, U170.

28 *Freeman's Journal*, 23 August 1922.

29 *Ibid.*

30 Regan, *The Irish Counter-revolution*, p. 76; Lee, *Ireland 1912–1985*, p. 66.

31 Lee, *Ireland 1912–1985*, p. 66.

32 Charles Townshend, *The Republic: The Fight for Irish Independence* (London, 2013), p. 432.

33 'General Michael Collins 1922', British Pathé, film id 276.28; Lee, *Ireland 1912–1985*, p. 66.

34 Dalton quoted in Coogan, *Michael Collins*, p. 410.

35 Florence O'Donoghue's account of Dalton's views, Florence O'Donoghue, Ernie O'Malley notebooks, UCDA, O'Malley papers, P17b/95.

36 *Sunday Pictorial*, 27 August 1922.

37 Signed certification by Oscar Traynor, 3 May 1954, MAI, Dependent's allowance application, Military service pension papers, Mary Collins Powell, DP23755, 1953, http://mspcsearch.militaryarchives.ie/docs/files//PDFPensions/R2/DP23755MICHAELCOLLINS/WDP23755MICHAELCOLLINS.pdf (viewed on 12 December 2016).

38 Deasy, *Brother Against Brother*, p. 81.

39 *Ibid.*, p. 82.

40 *Sunday Pictorial*, 3 September 1922.

41 Flor Begley quoted in Coogan, *Michael Collins*, p. 405.

42 A/G, 1st Southern Division, to Chief of Staff, 24 August 1922, UCDA, Twomey papers, P69/93(177).

43 Hart, *Mick*, p. 410.

44 Deasy, *Brother Against Brother*, p. 82.

45 Margery Forester, *Michael Collins: The Lost Leader* (London, 1972; 1st ed. 1971), p. 334; Younger, *Ireland's Civil War*, p. 436; O'Connor, *The Big Fellow*, p. 211.

46 Lee, *Ireland 1912–1985*, p. 66.

47 Hart, *Mick*, p. 356; Forester, *Michael Collins*, p. 333.

48 F.S.L. Lyons, *Ireland Since the Famine* (London, 1989; 1st ed. 1971), p. 466.

49 Florence O'Donoghue, Ernie O'Malley notebooks, UCDA, O'Malley papers, P17b/95; John Borgonovo, *The Battle for Cork: July–August 1922* (Cork, 2011), p. 131.

50 Winston Churchill, *The Collected Works of Sir Winston Churchill: vol. 11, The World Crisis, part 4: The Aftermath* (London, 1974), p. 348 & p. 336.

51 Hart, *Mick*, p. 42; O'Connor, *The Big Fellow*, p. 210; Coogan, *Michael Collins*, p. 399; Meda Ryan, *Michael Collins and the Women in His Life* (Cork, 1996), p. 42 & p. 184.

52 Younger, *Ireland's Civil War*, p. 433.

53 For example, Coogan refers to Collins's gun going off just before he left Dublin as an 'ill-omen', Coogan, *Michael Collins*, p. 400. Calton Younger wonders if Collins, in recording the death of his

namesake, 'was he perhaps recording a presentiment of his own fate?' amongst other ominous signs. He also wonders if he knew his end was near when he picked up a rifle off the floor of the touring car as they approached Béal na mBláth, Younger, *Ireland's Civil War*, p. 433 & p. 436; Mackay considers several presentiments of death, from ripping a button off his jacket to give to Kitty Kiernan to pondering whether he would live, Mackay, *Michael Collins*, pp. 278–80, and stopping to look at the headstones, p. 286; even F.S.L. Lyons gives in to this instinct: 'he may even have had a premonition', Lyons, *Ireland Since the Famine*, p. 466.

54 Lee, *Ireland 1912–1985*, p. 66.

55 See letter from M. McManus possibly to John Devoy, 31 August 1922, NLI, Devoy papers, Ms 18,007 (34).

56 Hart, *Mick*, p. 410; Regan, *The Irish Counter-revolution*, p. 76.

57 Regan, *The Irish Counter-revolution*, p. 77.

58 Coogan, *Michael Collins*, p. 409.

59 Harry Boland died on 1 August 1922; Arthur Griffith on 12 August 1922; Cathal Brugha died on 7 July 1922. Reginald Dunne and Joseph O'Sullivan were hanged on 16 August 1922 for the murder of Sir Henry Wilson, the day of Griffith's funeral. Forester records that Collins 'wept unrestrainedly' when he heard of Brugha's death. Forester, *Michael Collins*, p. 324.

60 Younger, *Ireland's Civil War*, p. 424 & p. 430.

61 Mackay, *Michael Collins*, p. 278, p. 281; Hart, *Mick*, p. 264, p. 408; *Daily Mail*, 24 & 25 August 1922; *Westminster Gazette*, 25 August 1922; *Sunderland Daily Echo and Shipping Gazette*, 23 August 1922.

62 See Coogan, *Michael Collins*, p. 408; Mackay, *Michael Collins*, p. 287.

63 Sean Boyne, *Emmet Dalton: Somme Soldier, Irish General, Film Pioneer* (Sallins, 2015), pp. 218–19; Coogan, *Michael Collins*, p. 408.

64 Quoted as a private source, Coogan, *Michael Collins*, p. 408.

65 Coogan, *Michael Collins*, p. 408; Boyne, *Emmet Dalton*, pp. 300–1, 304–5.

66 Coogan, *Michael Collins*, p. 408.

67 Younger, *Ireland's Civil War*, p. 436.

68 On the poison bullet rumour see Rex Taylor, *Michael Collins* (London, 1964; 1st ed. 1958), p. 199; Coogan states the report was placed in the safe of the Royal College of Surgeons, but was not to be found. Coogan, *Michael Collins*, p. 418; for a variety of rumours and conspiracies see NLI, O'Mahony papers, Ms 44,103–Ms 44,105.

69 *Westminster Gazette*, 25 August 1922.

70 Coogan, *Michael Collins*, p. 401.

71 See Boyne, *Emmet Dalton*, chapter 10; Cathal O'Shannon, 'Who shot Michael Collins?', in Justin Nelson, *Michael Collins: The Final Days* (Dublin, 1997), pp. 100–2; Cathal O'Shannon, 'Béal na mBláth – no easy road back', *An Cosantóir*, 50, 11 (November 1990), pp. 10–11; on McPeak see NLI, O'Mahony papers, Ms 44,103 (4); Dónal Ó hÉalaithe (ed.), *Memoirs of an Old Warrior: Jamie Moynihan's Fight For Irish Freedom 1916–1923* (Cork, 2014), p. 249; *The Shadow of Béal na mBláth* (1991), directed by Colm Connolly. Gerard Murphy disputes Sonny O'Neill's role in Collins's death. See Murphy, *The Great Cover-Up*, p. 127.

72 Coogan, *Michael Collins*, p. 411, p. 419, p. 421.

73 Military Service Pension application, Denis O'Neill, MAI, MSP34REF4067.

74 *Irish Times*, 3 October 2014; *Irish Examiner*, 3 October 2014.

75 For the full text of Hickey's findings see *Limerick Weekly Echo*, 26 August – 16 September 1972 & Murphy, *The Great Cover-Up*, pp. 201–24. Richard Lucid to Florence O'Donoghue, 8 December 1964, NLI, O'Donoghue papers, Ms 31,305 (1).

76 Florence O'Donoghue to Sean Feehan, 8 January 1964, NLI, O'Donoghue papers, Ms 31,305(1).

77 Note on the 'Death of Michael Collins', meeting at the Metropole Hotel, Cork, 15 February 1964, NLI, O'Donoghue papers, Ms 31,305 (1).

78 *Ibid.* O'Donoghue would later send on paragraphs of text to replace what he felt were offending passages of the text. Florence O'Donoghue to Capt. Sean Feehan, Mercier Press, 8 January 1965, NLI, O'Donoghue papers, Ms 31, 305 (1).

79 *Ibid.*

80 *Ibid.*

81 Jim Hurley to Florence O'Donoghue, 8 January 1964; Memo on meeting with Neeson, 17 February 1964, NLI, O'Donoghue papers, Ms 31,305 (1). For a lengthy consideration of O'Donoghue's memo and the plan to kill Collins see Murphy, *The Great Cover-Up*.

82 Memo on visit to the editor of the *Sunday Review*, 20 April 1964, NLI, O'Donoghue papers, Ms 31,305 (1).

83 Coogan, *Michael Collins*, pp. 419–21; Kissane, *The Politics of the Irish Civil War*, pp. 82–98.

84 Tom Barry expressed the same sentiment in *Guerilla Days in Ireland* (Cork, 1997 edn), p. 184. Gerard Murphy makes extensive use of a British intelligence summary which noted that 'It has been reliably reported that the Inner Circle of the Irish Republican Brotherhood in Ireland have tried MICHAEL COLLINS and SEAN McKEON for treason to the IRB and sentenced them to be shot.' Murphy builds this into his argument that there was clear intention to kill Collins. See Dublin Castle Files, Sinn Féin Activists: Michael Collins, TNA, WO35/206/35 & Murphy, *The Great Cover-Up*.

85 *Sunday Express*, 26 February 1956; *Irish Independent*, 6 February 1957.

86 See Boyne, *Emmet Dalton*, chapter 10; O'Shannon, 'Who shot Michael Collins?', pp. 100–2; O'Shannon, 'Béal na mBláth – no easy road back', pp. 10–11.

87 Boyne, *Emmet Dalton*, pp. 242–4. It is believed that Dalton resigned his commission in the National Army for a variety of reasons, these included: frustration with inadequate resources, indiscipline amongst his men and his own unease about the execution of anti-Treaty prisoners.

88 Postcards of Collins's funeral, various scenes, including the procession through O'Connell Street, Sean and Hannie Collins at the funeral, NLI, Dalton papers, Ms 46,687 (2).

89 Statement by Robert Flynn, 1977, NLI, O'Mahony papers, Ms 44,103 (1).

90 *Ibid.*

91 *Ibid.*

92 'Emmet Dalton remembers', interview with Cathal O'Shannon, RTÉ, March 1978.

93 Report on interview with Bill McKenna, 16 March 1981, NLI, O'Mahony papers, Ms 44,103 (6).

94 *Ibid.*

95 Dan Ryan to John Feehan, 9 November 1981, NLI, O'Mahony papers, Ms 44,103 (4).

96 Fr Sean O'Donoghue to John Feehan, n.d., NLI, O'Mahony papers, Ms 44,103 (4).

97 Fr James Redmond to John Feehan, 4 November 1981, NLI, O'Mahony papers, Ms 44,103 (4).

98 Copy of signed affidavit by Simon Joseph Dalton, 25 February 1987, NLI, O'Mahony papers, Ms 44,104 (2).

99 Notes of meeting with Larry Murphy, 11 September 1989, NLI, O'Mahony papers, Ms 44,104 (3).

100 *Ibid.*; allegations suggested that 'Dalton's main job was to pick up young privates for Collins', see Jordan, *Michael Collins Film Diary*, p. 29.

101 Notes of meeting with Larry Murphy, 11 September 1989, NLI, O'Mahony papers, Ms 44,104 (3).

102 *Ibid.*

103 Jordan, *Michael Collins Film Diary*, pp. 28–9.

104   *Ibid.*, p. 29.

105   Liam Collins to James McAllister, 31 August 1993, NLI, O'Mahony papers, Ms 44,103 (4).

106   *Ibid.*

107   Younger, *Ireland's Civil War*, p. 437.

108   Forester, *Michael Collins*, p. 333; Coogan, *Michael Collins*, p. 416. Calton Younger wrote: 'It can be wondered … whether he made any very serious effort to keep his guns going.' Younger, *Ireland's Civil War*, p. 437.

109   Edward Timlin to the *Sunday Independent*, 18 September 1981, NLI, O'Mahony papers, Ms 44,103 (4); Ó hÉalaithe, *Memoirs of an Old Warrior*, p. 249.

110   *Irish Independent*, 21 May 1971.

111   John Brennan to Michael Collins Jr, 28 September 1983, NLI, O'Mahony papers, Ms 44,104 (1); Brennan to Collins Jr, 28 September 1983, NLI, Collins Jr papers, Ms 40,423 (6).

112   *Ibid.*

113   Report by Lt Col. Patrick Collins on meeting with John Brennan, 25 August 1984, NLI, O'Mahony papers, Ms 44/104 (1).

114   Interview of Tom Foley by Fr Aiden O'Driscoll, 2 September 1989, NLI, O'Mahony papers, Ms 44,104 (4); Coogan, *Michael Collins*, p. 420.

115   *Ibid.* For a broader discussion of the confusion of ambushes in the Irish revolution see William H. Kautt, *Ambushes and Armour: The Irish Rebellion 1919–1921* (Dublin, 2010).

116   *The Canberra Times*, 23 August 1992.

117   Forester, *Michael Collins*; Lee, *Ireland 1912–1985*, p. 404.

118   Copies of Dublin District Weekly Intelligence Summaries by General Boyd for weeks ending 26 August 1922 & 2 September 1922, NAI, DT S1,784.

119   Sir Hugh Jeudwine to Judy, n.d., IWM, Jeudwine papers, 72/82/2.

120   Kissane, *The Politics of the Irish Civil War*, p. 84.

121   'Position of the Irish Provisional Government', 21 September 1922, UL, Templewood papers, i, 13, 26.

122   Ramsden (ed.), *Real Old Tory Politics*, p. 181; Report by Major W.E. de B. Whitaker, King's Regiment & special correspondent of the *Daily Express*, circulated to Cabinet Situation Committee on Ireland, 19 September 1922, TNA, CO 739/16.

123   Copy of Dublin District Weekly Intelligence Summary by General Boyd for week ending 16 September 1922, NAI, DT S1,784.

124   Derby to Rawlinson, 26 August 1922, BL, Rawlinson papers, Ms EUR D 605 f.112.

125   *Manchester Guardian*, 6 September 1922. He promised to attend or send a representative if he was not in London.

126   Andy Cope to Tom Jones, 23 August 1922, PA, Lloyd George papers, LG/F/26/2/20.

127   Lionel Curtis to Hugh Kennedy, August 1922, UCDA, Kennedy papers, P4/1456.

128   Keith Middlemas (ed.), *Whitehall Diary: vol. 3 Ireland 1918–1925* (London, 1975), p. 215.

129   Clementine Churchill to Winston Churchill, 14 August 1922, CA, Churchill papers, CHAR 1/158/49-50.

130   *Daily Mail*, 24 August 1922; *Westminster Gazette*, 24 August 1922.

131   Macready, *Annals of an Active Life*, pp. 662–3.

132   Memoir of Harold William O'Riley, n.d., National Army Museum, London (NAM), O'Riley papers, 2008–10–32–1.

133   Deasy, *Brother Against Brother*, p. 80.

134   *Ibid.*, pp. 77–8.

135   Account of escorting de Valera in late August 1922, recorded by Lt Col. P. Collins, 26 March 1990, NLI, O'Mahony papers, Ms 44,104 (5); Barry, *Guerilla Days in Ireland*, p. 183.

136   Quoted in Coogan, *Michael Collins*, p. 419.

137   Lee, *Ireland 1912–1985*, p. 270; Dorothy Macardle, *The Irish Republic* (London, 1937), p. 809.

138   'A comparison', 1923, NLI, EPH D112; Letter from D.F. Cronin to Gogan, 26 August 1922, NLI, Ms 49,671 (5); O'Leary letter, n.d., CAI, O'Leary papers, U291.

139   *Irish Times*, 14 November 1996.

140   Frank O'Connor, *An Only Child* (Belfast, 1993; 1st ed. 1961), p. 232.

141   O'Connor, *The Big Fellow*, p. 9.

142   Maire Comerford quoted in Kenneth Griffith and Timothy O'Grady (eds), *Ireland's Unfinished Revolution: An Oral History* (Colorado, 1999), p. 296.

143   Liam Lynch to Ernie O'Malley, 27 August 1922, UCDA, O'Malley papers, P17A/61; Con Moloney to Ernie O'Malley, 3 October 1922, UCDA, Twomey papers, P69/77(67); Cormac K.H. O'Malley and Anne Dolan (eds), *'No Surrender Here!': The Civil War Papers of Ernie O'Malley 1922–1924* (Dublin, 2007), p. 127, p. 253

144   Liam Lynch to Ernie O'Malley, 30 August 1922, UCDA, O'Malley papers, P17A/61.

145   Ernie O'Malley, *The Singing Flame* (Dublin, 1992; 1st ed. 1978), p. 151.

146   *Ibid.*

147   C.S. Andrews, *Man of No Property* (Dublin, 2001; 1st ed. 1982), p. 14; Andrews, *Dublin Made Me*, pp. 291–2.

148   Deasy, *Brother Against Brother*, p. 80.

149   *Irish Times*, 25 August 1922; *Daily Mail*, 25 August 1922; *Times of India*, 26 August 1922; *Manchester Guardian*, 25 August 1922.

150   Interview with Dan Breen, *The Word*, December 1968, TCD, J.R.W. Goulden papers, Ms 7,379.

151   Martin Walton quoted in Griffith and O'Grady (eds), *Ireland's Unfinished Revolution*, p. 296.

152   Máire Cruise O'Brien, *The Same Age as the State* (Dublin, 2003), p. 52.

153   Evidence of Colonel Charles Russell to the Army Enquiry, 10 May 1924, UCDA, Mulcahy papers, P7/C/29; *The Free State*, 29 August 1922; 'An appreciation of Michael Collins', NLI, Dalton papers, Ms 46,687 (4); Report on interview with Bill McKenna, 16 March 1981, NLI, O'Mahony papers, Ms 44,103 (6).

154   *Evening Herald*, 2 July 1971, NLI, O'Mahony papers, Ms 44,103 (2).

155   Patrick McCartan, quoted in Sean Cronin, *The McGarrity Papers* (Tralee, 1972), p. 123.

156   Middlemas (ed.), *Whitehall Diary*, p. 218.

157   'Emmet Dalton remembers', interview with Cathal O'Shannon, RTÉ, March 1978; Boyne, *Emmet Dalton*, p. 236; for reports of Mulcahy's message to the army, see *Evening Herald*, 28 August 1922; Hart, *Mick*, p. 412.

158   Quoted in Townshend, *The Republic*, p. 433.

159   O'Halpin, *Defending Ireland*, p. 14.

160   *Sunday Independent*, 25 August 1946.

161   Boyne, *Emmet Dalton*, p. 234; other sources put the offer at £1,000. Mackay, *Michael Collins*, p. 291. There are various accounts across the newspapers with slightly different details about where Hannie Collins was at the time she found out about her brother's death. See, for example, *Daily Mail*, 24 August 1922, *Westminster Gazette*, 24 August 1922; Hart, *Mick*, p. 412.

162   *Daily Mail*, 26 August 1922; *Illustrated Sunday Herald*, 27 August 1922.

163   *Daily Mail*, 26 August 1922.

164 'Farewell token of Michael Collins' sweetheart', *Daily Express*, 29 August 1922; *Illustrated Sunday Herald*, 27 August 1922; *Illustrated London News*, 2 September 1922.

165 *The Free State*, 29 August 1922; Forester, *Michael Collins*, p. 344; M. Connolly to Joseph Connolly, n.d., UCDA, FitzGerald papers, P80/340(2/2).

166 A record of over 12,000 words were transmitted on the night of 23–24 August 1922, and over 56,000 in the days that followed, a record from the Oxford to Nova Scotia telegraph, *Manchester Guardian*, 6 September 1922.

167 *Irish Independent*, 16 August 1924; *Westminster Gazette*, 24 August 1922; *Manchester Guardian*, 5 September 1922; for details of day of mourning see *Irish Independent*, 26 August 1922; funeral and day of mourning arrangements, NAI, DT S2,967.

168 The Dublin Building Trade Employers' Federation was reported as deferring a wage reduction for one week out of respect for Collins. *Manchester Guardian*, 25 August 1922.

169 Sir John Lavery, *The Life of a Painter* (London, 1940), p. 217.

170 British Pathé footage captures the crowds waiting to see him lying in state, 'Michael Collins crowds', film id 280.12.

171 British Pathé estimated 'more than half a million mourners', 'Funeral of Michael Collins', film id 280.18; '800,000 at Funeral of Michael Collins' was the *Daily Mirror* headline, 29 August 1922; *Manchester Guardian*, 26 August 1922; *Evening Herald*, 28 August 1922; *Sunday Independent*, 25 August 1946; *The Separatist*, 2 September 1922.

172 Patrick McCartan, quoted in Cronin, *The McGarrity papers*, p. 123.

8: Collins's Afterlives

1 Louis D'Alton, *This Other Eden* (Dublin, 1954), II:2, p. 45.

2 *The Western People*, 29 August 1931.

3 For de Valera's conditions see Coogan, *Michael Collins*, pp. 429–30.

4 For the saga of the Cenotaph on Leinster Lawn, see Anne Dolan, *Commemorating the Irish Civil War: History and Memory, 1923–2000* (Cambridge, 2003), chapter 1.

5 For the erection of the wooden cross see *Cork Examiner*, 22 June 1923; for speeches at the unveiling of the cross at Béal na mBláth see *Cork Examiner, Irish Independent, Freeman's Journal* 23 August 1924, *An t-Óglách*, 2:15 (30 August 1924), pp. 10–13.

6 Timothy Healy to Richard Mulcahy, 22 February 1923, UCDA, Blythe papers, P24/152(4).

7 For the long-drawn-out financial wranglings see NAI, Department of Finance (DF), s004/0264/24 & DF s005/0057/24.

8 Memo by D. O'Sullivan, Army Finance Office, 18 August 1924, NAI, DF, s004/0013/24.

9 Department of Finance memo, May 1931, NAI, DF, s004/0013/24; Islandbridge memorial, NAI, DT S4,156b. For reasons why the £25,000 was never fully spent see David Fitzpatrick, 'Commemoration in the Irish Free State: a chronicle of embarrassment' in Ian McBride (ed.), *History and Memory in Modern Ireland* (Cambridge, 2001), pp. 191–2.

10 See Keith Jeffery, *Ireland and the Great War* (Cambridge, 2000), pp. 115–25.

11 Seán Lester to the Executive Council, 3 July 1924, NAI, DT S3,913.

12 Secretary to the President to Richard Mulcahy, 23 February 1923, NAI, DE/5/83.

13 Seán Lester to the Executive Council, 3 July 1924, NAI, DT S3,913.

14 *One Million Dubliners* (2014), directed by Aoife Kelleher.

15 Dolan, *Commemorating the Irish Civil War*, pp. 172–94.

16   For some interesting views on de Valera's treatment of Collins's memory see Coogan, *Michael Collins*, chapter 13 'Honouring the dead?'.

17   Ceremonial – commemoration ceremony – General Michael Collins, MAI, Department of Defence, 3/6427; Memo by N.S. Ó Nualláin to the Taoiseach, 10 July 1951, NAI, DT S5,734D.

18   Ceremonial – commemoration ceremony – General Michael Collins, MAI, Department of Defence, 3/6427; Anniversary of the death of Michael Collins – army or government participation in annual ceremony at Béal na mBláth, NAI, DT S15,136A.

19   Dolan, *Commemorating the Irish Civil War*, p. 194.

20   *General Michael Collins 1922–1972* (Cork, n.d.), p. 6.

21   Summed up in the comment in 1996 that 'against the background of the Northern conflict, Beal na Bla [*sic*] orators … have been doing some fancy footwork to deflect attention from Collins the man of violence, asking us rather to consider Collins the administrator and the man of ideas.' *Sunday Independent*, 25 August 1996.

22   IRA commemoration ceremony at Benbulben mountain, County Sligo, report of Chief Superintendent Seán Liddy, 26 September 1940 & 2 October 1942; report of Superintendent Peter Fahy, 26 September 1944, 21 September 1945 & 1 October 1946, NAI, Department of Justice, DJ Jus8/865.

23   Deirdre McMahon, *Irish Times*, 22 October 2005.

24   Hart, *Mick*, p. vii.

25   Peter Hart (ed.), *British Intelligence in Ireland, 1920–21: The Final Reports* (Cork, 2002), p. 13.

26   Regan, 'Looking at Mick again', p. 22 & p. 17; Regan, 'Michael Collins: the legacy and the intestacy', p. 118.

27   See 'Introduction: the story of Michael Collins', Hart, *Mick*, pp. xiii-xxi.

28   See most explicitly the subtitle of Hart's biography *Mick: The Real Michael Collins*.

29   *Times of India*, 30 December 1939.

30   *Jezebel* (1938), directed by William Wyler; William Murphy, 'George Brent' in McGuire and Quinn (eds), *Dictionary of Irish Biography*, I, pp. 820–1.

31   *Beloved Enemy* (1936), directed by H.C. Potter.

32   Talbot, *Michael Collins' Own Story*; Béaslaí, *Michael Collins*.

33   Béaslaí to McDunphy, 26 October 1922, NAI, DT S1,760a.

34   Béaslaí to Eamon Duggan, 3 November 1922, NAI, *ibid*.

35   Seán Collins to W.T. Cosgrave, 7 November 1922, *ibid*; Publicity Department to Béaslaí, 31 October 1922, NLI, Béaslaí papers, Ms 33,930 (14).

36   Cosgrave to Joe McGrath, 15 March 1924, NAI, DT S1,760a.

37   Dolan, *Commemorating the Irish Civil War*, pp. 73–5.

38   Diamuid Lynch, New York, to Béaslaí, 7 August 1925, NLI, Béaslaí papers, Ms 33,930 (4).

39   For reviews and advertisements of Béaslaí's book see: *Times of India*, 17 December 1926, 9 June 1927; *The North China Herald*, 14 August 1926; *The Observer*, 14 November 1926. For notice of the serialisation of Béaslaí's book see *Manchester Guardian*, 26 July 1926 & 23 August 1926; newspapers and fan mail; *The Path to Freedom*; Review of *The Path to Freedom*, *Manchester Guardian*, 27 January 1923; Frank O'Connor's *The Big Fellow* was also widely reviewed. See, for example, *The Catholic Press*, Sydney, 22 July 1937. Rex Taylor's book was also reviewed in the *Times of India*, 9 November 1958.

40   Peter Hart, 'How did he get it? How did he use it?', *The Dublin Review*, 20 (Autumn 2005), p. 26.

41   Foster, *Vivid faces*, p. 292.

42 *Ibid.* Béaslaí's diary had been damning as well: 'Again and again I wonder how she attracted Michael. I can discern in her no brains, no beauty, no charm of manner.' See Deirdre McMahon, '"A worthy monument to a great man": Piaras Béaslaí's life of Michael Collins', *Bullán*, 2:2 (Winter/Spring 1996), p. 59.

43 Flanagan, *Remembering the Revolution*, p. 41.

44 Piaras Béaslaí, *Michael Collins: Soldier and Statesman* (Dublin, 1937).

45 Frank Pakenham, *Peace by Ordeal: The Negotiations of the Anglo-Irish Treaty* (London, 1935).

46 Macardle, *The Irish Republic*; Flanagan, *Remembering the Revolution*, p. 38.

47 Frank O'Connor, *The Big Fellow: A Life of Michael Collins* (London & New York, 1937).

48 Batt O'Connor, *With Michael Collins in the Fight for Irish Independence* (London, 1929); H.V. Morton, *In Search of Ireland* (2nd ed., London, 2000), p. 21.

49 Morton, *op. cit.*, p. 21.

50 *Ibid.*, pp. 20–1.

51 Frank O'Connor, *The Big Fellow* (5th ed., Dublin, 1996), p. 10.

52 *Ibid.*, p. 214.

53 Frank O'Connor, *The Big Fellow: Michael Collins and the Irish Revolution* (2nd ed., London, 1965).

54 *This Other Eden*, directed by Muriel Box and produced by Emmet Dalton, was released in 1959. It was based on a play of the same title by Louis D'Alton (Dublin, 1954).

55 *This Other Eden* (1959), directed by Muriel Box.

56 *Ibid.*

57 Rex Taylor, *Michael Collins* (London, 1958) (2nd ed., London, 1961, reprints 1963, 1964), (3rd ed., London, 1970); Margery Forester, *Michael Collins: The Lost Leader* (London, 1971).

58 Forester published a paperback edition in 1972. Gill & Macmillan also published an edition in 1989. León Ó Broin, *Michael Collins* (Dublin, 1980). It was reprinted in 1983, 1987 and again in 1991. Tim Pat Coogan, *Michael Collins: A Biography* (London, 1990). There have been many reprints, and a 2015 edition by Arrow books.

59 See for example, John M. Feehan, *The Shooting of Michael Collins* (Cork, 1981) (reprinted 1981, 2nd ed., Cork, 1982, reprinted 1987, 1988, 1989) (3rd ed., Cork, 1991); T. Ryle Dwyer, *Michael Collins and the Treaty: His Differences With De Valera* (Dublin, c. 1981); Dwyer also published a German translation of one his Collins books as *Michael Collins: biografie* (1997); Meda Ryan, *The Day Michael Collins Was Shot* (Swords, 1989); T. Ryle Dwyer, *Michael Collins: 'The Man Who Won the War'* (Cork, 1990); Patrick J. Twohig, *The Dark Secret of Béalnabláth* (Cork, 1991), (further editions 1991, 1995, 1997); James Mackay, *Michael Collins: A Life* (Edinburgh, 1996); Meda Ryan, *Michael Collins and the Women in His Life* (Cork, 1996); Justin Nelson, *Michael Collins: The Final Days* (Kilkenny, 1997); T. Ryle Dwyer, *Big Fellow, Long Fellow: A Joint Biography of Collins and de Valera* (Dublin, 1998); Chrissy Osborne, *Michael Collins: Himself* (Cork, 2003) & (Cork, 2015); T. Ryle Dwyer, *The Squad and the Intelligence Operations of Michael Collins* (Cork, 2005); T. Ryle Dwyer, *'I signed my death warrant': Michael Collins and the Treaty* (Cork, 2006); Meda Ryan, *Michael Collins and the Women Who Spied for Ireland* (Cork & Dublin, 2006); Michael Foy, *Michael Collins's Intelligence War: The Struggle Between the British and the IRA, 1919–1921* (Stroud, 2006) (2nd ed. 2008); Chrissy Osborne, *Michael Collins: A Life in Pictures* (Cork, 2007); S.M. Sigerson, *The Assassination of Michael Collins* (2009) (reprints in 2013 & 2014); T. Ryle Dwyer, *Michael Collins and the Civil War* (Cork, 2012).

60 Mary Banotti, 'Introduction', and Lee, 'The challenge of a Collins biography' in Doherty and Keogh (eds), *Michael Collins*, pp. 17–18 & p. 19.

61 O'Connor, *With Michael Collins in the Fight for Irish Independence*; David Neligan, *The Spy in the Castle* (London, 1999; 1st ed., 1968), p. 7.

62 Seán Moylan to Florence O'Donoghue, n.d., NLI, O'Donoghue papers, Ms 31,421 (15), quoted in Michael Hopkinson, 'Review article: biography of the revolutionary period Michael Collins and Kevin Barry', *Irish Historical Studies*, xxviii:111 (May 1993), p. 312.

63 Barry, *Guerilla Days in Ireland*, p. 185.

64 *Cork Examiner*, 19 April 1965.

65 Ernie O'Malley, *The Singing Flame* (Dublin, 1992; 1st ed. 1978), p. 285.

66 Brennan, *Allegiance*, pp. 152–3.

67 See Flanagan, *Remembering the Revolution*.

68 See Risteárd Mulcahy, 'Michael Collins and the making of a new Ireland', *Studies*, 67:267 (Autumn, 1978), pp. 187–200; Roy Foster estimates that his commentary on the book was over 400 pages long. Foster, *Vivid faces*, p. 293.

69 O'Hegarty, *The Victory of Sinn Féin*.

70 Flanagan, *Remembering the Revolution*, p. 99

71 O'Hegarty, *The Victory of Sinn Féin*, p. 99.

72 *Ibid.*, p. 38.

73 *Ibid.*, p. 100.

74 Elizabeth, Countess of Fingall, *Seventy Years Young: Memories of Elizabeth, Countess of Fingall Told to Pamela Hinkson* (Dublin, 1991), p. 410; Gogarty, *As I Was Going Down Sackville Street*, p. 195.

75 Pihl, *Signe Toksvig's Irish Diaries 1926–1937*, p. 376.

76 Douglas V. Duff, *Sword for Hire: The Saga of a Modern Free Companion* (London, 1934), pp. 78–81; Duff, *May the Winds Blow!*, pp. 79–81.

77 Coverage of Birkenhead's death as far afield as India mentioned anecdotes of Collins, *Times of India*, 2 October 1930. See also Birkenhead, *Frederick Edwin Earl of Birkenhead*; Eleanor Smith, *Life's a Circus* (London, 1940).

78 Jones, *Lloyd George*; Wilson (ed.), *The Political Diaries of C.P. Scott*; Lord Riddell, *Lord Riddell's Intimate*; *The Argus* (Melbourne), 15 January 1949.

79 See, for example, Sir Charles Petrie (ed.), *The Life and Letters of the Right Hon. Sir Austen Chamberlain* (London, 1940; Robert C. Self (ed.), *The Austen Chamberlain Diary Letters* (Cambridge, 1995); Ramsden (ed.), *Real Old Tory Politics*.

80 Crozier, *Ireland For Ever*. Crozier, who had resigned as head of the Auxiliaries, found it very difficult to get employment and later sought work from the Irish Free State. Macready, *Annals of an Active Life*.

81 Hart, *Mick*, p. 350.

82 Churchill, *The Collected Works of Sir Winston Churchill*, p. 336 & p. 349.

83 *Ibid.*, p. 348; The comment was attributed to Hazel Lavery, E. to Churchill, n.d., CA, Churchill papers, CHAR 22/14/56.

84 Quoted in Peter Clarke, *Mr Churchill's Profession: Statesman, Orator, Writer* (London, 2012), p. xiv.

85 John Anderson to Churchill, 29 November 1928, CA, Churchill papers, CHAR 8/217/143.

86 Lionel Curtis to Churchill, 17 November 1928, CA, Churchill papers, CHAR 8/217.

87 Churchill to Curtis, 27 December 1928, Bod., Curtis papers, Ms 89.fp. 76–83.

88 W.T. Cosgrave's comments on the draft, n.d., UCDA, Hayes papers, P53/222(160).

89 W.T. Cosgrave, 'Michael Collins', J.R.H. Weaver (ed.), *Dictionary of National Biography 1922–1930* (Oxford, 1937), pp. 199–201; see Dolan, *Commemorating the Irish Civil War*, pp. 105–10.

90 Béaslaí managed to get the *Sunday Express* banned in September 1922, *Daily Express*, 9 September 1922; on Béaslaí and O'Faoláin see Flanagan, *Remembering the Revolution*, p. 41.

91 Mulcahy, *Richard Mulcahy*, p. 94.

92 Quoted in Diarmaid Ferriter, *Occasions of Sin: Sex and Society in Modern Ireland* (London, 2009), p. 93; Constantine Fitzgibbon, *High Heroic* (London, 1969), p. 15.

93 *Times of India*, 8 August 1933; see Dolan, *Commemorating the Irish Civil War*, chapter 5.

94 Lee, 'The challenge of a Collins biography', p. 20.

95 *Seanad Éireann Debates*, 23:12 (25 October 1939); 96:5 (20 October 1981).

96 For example, see statements in the Dáil on the 'Joint declaration of peace in Northern Ireland', *Dáil Éireann Debates*, 437:3 (15 December 1993).

97 Northern Ireland, see, for example, *Financial Times*, 31 December 1994, 23. December 1995, 13 February 1996, 8 December 1997

98 Brian Lenihan's speech, 22 August 2010 (www.finance.gov.ie/ga/news-centre/speeches/former-ministers/michael-collins-commemoration-beal-na-mblath-address-minister) (viewed on 15 July 2016).

99 *Irish Times*, 17 October 2013.

100 An Taoiseach, Enda Kenny, Béal na mBláth speech, 19 August 2012. His error was quickly corrected on the copy of the speech on the Department of An Taoiseach's web page; see for example 'Kenny spins his old guff at Beal na Blah Blah Blah', *Sunday Independent*, 26 August 2012.

101 Speech by Leo Varadkar, 14 November 2017 (www.finegael.ie/speech-taoiseach-leo-varadkar-leader-fine-gael/) (viewed on 6 December 2017).

102 *Irish Independent*, 16 August 1924.

103 *Michael Collins – A Musical Drama* (written & directed by Bryan Flynn), first performed in Cork in 2006; *Munster Express*, 17 July 2008.

104 Staged by the Kilkenny Musical Society at the Watergate Theatre, Kilkenny, April 2014 (www.thejournal.ie/life-size-posters-of-michael-collins-promoting-upcoming-play-stolen-during-the-night-1380935-Mar2014/) (viewed on 12 February 2016).

105 See, for example, www.generalmichaelcollins.com/; http://sarasmichaelcollinssite.com/ (viewed on 15 July 2016).

106 See, for example, www.cafepress.co.uk/+michael-collins+gifts; www.redbubble.com/shop/michael+collins (viewed on 15 July 2016).

107 For details of Michael Collins tours see www.michaelcollinscentre.com/ (viewed on 15 July 2016); the Michael Collins House Museum was opened in April 2016 http://thecork.ie/2016/04/28/michael-collins-house-museum-opens-in-clonakilty-west-cork/ (viewed on 15 July 2016).

108 See Diarmaid Ferriter, 'Trading history: auction houses trumpet Irish "independence sales"', *Irish Times*, 26 October 2014, www.irishtimes.com/culture/heritage/trading-history-auction-houses-trumpet-irish-independence-sales-1.1976120 (viewed on 24 February 2016).

109 See, for example, *Irish Times*, 6 April 2011; http://whytes.ie/i6.asp?Auction=20090314 (viewed on 11 February 2016).

110 The Bible and revolver were sold on 14 March 2009 at Whyte's auction house, http://whytes.ie/i6.asp?Auction=20090314 (viewed on 12 February 2016).

111 *Irish Examiner*, 25 July 2013; www.irishexaminer.com/ireland/buttons-in-collinss-pocket-sell-for-5k-237844.html (viewed on 12 February 2016).

112 *Irish Times*, 18 April 2012.

113 *Nottingham Evening Post*, 4 May 1923.

114 'Collins film epic hits £3m record – all time Irish box office record', *Irish Times*, 4 December 1996; *Irish Times*, 3 November 1996.

115 *Financial Times*, 2 September 1996.

116 *Schindler's List* (1993), directed by Steven Spielberg; *Rob Roy* (1995), directed by Michael Caton-Jones; *Robin Hood: Prince of Thieves* (1991), directed by Kevin Reynolds; *Die Hard* (1988), directed by John McTiernan.

117 *Irish Independent*, 23 August 2002.

118 Dolan, *Commemorating the Irish Civil War*, p. 97.

119 See www.discoverireland.ie/Activities-Adventure/the-michael-collins-drive-wicklow/12865 (viewed on 15 July 2016).

120 See www.facebook.com/MichaelCollinsAdventures/; https://mobile.twitter.com/micksadventures (viewed on 15 July 2016). In 2013 they applied, but failed to win, an Arthur Guinness Project arts bursary: Collins was almost post-modern too. www.arthurguinnessprojects.com/arts/michael-collins-adventures (viewed on 23 July 2013).

121 Cecil Day Lewis, *The Whispering Roots and Other Poems* (New York, 1970); Denis Devlin, 'The tomb of Michael Collins', in J.C.C. Mays (ed.), *Collected Poems of Denis Devlin* (Dublin, 1989), pp. 283–5; Tom Paulin, *All the Way to the Empire Ballroom*, Radio 4, 1994; Seamus Heaney, *Electric Light* (London, 2001); Sebastian Barry, *Plays I* (London, 1997); Jane Purcell, *Cooking for Michael Collins*, Radio 4, *Financial Times*, 9 January 2006; Mary Kenny, *Allegiance* (Dublin, 2005). The play was performed in Edinburgh in August 2006. For review of the Edinburgh performance in 2006 see *Financial Times*, 11 August 2006; Roddy Doyle, *A Star Called Henry* (London, 1999); Dermot McEvoy, *Terrible Angel: A Novel of Michael Collins in New York* (Guilford, Conn., 2002).

122 Gerry Hunt, *At war with the empire* (Dublin, 2012); for Mick O'Dea's work see https://mickodea.carbonmade.com/ (viewed on 15 July 2016); Vincent McDonnell, *Michael Collins: most wanted man* (Cork, 2008); Gerard Whelan, *A winter of spies* (Dublin, 1998); Gavin Friday, *Catholic* (Rubyworks, 2011). The cover recreates the portrait of Collins lying in state. For the making of the art work for the album cover see http://gavinfriday.com/discography/album-catholic/album-cover-video/ (viewed on 15 July 2016).

123 David Puttnam asked Jordan to write a Collins script, but Warners did not wish to make it. See *Irish Times*, 17 Mar. 2016; on Cimino and Costner, see Eoghan Harris, *Sunday Independent*, 28 Oct. 2012; on Robert Redford see RTÉ, 30 January 2009 at www.rte.ie/entertainment/2008/0712/413966-redfordr/ (viewed on 15 July 2016). Other Collins-inspired works include a musical score 'The big fellow' by Leo Maguire; a play by the writer of Rab C. Nesbitt, Ian Pattison entitled 'A terrible beauty', *The Herald*, 2 September 2014.

124 *Irish Times*, 31 December 2010; *Irish Independent*, 25 March 2011.

125 'Big Fella's love letters on show', *Irish Independent*, 6 June 1998; on Norris see *Irish Times*, 8 October 2012; Diarmaid Ferriter, 'In such deadly earnest', *The Dublin Review*, 12 (Autumn 2003), p. 60.

126 Hart, *Mick*, p. xix.

127 According to Coogan she sent a draft to Batt O'Connor, who showed it to Liam Tobin and Frank Thornton, who sent her a death threat. Coogan, *Michael Collins*, p. 286; Pihl (ed.), *Signe Toksvig's Irish diaries*, p. 317; *Irish Times*, 4 April 2007.

128 Notes in Sean O'Mahony papers, NLI, Ms 44,104/7.

129 See, for example, *Irish Times*, 15 June 1995, 17 January 1997; see Ryan, *Michael Collins and the Women in His Life*; McCoole, *Hazel*.

130 See Ó Broin, *In Great Haste*.

131 *Irish Times*, 22 October 2005.

132 For details of the Lavery portrait Kitty Kiernan kept see Dolan, *Commemorating the Irish Civil War*, p. 78; for the button see Mackay, *Michael Collins*, p. 278; for the shamrock, which was kept in an envelope labelled 'where Michael fell', see McCoole, *Hazel*, p. 101; for the lock of hair see Ryan, *The Day Michael Collins Was Shot*, p. 121. O'Reilly began using Collins's room at Portobello, NAI, Department of Finance, DF f200/16/24. O'Reilly could not afford the £22-2-10 ½ cost he was asked to pay. The furniture was later bought by Collins's sister, Margaret, for £18-9-1. Report of christening of Dalton's son, *Freeman's Journal*, 17 December 1923. Kitty Kiernan christened her son Michael Collins Cronin. Bishop Fogarty was sent Collins's 'writing cabinet' as a gift, NLI, Collins Jr papers, Ms 40,420 (16).

133 *Irish Times*, 31 January 2000; National Army Museum, 'Enemy commanders: Britain's greatest foes', www.nam.ac.uk/exhibitions/online-exhibitions/enemy-commanders-britains-greatest-foes (viewed on 10 February 2015).

134 Elizabeth, Countess of Fingall, *Seventy Years Young*, p. 429.

Conclusion

1   Cathal O'Shannon, *Dáil Éireann Debates*, 1:2 (11 September 1922), col. 79.

2   W.T. Cosgrave, 'Statement by the President', *Dáil Éireann Debates*, 1:2 (11 September 1922), col. 69 & 77.

3   Cathal O'Shannon, *ibid.*, col. 79.

4   Lee, *Ireland 1912–1985*, pp. 63–4.

5   Regan, *The Irish Counter-revolution*, p. 78; Regan, 'Michael Collins – the legacy and the intestacy', p. 125.

6   Regan, *Myth and the Irish State*, p. 135.

7   Liam de Róiste's diary, 29 November 1922, quoted in Laffan, *Judging W.T. Cosgrave*, p. 116 & p. 156.

8   See letter from M. McManus possibly to John Devoy, 31 August 1922, NLI, Devoy papers, Ms 18,007 (34).

9   James A. Burke quoted in Regan, *The Irish Counter-revolution*, p. 85; *Dáil Éireann Official Report: Debate on the Treaty*, Kevin O'Higgins, 19 December 1921, p. 45; Mulcahy, *Richard Mulcahy (1886–1971): A Family Memoir*, p. 110.

10 Regan, *The Irish Counter-revolution*, p. 78.

11 See Regan, *The Irish Counter-revolution*, p. 80; Lynch, *The northern IRA*, pp. 193–5; McGarry, *Eoin O'Duffy*, pp. 112–13; Cronin, *The McGarrity Papers*, p. 123.

12 Hart, *Mick*, pp. 423–4.

13 *Ibid.*, p. 425.

14 Hayes, 'Michael Collins', p. 282.

15 Mark Mazower, *Dark Continent: Europe's Twentieth Century* (London, 1998), p. 5.

16 Lee, 'The challenge of a Collins biography', p. 37.

17 *Times of India*, 28 December 1925.

18 John Le Carré, *Tinker, Tailor, Soldier, Spy* (New York, 1974), p. 377.

19 Hart, *Mick*, p. 423.

20 Statement by Colonel Charles Russell, 10 May 1924, UCDA, Mulcahy papers, P7/C/20.

Picture Credits

The Board of Trinity College Dublin

p. 69	OLS Samuels Box 4_313
p. 169	OLS Samuels Box 2pt3_117
p. 192	OLS Samuels Box 4_021
p. 336	OLS Samuels Box 4_317

British Library & *Birmingham Daily Gazette*

p. 286	*Birmingham Daily Gazette* 24 August 1922

British Pathé

p. 209	Film id 270.31
p. 225	Film id 250.08
p. 227	Film id 248.40
p. 284	Film id 280.12

Churchill Archives Centre, The Papers of Sir Winston Churchill

p. 311	CHAR 22/14/56
p. 312	CHAR 8/217/143

Daily Express/N&S Syndication

p. 211	*Daily Express* 17 March 1921

David Low/Solo Syndication, British Cartoon Archive

p. 217	LSE 6649

Getty Images (Carl Mydans, the Life Picture Collection)

p. 317	50416572

Imperial War Museum

p. 67	IWM PST 5044
p. 321	EPH 7941

Hugh Lane Gallery

p. 287	Reg.751

Library of Congress

p. 48	LC-USZC4-10971

London Transport Museum Collection

p. 23	1998/75408
p. 25	1983/355

Mercier Press Cork

p. 111	

Military Archives of Ireland

p. 49	BMH CD152
p. 63	CP-41-001
p. 108	IE/MA/CP/5/2/20(xxix)
p. 136	IE-MA-ACPS-GPN-078
p. 156	MA_057_042
p. 242	MA_057_030
p. 254	DP23755

Museum of London

p. 39	LIB5333/MH7a

The National Archives, London

p. 14	Co904/196/65
p. 15	Co904/196/65
p. 29	CSC 11/63
pp. 54–55	Co904/196/65
p. 80	Co904/196/65
p. 137	Co904/196/65
pp. 138–9	Co904/196/65

National Archives of Ireland

p. 61	DE/2/530
p. 91	DE/2/530
p. 97	DE/2/244
p. 147	DE/2/530
p. 148	DE/2/530
p. 157	DE/4/5/7
pp. 184–5	DT S595
p. 193	DE/2/443

p. 198	DT S9,241
p. 212	DE/2/326
p. 219	DE/5/2/35
p. 281	DT S1,628
p. 296	DT S3,913
pp. 304–5	DT S1,760A

National Library of Ireland

p. ii	HOG140
p. xii	INDH398
p. 3	Ms 11,409/4/4
p. 6	HOGW126
p. 8	Ms 5,848
pp. 10–11	NPA POLF32
p. 13	INDH403
p. 20	INDH396
p. 22	L_IMP_3248
pp. 30–31	Ms 33,929(15)
p. 36	EPH G11
p. 38	Ms 13,329(4)
p. 56	Ms 23,469
p. 57	Ms 24,387
p. 71	HOGW 59
p. 79	EPH F306
p. 81	ILB 300 p5 [item 75]
p. 82	ILB 300 p12 [item 77]
p. 83	NPA POLF4
p. 88	PD3064TX(A)
p. 92	NPA POLF20
p. 94	BEA10
p. 102	EPH C184
p. 113	PD4309TX139
p. 115	HOGW 118
p. 116	Ms 22,613
p. 120	HOGW 117
pp. 126–7	Ms 17,424/2/7
p. 133	NPA POLF45
p. 135	ILB 300 p5 [item 7]
pp. 142–3	MS 5,848
p. 144	MS 17,090
p. 146	EPH E2
p. 149	MS 8,426/2
p. 159	NPA CIVP4
p. 163	EPH F27
p. 164	Ms 17,424/2/4
p. 165	ILB 300 p8[item 85]
p. 170	HOGW 65

p. 171	EPH D22
p. 176	Ms 35,823/5/14/10
p. 175	PD GREE-AL(i) II
p. 181	EPH G18
p. 183	OPIE R/10/8
p. 186	HOG 226
p. 197	EPH F236
pp. 202–4	Ms 49,618
p. 205	Album 472
p. 215	HOGW 141
p. 220	INDH397
p. 221	Ms 22,779
p. 228	Ms 33,916(1)
p. 231	Ms 33,915(7)
pp. 232–3	Ms 33,916(1)
p. 239	ILB 300 p13 [item 124]
p. 240	PD3060TX
p. 243	PD2159TX
p. 251	Ms 48,281(6)
p. 252	PD C86
p. 262	Ms 43,556(2)
p. 265	Ms 46,687(2)
pp. 272–3	Ms 17,489(4)
p. 275	EPH D112
p. 276	Ms 17,654/3/2
p. 279	PD 4309 TX 145
p. 280	INDH319
p. 283	Ms 33,929(15)
p. 294	Ms 40,422(18)
p. 297	BEA84
pp. 300–1	NPA POLF47
p. 307	Ms 49,667
p. 315	EPH F43
p. 320	Ms 33,930(16)
p. 323	EPH C47
pp. 324–5	Ms 41,780
p. 327	HOGW 8
p. 331	INDH 401
p. 332	HOGW 135
p. 335	INDH 400A
p. 339	Ms 18,001/12/2
p. 340	Ms 18,001/12/8
p. 341	Ms 11,374/19/8
pp. 342–3	NPA POLF28
Jacket –	front: NPA POLF30;
	back: HOGW 59;
	spine: NPA CEA132

National Museum of Ireland

p. vii	HE: EW 5720
p. 62	HE: EWL 227.8
pp. 64–65	HE: EW 1351
p. 66	HE: EW 370
p. 78	HE: EW 3804
p. 101	No reference available
p. 124	NMI 3052
p. 158	HE: EW 722(a)
p. 248	HE: EW 3059
p. 259	HE: EW 3057
p. 291	HE: EW 5024
p. 293	HE: EW 1027(b)

Parliamentary Archives, London

p. 99	LG/F/45/6/39
p. 270	LG/F/26/2/20

Royal Irish Academy

p. 258	P285/307

Royal Mail Group, Courtesy of the Postal Museum

p. 26	POST 118/248

Trinity Mirror Publishing Ltd

p. 236	*Daily Mirror* 24 August 1922

UCD Archives

p. 5	P123/43(1)
p. 32	P123/14(2)
p. 37	P123/25(1)
pp. 44–45	P123/6(4–5)
pp. 46–47	P123/46(1–2)
p. 105	P123/40
p. 121	P80/PH/49
p. 189	P123/42(1)
p. 190	P123/53(1)

Wikimedia Commons

p. 21	https://en.wikipedia.org/wiki/File:Michael_Collins_at_8_years_old.jpg

Index

Note: Pages in *italics* refer to illustrations or captions.

Frongoch camp 51, 58–60, *62*, *66*
funerals, political 74–5, *83*

Gaelic Athletic Association *39*, 40–1, 177
   Geraldines Club 34–5, *38*, 40, 103
   'the ban' 40
Gaelic League 34, *36*, *37*, 60, 68, 173, 174, 177
   Inis Fáil 24, 34–5, *175*
Garvin, Tom 19, 162
Gavan Duffy, George 134, *156*
Gellner, Ernest 33
Glasnevin Cemetery
   grave 292, *294*, 295, *296*, *297*
Gogarty, Oliver St John 98, 260, 264, 309
Good, Joe 28, 42, 68
gossip 4, 12, 98, 208, 210, 213, 214, 222, 224, 226,
   229, 322
grave 292, *294*, 295, *296*, *297*
Griffith, Arthur 28, 73, 86, 87, 89, 92, 130, 132, 141,
   152, 154, 155, *156*, *158*, 161, 182, 216, 226, 257,
   269, 271, 274, 292, 313, 329, 330, *335*, 338

Hales, Sean 60, 247, 263
Hales, Tom *108*, 112, 247, 274
Hankey, Maurice 117
Hart, Peter 2, *7*, 27, 35, 42, 87, 93, 118, 122, 145–50,
   155, 187, 200, 210, 226, *231*, 249, 256, 298, 306,
   322–6, 333, 337
Harte, Pat 160
Hayes, Michael 333
Healy, Tim 155, 263–4
Heaney, Seamus 319
Heffernan, Dr 289–90
Heygate Lambert, F.A. 60
Hickey, John 261
historical analogy 140
historical figures
   comparisons to 1, 326
history, importance of 174
Holland, Dan 261
Holohan, Brendan 278
Hughes, Edwin 278
Hurley, Agnes *259*
Hurley, Denis 250
Hurley, Jim 261, 274
Hutchinson, John 33
Hyde, Douglas 174

hydroelectric power 182

Illustrated Sunday Herald 237, 282
Inis Fáil 24, 34–5, *175*
inspection, tours of 246–7, 256
internet 316
Irish Independent 20, 229
Irish-Ireland ideals 182
   adherence to 33–40, 173–4
   Collin's father, 18
   Gaeltacht 177
   idealising the rural 174–7, 180
   Irish language 34, *37*, 172
Irish Nation League 72, 73
Irish National Aid Association 53–8
Irish National Aid and Volunteer Dependents'
   Fund 7, 51–3, *56*, 60, 68, *71*, 72–7, 174, 200
   merger 53–8
   prisoner aid 52–3
Irish National Relief Fund 52, 60
Irish Party 134, 172, 179, 191, *192*
Irish Relief Fund 52, 53–8
Irish Republican Army 18–19, 90, 93, 109, 112,
   117–18, 151, 210, 247, 257, 264, 292, 298, 338
   anti-Treaty 249, 255, 260, 266, 267, 274, 308
   Northern 194–6, 333
Irish Republican Brotherhood 40–1, 42, 52, 53,
   58, 60, 68, 72, 73, 74, 75, 89, 100, 118, 130, 131,
   134, 140, 150, 151, 152, 177–8, 188, 191, 199,
   200, 333
   President of Supreme Council of 89
   Treasurer 89
Irish Republican Prisoners' Dependents Fund
   71, 75–6, *82*, 131
The Irish Times 98, 326
Irish Volunteer Dependents' Fund 53–8
Irish Volunteers 42, 43, *49*, 52, 59, 60, 68, 74, 76,
   95, 100, *102*, 130, 131, 132, 134, 150

Jeudwine, Hugh 235, 268
jobbery 73–4, 191, *192*, *193*
Jones, Tom 154, 224–6
Jordan, Neil 1, 89–90, 109, 246, 250, 262, 266,
   306, 318–19, *323*, 334–7, 338

Kearney, Jim 267
Kearney, Pete 261

Keating, Michael 266
Kelleher, Denis 117–18
Kelleher, Tom 261
Kelly, Denis 73, 200
Kenny, Enda 316
Kenny, Mary 200, 319
Kettle, Tom 278
Kiernan, Kitty 200, *202–4*, 226, *236*, 238, 264,
　　282, *283*, 302, 322, *324*, 326
Kissane, Bill 177, 196, 268
Kivlehan, Alphonsus 73
Kostick, Conor 188

Laffan, Michael 145, 196, 199
Lavery, Hazel *311*, 322, *324*
Lavery, John *287*, 290, *291*
Lawrence, T.E. 229, 310
Le Carré, John 337
Lea Wilson, Percival 107
leadership 1, 110, 118–19, 122–3
Lee, J.J. 199, 249, 250, 255, 306, 314, 334
Lehane, Sean 277
Lenihan, Brian 314–16
Leonard, Joe 109
libel 263
Liberty League 72
Lindsay, Mrs 106–7
Llewelyn Davies, Moya 322, *324–5*
Lloyd George, David 98, 117, 152, 154–5, *158*, 162,
　　217, 222–3, 238, 269, *270*, 310
Loch, Sydney 222
Logue, Cardinal 134
London 19–24, 28, *30–1*, 33–43, *48*, *49*, 100, 177
Low, David *217*, 218
Lucid, Richard 261
Lutyens, Sir Edwin 295
Lynch, Diarmuid 68, 131
Lynch, Fionán 68, 131
Lynch, Liam 266, 274–7, 308
Lynch, Michael 140
Lynch, Robert 194
Lyons, Denis 27, 29

Macardle, Dorothy 274, 302
Macartney, W.H.S. 229
McCabe, Alec 76
McCan, Pierce 75

McCartan, Patrick 278
MacCarthy, Liam 40
McCarthy, Myra 68
McCormack, John *293*
McCormack, Kate 93–5
McCullough, Denis 132
Mac Curtain, Tomás 112
MacDonagh, Joe 132, 150
MacDonagh, Thomas 28
McDonnell, Mick 109
McDonnell, Vincent 319
Mac Dubhghaill, Cathal *66*
McEntee, Harry *275*
MacEntee, Máire 278
MacEoin, Seán *71*, 117, 122, 123
McEvoy, Dermot 319
McGarry, Fearghal 24, 27, 196
McGrath, Joe 255
McGuinness, Frank 73
McGuinness, Joe 72–3
McGuinness, Martin 314
McKee, Dick 93, 109
McKenna, Bill 264
Mackey, Anthony 74
MacNeill, Eoin 140, 174
MacNie, Isa *158*
McPeak, Jock 257, 260, 266–7
Macready, Nevil 123, 222, 223, 271, 310, 313
MacSwiney, Annie *276*
MacSwiney, Mary 180
MacSwiney, Terence 24, 117, 145, *276*
Maguire, Sam 40, 41, 42, 43, 100, 122
Manchester Guardian 214, 223, 234, 302, 310
Mann, Thomas 18
Markievicz, Countess Constance *88*, 237
Marsh, Edward 223, *311*
martial law 93
masculinity 23–4, 132, 155, 226, 319–20
Mason, Sinéad 256, *307*
Mellows, Liam *315*
memoirs
　　appearances in Irish 306–8
　　of British forces and politicians 310
　　offers for 226–9, 230
　　see also biography
memorials 292–5, *327*
　　see also commemorations

merchandise 316, *321*
Michael Collins (Neil Jordan, director) 1, 89–90, 109, 246, 250, *262*, 266, 306, 318–19, 323, 334–7, 338
military acumen 246, 250–5
Minister (Secretary) of Finance 140–1, 150, 191
mobbed 224
moderation 134–40, *142–3*
Molloy, Patrick 93
Moloney, Con 274
Moore, Maurice 58
Moran, D.P. 173–4
Morning Post 214, 223, 234–5, *240*
Morton, H.V. 226, 302–3
Moylan, Seán *115*, 308
Mulcahy, Richard 19, 60, 75, 90, 92, 109, 123, 134, 140, 161, 162, 196, 278, 308–9, 314, 333
Murphy, Fintan 59
Murphy, Larry 266
Murphy, Michael 59
museum 316
music: album cover 319
musical drama 316
Mydans, Carl *317*

Nankivell, J.M. 222
nationalism 27, 33–43, 172, 177, 187
nationality, conception of 172–3, 174–7, 179–80
Neenan, Connie 112
Neeson, Eoin 261
Neeson, Liam 246, 318–19
Neligan, David 308
News of the World 208, 214
newspapers 210–24, 226, 229–41, 316
  death of MC 234–5, *236*, 249, 250, *251*, *252*, 282
  see also individual newspapers
Nicholls, George 191
Nolan, Seán 145
Norris, David 319
northern Catholics and nationalists, defence of 122
northern constituencies: candidates in 1918 general election 134, 194
Northern Ireland 114, 119, 122, 125, 155, 298, 314, 330, 334
  Craig-Collins pacts 194
  election to parliament (1921) 194, *197*

policy on 194–6, *198*
northern unionists 134, 194
Nunan, Seán 110

Oberon, Merle 245
O'Brien, Art *36*, 60, 76, 150–1, 160
Ó Broin, León 306
O'Connell, Daniel 140
O'Connell, Sean 250, 278
O'Connor, Batt 130, 168, 303, 308, 322
O'Connor, Frank 2, 119, 125, 134, 145, 151, 155, 172, 180, 224, 274, 302, 303
O'Connor, James *142*
O'Connor, Rory 118, *315*
O'Connor, T.P. *217*
O'Connor, V.L. *175*
O'Daly, Paddy 107, 109
O'Dea, Mick 319
O'Doherty, Kitty 76
O'Donoghue, Daithí 140
O'Donoghue, Florence 125, 247, 249, 255, 261–3, 308
O'Donoghue, Fr 264
O'Donovan, Con *57*
O'Duffy, Eoin 19, 123, 196, 314, 333
O'Faoláin, Seán 90, 302, 313
O'Gara, Ronan 319
O'Hegarty, Diarmuid 19, 68
O'Hegarty, P.S. 24, 34–5, 40, 41, 42, 90, *113*, 122, 173, 309
O'Hegarty, Seán 24
O'Herlihy, Bill 172
O'Higgins, Kevin 145, *159*, 191, 249, 292, 313, 333
O'Kelly, J.J. 173–4
O'Kelly, Seán T. 161
O'Leary, Jeremiah 42
O'Malley, Ernie 89, 119, 274, 277, 308
O'Mara, Stephen 73
Ó Murthuile, Seán 95
O'Neill, Sonny 246, 260, 267–8
Oranmore and Browne, Lord 235
O'Reilly, Joe 256, 278, 326
O'Reilly, 'Skinner' 110
organisational skills 7, 118, 130, 141
O'Riley, Harold William 271
O'Shannon, Cathal 264, 266, 329–30
O'Shiel, Kevin 196

socialism 187, 188
The Spectator 235
The Squad 107, 109–10, 145, 278, 337–8
Stack, Austin 131, 132, 150, *272–3*
Stafford prison 58, *63*, *64–5*
Staines, Michael 60, 68, 73, 75, 76, 132, 191
stamps *186*
Stanley, Edward 269
The Star 217, 218
stockbroking 33, 42, 214
Stopford Green, Alice 174, *175*
Strachey, John St Loe 235
Strickland, General 106
Stuart, Francis 274
Sturgis, Mark 153
Sunday Chronicle 302
Sunday Express 229, 230, 237, 263
Sunday Independent 266, 278
Sunday Pictorial 224, 253
Sweeney, Joseph 107
Swindlehurst, J.P. 222

Tailteann Games 295
Talbot, Hayden *xii*, 1, 132, 216, 229, 230, 299, 313
taxation 187
Taylor, Rex 106, 261, 263, 306
This Other Eden 303–6
Thornton, Frank 76, 93, 95–6
tillage 182, 187, 314
The Times of India 182, 187, 218, 224, 245, 299, 334
The Times 214, *215*, 222, 234, 235
Tobin, Liam 95, *111*, 125
Toksvig, Signe 208, 309–10
tourism 319
tours 316
Townshend, Charles 250–3
Traynor, Oscar 68, 253
Treacy, Seán 114, 277
Truce 107, 112, 119, 151, 153, 161

unification 194
United States 141, 229

Varadkar, Leo 316
Villa, Pancho 9, 213

violence 9, 19, 41, 85–125, 177, 194–6, *198*, 249, *336*, 337–8
  attitudes to 103–4, 109–12, 117–18
  defences of 104–9
  and propaganda 112, 117–18
  scale 112
  sense of victimhood 112–14
  terror 117
von Lettow-Vorbeck, P.E. 104

Wall, Seán 145
Walsh, Ed 168
Walton, Martin 277–8
War of Independence 86–93, 112, *113*, 338
  financing of 89
  limited control 112, 119
  'the man who won the war' 86–7, 89
war record 86–93
weapons 89, *91*, 110–12, 119
West of Ireland 174–7, *176*
Westminster Gazette 249
Whelan, Gerard 319
Whelan, Leo *101*, 132
Whitman, Walt 104
Wigram, Clive 118–19
Wilde, Oscar 318
Wilson, Sir Henry 122–3, 230, 237, *258*
Winter, Ormonde de l'Épée 235
women 199–200, 322
Woods, Mary *320*
Woolf, Virginia 107
work 19, *26*, *29*, 51–3, *56*, 59, *61*, 76
  civil service 33
  stockbroking 33, 42, 214
  see also Irish National Aid and Volunteer
    Dependents' Fund
World War One 42–3, *48*, 104, 292–5, 338
The World's Pictorial News 229–30

Yeats, Jack Butler *176*
Yorkshire Post 208, 213, 234
Younger, Calton 266

Also from The Collins Press

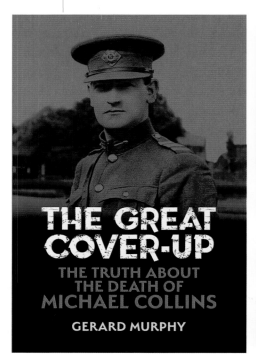

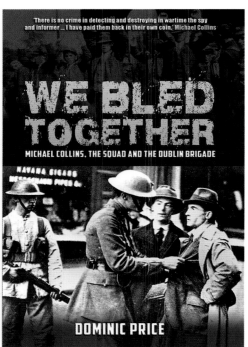

www.collinspress.ie

the Rear h
improved
comfortan
much old
for send
it

Remember m
Miramagne

Dear Mollie

    Very many thanks
indeed for that parcel. The
fruit especially was
beautiful. Indeed I dont
know in the world what I
shall ever be able to do for
all my friends who are being
so kind.

    I think we shall be
off to the old camp sometime
during this coming week.